Marlborough's Cameronians

Marlborough's Cameronians
Two British Officers During
the War of Spanish Succession

The Life and Diary of Lieut. Col. J. Blackader

Andrew Crichton

Brigadier Ferguson: A Soldier of 1688 and Blenheim

James Ferguson

Marlborough's Cameronians
Two British Officers During the War of Spanish Succession
The Life and Diary of Lieut. Col. J. Blackader
by Andrew Crichton
Brigadier Ferguson: A Soldier of 1688 and Blenheim
by James Ferguson

FIRST EDITION

First published under the titles
The Life and Diary of Lieut. Col. J. Blackader
and
Two Scottish Soldiers and a Jacobite Laird
(Extract)

Leonaur is an imprint
of Oakpast Ltd

Copyright in this form © 2014 Oakpast Ltd

ISBN: 978-1-78282-303-2 (hardcover)
ISBN: 978-1-78282-304-9 (softcover)

http://www.leonaur.com

Publisher's Notes

The views expressed in this book are not necessarily those of the publisher.

Contents

The Life and Diary of Lieut. Col. J. Blackader   7

Brigadier Ferguson: A Soldier of 1688 and Blenheim   395

LIEUT. COL. JOHN BLACKADER

The Life and Diary of Lieut. Col. J. Blackader

Contents

Preface	11
Genealogical and Biographical Remarks	15
The Cameronians	27
The Revolution	39
Cameronian Regiment	51
Battle of Dunkeld	63
War in Flanders	79
The Diary	100
War of the Succession	118
Campaign Second, 1703	131
Campaign Third, 1704	142
Campaign Fourth, 1705	162
Campaign Fifth, 1706	188
Campaign Sixth, 1707	203
Campaign Seventh, 1708	213
Campaign Eighth, 1709	234
Campaign Ninth, 1710	258
Campaign Tenth, 1711	279

Domestic Sketches, 1712-1714	302
Rebellion in Scotland, 1715-1716	315
Miscellaneous Extracts, 1716-1721	332
Conclusion, 1722-1729	360
Appendix	395

Preface

The principal materials from which the following *Life* is compiled, are the diary and letters written by the colonel himself during the campaigns in which he was engaged. These manuscripts, it would appear, were committed to the hands of his widow, who was married to Sir James Campbell of Ardkinglas, Bart. After her death, they were thrown aside, as papers of no value, and lay neglected for many years. When the descendants of Sir James quitted the family residence near Stirling, a quantity of papers, supposed to be useless, were sold to a tobacconist in that town; and among these, his curiosity discovered, and rescued from destruction, the diary and letters referred to. The manuscripts thus, as it were, accidentally preserved, happily came into the possession of those who perceived their worth, and were anxious to make their usefulness more extensively known. Part of them were shewn to the Rev. John Newton, them (1799) Rector of St. Mary's, Lombard Street, London, who expressed his opinion that their publication might do good, and agreed to write a recommendatory preface.

With this view they were put into the hands of Mr. John Campbell, then resident in Edinburgh, now minister of Kingsland Chapel, near London, and well known by his Missionary Travels in South Africa. Mr. Campbell transcribed many of the letters and made several extracts—a task of no small difficulty, from the smallness and faintness of the character in which they are written; but his various engagements hindered him from preparing them for the Press. He committed them to the care of Dr. Charles Stuart, of Dunearn, who, every ready and zealous to promote the interests of religion, willingly undertook to superintend their publication. The volume made its appearance about twenty years ago, (as at 1824), and was printed for the benefit of the Magdalene Asylum, Edinburgh, as originally intended by Mr. Campbell. It comprehended, however, only twelve years of the diary, being, as appears, all that had come into the editor's possession at the time of publishing.

By his diligent inquiries among the colonel's surviving friends and relatives. Dr. Stuart collected various particulars of his family and parentage, which he prefixed to the *extracts*; illustrating the whole with short historical notes and explanations. He likewise recovered twelve additional years of the diary, which made the series complete from 1701 to 1725. For these he acknowledged himself indebted to the colonel's grandnephew and representative, the late John Blackader, Esq. Accomptant General of Excise.

The whole of the original manuscripts, comprising many unpublished letters, and the remainder of the diary from 1700 to 1728 inclusive, are in the hands of the present compiler. The former extracts have been revised and enlarged, various letters and select passages inserted, so as to render the *Life* as complete and interesting as the nature of the materials will admit. A chasm of fifteen years in the colonel's history is here supplied; historical illustrations have been more copiously introduced, so as to render the subject intelligible without the labour of consulting the political or military annals of the times. The peculiar formation of the Cameronian Regiment—the character of the religious Sect from which it was originally composed—and the distinguished share they took in the memorable Revolution, are dwelt upon at considerable length; not altogether from their connection with the colonel's personal history, for he then acted in a very subordinate capacity; but because they throw light on the principles and conduct of the party with whom he was associated in arms—a party which has been much traduced and misunderstood.

Of the execution of the work, the public must judge; of its fidelity to truth and fact the author can speak with confidence. The dates and form of the diary have been preserved; which may give it a desultory and disconnected appearance; but the spirit and expression of the original must have been impaired had it been thrown into the form of a continued narrative.

Of the utility and entertainment to be derived from biography in general, no a work need be said—more especially from the lives of those military men who have acted upon Christian principles, and while fighting under the banners of an earthly sovereign, have not forgotten that they were soldiers of the Cross.

The favourable reaction of Dr. Stuart's extracts, encouraged the present Publisher to undertake the work on a more full and comprehensive plan. He had, besides, other inducements; as various attempts to republish Colonel Blackader's *Life and Diary* have, from time to time, been made, by those who had not access to the original sources of information, and were therefore in danger of obtruding upon the world defective and inaccurate editions. In the present work, these faults have been avoided, so far as care and research could accomplish it.

The engraving of the colonel is taken from the original family painting; which appears from the style and superior manner of execution, to be the workmanship of some foreign artist.

Edinburgh
September 10, 1824

Chapter 1

Genealogical and Biographical Remarks

Lieutenant Colonel John Blackader was a native of Dumfriesshire. He was born in the parish of Glencairn, on the 14th of September, 1664. His father, the Rev. John Blackader, was minister of Troqueer in the presbytery of Dumfries; and expelled at the restoration of Charles II, for refusing to comply with Episcopacy, which the government had imprudently introduced in opposition to the wishes of the church and the nation. Of his early life, very little is known beyond a few incidental notices, until he entered the army in his 25th year. It is then, chiefly, that our acquaintance with him must commence: But as there is, in general, a curiosity to know more of the history of a distinguished individual than his personal adventures, some preliminary notices of his family will not, I am persuaded, be unacceptable to the reader. Genealogical detail is not our purpose, and has been given elsewhere; yet on this subject, a few observations may be promised, without overstepping the restrictions of biography.

Colonel Blackader's parentage was highly respectable. He had the honour to be connected, by propinquity of blood and hereditary descent, with the ancient baronage of Scotland. The original family was Blackader of that ilk in Berwickshire, who had acquired considerable renown for their military achievements in the Border feuds, so early as the minority of James II towards the middle of the fifteenth century. The lands from which they derived their name were the gift of that prince, conferred as a reward for their patriotic and enterprising activity in defending the eastern frontier, against the frequent and often sanguinary depredations of the English. An extensive addition was afterwards made to their property, by a marriage with the heiress of Tulliallan, an estate in Perthshire. This became afterwards the seat of the family, when the avaricious pretensions of a rival clan, the Homes of Wedderburn, had violently dispossessed them of their patrimonial estate in the Merse. The castle, now in ruins, stands on the northern bank of the Forth, near Kincardine. It belonged to the late Lord Keith, and was for several generations, the residence of the Blackaders, Barons of Tulliallan.

The House of Blackader formed at various times matrimonial connexions of the first respectability. They were allied, by intermarriage, to the noble family of Douglas of Angus, Graham Earls of Monteith, and Bruce of Clackmannan, whose line still survive in the Earl of Elgin and Kincardine.

Living in the days of war and chivalry, they seem to have imbibed, in no inconsiderable proportion, the martial spirit of those heroic ages. Stimulated by the maxims of a perverse errantry, which made it fashionable to court danger for the love of fame,—to seek military glory in every perilous enterprise, their romantic courage led them to wander in search of honourable adventures under that standard of foreign princes. A small body of them volunteered for the cause of Henry VII. in the wars of York and Lancaster. They were present at the Battle of Bosworth, the field that terminated the life and reign of the ambitious Richard, and restored the Red Rose to its ancient ascendancy.

The heir of Blackader followed the banner of the Douglases at Flodden,[1] and perished, with many of his kinsmen, in that disastrous contest. They espoused the part of the unfortunate Mary, and sided with the Cavaliers in the parliamentary wars of Charles I. There was a cadet of this family in the Spanish service, under Ludovic, Earl of Crawford; and another served with Gustavus Adolphus, King of Sweden, in his campaigns for relief of the distressed Protestants in Germany. One of their last lineal representatives, raised a body of troops, and joined the Earl of Glencairn, who, with some of the Highland chiefs in 1653, assembled a considerable force in the North to repel the usurpation of Cromwell—the last effort that was made to retrieve the departing liberties, and preserve the ancient independence of Scotland.

The Blackaders made some figure in the ecclesiastical, as well as in the military annals of their country. Prior to the Reformation, they possessed official jurisdiction and monkish dignities in various churches and monasteries. In those days, the rich patrimony of the

---

1. *The Battle of Flodden Field* by Robert Jones is also published by Leonaur.

church offered a prize worthy of competition. Spiritual titles and monastic revenues were contested with the same arms. The lucrative endowments of religious foundations were either monopolised by the nobles, or seized by those who could back their claims with force, and by casting the sword in the scale, make the balance of justice turn in their favour. The Priory of Coldingham was filled repeatedly by members of the Blackader family, one of whom was murdered, with six of his domestics, to make way for William Douglas, brother to the Earl of Angus.

Another of them was Dean of Dunblane, and suffered the same fate; another, Archdeacon of Glasgow, fell in a skirmish at Edinburgh with the rival faction of the Homes; and another, Abbot of Dundrennan in Galloway. Of this House also was Robert, Bishop of Aberdeen, who was afterwards translated to Glasgow, and became the first Metropolitan of that See. It was during his incumbency, and chiefly through his interest with Pope Sextus IV. and his successor Innocent VIII. that this new archbishopric was erected,—a measure, resented with jealous indignation by his Grace of St. Andrews, and like to have occasioned a dangerous schism in this remote province of the Catholic dominions.

The last Baron of Tulliallan, Sir John, was, in 1626, created by Charles I. One of the Knights Baronets of Nova Scotia,—a dignity which none of his posterity every enjoyed. Being of a wasteful and extravagant turn, he impoverished his estate, and retired to the continent. He bore a commission for some time in the French Guards, and died in America about the year 1653. To the title of this Knight Baronet, Colonel Blackader's father lived to be the lineal heir, having survived all nearer claimants. But as the prodigality of its first possessor had reduced it to an empty honour, it was never assumed either by himself, or any of his descendants.[2]

Colonel Blackader was from a younger branch of the Tulliallan family, who possessed the lands and barony of Blairhall, near Culross. One of his immediate progenitors, his great grandfather, married a daughter of the celebrated Robert Pont, minister of the St. Cuthberts, near Edinburgh, an eminent Reformer, son-in-law to John Knox, and one of the last of the clerical order that sat as a Lord of Session.

But of all this remote and once opulent ancestry, nothing remained to Colonel Blackader except the name. He inherited no other advantage from it than the frivolous boast of an ancient and honourable

---

2. For a more particular account of the family, see *Blackader's Memoirs*, chap. 1.

pedigree. Long before his birth, the fortunes of his family had become extinct, partly through domestic embarrassments, and partly from the desolating effects that always follow the storms and convulsions of political or religious hostilities, in a kingdom divided against itself. These deficiencies, however, he repaired by the celebrity of his own character. His reputation as a brave officer, is a monument that will survive when the glory of hereditary distinctions has perished. His piety, as a devout Christian, has earned him a more illustrious title than any he could have derived from antiquity of blood, or elevation of birth

His father, as has been already noticed, was a minister of the church of Scotland. The history of this worthy and excellent man, besides his personal sufferings, exhibits, at considerable length, a detail of the various cruelties and oppressions to which this country was subjected for twenty-eight years, under the Episcopal persecution. He bore a proportional share of the toils and harassing of that unhappy period, being one of the most indefatigable and intrepid preachers of his time. Though expelled from his charge at Troqueer, he did not renounce the ministerial privileges of his office when deprived of its temporalities. Denied access to the established pulpits, he erected the standard of religious liberty in the fields, and was one of the first three who ventured their lives for the free preaching of the gospel.

His itinerary labours were continued for nearly twenty years, with a zeal and perseverance truly apostolical, and a success altogether astonishing. His exertions were not circumscribed to Dumfriesshire or Galloway, but extended to almost every county south of the Tay. There was scarcely a hill, a moor, or a glen in the southern and western districts of Scotland, where he did not hold a conventicle, or celebrate a communion. In these excursions he was frequently the companion and coadjutor of Welsh, Peden, Cargill, and other undaunted Covenanters, who maintained the rights and the freedom of their national worship in the face of peril and sword. In 1674, he was proclaimed rebel and fugitive, and a premium of a thousand *merks* offered to any that should kill or apprehend him. But the goodness of providence, with every danger, made a way for his escape, preserving him from the violence of barbarous edicts, and bloody executioners.

After the defeat at Bothwell Bridge, he went over to Holland, where he made a short stay, and proved eminently serviceable in allaying those irritations and ill-natured debates that had sprung up among the refugees, from want of proper information on the true state of Scottish affairs. On his return, he was apprehended at Edinburgh, in his own house, and sent a prisoner to the Bass Rock, then employed as a convenient receptacle for the persecuted victims of Prelacy. In this bleak and solitary isle, he lingered several years in rigorous captivity. The harshness of his treatment, and the ungenial air of the place, terminated his days. He died in 1685, and was buried in the churchyard of North Berwick, the adjacent parish.

It was about two years after his father's ejection, that Colonel Blackader was born. He was the youngest of five sons, all of whom he survived. (See note following)

******

Note:—The family consisted altogether of six children. The eldest son William, was born in 1647. He studied medicine, and for his services at the revolution was made physician to king William; he died in 1704. The second son, Adam, was a merchant. He had been several years in Sweden, and at his return in 1685, settled in Edinburgh. He wrote an account of his father's sufferings which he transmitted to the historian Wodrow; and some political tracts concerning the Darien expedition, and the state of parties in Scotland. Robert, the third son studied Theology, and died at Utrecht in 1689. Thomas went to New-England, and died before his father. Elizabeth, the only surviving daughter, was younger than the Colonel. She married a Mr. Young, writer in Edinburgh, and appears to have been a lady of remarkable piety and superior learning. She kept a diary or "Short account of the Lord's providence towards her," which gives a summary of the memorable events of her life from 1700 until 1724. A further account of these, and some extracts may perhaps be given in an Appendix.

******

The act that extruded the Presbyterian ministers strictly forbade residence or intercourse with their vacant parishes. The penalties of the law, in case of nonconformity, were a total suspension of their salaries, banishment without the bounds of their respective presbyteries, and a prohibition to settle within ten miles of heir former churches. In compliance with these injections, Mr Blackader had retired to Glencairn, which was beyond the boundaries of the act. There he was accommodated with the house of Barndennoch, a seat of the Dowager Lady Craigdarroch, in the immediate neighbourhood of Minnyhive. In this retreat, he continued until the winter of 1666, when he was obliged, for greater security, to withdraw to Edinburgh, as reports of his boldness in field-preaching had reached the ears of the council, and attracted the notice of the military who were posted in the districts of Galloway and Nithsdale, to guard the new Episcopal incumbents, and compel the refractory parishioners to attend their sermons.

A party of Sir James Turner's men attacked his house, but fortunately he had made his escape. Disappointed of their prey, they threatened to wreak their vengeance on the object that remained. They burnt the furniture, destroyed or carried away books and provisions, and having pillaged the house, they left the helpless family to shift for themselves. The eldest son went to Edinburgh. The colonel, then a child, and the rest or his brothers, were secreted by such people in the neighbourhood as dared, on their account, to hazard the penalties of *Reset and Converse*. From the state of the country at that time, when it was peremptorily forbidden to hold intercourse with disaffected persons, or make charitable contributions for their support, it required both courage and humanity to afford them shelter or concealment.

All who were found guilty of these benevolent transgressions were punishable by fine, imprisonment, or death. But the rigour of the law could not shut up the channels of compassion, or extirpate the common sympathies of nature. Notwithstanding these legal prohibitions, charity was often brave enough to extend her relief, and sufficiently ingenious to elude detection. Many were ready to peril their own comfort and their own lives, in pity to those little victims of oppression. Hundreds of destitute and wandering fugitives found a sanctuary in the compassionate hospitality of their countrymen.

So soon as circumstances would permit, Mr Blackader collected his scattered family. They resided chiefly in Edinburgh, until his death, sharing with him his privacy and restraints, according as the storm of persecution raged or abated. In the midst of confusion and distraction, he seems to have paid every attention to their literary and religious attainments; employing the intervals of his professional engagements in storing their minds with useful instruction. He himself taught them the rudiments of classical learnings, and furnished them with an education, apparently beyond his means and opportunities. They had all attended the ordinary courses of Humanity and Philosophy in the College of Edinburgh, notwithstanding the political impediments with which academical studies were then fettered.

Shortly after the Restoration, the universities were subjected to the same restrictions as the church. It became a matter of the greatest importance to secure the seats of learning, and have the instructors of youth seasoned with proper principles. No professor, regent, or master was allowed to continue, or be admitted into office, unless he took the oath of allegiance to the king, and acknowledged the government of the church by bishops. And none, except persons thus qualified, were allowed, under pain of rebellion, to congregate any number of scholars, or teach such languages and sciences as were taught at the universities. The college of Edinburgh was more tardy in her compliance, than her sister seminaries. Disaffection was there more firmly rooted, and continued longer; and some of her members even chose deposition, in preference to conformity. Matters, however, were not urged with the same violence and precipitancy in the schools, as they had been in the church.

Impositions so adverse to the prevailing sentiments of the nation, greatly impaired the interests of learning, and the prosperity of the universities. Such as had adequate finances, repaired to the continent, and studied under foreign masters. At Edinburgh, about the time of Colonel Blackader's attendance, the number of students had fallen off exceedingly. So few were the candidates for the annual degrees, that it was sometimes thought needless to go through the ceremony of public laureation.[3] One reason of this extraordinary deficiency was, the conditions imposed upon all applicants for literary honours. No candidate was permitted to graduate without taking the oaths to the government, civil and ecclesiastical. This constrained many, after finishing their regular course of studies, to take their degrees in some foreign university, where letters were not shackled by any political disabilities.

For this purpose, Mr. Blackader sent two of his sons abroad, the eldest to graduate as a physician at Leyden, the most celebrated school of medicine in the world, and the other to study theology at Utrecht, where it would appear he had also designed to send his youngest son, the colonel, had he been in a capacity to defray his expenses. Whether his father had destined him for the church, may be uncertain, but he speaks of him as a youth of promise and abilities, and laments the degraded and neglected state of education in his own country.[4]

From Colonel Blackader's future life and reflections, it is manifest he had imbibed early impressions of religion. At twelve years of age, he is said to have been admitted a communicant to the sacrament of the Lord's Supper. He appears to have frequently attended conventicles and communions, which were celebrated in the open fields, and

---

3. Bower's *History of the University of Edinburgh*, vol. i.
4. *Blackader's Memoirs*.

which had begun about 1677, to attract immense crowds of hearers from all parts of the country. He speaks, in his diary, with rapture of those quickening and refreshing ordinances, and complains, that he felt not on Sabbaths, in army abroad, the same ardent desires and tender meltings of soul that he used to have in Scotland. Amidst the confusion of battles, and licentiousness of camps, he reverts, with a mixture of delight and regret, to the days of old, when he went with the multitude that kept solemn fast, and took sweet counsel together. His piety, though early, proved uniform and abiding.

Much, doubtless, in the formation of his character, must be ascribed to the influence of his father's instructions and example; yet devotion seems, as it were, to have been inherent in his constitution, and all his inclinations, from his tenderest years, happily predisposed to virtue. His infant steps were trained with care to the paths of righteousness. In his heavenly career, he marched on steadily and progressively, without straying or degenerating from his course,—his life advancing to perfection like the morning light, and shining to the last with increasing brightness. It was his glory and felicity to maintain his integrity in a station so replete with dangers and temptation, where the mind is so apt to contract a contrary bias, and where a negative innocence, or an exemption from the more flagrant vices, may be regarded as virtues of rare and difficult attainment.

We have not, in his instance, an example which we sometimes find in the histories of good men, of the subduing power of regenerating grace over a reprobate and unrenewed heart,—of the mysterious efficacy with which it operates in awakening and transforming sinners, to all appearance irrevocably lost, who, after having given in to every lawless excess, have been suddenly recovered, as by miracle, from the most daring profanity, or the grossest licentiousness. It is remarkable by what variety of means the plans of mercy are accomplished, and what trivial, and as it were, fortuitous incidents are often made the occasion of producing the most surprising and memorable changes. The hearing of a sermon, the accidental perusal of a book, an afflicting dispensation, or some unforeseen deliverance, has frequently been to many the instrument of removing the scales of error and darkness from their eyes, and altering the whole course and system of their lives.

We read of some, who, having outlived the religious impressions of their youth, and the companions of their folly, and after years spent in utter alienation from God, have been reclaimed from their long wanderings, back to the paths of virtue and piety. Conviction is made to rekindle those sparks of divine grace which seemed utterly quenched in the sink of depravity,—to touch, as it were, with a live coal from the celestial altar, that truth which had lain so long buried and captive in their hearts. We have seen the most devoted slaves of vice, arrested in their wild career of profligacy, while pursuing, with headlong eagerness, the phantoms of unworthy delights—overtaken with mercy at the solitary unexpected hour, when concerting with their own corrupt hearts some new scheme of guilty pleasures.

Even the sceptic and the infidel have been subdued in spite of all their reasonings and their railleries; remorse has touched their consciences, or a ray of heavenly light has penetrated their minds, and unveiled their danger in all its horrors to their terrified imaginations. Frequently has religion thus seen her bitterest enemies become her most zealous votaries, and transformed into her brightest ornaments. These truths require not the corroboration of particular instances, they are illustrated in the lives of departed saints, as well as in many living examples who still remain monuments to the victorious power of divine grace. Let none, however, take encouragement from such recoveries to continue in sin, that for this cause they may obtain mercy, or that a miracle of special grace may be wrought in their behalf. To reckon fearlessly on this interposition, is to tempt the Holy Spirit, and rely on the grossest presumption.

Such instances are recorded or permitted for our instruction, and not for our imitation: and though it be true that there may be joy in heaven over a repentant sinner, more than over ninety-nine righteous persons that went not astray; yet ought we to carry this caution along with us, that where one escapes the consequences of his presumption, nine hundred perish in their iniquities.

With such a religious cast of mind, it may appear singular that Colonel Blackader should have embraced a military life. It seems to be the profession, to which, by habit and education, he was least adapted, and which he was likely to encounter more occasions of annoyance and vexation than in any other. The army, however, may probably have been an object of necessity, more than of choice with him. Other situations might be more eligible, but considering the political and pecuniary circumstances of his family, we may suppose they were placed beyond his reach.. The government that had proclaimed his father a rebel, was not likely to open to him the gates of favour and preferment. But at the time he entered the service, there were inducements of a peculiar kind. The memorable Revolution was achieved, but not yet confirmed. The country, emerging from slavery, and still smarting under the rod of oppression, made an appeal to the patriotism of every citizen, to take arms in the common cause,—an appeal which must have been doubly enforced by the remembrance of past injuries, and the hope of a glorious deliverance.

These consideration laid an imperative command on every man of public spirit and right feeling, to stand forth, if not to avenge their common wrongs, at least to secure their recent victory. In this light, they must have appeared to Colonel Blackader, who had himself been a sufferer, and seems to have possessed an abundant share of natural bravery. A sense of duty alone, at such a juncture, might overcome that scrupulous reluctance to war and bloodshed, which is a characteristic of every true Christian.

Whatever dislike or aversion may be felt, and every humane spirit must feel a dislike to engage in civil or foreign hostilities, yet there are times of necessity when the public welfare rises paramount to every other consideration, when backwardness or negligence would be criminal. Although it is forbidden to propagate or maintain religion by force, the use of the sword is nowhere prohibited in defence of the established authorities. When the peace and safety of the state are in danger, the magistrate is not only empowered, buy obliged to employ arms for the suppression of anarchy and insubordination. The military profession, so far from being condemned as unlawful, is expressly countenanced and sanctioned in Scripture.

The manifest tendency of religion undoubtedly is, to disincline and restrain men from quarrellings and fightings; to abolish war, not by proscribing the use of carnal weapons, but by rooting out of the heart those passions of envy, hatred, and ambition that make them unlawful; by rendering men just, merciful, and peaceable; by inspiring them with that benevolence and philanthropy which is the distinguishing badge of Christian fellowship.

But, unfortunately, men do not yield themselves up to its dominion, nor allow its benign influence to predominate and take the lead in their affections. And so long as human nature is constituted in its present form, to expect the universal reign of peace and good-will, were to indulge a chimerical hope, a millennial dream, that will never be realised. Thus, while Christianity condemns decidedly unjust aggressions and unnecessary bloodshed; while it recommends strongly to keep the unity of the Spirit in the bond of peace, it inculcates, at the same time, energy and activity when the country requires the aid of defensive arms. Such being the case, every patriotic citizen will feel it his duty to make his private inclinations give way to the general interest. These were evidently the views and feelings which Colonel Blackader entertained upon the subject, and which alone could have reconciled him to an occupation to which he was naturally disinclined.

Previously to his entering the army, two of his brothers especially the eldest, had made themselves rather conspicuous by the active share they had taken in public affairs, and it is probable, had not the power of the Council been disarmed by the Involution, the whole family might have felt the effects of their vengeance.[5] Dr. Blackader was much in the confidence of the leading characters, both in Scotland and Holland, and had frequently been employed by them in negotiating political transactions. He had several times passed between the two countries on expeditions of intelligence; and twice narrowly escaped torture. The first time was in 1685, when he came over with the Earl of Argyle, who had made a descent on the western coast of Scotland. He and Spence, the earl's secretary, had put ashore at Orkney, to procure information, but were apprehended and despatched to Edinburgh to be examined.

On their landing at Leith, they were conducted by the guard for examination before the Privy Council. The sister of Dr. Blackader joined the crowd that followed them, anxious to be of service to him, for none of his brothers durst appear. But she was not allowed to approach near enough for conversation. The soldiers repulsed her with their muskets. Her person, however, had caught his eye, for she observed him looking at her with expressive steadfastness; and pointing at his hat, as if to draw her attention particularly to it. Struck with the idea that this was the mysterious symbol of some important secret in reference to his examination, she immediately returned to Edinburgh, and finding among his luggage, which had been forwarded to a private lodging, a hat belonging to him, she discovered papers concealed under the lining, of such a nature, that had they been detected, the consequence might have proved fatal to himself, as well as to several others. These she immediately destroyed, and by this well-timed resolution, averted the danger that threatened his life; for immediately a party of soldiers entered the house in search of papers, but without success, as nothing suspicious was to be found.

He and Spence, however, were closely imprisoned in separate rooms, in order to try if evidence could be expiscated by torture.[6] They were

---
5. *Balcarras' Memoirs.*
6. Spence had been apprehended and put in irons the year before, for holding a treasonable correspondence with the Earl of Argyle. (Continued next page)..

interdicted all communication with their friends, and denied the use of pen, ink, or paper.

Here again Dr. Blackader was rescued by an intrigue of his brother, who had but recently returned from Stockholm in Sweden. He had provided himself with a large tin or white-iron box, with a secret opening underneath, and a double bottom, between which writing material might be concealed. This he took with him, and ascending a common stair immediately opposite the prisoner's chamber, he remained there until he observed him through the grating of his window. He shewed him the secret opening, and the materials with which it was furnished. Next day he sent a servant with the open box, full of salad, in the one hand, and a shoulder of roasted mutton in the other, which were admitted by the keeper without suspicion. The doctor immediately wrote a letter to Holland to the Pensionary Fagel, who represented his case to the British Envoy, and by his means, an express was sent to the Council granting the prisoner a remission, and orderings his liberation.[7]

Dr. Blackader was apprehended a second time in the year 1688. He and Colonel Cleland were sent over by the banished lords and gentlemen in Holland, the former to Edinburgh, the other to the west country, to pave the way for the Prince of Orange's landing, by encouraging their friends, and sounding the dispositions of the people. The doctor had a commission to transmit to the prince a weekly account of all that passed, and let him know how the nation stood affected to his cause. He was also charged with the secret correspondence between Murray of Tibbermore, and Lord Murray, son to the Marquis of Athole.[8] Having imprudently ventured into the castle, he was seized by order of the governor, the Duke of Gordon. Some letters and mystical characters being found upon him, he was committed for trial, and threatened with the boot and thumbkins. His examination, however, was delayed, until the rumour spread that the Prince of Orange was landed, and had got possession of London. The fears of the Council then superseded their desires of revenge, and the prisoner was immediately set at liberty.

He was tortured by a barbarous and unprecedented method, but without making any discovery. He endured the boot with great fortitude; and after that, soldiers were employed to watch him in his cell by turns, and to prick him with sharp instruments, that he might be kept awake, and not suffered to sleep by night or day. *Wodrow* vol. II.

7. *Blackader's Memoirs. Wodrow*, vol. ii.
8. *Balcarras' Memoirs.*

CHAPTER 2

The Cameronians

The regiment in which young Blackader enrolled himself a cadet, was that raised at the Revolution by the Cameronians, under command of the Earl Angus. It is now the 26th Regiment of the line, British Infantry, and still retains the appellation of the sect from which it was originally formed. Both officers and men were remarkable for the strictness and propriety of their moral conduct, and for the most exemplary attention to the duties of religion, characteristics far from being incompatible, but unhappily too seldom found conjoined with the profession of arms. Their piety became proverbial, and so regular were they, under all emergencies, in keeping up the public exercises of devotion, that they were nicknamed in derision by their enemies, the Psalm-singing Regiment.[1]

But their seriousness abated nothing of their courage or their patriotism. No class of subjects was readier to offer their services in defence of their king and country, and none behaved with more gallantry in the field. If they were eminent for their superior morality, they were no less distinguished by their bravery and enterprise in the day of battle. Dunkeld, Steinkirk, Blenheim, and Ramillies, are names that sufficiently attest their valour, and have immortalised their renown. The peculiar conditions upon which they tendered their services, are perhaps not generally known: And the reader; I am persuaded, will not think it a needless digression, if we dwell a little upon the important events which occasioned its formation. The character and tenets of the religious sect from which it had its name and its origin, are, in the first place, worthy of notice.

The Cameronians, or, as they were sometimes called, the United

---

1. Defoe's *Memoirs of the Church. Faithful Contendings.*

Societies, or Hill-men, from their mode and place of worship, were a party that separated, about the year 1680, from the main body of the Presbyterians. The designation by which they are still known, was first applied to them as followers of Richard Cameron, one of their itinerant preachers, who fell in the rencounter at Airs-moss, where he and his little land were surprised and defeated by Bruce of Earlshall.[2] Among the earliest causes of this dissension was the king's indulgence to the ex-parochial clergy, allowing them to preach and exercise their ministerial function under certain restrictions. It was this subject that created those violent and contentions debates which inflamed the camp, and ultimately disconcerted the measures, of the insurgents at Bothwell Bridge.

Some imagined they might conscientiously accept of this liberty with all its restraints, and that it was better to avail themselves of this license, than to continue silent, or incur, by holding conventicles, the penalties of outlawry and rebellion. But the zeal of the Cameronians spurned these courtly terms of comprehension. They looked upon the indulgence as a crafty device, to rivet the chains of submission gradually and imperceptibly, and, by fomenting divisions in the Church, to make them pull down with their own hands the only remains of freedom that tyranny had left undestroyed.

Accepting liberty of worship from the bishop or the crown, they condemned as a criminal acknowledgement of Erastian supremacy, a base recognition of the Episcopal authority, which, instead of submitting to, they were bound to extirpate. On these grounds, they conceived themselves obliged to cast out of their fellowship all who were found guilty of temporizing and dishonourable compliances. There were various other reasons of secession upon which we cannot here enlarge, but the consequence was an irreparable breach in their sentiments and worship.

The Separatists formed but a very inconsiderable portion of the Presbyterians, comprehending such of them only as were of a more rigorous and uncompromising temper. Without doubting the integrity of their intentions, we may, in some things, question the propriety of their conduct. They certainly deserve the praise of firmness and

---

2. There was a party of Calvinists in France called Cameronians, who flourished about the beginning of the 17th century: It is curious they also had their name from a Scotsman, John Cameron, who was born at Glasgow in 1580, where he was sometime Professor of Divinity, as he was afterwards at Bourdeaux, Sedan and Saumur. Buck's *Throl. Dict.*

consistency, in resisting all attempts, whether by force or stratagem, to impose conditions on their religious liberties, which they abhorred as sinful and degrading. While others were content to exercise their privileges by royal grant, they had the felicity to preserve their conscience and their worship free and unshackled by oaths or restriction. But they adopted opinions, and urged matters to dangerous extremes, which were disapproved by their fugitive brethren, and even reprehended by the more sober and deliberate of their own party.

In rejecting the king's authority, they stood distinguished from all other Presbyterians, although the whole body of sufferers have often been falsely and injuriously involved in that aspersion. The severity with which they interpreted the religious obligations of the national convenants, and the unsocial disdain they cherished towards those who did no choose to go the same length in maintaining the superior and exclusive rights of their own particular system, infused into all their proceedings a spirit of illiberality and intolerance. They dealt their censure with unsparing hand, against such as they alleged had yielded to the sinful defections of the times, or who did not think themselves called upon to strain their resistance to an equal pitch. Many, on this score, both indulged and nonindulged, were included in their reprehensions and solemnly interdicted their community.

These narrow and scrupulous jealousies, it is to be regretted, did not altogether abate or subside on the return of a milder and more tolerant administration. Whatever grounds they may have had for separation or reproof in times of persecution, when some from policy or weakness might be induced to temporize, there certainly existed no valid reason for this apostasy, after the Revolution had proclaimed liberty of conscience, and re-established the church in her ancient privileges. To have then enforced such stem unaccommodating maxims, would have been to perpetuate those very miseries and oppressions from which they themselves displayed so laudable an eagerness, and made such meritorious exertions to be delivered.[3]

But though their conduct cannot, in all points, be defended, their excesses, we are convinced, may be explained—many of them justified by the peculiarity of their circumstances. And while upon this subject, it would be acting unfairly and unjustly to pourtray only their harshest features, or contemplate, exclusively, the darker shades of their character. We ought not to refuse them the advantage of pleading in

---
3. For a larger view of their principles and transactions, see *Fatihful Contendings Displayed*.

their own behalf the specialities of their case—to deprive them of those palliations, or shut them out from the benefit of those sympathies to which the extraordinary difficulties and complicated hardship of their situation fully entitle them. Their worst deeds were greatly exaggerated, and their sentiments misinterpreted. Strangers, ignorant of what they suffered, and mistaking the principles on which they acted, believed them to be those traitors, rebels and murderers which their enemies represented them. Better information would have refuted and dispelled many of those calumnies. Men of candour and humanity, who know their history, will be more disposed to pity, than to censure them. They will treat their foibles with leniency, and throw a veil of charitable construction even over their extravagances.

They will see in those indiscretions or crimes of which they were guilty, only the natural result, or rather the unavoidable consequences of their treatment. They will find their obstinacy to be an honest, but inflexible adherence to what they believed to be the imprescriptible rights of all free-born citizens. They will attribute their rejection of authority, to the abuse of it, on the part of their rulers, and not to any factious dislike of royalty, or a turbulent impatience of order and subordination. They disclaimed the taking of arms, for any other purpose, but that of self-defence; and not until the rigour of government had compelled them to adopt that last and desperate resource. They did not disown the king, until they were persuaded he had forfeited his claim to their allegiance, by perfidiously violating ever solemn and constitutions stipulation. He had assumed a prerogative inconsistent with the safety and freedom of the people, and subversive, both of their natural and civil rights.

They did not openly announce their revolt from government, until they were provoked and exasperated to a degree of madness, by its oppressive exactions and brutal inhumanities. The law, by placing their lives and properties at the mercy of every ruffian soldier, or every hireling informer, had laid them, as it were, under an absolute necessity of entering into leagues and compacts for their mutual security. In the heat and frenzy of their spirits, they published treasonable and sanguinary declarations, denouncing vengeance on their persecutors, and warning them, at their peril, not to molest their worship, or "stretch forth their hand against them while maintaining the cause and interest of Christ against his enemies."

These principles, hastily and rashly adopted, if taken in the abstract, would have opened a way to all the atrocities of lawless bloodshed, and clandestine murder: But we find them, upon more cool and dispassionate refection, endeavouring to alter and modify those expressions that were liable to misconstruction. They disown and deprecate the thought of killing any, because of a different persuasion or opinion from them. They were careful to mark the different shades of guilt in their oppressors, distinguishing "betwixt the cruel and bloodthirsty, and the more sober and moderate." Their chief design seems to have been, to appal their adversaries by threatening admonitions, and at the same time, to throw around their societies the fence of a mysterious and repulsive terror.[4]

These excesses, instead of being viewed in their proper light as the effects of tyrannical violence, were converted into an apology for the most shocking barbarities, and used as a pretext for multiplying those very rigours from which all the mischief had originated. The wretched Cameronians became a butt for the vengeance and fury of the government. They were decried, in edicts and proclamations, as a race to be abhorred by all Christians, and extirpated from the face of the earth. Such as escaped the axe or the dungeon, were outlawed and intercommuned. The state laid them under a political ban. Their character was branded with the mark of general execration, and tainted with a sort of pestilential treason, which rendered their very presence contagious, and spread infection wherever they went. No person was allowed to harbour or conceal them, to correspond, or even to talk with them on the public way, under pain of High Treason, and at the hazard of being prosecuted as equally guilty with the criminal. The military were dispersed over the country to search for, and hunt them like wild beasts of the desert. Spies were ready to give information, and diligent in employing every crafty and insidious artifice to discover their retreats.

Driven, as it were, beyond the pale of civilized society, and the privileges of human beings, they betook themselves to woods, and hills, and solitudes; wandering about like the primitive martyrs, in deserts and mountains, or lurking in the dens and caves of the earth. They rarely ventured from their hiding-places by day, for the *hue and cry* was instantly raised against them. They met for worship by stealth, and at dead of night. Often, especially in the winter season, they were reduced to incredible hardships for want of shelter and support. Unprovided with sustenance, and not daring to ago abroad to seek it, but at the peril of their lives, they endured extremities of hunger and cold,

---
4. *Vide, Sanquhar Declaration,* 1680. *Lanark Declaration,* 1682. *Informatory Vind.* 1684.

beyond what nature seemed capable to bear.⁵

But though their enemies had vowed their extirpation, and put in practice all the ingenuity of violence and stratagem it increased, rather than diminished their numbers. Ships, prisons, and gibbets could not exhaust them; nor the sword destroy them, though its edge was doubly whetted by avarice and cruelty. The more they were afflicted, the more they grew and multiplied. They sprung up under the scythe of the mower; and their blood served to water the roots of the *plant of renown*, which was soon to spread its branches, and cover the land with its peaceful shadow. The murderous edicts levelled against them, never shook their constancy, nor thinned their ranks. They courted the glory of martyrdom with an eagerness that astonished their oppressors.

They suffered torture and execution, not only with firmness, but with alacrity; for the sacred justice of their cause had, in their eyes, stripped the most appalling implements of death of their usual terror and ignominy. The aged seemed to forget their years and infirmities. Parents and relatives felt the obligation s of religion, stronger than all the ties of blood, and attachments of life. Women laid aside the timidity and the weakness of their sex. Their very executions turned rebels to their office: from enemies, they became converts and associates, ready to offer their necks on the same block, and fall the next victims to the cause they had persecuted.

Thus did these spirited and oppressed fugitives maintain their principles and their party; leaving, in their example, a salutary lesson on the rash and illiberal policy of assailing conscientious opinions by force, or attempting to alter or subdue them by cruelty. They were a remnant that had not bowed the knee to Baal. From the midst of the fiery furnace, they came out untouched, and unchanged in their sentiments. They were resolved, whatever it might cost, to hold fast their integrity—to vow perpetual hostility, and wage a defensive warfare, against their inhuman spoilers.

Considering their circumstances, it is not surprising that they assumed an attitude of defiance, or spoke in language which their rulers deemed seditious and insulting. The wonder would have been had they acted otherwise—had they felt no resentment for past indignities, or expressed no inclination to retaliate. And who, we are tempted to ask, in the same situation, but would have pursued similar steps? Is it possible to put on bowels of compassion towards murderers and incendiaries, or speak of their atrocities with affected tenderness? It is

---

5. *Wodrow*, vol. ii. *passim*. De Foe's *Memoirs*.

a surer mark of an honest mind, to avow its indignation openly and boldly, to be ingenuous and undisguised in word as well as in deed. If we do discover fierceness in their expressions, or asperities in their temper, we may well suppose that their sensibilities must have been a little impaired, and their kindlier feelings worn off amidst the storms of persecution, and the strife of party contentions.

Taking these into account, there is a tone of sobriety, of indulgence and forbearance, which we could scarcely have expected, and which may be thought almost incompatible with their stern principles, or the unavoidable irritation of their spirits. Towards the established authorities, they manifested disrespect and aversion; but this, as we have said arose from the accumulation of intolerable grievances, of which they saw no prospect either of termination or redress. They could not reverence the emblems of official power, when borne by hands that were polluted by extortion, and reeking with human blood. They could not pay reciprocal homage to a government, which had not only refused them the benefits of justice and protection, but driven them beyond the reach of clemency and forgiveness. They could not respect laws that had violently overturned all the fences about their lives, properties, and religion; laws that had delegated a justiciary power to the meanest soldier, and planted the assassin's dagger in the hand of every mercenary spy; that had ruined their estates by enormous exactions, and laid their conscience under an absolute and inextricable subjection to the crown. Change of administration produced no relaxation or abatement of their sufferings. To the character of being vindictive, their persecutors added that of being implacable and remorseless in their vengeance.

The history of this sect cannot by excite strong and mingled emotions in every unprejudiced and reflecting mind. While we censure the intemperance of their zeal, or the dangerous extreme to which they pushed the doctrine of self-defence, we must applaud the open and fearless honesty with which they acted. We must admire their courage, their patience and forbearance. Above all, they merit our praise and our gratitude for their enthusiastic love, for their generous and devote efforts in the cause of civil and religious liberty. They were highly instrumental, under the blessing of Providence, in bringing about that happy change of constitution, which adjusted the long-disputed balance between privilege and prerogative, and settled each by their proper limitations.

We are far from saying, that they are here entitled to engross exclusively the encomiums of posterity. It is an honour which they share in common with hundreds of their countrymen. But it is pleasant to contemplate the unconquerable and incorruptible ardour of this hardy and veteran band, struggling, with success, to rescue their inalienable rights from the iron grasp of tyranny and superstition. While others were making flattering addresses and abject concessions to the throne—while the degenerate nobles were bowing their necks to the yoke with a disgraceful servility—while the Scottish Parliament, forgetting the dignity and the glory of their ancient independence, were resigning up the last fragments of their national liberties; a few wretched and harassed fugitives had the integrity and the boldness to resist with arms, the gigantic encroachments of despotism—to assert, in the face of every danger, their rights as Christians and as freemen.

Contrasting their conduct with all its extravagance, with the sycophancy of those, who, in a free country, could wear the chains of slaves, and lick the dust at the feet of arbitrary power and insolent usurpation, we need not ask who has the better reason to triumph, and be proud at the comparison. Their example served to keep alive a wholesome spirit of resistance in the nation. It was the hidden leaven that fermented the mass of public opinion. Amidst the solitude of caves aid deserts, they fanned the feeble spark of opposition, and cherished on their lonely altars in the wilderness, the vestal fires of expiring liberty; unconscious, perhaps, that the flame was so soon to burst forth, and wrap, not only the British Isles, but the Continent of Europe in the general conflagration. A reverend and elegant writer says:

> Their standard on the mountains of Scotland indicated to the vigilant eye of William, that the nation was ripening for a change. They expressed what others thought, uttering the indignation and the groans of a spirited and oppressed people. The investigated and taught, under the guidance of feeling, the reciprocal obligations of kings and subjects, the duty of self-defence, and of resisting tyrants, and the generous principle of assisting the oppressed. These subjects, which have been investigated by philosophers in the closet, and adorned with eloquence in the senate, were then illustrated by men of feeling in the field.
> While Russel and Sidney, and other enlightened patrons in England were plotting against Charles (and James) from a conviction that their right was forfeited, the Cameronians in Scotland, under the same conviction, had the courage to declare

war against them. Both the plotters and warriors fell; but their blood watered the *plant of renown*, and succeeding ages have eaten the pleasant fruit.—Dr Charters' *Sermons*.

The part they acted at the Revolution, while it wiped off reproaches from their past conduct, extorted approbation even from their enemies. Their general political principles were recognized by the whole kingdom. Many commended their zeal, their sincerity, and consistency, who had shrunk, with irresolution, from the same dangers, and were then anxious to bury the memory of their delinquencies in silence and forgetfulness. The language they employ in their memorial to King William for redress of grievances, and their activity in his service, shews that they could be peaceable subjects, as well as factious rebels, that they could bow with submission to the sceptre when swayed by proper hands, for the good of the people, and the prosperity of religion. We find those turbulent subverters of thrones and authorities, not only acquiescing, without a murmur, in the restoration of magistracy and limited monarchy, but cheerfully expending their lives and fortunes in their support.

They say:—

We are represented by our enemies as antipodes to all mankind, enemies to government, and incapable of order: but as their order and cause is diametrically opposite to the institutions and cause of Christ; so they must have little wit and less honesty, who will entertain their reproaches, who are as great rebels to this government, as we avowed ourselves to be to the former. Our sufferings for declining the yoke of malignant tyranny, and Popish usurpation, are generally known; and all that win be pleased to examine and consider our carriage since the king did first appear in his heroic undertaking to redeem these nations from Popery and slavery, will be forced to acknowledge, we have given as good evidence of our being willing to be subjects to King William, as we gave proof before of being unwilling to be slaves to King James.

For upon the first report of the Prince of Orange's expedition, we owned his Highness' quarrel, when the Prelatic Faction were in arms to oppose his coming to help us. We prayed openly for the success of his arms, when, in all the churches the prayers were for his ruin. We associated ourselves to contribute what we could to the promoting of his interest, and were the first that declared a desire to engage for him, and under him; while they were associating with, and for his enemies—But before we offered to be soldiers, we first made an offer to be subjects. We made a voluntary tender of our subjection in a peculiar petition by ourselves.[6]

This petition was addressed to the Meeting of Estates of the Kingdom of Scotland, the Noblemen, Barons, and Burgesses, assembled at Edinburgh, for establishing the government, restoring the religion, laws and liberties of the said kingdom. After a brief statement of their sufferings, and the reason why they refused to own allegiance to King James, they proceed:

> We prostrate ourselves, yet sorrowing under the smart of our still bleeding wounds, at your Honours' feet, who have a call, a capacity, and we hope, a heart to heal them: And we offer this our humble petition, enforced. By all the formerly felt, presently seen, and, for the future, feared effects and efforts of Popery and tyranny: By the cry of the blood of our murdered brethren: By the slavery of the banished free-born subjects of this realm: By all the miseries that many forfeited, disinherited, harassed and wasted families have been reduced to, for adhering to the ancient establishment of religion and liberty: And by all the arguments of justice, necessity, and mercy that ever could excite commiseration in men of wisdom, piety, and virtue: Humbly beseeching, and craving of your Honours, now when God hath given you this opportunity of acting for his glory—the good of the church and nation—and the happiness of posterity.
>
> Now when this kingdom, and all Europe have their eyes upon you, expecting you will acquit yourselves like the representatives of a free nation in redeeming it from slavery, otherwise inevitable, following the noble footsteps of your renowned ancestors, and the example of the present convention and parliament, now sitting in England: That you will proceed without farther delay, to declare the late iniquitous government dissolved, the crown vacant, and James VII. whom we never have owned, and resolve, with many thousands of our countrymen, never again to own, to have really forfeited and deprived himself of all right and title he could ever pretend thereunto: And to provide, that

---

6. "Memorial of sufferings and grievances of the Presbyterians in Scotland, particularly of those nicknamed Cameronians."

it may never be in the power of any succeeding governor, to aspire unto, or arrive at such a capacity of tyrannizing.

"Moreover, since anarchy and tyranny are equally to be detested, and the nation cannot subsist without a righteous governor; and none can have a nearer claim, or fitter qualifications than His Illustrious Highness the Prince of Orange, whom the Most High both signally owned and honoured to be our deliver: We cry and crave that King William may be chosen and proclaimed king of Scotland, and that the regal authority may be devolved upon him, with such necessary provision, limitations, and conditions of compact, as may give just and legal securities for the peace and purity of our religion—the stability of our laws—privileges of parliament—liberties of the people, civil and ecclesiastic; and thus make our subjection both a clear duty and a comfortable happiness.

And we particularly crave, that he and his successors be bound in the royal oath, to profess, protect and maintain the Protestant religion—that he restore and confirm by his princely sanction, the due privileges of the church, and never assume to himself an Erastian supremacy in matters ecclesiastic, nor unbounded prerogative, in civil: Upon these, or the like terms, we tender our allegiance to King William, and hope to give more pregnant proof of our loyalty to His Majesty, in adverse, was well as prosperous providences, than they have done or can do, who profess implicit subjection to absolute authority.[7]

That their profession of loyalty might not evaporate in idle words, they stood forth in arms to realise their declaration the moment their interposition could be of service. As they had been eminent for their sufferings under tyranny, they were not less conspicuous as the first to take the field in the war of emancipation. They continue:—

> In order to make good our intentions, we modelled ourselves into companies, that we might be in readiness to offer our assistance. This we did offer, and had the honour done us to be accepted. We were admitted to guard and defend the Honourable Meeting of Estates against all attempts of the Duke of Gordon, Viscount Dundee, and other enemies. Thereafter, understanding that the government required the raising of forces, for its defence, against intestine insurrections, and foreign invasions

---

7. Grievances of the Cameronians.

of the late King James and his accomplices: Upon this occasion, we were the first that offered to furnish a regiment for his Majesty's service, and accordingly did make up the Earl of Angus' Regiment of 800 men, all in one day, without beat of drum or expense of levy money, having first concerted with Lieutenant Colonel Cleveland, such conditions and provisions as we thought necessary for clearing our conscience, and securing our liberty and safety.

These conditions shall be stated when we come to speak more particularly of the regiment. Meantime, it will be proper to give some account of the share they took in the Revolution, and the service they rendered the Convention, before they were regularly embodied, or had agreed to any special proposals.

CHAPTER 3

The Revolution

The encroachments of arbitrary power had so far exceeded all the reasonable grounds of prerogative, as to make revolt the indispensible duty of every subject. In the propriety of imposing some restraint upon its enormous aggressions, all ranks acquiesced with one general consent. A revolution they felt to be not merely a desirable, but a necessary measure—a remedy which nature, reason and religion equally suggested, and which all nations have had recourse to, when that power which had been delegated for their happiness and security, has been wrested from its original purposes, and turned to the extinction of their liberties or their lives.

It is a fundamental law of policy, as well as a kind and wise provision in nature, that no authority can be permanent that is built on violence and terror. If not founded in the rules of justice, and the hearts of the people, it stands on hollow and volcanic ground. The growth of faction may be checked for a time, or suppressed by force, but the latent seeds of resistance still remain, too deeply rooted ever to be eradicated. In this state of combustible and jealous discontent, the national feeling is always ready, on sufficient provocation, to burst out into open insurrection. There can be no lasting dominion, and no real security where such suspicions exist—where there is not a mutual and mistrustless confidence between the governed and their governors; which alone can prevent those scruples and apprehensions, that mankind are naturally inclined to, in reference to those placed in authority over them. But when this mutual assurance and good faith subsist, they will be a sufficient guarantee for the stability of power, and dispel those doubts and misgivings that haunt the public tranquillity with the perpetual terrors of infringement.

Possessing the love, and supported by the universal opinion of his subjects, a prince is better fortified than he could ever be, though environed with all the acts of the most despotic legislature. He reigns independent of changes and revolutions. He dreads no rebellion, as he is not conscious of doing anything to provoke or deserve it. He has all the real authority a magistrate can ever be invested with; and, by a natural consequence, is more absolute than the most unlimited measures of power could make him. Though law were abolished, his reign would continue in force, for his wisdom would act, voluntarily, without direction or constraint, in the same manner as if guided by the statute. Then, and only then, a king can truly and safely great. He is united to his subjects by a more sacred and durable interest, than the cold and formal ties of political relationship. His throne is exalted above the fears of popular commotion; for the people have no temptation, and no cause to raise their thoughts beyond the sphere of their obedience. Their wishes and their benedictions will ascend towards him like perpetual incense, and the error they are most likely to commit, were they to follow the bent of their inclinations, would be the sin of idolatry, rather that of treason or rebellion.

As there can be no real empire, but in the affections of the people; so there can be no allegiance, but on the same principle. Abstract this quality, and allegiance is reduced to a heartless ceremony, if not a burdensome and ungracious task. Laws may be imposed, but they will be imperfectly obeyed. The people will consider themselves as the vassals, and not the subjects of the crown. The prince, instead of receiving the willing sacrifice of duty, win be served with the reluctant homage of slaves and tributaries; and, though he should bend his refractory subjects by force, into the most abject servility, he will never be able to overcome his own fears. These are enemies that he can not subdue, and which win make his own kingdom as dangerous and insecure, as if he lived in a hostile country.

If men stand in awe of his authority, it is only because he can punish. His power which ought to be terrible to none but offenders, will carry to all indiscriminately, a frightful and repulsive aspect. And though men do pay it an external respect, their submission will be like the worship which some of the ancients paid to noxious animals, more out of terror than reverence. When he has thrown aside the robes of mercy and justice, he has lost all the attributes that can make him venerable in the eyes of the people.

These remarks are not inapplicable to the state and feelings of the British nation, at the Revolution of 1688. The arbitrary principles, and Popish bigotry of James, had generated in the minds of his subjects, a degree of mistrust and aversion which was beyond the power of law to remedy. For it was impossible they could ever dismiss their jealousies and apprehensions, so long as a king kept possession of the throne, who believed his power to be indisputable, and superior to the control of laws or parliaments. Nothing could restore the public confidence and tranquillity, but the radical extirpation of despotism. For this change, the nation were fully ripened and prepared in their sentiments, long ere a foreign invader had reached their shores. James, in effect, though he had not abdicated the throne, had ceased to reign; and William was virtually king of England, before he had quitted his own territory.

It is true, with the exception of the outlawed Presbyterians, there were but feeble and partial efforts at resistance or open revolt. Many were restrained from mere dislike of innovation, or the ties of settled and established customs; others from a dread of hazarding the uncertainties of a doubtful and perilous enterprise. But the event proved, that this smothered discontent only wanted opportunity to discharge itself; that the people were ready to embrace freedom under any leader, to rally round any adventure that held out a likely prospect of success. And when they saw the projector of their deliverance once fairly embarked in his heroic undertaking, there was a simultaneous movement, a systemic co-operation in his favour, that overpowered all opposition. The infection spread from one end of the island to the other. All classes fervently prayed for his success, or eagerly flocked to his standard. The defection of the nation, from their former masters, was not only universal, but also instantaneous. The Revolution was accomplished with all the celerity and surprise of a dramatic representation.

Nothing could more strikingly evince the unstable and unnatural foundation on which James had built his overgrown tyranny; and how little hold he had, in reality, over the sympathies and attachments of his subjects. Few, in adversity, adhered to his fallen interests, all of whom he had loaded with his favours, or honoured with his personal friendship. The fleet mutinied, and refused to counteract the invader. The military which he had carefully trained to be the Praetorian guard of his authority, almost to a man deserted him. His generals, one by one, turned rebels. The calls of honour and fealty, esteemed by the soldier as the most sacred of all engagements, were found but slender obligations, when put in competition with the safety of their country and their religion.

The spirit of disaffection which terror had formerly silenced and kept down, now burst out on all sides without disguise, and without fear. The unfortunate monarch saw himself on the brink of a precipice, which the delusions of flattery and superstition had concealed from his eyes. As the tide of invasion approached his capital, the bulwarks of royalty fell to pieces of their own accord. He was dislodged, without striking a single blow, from the strongholds of despotism, where he had vainly imagined himself fenced securely with oaths and tests, beyond the fear or the possibility of assault. Struck with astonishment and consternation, he abandoned a throne which he had neither policy to fill, nor courage to defined; leaving to his successor a victory without blood, and a crown without a competitor. With a few adherents, he escaped to France, which had already been the asylum of his own, and his brother's misfortunes. There he outlived his former *grandeur*, and had the unspeakable felicity, after an exile of twelve years, to expire in the arms of that religion which had cost him three kingdoms.[1]

The prevailing genius of the two nations is well exemplified by their conduct at the Revolution. In England, where there was a more ceremonious awe for royalty in the abstract, and a greater venation for the names and forms of official dignities, the public mind was held to the current order of events, by an influence which it was difficult to shake off. Political reasons seemed incapable of stirring it into action, without the addition of ecclesiastical motives; and it is probable, had not he English Episcopacy been treated with extinction, matters might have lingered on without redress, and the crown ultimately succeeded in its arbitrary projects. But here the bigoted zeal, and eager temerity of James luckily frustrated the completion of his purposes.

The most unpopular and alarming feature of his reign was, his undisguised attempt to abolish Prelacy, and substitute Catholicism, which was universally abhorred as the religion of slavery, and proscribed by repeated acts of the legislature. He had imbibed, with his mother's milk, a fatal predilection for the Romish Communion, which neither policy nor experience could teach him to conceal. It was not an age for experimenting on religion. Church controversies were agitated with the greatest keenness; and there was not one inviting symptom, throughout the empire, for putting the faith of the nation to this criti-

---

1. James' blind and bigoted attachment to the Romish religion was the subject of raillery and pasquinade, even among Catholics themselves. A witty prelate at the court of St. Germains, exclaimed aloud: *Voilà un bon homme qui a quittè trois royaumes pour une messe.*—*Volt. Siecle de Louis* XIV. chap xv.

cal trial.

To change the religion of a state, is an enterprise always hazardous, and seldom practicable. It requires a conjunction of favourable circumstances, and the most consummate political skill, neither of which James possessed. Nevertheless, his intemperate zeal hurried him, by a singular infatuation, blindly on to destruction, without even awakening him to a sense of his own danger. The partiality he shewed to Catholics, at once disgusted and alarmed his Protestant subjects. The pope's *Nuncio* was publicly entertained at his court. Swarms of priests and Jesuits were imported, and employed in making proselytes. Fransiscans, Benedictines, Dominicans, Capuchins, and Carmelites overran the whole country. They engrossed the royal favour, and were rapidly advancing to monopolize all place of official trust. Psalters and manuals, beads, rosaries, and other Popish trinkets became staple articles of traffic, and were exposed for sale in every place of public resort. Popery had begun to erect her seminaries, to set altar against altar, and bring her odious mysteries fearlessly into open light. This bold effrontery startled all parties in England; and in opposing it, wig and Tory, churchman and dissenter unanimously coalesced.[2]

In Scotland, there was not the same unanimity. The ties of interest bound many to the throne, who, if they had not been self-concerned, would not have adhered to it so tenaciously, from an exclusive veneration for majesty. The Episcopalian party, whose very existence was linked to the crown, and who seemed ready to adopt any creed the court chose to impose, and several of the nobility, stood out for James. The revolution was accomplished by Presbyterians alone, in the face of their adversaries, and in spite of all their efforts to interrupt and embarrass their proceedings. From their secret correspondence with William, they were aware of his projected invasion, and prepared to expect his arrival. Their situation at home was equally known to the prince, who had correct intelligence from special agents, as well as from the religious emigrants of both kingdoms who had fled to his dominions, and found a secure asylum under his protection.

So soon as he had got possession of the capital, a body of their country men, in London, made a formal proffer of their allegiance, requesting him to assume the government of Scotland, and summon a Convention of the Estates. The news of his sudden and peaceful accession, was the signal for a general commotion in his favour. Edinburgh became the centre of resort from all places in the kingdom.

---

2. Letter to a Member of Parliament on the great growth of popery.

Private deliberations were held in every corner of the city. Taverns and coffee-houses were crowded with politicians.[3] Their numbers were daily augmented, and their confidence emboldened by the growing timidity of their antagonists. Meetings, which had been prescribed as treasonable, were now held, unmolested, within the very precincts of that authority which had lately spread terror and flight over the whole country. The anathemas of Prelacy were totally disregarded. The formidable jurisdiction of the Council and the Bench, had dwindled into contempt. Their confusion was increased by contradictory reports, rumours of invasions, and false alarms of Popish massacres. To add to their trepidation, they lost the support of the regular forces, which were partly disbanded through the intrigues of a few Presbyterian leaders, and partly summoned to England to defend their master, but in reality, to swell the train of their conqueror.

In this destitute and abandoned condition, their power became languid, and seemed to expire of its own accord. The symbols of office dropt insensibly from their hands. Their fears even constrained them to consult their own safety, by obliterating, as far as they could, the remaining vestiges of despotism, and abolishing the public monuments of their cruelty. They hastened to set at liberty prisoners illegally detained, whose wrongs they dreaded as evidence and witnesses against themselves. They took down the heads and hands of martyrs, some of which had stood for eight and twenty years on the gates and market-crosses of the city, lest the horrid spectacle might revive the memory of their guilt, and occasion the question to be agitated, for what, and by whom they had been set up?[4]

Relieved from the terror of the military, the Revolutionists seemed to dismiss all other apprehensions. The panic of their enemies, they wisely improved to their own advantage, and hastened to secure the easy conquest it had given them. To intercept communication with the English Jacobites, they shut up the channels of intelligence, dispersing emissaries throughout the kingdom, who opened all packets and expresses, and suffered no letters of importance to pass. To supply the place of the disbanded troops, they ordered militias to be raised and accoutred, and given in command to such officers as could be relied on. Every precaution was adopted, that policy could suggest. The reins of the legislature were now seized by other hands; while Liberty and Justice, returning from exile prepared to mount those seats which

---

3. *Balcarras' Memoirs.*
4. Grievances of the Cameronians.

persecution and arbitrary power had left vacant.

The Convention of Estates had been summoned to meet at Edinburgh, and met accordingly on the 14th of March, 1689. Lord Angus' Regiment was not yet embodied, but many of them served in the Cameronian Guard, that volunteered for the temporary protection of the estates. In the honourable struggle for independence, this sect had not remained idle or unconcerned spectators.[5] Their activity was pre-eminent, and their general conduct marked with a forbearance surprising expectation. When the rumour spread that the Irish Catholics had commenced a general massacre, and burnt the town of Kirkcudbright, they ran to their arms; but finding no enemy to oppose, they turned their weapons against the images and idolatries of popery. They afterwards distributed themselves in small parties along the borders, to cut off the enemies sources of information, by preventing all strangers, without passes, to enter or leave the kingdom. (See note following).

★★★★★★

Note:—In the month of December, 1688, a sudden and surprising report was spread all over Scotland, that 10,000 Papists were landed from Ireland, with strange instruments of death for despatching Protestants. Concerning which, a letter was writ from the magistrates of the city of Glasgow, to the magistrates of Hamilton, bearing, that they had already burnt down the town of Kirkcudbright, and were come within twenty-two miles of Hamilton, in order to use them at the same rate. This letter came to Edinburgh upon Friday night, before Christmas; and all the night after, the citizen's wives were running about the streets with their children in their arms, with hideous cries, what should become of them and their poor young ones? Upon Saturday, the contrivance being speedily and warily managed against eleven o'clock, there were got together, in Douglasmoor, some 6000 Presbyterians, well armed, for pretence of defending the country from these invaders. But their design was quickly discovered; for by three in the afternoon, they were all divided in small detachments of two or three hundred in a company, whose business it was to disarm all that were disaffected to their cause, and which effectually they did.—*Case of Epis. Cler. in Scotland Truly Represented, Somers' Tracts*, vol. xi.

★★★★★★

---

5. *Faithful Contendings*. Dalrymple's *Memoirs*.

Some days before the sitting of the Convention, several companies of them had come to Edinburgh, with the Duke of Hamilton, the Laird of Binny, and other gentlemen, and were quartered about the Parliament House.

There were great numbers, besides which, they kept hid in cellars, and houses below the ground, which never appeared till some days after the Convention was begun, though they were generally believed to be thrice as many as they were.[6]

A considerable body of them were stationed as a regular guard on the castle hill, to intercept intelligence and provision for the garrison, and others were employed in digging trenches preparatory to the siege.

These precautionary defences tended greatly to maintain the tranquillity, and expedite the deliberations of the Conventional Assembly. The majority, which had been secured at the election by a manoeuvre of Sir John Dalrymple, left the Episcopal members but a feeble chance of opposition. The principal source of their danger and disturbance, was from enemies without. The Duke of Gordon, a Roman Catholic, held the castle: but it is probable he would speedily have come to terms of capitulation, had he not been instigated by a bolder spirit than his own, for his garrison was disaffected, and his supply of stores entirely dependent on the town.

The prime abettor of rebellion, and the adversary most to be dreaded, was the Viscount Dundee, already notoriously odious to the Presbyterians, under the name of Claverhouse. He and the Earl of Balcarras had been commissioned to act, the one as the civil, the other as the military agent of the Jacobites. Dundee arrived in Edinburgh with about fifty horsemen, who had deserted from his old regiment, then in England. He endeavoured to excite tumult and division in the Convention, and failing in that attempt, he urged the Duke of Gordon to fire upon the city and disperse them. But the irresolution of the governor balked him in this expectation.

Disappointed in all his schemes, and enraged equally at friends and foes, he determined to repair to Stirling, and summoned a counter-convention, which his instruction authorised him to do. In this project, he was also frustrated by the infidelity of Mar, who command of the castle, and deserted him to join the Revolutionists. To prevent the alarm his departure from Edinburgh would occasion, he gave out that

---

6. Balcarras' *Memoirs*. Dalrymple's *Memoirs*. Mackay's *Memoirs*. MS. *Adv. Lib.*

his life was in danger, that the western fanatics had threatened to assassinate him, in requital of his former cruelties. He applied to the Convention for justice and protection; but they were too much occupied with weightier matters, to investigate the evidence of an imaginary conspiracy.[7] Chagrined by neglect and disappointment, he quitted the house and the city, breathing threats and revenge. As he lode past the castle, on the west side, the Duke of Gordon observed him, and made a signal for an interview. He dismounted, climbed up the steep rock, to the foot of the walls, and at a small postern, remained in conference with the duke for some time.

The novelty of the spectacle attracted a crowd down below. The number increasing, spread the alarm of some hostile design, as they were mistaken for Dundee's adherents. Messages were repeatedly sent to the Convention, that an army was at the gates, and the governor of the castle preparing to fire upon the town. The president, Duke of Hamilton, though he had better intelligence, resolved to improve this sudden panic, into an occasion to encourage his friends, and intimidate their opponents. In a tone of counterfeited rage, he told the Convention that it was high time to look to their own safety, since Papists and enemies to the government were so bold, as to assemble at their very gates; that doubtless, there were some among themselves privy to the design, and that the traitors within must be held in confinement until the danger was over: But that the friends of liberty had nothing to fear, since thousands were ready to start up in their defence at the stamp of his foot. He ordered the doors immediately to be bolted, and the keys laid on the table before him. He caused drums and trumpets to sound to arms, and despatched the Earl of Leven to collect and embody the Cameronians, who only waited the signal to emerge from their concealments.

> In an instant, vast swarms of those who had been brought to town from the western counties, and who had been hitherto hid in garrets and cellars, appeared in the streets, not indeed in proper habiliments of war, but with arms, and with looks fierce and sullen, as if they felt disdain at their former confinement.[8]

All was noise, hurry, and confusion in the town, especially about

---
7. That this was an affected alarm, is manifest, see Laing's *Hist*. Vol. iv. Balcarras himself seems scarcely to believe it. "It is not to be doubted," says he, "but the made several such things to pass, purposely to frighten us, as all they desired was, to have the house alone." *Memoirs*.
8. Dalrymple's *Memoirs*. Balcarras' *Memoirs*.

the Parliament Square. The Jacobite members hearing the clamour without, and ignorant of the cause; and finding themselves locked in the hands of their enemies, looked upon their hopes as blasted, and lost all resolution in the midst of tumult and conjecture. When the doors were thrown open, the Presbyterian members were hailed, as they passed, with acclamations, while those of the opposite party were received with the hisses and execrations of the populace. Terrified by the apprehensions of unknown dangers, many changed sides, and joined the Convention; others left town, and returned to their homes in despair.

When the Revolutionists, by their superior policy, had thus freed themselves from turbulent opposition, they acted with the greatest promptitude and unanimity. Their proceedings savoured nothing of that tardy and scrupulous ambiguity, which marked the debates of the English Convention. There, it was disputed, whether a king could, by misgovernment, or on any other account, forfeit his sacred title to the crown. The doctrine of dethronement, and of altering, by election, the ancient hereditary line, seemed like introducing an unnatural chasm into the constitution. Hence the delicate and equivocal terms in which their vote of deposition is couched: That James, having endeavoured to subvert the constitution, and withdrawn himself out of the kingdom, had *abdicated* the government. The Scottish Convention, who were not shackled by the same dread of innovation, or the same attachments to a settled unbroken succession, declared their sentiments at once, without fear, and with ceremony. Entering into no verbal criticisms or refined distinctions, they came boldly to the resolution:—

> That James, being a professed Papist, had assumed the royal power, and acted as king, without having taken the oaths required by law; and had, by the advice of wicked and evil counsellors, invaded the fundamental constitution of the kingdom—altered it from a limited and legal monarchy, into an arbitrary and despotic power, and had exerted the same, to the subversion of the Protestant religion, and the violation of the laws and liberties of the kingdom; whereby he had *forfeited his right* to the crown, and the throne had become vacant.

The crown was then offered to William and Mary, who were proclaimed at the market-cross of Edinburgh, king and queen, with the greatest demonstrations of joy that had ever been seen in Scotland.

The Meeting of Estates was converted into a parliament, and everything promised an amicable conclusion. It is probably the Revolution in Great Britain would have been achieved without a single drop of blood, but for the haughty and rebellious temper of one man.

The Viscount Dundee was certainly the life and spirit of the Jacobite party; but he has evidently got far more credit for his disinterested loyalty and devoted attachment to his master, then he is entitled to. Historians have romanced upon his exploits, and lavished their panegyrics on the gallantry and generosity of his character. His bravery was undoubted; but the honesty of his intentions, and the integrity of his principles, admit not of unqualified praise. If he was loyal, it was more to serve his own interest, than from any inherent or steady affection to the existing dynasty. Pride, ambition, and revenge were his master passions; and he would have fought under any banner, and for any cause that had honours and emoluments to bestow. He had been originally a soldier of fortune, and his conduct veered with the caprices of that fickle divinity.

At his first outset, when a volunteer in the French service, he carried arms in opposition to William. He afterwards joined his standard, was made a cornet in the Royal Guards; and at the Battle of Seneffe, in 1674, he had the honour to save the prince's life. This brave action, His Highness instantly requited with a captain's commission; a generosity which left no room for the reflection he afterwards made, that William was ungrateful.[9] One of the Scottish Regiments, in Holland, becoming vacant, his ambition aspired to the command; but the prince was pre-engaged. This refusal he construed into an affront, and quitted the Dutch service. He returned to his native country in 1677, again to become the enemy of William, by persecuting his interest in Scotland.

At the Revolution, his conduct at first was ambiguous. If he did not actually offer his services to the prince, as some have thought, he seemed inclined, at least, to remain neuter.[10] His panegyrists, I know, deny this;[11] but others, affirm it without hesitation. The candid writer of a life of King William says:—

> It is most certain that my Lord Dundee did not originally design to break with the prince. He had served under him in Flanders, was a Protestant, and as is generally believed, had no

---

9. Dalrymple's *Memoirs*
10. Oldmixon's *Hist. Eng. ii.*
11. Dalrymple's *Memoirs*. M'Pherson's *State Papers* vol. i.

great inclination for James; but he was in a manner forced upon what he did, by the carriage of a fine gentleman, and a very good officer, (Colonel Cleland,) who afterwards lost his life in the quarrel.—Somers' *Tracts*, vol. xi.

The nature of this provocation, it is to be regretted, cannot now be ascertained; but it was probably some accidental rencounter about the streets of Edinburgh, and might give rise to the report of his assassination, as he and Cleland were acquainted of old, having commenced an intimacy at Drumclog, which Dundee was not likely to forget. Thus, wounded pride, and the desire of revenge, it would appear, contributed as much as loyalty, to kindle and prolong the flames of civil war.

CHAPTER 4

Cameronian Regiment

For more effectually maintaining tranquillity in the absence of regular troops, three Scots Regiments, which had been in the Dutch service, were ordered for Edinburgh, under command of General Mackay, *viz* his own. Brigadier Balfour's, and Colonel Ramsey's, (see note following). They landed in Scotland towards the end of March, and were quartered about Leith and the suburbs. Their arrival relieved the Cameronian Guard, who were chiefly inhabitants of Glasgow, or its vicinity; and they were dismissed with the thanks of the Convention, for their seasonable assistance; for having, as it is expressed, taken up arms, and continued watching and warding; during which time, they had demeaned themselves soberly and honestly, been active and instrumental in preventing tumults, and in securing the peace and quiet, both of the meeting and of the place.[1]

******

Note:—These regiments were long and well known on the Continent, under the name of the Scots Brigade, having ex-

---

1. Minutes of convention, 28 March. After the Cameronians were relieved from guarding the Convention, they were ordered to go to Stirling Castle, to guard the arms and ammunition, appointed by the estates, to be carried from thence to Glasgow, for the use of the country. "Yet though they had the warrant of the estates, the magistrates of Stirling did violently keep them from entering of the said town, and shut the gates against them, causing them stand a long time in their arms, wearied after a tedious journey, and would not suffer them to enter, until by long solicitation, and their officers giving bond for their peaceable behaviour, they were prevailed with. And after the said arms and ammunition were loaded, the people gathered together in companies, designing to stop them, until their fury and malice was allayed by the storekeeper." The magistrates of Stirling, for their "rude and indiscreet carriage," were obliged to convey the arms to Kilsyth, at their own expense. *Thomson's Acts of Scottish Parliaments, 2nd April,* 1689.

isted since the year 1572. They were the only standing forces belonging to Scotland, and among the oldest regular troops in Europe. They were always in the Dutch service until the Revolution, and had fought many campaigns under the princes of the House of Orange. They sustained the brunt of the action at the Battle of Reminant, near Mechlin, in 1578, against the Spaniards, where they fought without armour, and in their shirts. In 1688, they formed part of the armament that came over with King William. They were at the Battle of Killicrankie, where it is rather remarkable, that the commanders, on both sides, Mackay and Dundee, had once been fellow-officers, having served together in the Scots Brigade in Holland. When the Rebellion in the Highlands was quelled, they went to Ireland. At the siege of Athlone, they were the first that entered the breach in the ramparts, and stormed the place. In 1690, they were sent to the army in Flanders, where we may probably have occasion to mention them again." *Vide, Hist. Account of British Regiments in the Dutch Service.*

******

A proclamation, requiring all men between sixteen and sixty to be ready in arms, was issued, and at the same time, warrant granted to General Mackay to raise, by beat of drum, four regiments of foot, and one of dragoons. The Cameronians in the west country, chiefly in and about Douglas, had already deliberated with their friends, on the propriety of furnishing a regiment of infantry for his majesty's service; and it is to their voluntary resolutions, principally, that Lord Angus' Regiment owes its origin, of which we are now to give the reader some account.[2]

The first and most active leaders in the affair, were Laurie of Blackwood, who had suffered by a most iniquitous process under the late reign;[3] and Captain William Cleland, a gallant youth, who had served

---

2. "Meantime, arms had been distributed to the Presbyterians of the west country, who shewed themselves, of all the kingdom, the most zealous for their majesty's government, and the Protestant interest; and the most popular and leading men among them, came to wait on the general, and gave him, from time to time, account of these matters, who encouraged them in their method of forming themselves into companies, and continuing their weekly exercises, of the handling of their arms; whereof, so far as the government could not do it, they provided themselves, so zealous were they for the cause." M'Kay's *Mem. MS. Advocate's Library.*
3. *Wodrow*, vol. ii.

in the army of the Covenanters. So soon as the proposal was agreed to, they made an offer to the Meeting of Estates, to levy, in fourteen days, two battalions, each to consist of ten companies of sixty men. A general meeting for concerting and adjusting the necessary measures, was appointed to convene on the 29th of April, at the Kirk of Douglas. As a useful preparative in so important a matter, recourse was had to the exhortations of the pulpit.

On the day before the meeting, vast crowds had assembled. Three of their most popular preachers. Shields, Boyd, and Lining, alternately addressed the congregated multitudes, on a field or holm close by the town. The eloquence of the speakers, aided by the force and pertinence of appropriate texts, gave a new edge and ardour to their patriotic zeal.

The scope of their arguments was, to rouse the audience to a vigorous and simultaneous movement—to clear away certain doubts that had been started, respecting the lawfulness of expediency of admitting such as had not owned or faithfully adhered to their cause, or who differed from them any way in principles and profession.

It was a point on which they were extremely scrupulous, and a question that had been agitated with some bitterness, whether it was not a sinful association, to enlist under the same banner with those who had been the instruments and abettors of tyranny, or who had not kept their conscience clear of oaths, tests, and declarations. This diversity of opinion prevented the adoption of any express conditions, and the meeting was prorogued till the 13th May.

Meantime, several petitions and copies of resolutions were drawn up, and submitted for the approbation of their intended officers, stating, in special terms, the motives of their undertaking, and the conditions upon which they were willing to tender their services. These conditions, however, though honestly intended, were too exceptionable to meet with the concurrence of the officers; some of them being beyond the power of subjects to grant, others inconsistent with the laws of military discipline.

A brief declaration was then drawn up by Hume of Polwart, which met the views of both parties, and on the 14th of May the regiment, consisting of 1200 men, was mustered on the holm of Douglas. Cleland, who was now chosen their lieutenant colonel, went through the whole battalion, addressing each company separately in a short speech, and causing the terms of agreement to be read and explained. James, Earl of Angus, a youth under twenty, and only son to the Marquis of Douglas, was appointed colonel.[4] The two brothers, Michael and Alexander Shields were chosen, the former clerk, the other chaplain to the regiment, for it was expressly stipulated, that they should be provided with a minister of their own persuasion, and each company with an elder, for promoting piety and reproving offenders. The following is a copy of the articles referred to.

> 1. That all the officers of the regiment shall be such as in conscience and prudence, may, with cordial confidence, be submitted unto and followed; such as have not served the enemy in destroying, nor engaged by oaths and tests to destroy the cause, now to be fought for and defended.
>
> 2. That they shall be well affected, of approven fidelity and of a sober conversation.
>
> 3. They declare: That the cause they are called to appear for is, the service of the king's majesty, in the defence of the nation; recover and preservation of the Protestant religion; and in particular, the work of reformation in Scotland, in opposition to Popery, prelacy, and arbitrary power, in all its branches and steps, until the government of church and state be brought back to their lustre and integrity, established in the best and purest times.[5]

Such were the conditions of their formation; and upon the same terms they offered, if necessary, to equip two or three regiments more, without beat of drum or expense of levy-money.

It was in this patriotic corps that young Blackader volunteered as a cadet, and served for sixpence a day. Through what peculiar interest or connexion he entered this regiment, is not known. But most probably it was owing to his intimacy with the lieutenant colonel, who had been a fellow-student with him at the University. Cleland was well acquainted with his family, having been occasionally on the patrol that guarded his father at Conventicles, and as we have seen, was a conjunct agent with his eldest brother, in promoting the Revolution.[6] His noviciate seems, however, to have been but short, as in less than two months he carried a lieutenant's partisan.[7] It does not appear that

---

4. The Commissions of Lord Angus, and the other officers, are printed in Proceedings of Convention, in the Appendix to Thomson's *Acts of Scottish Parliament*.
5. *Memorial of Grievances. Faithful Contend.*
6. Blackader's *Mem.*
7. A weapon somewhat like a halbert.

he had ever been a member of the United Societies; and he certainly did not entertain their peculiar views of ecclesiastical affairs: But in other respects, he possessed all the necessary qualifications. He could plead exemption from the prevailing defections and compliances of the times. He had never been guilty of hearing curates or indulged clergymen; of supporting the cause of antichrist by paying cess, or debauching his conscience by oaths and tests. These, at the formation of the regiment, were deemed exclusive and insuperable objections; although they became afterwards less scrupulous in filling up their ranks.

Each company, on being mustered, was paid £35, sterling, per advance, to be collected from the shires of Lanark and Peebles. Towards the end of May, they were ordered to march under Lieutenant Colonel Cleland to Perth, where they were to quarter, and on their way to halt at Stirling, that such as had not arms and accoutrements, might be provided from the magazine in the castle. The commanding officer had orders to furnish them with powder and ball, and matches for their firelocks. Brigadier General Balfour delivered to them 400 pikes, and the same number of muskets, with halberts for forty sergeants. Before marching to Perth, they were commanded to rendezvous for some time about Falkirk, Larbert, St. Ninians, Doune, and Kilsyth, in order "to clear the braes of Stirlingshire of lowse and ill-affected men, who might be found in arms."[8] In the month of July, they lay at Perth as a check on the Viscount Dundee, who had made several irruptions into the Lowlands, to plunder and levy contributions.

The activity and artifices of that enterprising rebel had begun to diffuse a spirit of insurrection over the North, which was become formidable to the government. He had quitted Edinburgh, as was mentioned, under pretence of assassination; but, in reality, to summon the Clans to arms. For some weeks he remained inactive at his own house of Disdope, in Angus-shire, expecting succours from Ireland. The Convention, dreading his designs, had summoned him to return, which he refused in a disrespectful letter, and was outlawed. The Earl of Leven with 100 foot, and some troops of dragoons, were despatched to apprehend him, but he made his escape to the mountains. He repaired directly to the Duke of Gordon's territory, with the intention of raising, in a body, the vassals of that nobleman.

His purpose being known, Mackay himself went in pursuit of him, leaving charge of Edinburgh Castle, then under siege, to Brigadier

---

8. Thomson's *Acts of Scottish Parliament*, Appendix.

Balfour and Sir John Lanier, not so much for reducing that fortress, as for preventing the Duke of Gordon from joining his friends in the Highlands, as his extensive interest might have proved dangerous. He took with him four troops of Lord Colchester's Regiment, and Sir Thomas Livingston's dragoons; and marched rapidly by Brechin, Fettercairn, and Strathbogie, to Elgin. Dundee made his way to Inverness, 1st May, and by this time his party had greatly increased, being joined by M'Donald of Keppoch with 900 men.

Not daring to offer battle to Mackay, and disappointed in raising the number of adherents he expected, he withdrew to Lochaber, where he appointed a general rendezvous of the clans, to meet against the 18th day of May. Here his force increased immensely: Glengarry joined him with nearly 300 men; Clan Rannald with 200; Stewart of Appen, and M'Donald of Glenco with 200; M'Donald of Keppoch with 200, and Lochiel with 600 of the Camerons. He was unexpectedly joined by 1000 of the Athol-men, whom Lord Murray Marquis' son, had raised on his father's estate for the service of William; under pretence, however, of espousing the opposite interest. When their real destination was explained to them, they quitted their ranks, and their hereditary chieftain—a rare instance of feudal infidelity—and running to the nearest brook, they filled their bonnets with water, drank to the health of King James, and marched off to Lord Dundee.[9]

With these, and other reinforcements, and the addition of 500 recruits from Ireland, Dundee saw himself at the head of nearly 6000 men.

Many motives concurred to attract the roving Highlanders to his standard, besides their romantic admiration of his character, their attachment to James, or even their natural love of war. Plunder had more captivating charms in their eyes than either. All the arts and discipline of their commander could not restrain their predatory habits. Not withstanding every precaution of sentinels and rearguards, "they were marching off every night by forties and fifties, with droves of cattie, and loaden with spoils."[10] Some of the chiefs had no other concern, than to retain those forfeited estates of which they had gotten possession; others were hopeful to enrich themselves by new attainders. Mackay says:

> In all the progress of the army benorth the Tay, the people seemed to bear little sense of their deliverance, except a few.

---
9. *McPerson's State Papers*. Balcarras' *Memoirs*.
10. *M'Person. Balcarras.*

They seemed more disposed to submit to, and embrace the party which they judged most likely to carry it; their zeal for the preservation of their goods going with them, far beyond the considerations of religion and liberty.—It was neither out of love for King James, nor hatred for King William, that made them rise; at least, the wisest of them, as Lochiel of the Camerons, whose cunning engaged others that were not so much interested in his quarrel. But it was out of apprehension of the Earl of Argyle's apparent restoration and favour, because he had some of his forfeited estates, and several combined Highlanders held lands of the Earl's.[11]

A general expectation was entertained by the Jacobites, that the estates of their opponents would recompense the, and the most golden prospects were held out repeatedly in letters to Lord Dundee, from the Earl of Melfort, secretary to James.[12] Happily, however, these expectations were frustrated, and this formidable insurrection eventually quelled by the defeat of the rebels, 17th June, at Killicrankie. That defeat, though it can scarcely be termed a victory, proved sufficiently decisive by the death of Dundee. He fell early in the action, by a musket-ball which entered at an opening of his mail, beneath the arm, while elevating it in the act of giving command.[13] His followers, though they had broken the lines of the enemy, and by the impetuosity of their attack, spread terror and flight on all sides, lost a victory within their reach, by their eagerness for spoil and pillage.[14] They stripped the slain of their own party, and even their own general, leaving his body on the field, which could not for some time be distinguished from those of the common soldiers. (See note following).

★★★★★★

Note:—Sir Duncan Campbell of Auchenbreck, being at the Blair of Athol, had the curiosity to go and view the bodies of the late deceased Viscount of Dundee, the Laird of Pitcur, and

---

11. MSS. *Adv. Lib.*
12. Dal. *Mem.* lib. viii. Bal. *Mem.*
13. It has generally been supposed that Dundee's death happened towards the close of the action. This appears to be a mistake. "He fell by a random shot at the beginning of the action; yet his men discovered it not till they had obtained the victory." *Memoirs of Captain Creichton.* This is confirmed by King James' letter to the Laird of Ballachen. *Vide,* Col. Stewart's *Sketches of the Highlanders,* vol. i. He survived, however, to write King James a short account of the battle. M'Pherson's *State Papers.*
14. Balcarras.

M'Donald of Largie, who were killed at Killicrankie, and saw their bodies lying in an aisle of the church of Blair, and not yet interred, but wrapt up in coarse linen cloth, in very ordinary coffins, where anybody that pleases may see them: That Dundee's body, at first, was, with much difficulty, distinguished from the rest of the bodies that fell that day; for he, dying of his wounds in a very little time after the engagement, his body was presently stripped by his own party, and left naked amongst the rest of the field. *Proceedings in Scotland, 7th September.*

Some of the officers that came to town with the major general, declare, that being at Blair Castle, they had the curiosity to view the corpse of the late Lord Dundee, which they found lying in a vault in one of the aisles of the church there. The mortal wound he received, and of which he soon died, was by a shot in his left eye. *Proceedings in Scotland, 14th September*

******

Though Mackay had the superiority in numbers, he sustained a very considerable loss; the main causes of which were, the disadvantage of the narrow pass where they fought his want of dragoons, which were the only troops the enemy was afraid of, and the extraordinary mode of fighting practised by the Highlanders, with which his men were totally unacquainted. Of their singular method of attack, he gives the following description:—

The Highlanders never fight against regular forces, upon any thing of equal terms, without a sure retreat at their back, particularly if their enemy be provided with horse. And to be sure of their escape, in case of a repulse, they attack barefooted, and without any clothing but their shirts, and a little Highland doublet, whereby they are certain to outrun any foot; and they will not readily engage, where horse can follow the chase to any distance. Their way of fighting, is to divide themselves by clans; the chief, or some principal man being at their heads, with some distance to distinguish betwixt them.

They come on slowly until they be within distance of firing, which, because they keep no rank or file, doth ordinarily little harm. When their fire is over, they throw away their firelocks, and every one drawing a long broadsword, with his targe in his left hand, they fall a running towards the enemy, who, if he stand firm, they never fail of running with much more speed back again to their hills, which they usually take at their back, except they happen to be surprised by horse or dragoons, marching through a plain, or camping negligently. All our officers and soldiers were strangers to the Highlanders' way of fighting, which mainly occasioned the consternation they were in. To remedy this for the future, having taken notice on this occasion, that the Highlanders are of such a quick motion, that if a battalion keep up firing till they be near to make sure of them, they rush upon it before our men can come to their second defence, which is with the bayonet fixed withinside the muzzle of the musket. The general having observed this method of the enemy, he invented the way to fasten the bayonet to the muzzle on the outside, by two rings, that the soldiers might safely keep up their fire till they pour it into the enemy's breast, then have no other motion to make but to push with it as with a pike.[15]

The castle of Edinburgh had by this time surrendered, after a siege of more than two months. On the 6th of April, Mackay had erected four batteries, intending to storm it in a few days. One of them was raised at Multrassie's hill, another at Castle Collups, and a third at Heriot's Hospital, near which was a mortar for throwing bombs.[16] On the 17th, the cannonading commenced briskly on both sides. But in the beginning of May, Mackay having gone north in pursuit of Dundee, the siege was left in charge of the Earl of Leven and the Cameronians, who, with immense labour, drew a deep trench around the whole west side of the rock, extending from the West-Port to St. Cuthbert's Kirk.

In a few weeks. Sir John Lanier, having arrived from England, undertook to reduce the fortress, and converted the siege into a regular blockade. An attempt was likewise made to assault it on the side next to the town, by raising a breastwork of wool sacks on the Castle-hill, near the place called Blue-stone. The city of Edinburgh was required to furnish whatever number of packs might be necessary for the service, to be reimbursed for any damage the wool might sustain. This project, however, was found impracticable, and abandoned. Operations

---

15. Mackay, *Mem.* MSS.
16. Multer's, or Multrie's, or Multrassie's hill, is the rising ground west side of James' Square, immediately behind the Register Office. It was at this time sprinkled over with cottages, forming a sort of country village, where the citizens used to regale themselves with Curds and Cream. Descriptions of Old Houses in Edinburgh. Castle Collups lay on the south side of the town. *Grose's Antiq.* vol. i.

were conducted with so much vigour, that in a short time the walls were battered down in several places, and the fortifications rendered almost ruinous. The duke found himself compelled to beat a parley, and on the 30th of May he wrote to Lord Ross desiring a conference. His Lordship not thinking it safe to venture within the gates, proposed to meet His Grace on the Castle-hill, which the duke refused, it appeared however that this was a mere contrivance to gain time, and that he only wanted a temporary suspension of arms, in order to repair the bartizans and cover the roofs of the houses with earth; for the bombs had destroyed most of the stores and magazines, and penetrated to the very cellars. He pretended also that the public registers were sustaining injury, and desired they might be removed, with a design, it was supposed, either of despatching or receiving private intelligence.

Hostilities were immediately renewed with increased activity. The besiegers kept up an incessant fire, throwing in shells night and day, with a design to keep the garrison in perpetual alarm, and weary them out through the want of sleep and necessary repose. They had sunk mines, and advanced their trenches to the very bottom of the walls. They endeavoured to cut off their supply of water by draining the North Loch, thinking it would dry up the well in the castle. But notwithstanding all their vigilance, the garrison contrived to get stores and intelligence secretly conveyed to them by means of spies and partisans which they had in the town. Women were nightly employed either in furnishing information, or in procuring fresh provisions. A regular correspondence with the rebels in the North was held, through the medium of a rude and rather singular telegraph.

This mode of communication was the contrivance of a woman, a grand—daughter of the Bishop of Galloway. She inhabited the upper flat of one of the highest houses in the street that runs from the Lawn-market to the Castle-hill. Whatever intelligence she wished to communicate, she was in the habit of writing, in large capital letters, on a tablet or board, which she exposed at her window, so that the duke, with the aid of a telescope, could easily read it from the castle walls. The signal of good news was a white cloth which she hung out at the same place, and a black one when she heard anything unfavourable. (See note following).

******

Note:—A regular system of espionage was carried on, under the pretext of supplying the garrison with medicines, midwives, and other indispensibles. *Grose's Antiq.* vol. i. Several ladies of quality were also concerned; among these the Countess Dowager of Errol was one. She was apprehended and committed to custody, owing to the discovery of one of her messengers. This emissary had been in the habit of conveying intelligence while travelling the country in the humble character of a mendicant. Going, upon one occasion, in the tattered guise of a beggar with a bag of meal upon his shoulders, to the house of the Viscount Stormont, near the castle, he happened to excite the suspicion of some of the guard. After he had passed several of the sentinels, he was at last challenged and stopped by one of them, who, putting his hand into the bag among the meal, found several letters, and the sum of fifteen pounds sterling in gold. These letters discovered the fair conspirator and her correspondents, with her orders for distributing the gold among Dundee's officers.

The lady and the gold were sent up to the council, who ordered the countess to be committed to prison, and the money to be employed for the service of King William. *Hist of Revol. in Scotland.* The telegraphic lady was a Mrs. Anne Smith. Her grandfather was a Dr. Atkins. The spies were usually secreted in her house, until they could be privately conveyed into the castle, which was done by a newly discovered passage across the North Loch; the ordinary entrance being filled up with earth, and closely blockaded from without. When they had got safe into the garrison, a signal was given to Mrs. Smith by firing a musket off the half-moon.—*Vide, Account of the Siege, Grose,* vol. i.

★★★★★★

The secret mystery of these intrigues was at length discovered, and the true state of the garrison made known by means of some deserters who had been apprehended while making their escape. It appeared that their ammunition and provisions were nearly expended, being scarcely sufficient for three weeks consumption, and that they would have wanted water had they not been providentially relieved by a late extraordinary fall of snow. The bombs had destroyed the greater part of the bread, wine, and beer in the cellars, and forced the duke, with the principal officers, to retire and lodge within the strongest vaults. Threatened with ruin and starvation, and despairing of relief, the duke found himself obliged to capitulate. For this purpose he hung out a white flag as the signal of surrender; upon which. Commissioners were immediately sent up to treat with him. While they were debating together upon the terms of capitulation, which, on the part of the duke, were deemed rather high and unreasonable, a certain person ran suddenly into the castle and delivered several letters to the duke, either from Dundee, it was alleged, or the late King James, then in Ireland. The commissioners, considering it unfair that any man, upon such an embassy, should have access to the castle during the truce, without their consent, insisted that the messenger should be delivered up to their hands. This the duke refused to do, and the treaty was in consequence broken off.

The garrison immediately began to discharge both their great and small shot, and continued all night to fire upon the city, and wherever they imagined they could do most mischief. May houses were much damaged, several persons were killed, and others wounded. Next day, however, the 13th of June, the duke agreed to surrender, and obtained honourable terms for the garrison, who marched to the Castle-hill, where they laid down their arms, and delivered up the keys; thousands of people having collected to witness that gratifying spectacle, and testify their joy by loud acclamations, who never could regard themselves as secure while that important fortress remained in the hands of their enemies.[17]

---

17. *Vide Proceedings of Scottish Parl. Mem. of Viscount Dundee, Hist, of late Revol. in Scotland.*

CHAPTER 5

Battle of Dunkeld

After the death of Viscount Dundee, the command of the rebel army devolved on Colonel Canon, an Irish officer, but destitute of the resolution and military talents of his predecessor. Their numerical loss, which had been but small, was speedily repaired by new accessions. On the Braes of Mar, he was joined by the M'Gregors, the Frazers, the M'Farlanes, and the Gordons of Strathdon and Glenlevit. But neglecting to improve his advantages, and failing in his first enterprises, he lost the confidence of his troops. He opposed the advice of the clans, who were resolute to engage the enemy immediately, and follow up their success at Killicrankie, by a more complete victory.

For this, the accidental panic into which the government was thrown, certainly offered a fair opportunity. On the first rumour of the battle that reached Edinburgh, the consternation was extreme. It was reported by those who fled, that Mackay was defeated, and all his army cut to pieces. But the terror of the fugitives had multiplied their own losses, and spread a needless alarm; for in a few days, a disclosure of the real state of matters quieted all apprehensions. Canon declined an engagement, and instantly marched northward to Aberdeenshire; coasting along the skirts of the hill, followed by Mackay, and afraid to descend to the open plain, knowing that his safety consisted in keeping a position where cavalry could be of no avail. In this way the two generals continued, for nearly a month, traversing the whole range of the Grampian mountains, each unwilling to quit his ground, or resign his advantages to the other. Every day the armies were in sight of each other, and exchanging bravadoes, but without venturing to fight.[1]

About the middle of August, Canon having gotten intelligence

---

1. *Memoirs of Viscount Dundee.* Balcarras' *Memoirs.*

that the Cameronian Regiment were come to Dunkeld, he resolved to attack them, without delay, expecting to cut them off to a man, being in a defenceless place, and remote from any immediate succour. This regiment, as the reader will recollect, shortly after its formation, had been ordered to the Highlands to join Mackay. While they lay at Dunblane, in the beginning of July, the soldiers emitted a petition and declaration to be presented to Parliament, vindicating themselves from some aspersions of their enemies, and craving, that the church might be purged of Episcopacy, and the more notorious of their late persecutors legally impeached and punished. In making this latter request, they were not actuated by any vindictive desire of shedding blood.

They considered themselves as called upon to demand justice on their oppressors; and that without being guilty of any criminal intentions, they might pray the vengeance of government to overtake those, who, though not arraigned before any human tribunal, were condemned to the punishment of murderers by the laws of God, and the justice of all nations. They were provoked and scandalised to see them, not only indemnified, but continued in authority, and crowded into the ranks of the army; for many, they alleged, had sought a sanctuary under the royal standard, not from any love to the cause, but to screen themselves from the consequences of their past crimes.[2]

These sentiments of the Cameronians were certainly just, though perhaps mistimed, considering the unsettled state of public affairs, and the growing progress of the insurrection in the North. The extreme leniency of William in not calling to some account the authors of the cruelties and extortions of the preceding reign, is unparalleled in the history of revolutions, and may be said to have left a political stain on his administration. Perhaps it may be attributed more to the unexpected difficulties with which the government had at first to contend, than to any extraordinary clemency, or culpable indifference in the crown; but assuredly the abettors of tyranny, who, by their flagitious counsels, had brought church and state to the brink of ruin, ought to have felt the weight of his resentment. It would have been no trespass against the rules of equity, had mercy been meted out to them according to their own measure. This was only what the wrongs of the nation, and the injured honour of the laws demanded.

The blood of Russel and of Sidney required expiation: the oppressions of Lauderdale called aloud for retribution: the atrocities of Dalzell and Claverhouse demanded investigation and redress: the tears

2. *Faithful Contendings.*

of many widows and orphans—the blood of martyrs that perished on fields and scaffolds—the miseries of those who languished in banishment or slavery in foreign plantation—should have prevailed with the government to make some retaliatory sacrifices to the public justice of the country.

From Dunblane, the regiment marched to Perth, and thence to Dunkeld, being ordered to defend that post, which was considered as important, being at the mouth of the Highlands. The propriety of this measure was doubted, both from the insufficiency of the place for defence, and the unlikelihood of any advantage that could result from it. Mackay says:—

> They were posted there separate from all speedy relief, and exposed to be carried by assault, without the least prospect of advancement to the service, but an assured expectation of being attacked; because the enemy had not such prejudice at any of the forces, as at this regiment, whose opposition, against all such as were not of their own sentiments, made them generally hated and feared in the northern counties: Whereby it might be easily judged, that the men of Athol, now fully declared for the rebellion, would not fail to lay hold of this occasion to cut them off, finding them so disadvantageously lodged; and therefore sent to give advertisement of the occasion to defeat them, to Colonel Canon, who, having passed the hills, thought to play his personage alone, in the County of Angus.
>
> Sir John Lanier had come to Brechin, but knew nothing that the Angus Regiment had been so disadvantageously posted, nor that Canon had received the message from the men of Athol concerning it, and the opportunity offered to cut it off. Meantime, if Providence had not blinded Canon, and disheartened his Highlanders for continuing their attack, the regiment had certainly been beat, for they had two full days time to carry them; and all their defence was but low garden-walls, in most places not above four feet high. But if a sparrow fall not to the ground without the permission of our heavenly father, much more may we conclude, that the lot of the children of men is overruled by his Providence.[3]

The description of this obstinate rencounter, in which an army of 5000 disciplined Highlanders was repulsed and defeated by a com-

---

3. Mackay's *Memoirs*, MSS.

pany of seven or eight hundred raw volunteers, who had never seen a pitched battle, and had scarcely been three months in the service, will be best given in their own language. As the document, I believe, is rare, and drawn up in a simple style, but with a picturesque and interesting minuteness, no apology win be required for inserting it at full length.[4]

> The said regiment being then betwixt seven and eight hundred men,[5] arrived at Dunkeld, Saturday's night the 17th of August, 1689, under the command of Lieutenant Colonel William Cleland, a brave and singularly well accomplished gentleman, with 28 years of age. Immediately they found themselves obliged to lie at their arms, as being in the midst of their enemies. Sunday, at nine in the morning, they began some retrenchments within the Marquess of Athol's yard-dykes, the old breaches whereof they made up with loose stones, and scaffolded the dykes about. In the afternoon, about 300 men appeared upon the hills, on the north side of the town, who sent one with a white cloth upon the top of a halbert, with an open unsubscribed paper, in the fashion of a letter, directed to the commanding officer, wherein was written as follows.
>
>> We, the gentlemen assembled, being informed that ye intend to burn the town, desire to know whether ye come for peace or war, and do certifie you, that if ye burn anyone house, we will destroy you.
>
> The Lieutenant-Colonel Cleland returned answer, in writ, to this purpose:
>
>> We are faithful subjects to King William and Queen Mary, and enemies to their enemies; and if you who send those threats, shall make any hostile appearance, we will burn all that belongs to you, and otherwise chastise you

---

[4] The original of this curious account is entitled, *The Exact Narrative of the Conflict at Dunkeld, betwixt the Earl of Angus' Regiment, and the Rebels, collected from several Officers of that Regiment, who were Actors in, or Eye-witnesses to, all that's here narrated in reference to these Actions.*" Vide Pamphlets Adv. Lib. FF. 7-11. A reprint of it appeared some years ago in one of the *Edinburgh Magazines*

[5] A party of 400 of them had been ordered by the Convention to be stationed about Lorn and Cantire, to guard the west coast, against the invasions of the Irish, who were expected to reinforce Lord Dundee. They sailed from Greenock on the 15 of May, and were quartered some time in Badenoch, with two days march of Inverlochy. *Proceedings of the Convention.*

as you deserve.

But in the meantime, he caused solemnly proclaim, in the mercat-place, His Majesties indemnity, in the hearing of him who brought the foresaid paper.

Monday morning, two troops of horse, and three of dragoons arrived at Dunkeld, under command of the Lord Cardross, who viewed the fields all round, and took six prisoners, but saw no body of men, they being retired to the woods.

Monday night they had intelligence of a great gathering by the fiery cross; and, Tuesday morning, many people appeared on the tops of the hills, and they were said to be in the woods and hills about Dunkeld, more than 1000 men. About eight of the clock, the horse, foot, and dragoons made ready to march out, but a detached party was sent before of forty fusiliers, and fifteen halbertiers, under command of Captain George Monro, and thirty horse with Sir James Agnew, and twenty dragoons with the Lord Cardross his own cornet; after them, followed ensign Lockhart, with thirty halbertiers.

The halberts were excellent weapons against the Highlanders' swords and targets, in case they should rush upon the shot, with their accustomed fury. They marched also at a competent distance before the body. One hundred fusiliers were under the command of Captain John Campbel, and Captain Robert Hume, two brave young gentlemen; and upon the first fire with the enemy. Captain Borthwick and Captain Haries, with 200 musquetiers, and pikes, were likewise commanded to advance towards them; the lieutenant-colonel having proposed, by that method, to get advantage of the enemy in their way of loose and furious fighting. The body followed, having left only 150 foots within the dykes.

The first detached party, after they had marched about two miles, found before them, in a glen, betwixt two and three hundred of the rebels, who fired at a great distance, and shot Cornet Livingston in the leg. The horse retired, and Captain Munro took up their ground, and advanced, firing upon the rebels to so good purpose, that they began to reel and break, but rallied on the face of the next hill, from whence they were about beat. About that time, the lieutenant-colonel came up, and ordered Captain Monro to send a sergeant, with six men, to a house on the side of a wood, where he espied some of the enemies.

Upon the sergeant's approach to the place, about twenty of the rebels appeared against him, but he was quickly seconded by the captain, who beat them over the hill, and cleared the ground of as many as appeared without the woods; and upon a command sent to him, brought off his men in order. Thereafter, all the horse, foot, and dragoons retired to the town; and that night, the horse and dragoons marched to Perth; the Lord Cardross, who commanded them, having received two peremptory orders for that effect. The second was sent to him, upon his answer to the first, by which answer, he told they were engaged with the enemy, and it was necessary he should stay.

In that action, three of Captain Monro's party were wounded, one of which died of his wounds. William Sandilands, a cadet, nephew to the Lord Torphichen, and a very young youth, being of that party, discharged his fusie upon the enemy eleven times. The prisoners taken the next day told, that the rebels lost about thirty men in that action.

After the horse and dragoons were marched, some of the officers and soldiers of the Earl of Angus's Regiment, proposed that they might also march, seeing they were in an open useless place, ill provided of all things, and in the midst of enemies, growing still to greater numbers; the vanguard of Canon's army having appeared before they came off the field. The brave lieutenant colonel, and the rest of the gentlemen officers amongst them, used all arguments of honour to persuade them to keep their post; and for their encouragement, and to assure them they would never leave them, they ordered to draw out all their horses to be shot dead. The soldiers then told them they needed not that pledge for their honour, which they never doubted; and seeing they found their stay necessary, they would run all hazards with them.

Wednesday with the mornings light, the rebels appeared, standing in order, covering all the hills about, (for Canon's army joined the Athole men the night before, and they were repute in all, above 5000 men.) Their baggage marched along the hills, towards the west, and the way that leads into Athole, consisting of a train of many more than 1000 horses. Before seven in the morning, their cannon advanced down to the face of a little hill, close upon the town, and 100 men, all armed with back, breast, and head piece, marched straight to enter the town, and a battalion of other foot close with them. Two troops of horse marched about the town, and posted on the south-west part of it; betwixt the ford of the river and the church, and other two troops posted in the northeast of the town, near the cross, who, in the time of the conflict, shewed much eagerness to encourage and push on the foot.

The lieutenant colonel had before possessed some outposts, with small parties, to whom he pointed out every step for their retreat. Captain William Hay and Ensign Lockhart, were posted on a little hill, and the ensign was ordered with twenty-eight men, to advance to a stone dyke at the foot of it. They were attacked by the rebels who were in armour, and the foresaid other battalion. And after they had entertained them briskly with their fire for a pretty space, the rebels forced the dyke, and obliged them to retire, firing from one little dyke to another, and at length to betake themselves to the house and yard-dykes; in which retreat. Captain Hay had his leg broken, and the whole party came off without any more hurt.

A lieutenant was posted at the east end of the town with men, who had three advanced sentinels, ordered, upon the rebels close approach, to fire and retire, which accordingly they did; and the lieutenant, after burning of some houses, brought in his party.

Lieutenant Stuart was placed in a *baricado* at the cross, with twenty men, who, seeing the other lieutenant retire, brought his men from that ground, and was killed in the retreat, there being a multitude of the rebels upon them.

Lieutenant Forrester, and Ensign Campbell were at the west end of the town, within some little dykes, with twenty-four men, who fired sharply upon the enemies horse, until great numbers of foot attacked their dykes, and forced them to the church, where were two lieutenants, and about 100 men.

All the outposts being forced, the rebels advanced most boldly upon the yard-dykes all round, even upon those parts which stood within less than forty paces from the river, where they crowded in multitudes, without regard to the shot liberally poured in their faces, and struck with their swords at the soldiers on the dyk, who, with their pikes and halberts, returned their blows with interest. Others, in great numbers, possessed the town houses, out of which, they fired within the dykes, as they did from the hills about:

And by two shots at once, one through the head, and another through the liver, the brave lieutenant colonel was killed, while he was visiting and exhorting the officers and soldiers at their several posts. He attempted to get into the house, that the soldiers might not be discouraged at the sight of his dead body, but fell by the way. (See note below). And immediately thereafter, Major Henderson received several wounds, which altogether disabled him, and whereof he died four days after. Captain Caldwal was shot in the breast, and is not like to recover. Captain Borthwick was shot through the arm, going with succours to the church; and Captain Steil got a wound in the shoulder, which he caused pance, and returned again to his post.

★★★★★★

Note:—Of Colonel Cleland's history, it is to be regretted, that so little is known; although he appears to have been one of the most gallant and accomplished leaders that the Covenanters had. Most of their champions have found a niche in the biography of the times. The industry of Howie and others, has preserved the names and exploits of many of their party from oblivion. Cleland, however, has passed unnoticed, and might have remained unknown, had he not, by his poetical talents, raised a monument to himself. This neglect, most probably, is to be ascribed to the defection he was alleged to be guilty of, in adhering to the government, after the Revolution, when he was regarded as an apostate from the Society's principles, no longer a pillar of the Covenant, but a supporter of Antichrist. He was a gentleman of a good family in the west country, though we have no notice of his parentage or connexions.

From certain allusions in his poems, it has been conjectured, but without proper foundation, that he was born about Dumfries. His rank, aided by his great bravery and military capacity, gained him considerable influence among the suffering Presbyterians. He was chosen one of their officers, immediately on his leaving the University, and before he reached his eighteenth year. He first distinguished himself at Drumclog or Louden-Hill—the only rencounter in which the Covenanters were successful, where Claverhouse was repulsed, and nearly taken prisoner. Hamilton was commander of the party, but the victory was, by many, ascribed to a stratagem of Cleland's, who, when the enemy presented their pieces, made his men fall flat on the ground, so that they quite escaped their fire. At Bothwellbridge, he held the rank of a captain. After that defeat he fled, and continued some time in Holland. In 1685, he was again in Scotland, "being under hiding among the wilds of Lanark and Ayrshire."

The failure of Argyle's expedition, obliged him to escape a second time to the Continent; and in 1688, as was already noticed, he was one of the commissioned agents, sent by the Scottish emigrants to prepare his countrymen for their long expected deliverance. From that time, until the raising of the Cameronian Regiment, he resided much with the Marquis of Douglas, at his castle, his son, the Lord Angus, having a great attachment to him. The colonel was father to William Cleland, Esq. one of the commissioners of the Customs in Scotland, author of the *Prefatory Letter to Pope's Dunciad*, and said to have been the original of the celebrated Will Honeycomb in the *Spectator*. As a poet, Cleland, considering the state of society, and the disadvantages under which he wrote, will rank very high.

His effusions are honourable to the Scottish Muse, and superior to anything produced in that age, in his own country. His vein seems to have been chiefly humorous and satirical, though he was capable of rising to the more elevated and dignified heights of poesy. His principal pieces are, *A Mock Poem on the Expedition of the Highland Host, in 1678. Effigies Clericorum. Halloo my Fancy, with Ballads and smaller Poems*. Of the rhapsody entitled *Halloo my Fancy*, which has been admitted by a competent judge of poetry, though a reviler of Cleland's party and principles, (*Minstrelsy of Scot. Border,* vol. i.) to display considerable imagination, only the later half is his.

It was written when he was a student, and very young. The part he wrote, begins at the *stanza*, "In conceit, like Phaeton, I'll mount Phoebus' chair," &c. His genius, however, considering his untoward and premature fate, must be estimated rather from what it promised, than what it performed. And if his talents have numbered him one of the Scottish Poets, his bravery will entitle him to rank among the Scottish Heroes. His career was short, but it closed with honour. His conduct, during the action narrated above, was marked by all the coolness, skill, and intrepidity of a veteran; and his effort to retire when he had received the fatal wound, lest the sight of his dead body might discourage his soldiers, throws an air of chivalry over his death, and discovers a species of heroism truly noble and sublime. This note has swelled to too great a length, and I quit the subject with this regret, that our limits admit not of paying a more worthy tribute to his memory; and that this brief notice will avail so little to draw from unmerited obscurity, the name of one who was at once a polite Gentleman, an able Poet, a devoted Patriot, a brave Soldier, and a pious Christian.

★★★★★★

The lieutenant colonel being dead, and the major disabled about an hour after the action began, (which was before seven in the morning) the command fell to Captain Monro, who left his own post to Lieutenant Stuart of Livingstone: And finding the soldiers galled in several places by the enemies shot, from the houses, he sent out small parties of pikemen, with burning faggots upon the points of their pikes, who fired the houses; and where they found keys in the doors, locked them, and burnt all within; which raised a hideous noise from these wretches in the fire. There was sixteen of them burnt in one house, and the whole houses were burnt down, except three, wherein some of the regiment were advantageously posted. But all the inhabitants of the town, who were not with the enemy, or fled to the fields, were received by the soldiers into the church, and sheltered there.

Notwithstanding all the gallant resistance which these furious rebels met with, they continued their assaults incessantly, until past eleven of the clock. In all which time, there was continual thundering of shot from both sides, with flames and smoke, and hideous cries filling the air: And, which was very remarkable, though the houses were burnt all round, yet the smoke of them, and all the shot from both sides, was carried every where outward from the dykes upon the assailants, as if a wind had blown every way from the centre within.

At length the rebels, wearied with so many fruitless and expensive assaults, and finding no abatement of the courage or diligence of their adversaries, who treated them with continual shot from all their posts, they gave over, and fell back, and run to the hills in great confusion. Whereupon, they within beat their drums, and flourished their colours, and hollowed after them with all expressions of contempt and provocations to return. Their commanders assayed to bring them back to a fresh assault, as some prisoners related, but could not prevail; for they answered them, they could fight against men, but it was not fit to fight any more against devils.

The rebels being quite gone, they within began to consider, where their greatest danger appeared in time of the conflict; and for rendering these places more secure, they brought out the seats of the church, with which they made pretty good defences; especially they fortified these places of the dyke which were made up with loose stones, a poor defence against such desperate assailants. They also cut down some trees on a little hill, where the enemy galled them under covert. Their powder was almost spent, and their bullets had been spent long before, which they supplied by the diligence of a good number of men who were employed, all the time of the action, in cutting lead off the house, and melting the same in little furrows in the ground, and cutting the pieces into slugs to serve for bullets. They agreed that in case the enemy got over their dykes, they should retire to the house, and if they should find themselves overpowered there, to burn it, and bury themselves in the ashes.

In this action fifteen men were killed, besides the officers named, and thirty wounded. The account of the enemies loss in uncertain; but they are said to be above 300 slain, amongst who were some persons of note.

That handful of inexperienced men was wonderfully animated to a steadfast resistance against a multitude of obstinate furies. But they gave the glory to God, and praised him, and sung psalms after they had fitted themselves for a new assault. Amongst many who shewed extraordinary courage, some young gentlemen, cadets, deserve a special testimony and remembrance; as William Sandilands, above named; James Pringle of Hultrie; William Stirling of Mallachen; James Johnstoun, a reformed lieutenant, and several others.

Diverse officers besides those above specified, *viz.* another Captain John Campbell; Captain Haries; Lieutenant Henry Stuart; Lieutenant Charles Dalzell; Lieutenant Oliphant; Lieutenant Thomas Haddo; ensign William Hamilton, and most of all the other officers behaved very worthily, at their several posts, throughout the whole action, and deserve well to be recorded, as men of worth and valour. And the whole soldiers did every thing with such undaunted courage, and so little concern in all the dangers and deaths that surrounded them, and stared them in their faces, that they deserve to be recommended as examples of valour to this and after ages, and to have some marks of honour fixt upon them. And it is expected, His Majesty will be graciously pleased to take notice both of officers and soldiers. Upon the Saturday immediately after those actions, the young Laird of Bellachan, came into Dunkeld, to treat for the benefit of His Majesties indemnity, for all those Athole. And he declared, that Lord James Murray was willing to accept thereof But Major General M'kay, who by his gallant and wise conduct, prevented the conjunction of ill-affected people with the rebels, and baffled all their designs upon the low countries, is now in the Highlands with a brave army: And, with the blessing of God, will shortly give a good account of them all, and put an end to the troubles of this kingdom.

This engagement gave rise to a great deal of surmise and discourse. The regiment was everywhere commended for their bravery and intrepid conduct. Their unparalleled courage was the subject of universal admiration. It so intimidated the rebels, that they never attempted to appear in any great body afterwards, or attempted to disturb the peace of the country. It lowered their esteem of Colonel Canon; for after the first repulse, the Highlanders could never be induced to offer a second attack.

Everything certainly operated to their discouragement, overwhelmed as they were with numbers, abandoned to the fury of their most implacable enemies, and intercepted from all possibility of retreat. Their friends, and some of themselves, were of opinion they had been betrayed, and sent to that remote, defenceless pass, with a design to be cut off. In this, the Duke of Hamilton was blamed, and Col. Ramsey, who, having sent three troops of dragoons from Perth for their assistance, had order them back, "judging that they could not add much to the defence of that post."[6] These charges, in all probability, were without any just foundation, and most likely originated

---

6. Mackay's MSS. *Faithful Contendings*.

from their own suspicions. There might be imprudence or impolicy in leaving so small a body to sustain the whole force of the enemy, but there is scarcely room to suspect treachery.

In addition to the foregoing account of the battle, I shall here give an original letter of Lieutenant Blackader, written on the spot, to his brother in Edinburgh, about two hours after the engagement. As it was printed and circulated in the periodical papers of the time, it is most probably one of the documents from which the preceding narrative was drawn up. I may venture, however, even at the hazard of making some repetitions, to insert it at full length, both on account of the neatness and modesty of expression, and as furnishing an early illustration of that piety and humility which marked his whole conduct in future life.[7]

(The copy of a letter written and sent by Lieutenant John Blackader, in E. of Angus his Regiment, about two hours after the engagement.)

Dunkell, Wednesday, Aug. 21, 1689

D.B.—I have taken this first opportunity to shew you I am in good health, because I believe may false reports will, by this time, be come to your ears anent our engagement, which was this same day; but for your certain information, the manner and way was this: On Saturday last we came to this town at night, and camped within some walls between the church, and a house belonging to the M. of Athol. On Sabbath morning, the country people, and Atholmen appeared on the Hills round us in tens and twenties; and about four afternoon a party of 60 or 80 men drew up on a hill above us, and within a little while, sent down a letter to our lieut. col. full of threatenings and boastings, the which he answered as briskly, and after carried up the indempnity, and proclaimed it in the messenger's hearing, and so he retired.

Meantime notice had been given to St. Johnstown, to the forces there, to come up to our help, and accordingly on Monday morning came Lord Cardros with four troops of dragoons and

---

[7]. I had in my possession a mutilated copy of this letter; but a complete transcript of it, (I believe from the collection of newspapers in the British Museum,) has been procured for me, through the kindness of Thomas Thomson, and David Constable, Esqrs. Advocates, gentlemen eminently distinguished for their profound knowledge and patriotic interest in Scottish Historical Literature.

one troop of horse; upon which, the lieut. col. detatched out the most part of the regiment, who, with the Horse, went to meet the enemy, who appeared in several parties, to the number of about 500 or 600 men (ours being about the same number) Some small parties went out and skirmished; but Cardros, after an hour or two's stay, brought in his men to the town; our lieut. coll. did the like. An hour after, Cardross told the lieut. coll. he must needs go back to St. Johnstown, being expressly ordered by Coll. Ramsay so to do. Our men were mightily discouraged to hear this; but whatever could be said, the Horse would not stay, and it was much for us to keep our men from going along with them whether we would or not, but the lieut. coll. compelled them and told them. That though every man went away, he resolved to stay himself alone; so we past Tuesday night also in arms.

This morning about six of the clock, the enemy appeared on the hills, and whereas we expected only the enemy we lad seen the day before, we saw to the number of 3 or 4000 Men draw up above us, which proved to be the whole force of Coll. Cannon, the which one of the prisoners we took, gave out to be 4000 men, besides the addition of the countrey. Our lieut. coll. making a virtue of necessity, being nothing discouraged, posted the men so as they might most annoy the enemy, planting them behind dykes and ditches, which he caused to be cast up, and in the church and steeple, and in Athol's house. When he had done so, the enemy approached very fast, the Highlanders came running on like desperate villains, firing only once, and then came on with sword and target; a troop of the enemies horse, (brave horse, and all gentlemen) beset one side, on purpose, we think to have cut us off when we fled, which they nothing doubted off.

A party was sent out under the command of Capt. Hay (Park Hay's son) to keep them up, which fired on them, and then retired, not being able to restrain their great number and fierceness, pressing in upon us to the very cross in the middle of the town, where another party of our men fired on them, and they retired in order. After which, the Highlanders came swarming in on all sides, and gave a desperate assault in four places all at once, first firing their guns, and then running in on us with sword and target. But it pleased God, that they were also bravely repulsed, our men still firing on them, where they came on thickest, in this hot service we continued above three hours, the

Lord wonderfully assisting our men with courage, insomuch that old soldiers, that were with us said.

They never saw men fight better, for there was not the least sign of fear to be seen in any of them, every one performing his part gallantly. But (which is never enough to be lamented) our dear and valiant lieut. coll. at the beginning of the action going up and down encouraging his men, was shot in the head and immediately died; our major also received three wounds, so that I fear he will not live.

Notwithstanding all these discouragements, our men fainted not, but fought so, that the enemy at last found themselves necessitated to flee back on all hands, leaving a number of their dead carkasses behind them, and a great many of them getting into houses to fire upon us, our men went and sett fire to the houses, and burnt and slew many of them. One of the prisoners we have taken, told us. That after they were gone off, their officers would have had them come back, and give us another assault, but they would not hear of it, for they said we were mad and desperate men. Upon their retreating, our men gave a great shout, and threw their caps in the air, and then all joined in offering up praises to God a considerable time for so miraculous a victory. I must really say.

The Lord's presence was most visible, strengthening us, so that none of the glory belongs to us, but to His own great name; for we clearly saw. It was not by might, or our power, nor by conduct, (our best officers being killed at first, or disabled) so that we have many things to humble us, and to make us trust and eye him alone, and not instruments. I pray God help me, not to forget such a great mercy I have met with, not receiving the least hurt, notwithstanding several falling on my right and left hand. This is a true and impartial account of the whole affair, which you may communicate to others in case of misrepresentation. The enemy retired, as we hear, to the castle of Blair, We expected still they would assault us again, but word being sent to St. Johnstown at 12 o'clock, we expect speedy help from thence. This in haste from

Your affectionate brother,

(*Sic Surscribitur*)   J. Blackader.[8]

---

8. *Vide, Continuation of the Proceedings of the Parliament in Scotland, &c.* No. 52. 31st Aug. to 3rd Sept. 1689.

The Cameronian Regiment, after the affair at Dunkeld, marched northward to Aberdeen, and thence to Montrose, where they remained most of the time they were in Scotland. They defeated a small party of the rebels near Cardross. The terror of their name served to keep the country in awe; for a body of Highlanders, having come to plunder about Montrose, so soon as the Cameronians shewed themselves, fled with precipitation, without daring to stand or offer the least resistance.[9]

---

9. *Faithful Contendings. Proceedings in Scotland.*

CHAPTER 6

War in Flanders

The reduction of the Highlands, and the abandonment of Ireland by James, left William at leisure to co-operate with his allies, in prosecuting the war on the Continent. All the troops that could be spared from the necessary defence of his kingdoms, were ordered to cross the seas, to join the confederate army, then assembled in the Netherlands. Of this number was Lord Angus', and other five Scottish Regiments, *viz*. the Scots Guards, Mackay's, Ramsey's Douglas', and O'Farrell's, now the 21st or Royal North British Fusiliers. These regiments suffered severely in the various sieges and actions of the Flemish campaigns. At most of the engagements in that sanguinary war. Lieutenant Blackader was present, and was so remarkably fortunate, as to escape without a single wound.

His diary, however, which does not commence until 1700, contains no account of these military operations, and only adverts occasionally to some of his own memorable escapes. We do not, therefore, think it necessary to give more than a brief outline of the more prominent actions in which he was engaged. His personal services, in the following campaigns, cannot indeed be distinguished from those of his regiment; but to have omitted them entirely, would have been to leave an important blank in his history, and detract from the merits of his well-earned reputation.

Meantime, we may here observe, that the affection and good understanding which had hitherto subsisted between the gallant Cameronians and their parent sect, was now to be interrupted by an irreparable breach. The United Societies had kept up a friendly correspondence with the regiment, ever since it was raised, and claimed a sort of spiritual charge over its religious and moral deportment. They repeatedly sent to the Highlands admonitory letters, exhorting the soldiers both to their private and public duties—to refrain from drunkenness, duels, swearing, and such other vices as soldiers are addicted to—to abstain from the sinful and scandalous games of cards and dice, of which some of them were occasionally guilty: They sometimes reprimanded the elders for being lax in administering reproof, and not keeping up sessional discipline in the regiment. To all, they recommended the propriety of laying down their arms, and quitting the profession, rather than be engaged in any service which did not end to advance the glory of God, and the work of reformation.

They applauded their resolution, not to serve with the malignant armies in Ireland, which they had refused to do, when the Scots Brigade were sent over. But they were highly incensed at their present conduct, for entering into foreign service, and especially for joining in association with what they considered a profane and Popish confederacy. By this step of defection, as it was called, the brave Cameronians incurred the displeasure of the United Societies, and were formally disowned by the more rigid brethren.

The truth is, being disappointed in their peculiar views of church government, and seeing their persecutors continued in office, instead of being brought to condign punishment, as they expected, they began to be disaffected to the government; and to cast out of their fellowship, all who adhered to it. They retracted their former declaration for the Prince of Orange, and their owning as queen, a daughter of the bloody Popish Duke of York, educated in the abjured principles of Prelacy. The gallant Cleland who had disciplined their troops, and led them on to victory against Claverhouse and Canon, was now branded as a betrayer of their cause, and a reviler of the great Mr. James Renwick. Shields the chaplain, with Boyd and Linning, who had assisted, by their eloquence, in levying the regiment, being charged with lapsing into these backslidings of the times, abandoned the Community, and were admitted into the bosom of the church.[1]

Their animating appeals to the patriotism of their countrymen on the holms of Douglas, were all construed into rhetorical subtleties, to

---

1. Acts of General Assembly, November, 1691. Mr. Boyd was afterwards settled at Dairy, and so zealous was he for the interests of the regiment, that his old friends, the Hill-men, accuse him of causing his elders in the night, to take out of their beds, several of the dissenters in that parish; and upon the Sabbath morning, shaved the old men's beards to make them look young, and presented them to the recruiting officer, that so they might pass for the parish: But in this he was disappointed, as the officer would not accept of them, because of their age. *Faithful Contendings*, App.

entrap and ensnare them into unlawful associations. Instead of going *To pull down the gates of Rome*, as the preachers had expressed themselves, they were going to espouse the cause of Antichrist, and fight for the rights of the *Holy See*, in league with malignant heretics and Popish idolaters—alluding to the alliance entered into by the treaty of Union, at the Hague, in 1690, which we shall shortly have occasion to mention. From this period, the Cameronian Regiment may be regarded as altogether disowned by the United Societies, or at least, in a state of alienation and apostasy from them.[2]

The war of 1690, against Louis XIV. was a confederacy of all Europe, which he had justly provoked by his insatiable ambition, and his regardless infringement of treaties. (See note following). His gigantic policy seemed to grasp at universal empire, and to enlarge the boundaries of his own dominions, he scrupled not to make the most flagrant aggressions upon the territories of his neighbours. Not only the faith of treaties and negotiations, but even the laws of religion and humanity were dispensed with, when they obstructed the accomplishment of his vainglorious projects. The English and the Dutch complained that he had oppressed their commerce, plundered their merchants, and encroached upon their fisheries and foreign colonies. By violence or artifice, he had made himself master of the chief fortresses on the side of Germany, and had laid his plans to seize every place of strength on the Rhine, from Basle to Mayence. He had wrested to himself two-thirds of the Spanish Netherlands, and eagerly sought a pretext to appropriate the remainder.

★★★★★★

Note:—This disastrous war, if we may believe St. Simon, originated in a dispute between the King of France, and his minister Louvois, about the proportion of a window! When the castle of Trianon was built, Louis imagined he discovered a defect in the relative symmetry of on of the windows. Louvois was of a contrary opinion. This insolence (the liberty of thinking for himself,) so enraged his royal master, that he reprimanded him very severely in presence of many of the courtiers. Louvois, with his mind agitated betwixt rage and shame, returned home to devise some scheme for averting the consequences of his obstinacy, which might have cost him his office, perhaps his life. "It is all over," said he, "I must have lost my credit with the king.

---

2. *Faithful Contendings*, Appendix.

I have no resource but in war, which will divert his attention from buildings, and render my assistance necessary. And war he shall have." The courtly minister kept his word. In a few months war was declared, and a flame kindled with raged for eight years—overran Ireland, France, Spain, Italy, Germany, Flanders, and the West-Indies—at the expense of millions of money, and many thousand lives. *Percy Anecd. of War.*

★★★★★★

The States beheld with alarm these frontier towns, which ought to have been a barrier to repel his ambition, filled with hostile troops, and converted into military stations, whence their enemies might annoy and oppress them at pleasure. On the Upper Rhine he had ravaged the whole country with fire and sword. Not content with possessing the fortifications, he ordered the towns and villages to be laid in ashes, and reduced the Palatinate to a desert. The wretched inhabitants, delivered up to the pillage of a lawless soldiery, were driven from their homes in the dead of winter, to wander in the fields without food or shelter. Twice in his reign did he desolate these fertile and populous provinces, involving, in one promiscuous ruin, the works of art—the monuments of antiquity, and the temples of religion.

Embowered amidst the luxuries and voluptuous pleasures of Versailles, he consigned, without pity or remorse, the lives and properties of a flourishing district, to the lusts and the swords of a barbarous military. These inhuman mandates found Lauderdales, Grahames, and Dalzells, ready to sanction and to execute them; and it may seem a strange anomaly in human nature, that the most cruel and oppressive acts that disgraced the annals of that period, issued from the two most effeminate courts in Europe, those of Charles II. and Louis XIV. Atrocities so remorseless and unprovoked, struck the nations with horror at the spectacle: Even the officers who were the instruments of them, were ashamed at their own barbarities.[3]

His severe persecution of the Huguenots or French Protestants, was a measure equally repugnant to humanity, and the principles of sound policy. By revoking the Edict of Nantz, which secured to them the free exercise of their religion, he had driven into exile above 400,000 of the most industrious and valuable inhabitants of France. The Huguenots being incapacitated by law from holding civil offices, had employed themselves chiefly in arts and ingenious manufactures;

---

3. Voltaire's *Siecle de Louis XIV.* chap. xvi. Ralph's *History of England*, vol. ii.

and by their skill, and the encouragement they received under Colbert, they had amassed very great opulence. But the cruelties and military executions to which they were exposed, forced them from their homes, to seek protection in foreign countries. Religious emigrants were scattered over the whole continent. Fifty thousand of them took refuge in England, and many more in Holland and Germany. Wherever they fled, they carried their wealth, their industry, and ingenuity along with them. Their miseries and complaints excited the compassion of strangers, and increased the general detestation at the tyrant who was the author of them. Numbers of these fugitive joined the ranks of the allied armies, in order to revenge their injuries, by retaliating on the persecutor. Louis had thus the mortification to see his own subjects become, not only rivals in arts and commerce, but enemies, and instruments to chastise him.

By his rapacious aggressions abroad, and his impolitic severities at home, Louis had thus raised up against him a formidable confederacy, such as Europe had never seen; comprehending nearly all the powers in Christendom, with the exception of Poland and Switzerland. England and Holland, the emperor, with all the princes and electors of Germany, Spain, Savoy, and almost the whole of Italy, were leagued in alliance against France. Of the confederacy, William was unquestionably the presiding genius and master-spirit. Besides his natural hatred of France, which had always been the oppressor of his House, he had at this time special reasons of enmity. Louis had attempted to drive him from the throne, and assailed his dominions in support of the abdicated monarch. He had invested Ireland with his fleets, and filled it with his armies. Emissaries were employed to foment opposition, and even to attempt his assassination. French gold, by which he had corrupted all the courts in Europe, was distributed among the rebels in he three kingdoms. England had thus a personal interest in this Continental Association. She was not entering into foreign connexions from a love of war, or embarking in any romantic speculation of chivalry, from which she was to derive no benefit. She took up arms in defence of her religion—the independence of her crown—and her very existence as a free nation. [4]

France never beheld such a combination of power leagued against her; and the hour seemed to be approaching, when she was to experience, in her turn, so many miseries and insults. With this formidable array, Louis had to contend single-handed. The most magnificent

---
4. Ralph, vol. ii., Burnet, vol. ii., Dalrymple's *Mem.* B. ii.vi.

preparations wee made to repel the invasions that threatened him on all sides. His resources seemed to increase in proportion to his difficulties, and to multiply with the purposes and demands he had to answer. The unlimited control he possessed over the finances of the mighty empire, enabled him to set in motion, and keep a-going a vast system of offensive war; and with a vigour that astonished the most sanguine of his adversaries. He had in regular pay, of land and marine forces, not less than 450,000 men. These he had divided into six armies, which were stationed round his dominions, and all at once in active operation.

One army was employed in Ireland, to support the interests of James, under Count de Lauzun, and the Duke of Berwick; another in Spain with the Duke de Noailles; and a third on the confines of Italy, commanded by Marshal Catinat; a fourth was stationed on the Upper Rhine, to oppose the Emperor Leopold, and the rest of the Germanic princes; a fifth, under Marshal Boufflers, was posted on the Moselle, as an army of observation, to act as circumstances might require; the sixth, commanded by Luxembourg, the ablest general in the French service, was opposed to the Dutch and British in the Netherlands; where the greatest efforts were to be made, and the greatest obstacles to be encountered.[5]

In the Congress which met at the Hague, January 1691, the Allies concerted their measures for opening the approaching campaign, and fixed the number of troops to be supplied by each of the contracting powers.[6] They published their resolution, not to lay down arms against France, until she should restore all she had taken from the neighbouring states since the peace of Munster. William, who presided, and opened the congress, harangued them in an eloquent speech, on the imminence of their danger, and the necessity of making a simultaneous effort, to snatch the liberties of Europe out of the hands of the Usurper. He promised to spare neither his credit, his fortune, nor his person; and undertook to furnish a quota of 20,000 men, at the head of which, he was determined to conquer or perish with his allies.[7]

Besides the six Scots Regiments mentioned above, which were

---

5. Voltaire. *Dalrymple*. Ralph, vol. ii.
6. The Emperor, Spain, Brandenburg, and England were to furnish each 20,000; the Dutch 35,000; Savoy and Milan 18,000; Bavaria same number; Saxony 12,000; the Palatinate 4000; Hesse, 8000; Suabia and Franconia 10,000; Wirtemberg 6000; Bishop of Liege, same; Bishop of Munster, 7000; the Princes of Lunenburg, 16,000. *Dalrymple's Memoirs*, Book vi.
7. Ralph, vol. ii.

shipped at Leith, about the end of February, but detained some weeks in the Frith by contrary winds, several others were about the same time embarked for Flanders, *viz.* Earl of Leven's, Argyle's, Lawder's, and Beveridge's.[8] His majesty sailed on the 3rd of May, and landed in Holland on the 18th. Next month he reviewed the whole of the royal confederate army, consisting of 184 squadrons of horse and dragoons, and 83 battalions of foot, each 800 men, amounting in all to 222,000.

In every quarter, fortune had attended the French arms. Victory had declared for them in Spain and in Italy. In Flanders, they had gained the Battle of Fleurus, July 1690, and in March, next year, they took the strongly fortified city of Mons. The summer was spent in marching and manoeuvring, in raising batteries and constructing bridges, without producing any thing of importance, each party forming projects that vanished before they could be put in execution. The allied army had advanced on the Sambre, between Huy and Charleroi; and although William was desirous to undertake some enterprise which might sustain his high reputation among the allies, and give a pledge for the confidence they had reposed in him, yet the enemy were content, merely to thwart his designs, without risking the decision of a battle. In the month of September he returned to England, leaving the army in charge of Prince Waldeck.[9]

As Louis had reaped little glory from the preceding campaign, he resolved to signalize the following year, 1692, by some enterprise, worthy of his power, that might strike terror into the allies, and compel them at once to sue for peace. Two grand projects he had in contemplation; the one was, to astonish the Confederates by the conquest of Namur; the other, to make a descent on England, to second the zeal of the Jacobites, and re-establish James on the British throne. A most splendid naval armament was fitted out at the ports of Brest and Toulon, which was opposed by preparation equally magnificent on the part of England and Holland. The two fleets met off Cape La Hogue; and after an obstinate engagement, which continued for six days, the French were completely defeated.[10]

In Flanders, Louis was more successful. He had withdrawn the greater part of his troops from his other frontiers, and sent them to join the army under Luxembourg, who invested Namur, towards the

---

8. *London Gazette.*
9. Beaurain *Hist. Militaire.* Ralph, vol. ii
10. *Dalrymple's Memoirs,* vol. i. book vii. Burnet.

middle of May. Lord Angus' Regiment had not yet been in any general action, though they were in active service all the preceding campaign. They were now with the army under King William, that covered this celebrated siege.

Namur, which was reckoned one of the best fortified cities in Flanders, is situated between two hills, at the confluence of the Meuse and the Sambre. Its natural strength was rendered still more impregnable by the subsidiary works of art. The citadel, built upon a rock, was considered one of the strongest in the Netherlands. Cohorn, the famous Dutch engineer, had constructed new fortifications, and was himself employed to defend them. The garrison, between nine and ten thousand men, was provided with all the requisites for a long and obstinate resistance. Few sieges had witnessed such a display of military talent and preparation. Here art was opposed to art; and the two great rivals in military architecture, Cohorn and Vauban, were brought into contact with each other, and set to exert all the powers and resources of their genius, as it were, to determine the point of superiority between them. It was, moreover, a spectacle but seldom witnessed, and which filled the nations with anxiety for the event, to see the two most powerful monarchs in Europe contending in person, each at the head of their respective armies.

Louis appeared first on the field, though he had left Versailles on the same day that William had quitted the Hague. His travelling retinue was rather unusual for a warrior, and altogether in the effeminate style of an Asiatic court. He had a train of carriages filled with his mistresses and ladies of quality; and was accompanied by musicians, dancers, opera singers, and all the voluptuous ministers of luxury. He immediately invested the town, being resolved to carry it before he attempted the citadel. His army, consisting of 120,000 men, he divided into two halves; with the one, he himself pressed the siege, while Luxembourg, with the other, was employed to cover it. On the night of the 29th of May, the trenches were opened, and next day. Marshal Boufflers made himself master of one of the suburbs. In two days more, the counterscarp was carried by assault; and after several attacks, in one of which, the grand magazine of the town took fire and blew up, the besieged found themselves obliged to capitulate, which they did on the 5th of June. But the garrison were allowed forty hours to retire into the castle.

When the city had surrendered. Fort Cohorn was next attacked with great fury, the batteries having played upon it for six days, without intermission, but though defended with the utmost resolution, it was reduced, after an obstinate contest, in which Cohorn himself, who commanded the fort, was dangerously wounded. The reduction of the citadel now only remained, and this was immediately undertaken by the besiegers, with all the spirit and intrepidity which the presence of their great monarch could inspire. From the 22nd until the 27th, bombs and balls were poured into it incessantly. The defendants made several bold attempts to dislodge the enemy, and kept them at bay by the briskness of their fire; but one of their bastions being taken by surprise, had such an effect on the governor, the Prince de Barbason, who was suspected, on this occasion, of cowardice or treachery, that he beat a parley, and agreed to evacuate the place, which was immediately taken possession of in the Name of His Most Christian Majesty.

William, who was assembling his troops near Louvain, had not begun to move when the city of Namur capitulated. On the 8th of June, he advanced on the small River Mehaigne, with intention to force the enemy to raise the siege. Luxembourg occupied the opposite bank, and the two armies continued many days in sight, and sometimes within cannon-shot of each other, without coming to any decisive action.

There was frequent and sharp skirmishing between them, and William made several efforts to dispost his antagonist, and decide the fate of Namur, by a battle. But the rains, having swelled the river, swept away his bridges, and rendered the low grounds a complete marsh, unfit for cavalry or artillery to pass. Besides, Luxembourg who had the start of him in preparations, had secured all the most advantageous posts, and made such dispositions, that it was scarcely possible he could have been dislodged, but by a force much superior to his own. It was with the greatest mortification, that William saw himself obliged, at the head of 80,000 men, to lie inactive, and witness, with his own eyes, the reduction of the most important fortress in the Netherlands—his presence serving only to give additional *éclat* to the triumph of his grand rival, who, considering this feat as the greatest action of his life, returned to Versailles, to be flattered with the pompous compliments of his court and nobility.[11]

In order to retrieve his lost honour, William determined immediately to anticipate, in his turn, the artifices of Luxembourg, who had retired to an encampment between Steinkirk and Enghien; his own camp being at Lambecq, about six miles distant. Hoping to attack the

---
11. Voltaire, Beaurain, Ralph, Burnet.

French by surprise, he sent them, by means of a spy, false intelligence of his destination; while, by the disposition of his troops, he left it uncertain whether Namur, Liege, or Dunkirk was to be the object of his attack. Eager for a battle, as the only means of sustaining his reputation, and consoling the allies for their ill success, he set out for Steinkirk on the night of the 2nd of august, with all secrecy: The army repassed the Senne at Halle, and marched in two columns, as the nature of the country, which was covered with thickets, and intersected by hedges and narrow defiles, did not admit of an extended front.

By daybreak they were close upon the enemy; but owing to the encumbrances of the ground, it was mid-day before they could make their necessary evolutions, or form in order of battle. The Prince of Wirtemberg led the van, supported by Lieutenant General Mackay, at the head of the Scottish Infantry, and several battalions of English. Count Solmes had the command of the centre, and the Elector of Bavaria, of the rear. The French were posted on a rising ground, with their right on Steinkirk, and their left towards Enghien. They were encompassed with hedges, and defended in front by a wood, so that there was no way of attacking them but by the side of the wood, or through the hedges which they were in possession of. About two in the afternoon, the battle commenced with a furious attack on the enemy's right wing, by the Prince of Wirtemberg, whose brave battalions charged up the hill with such vigour, that they drove the French from their hedges and trenches, and made themselves masters of the cannon which they kept possession of, for more than half-an-hour. Of the ten battalions that behaved with such gallantry, four were English and Scots, the rest Dutch and Danes.

At this time, the enemy's camp presented a scene of consternation and disorder; and had the panic been taken advantage of, the affair might have terminated in favour of the allies. But unfortunately. Count Solmes neglected to follow up this success, and either from a hatred of the English, or a jealousy of the Prince of Wirtemberg, purposely kept back the necessary succours, until Luxembourg had rallied his broken lines, and reinforced them with fresh troops.[12] The French soon recov-

---

12. "Though the Prince of Wirtemberg sent one of his *aides-de-camp* twice to require succours from Count Solmes, and at last procured a positive command from the king himself, so jealous was the said Count of the Prince's glory, and so thoroughly did he hate the English, that he ordered his horse, which he knew could not act for want of room, to march, and his foot to halt, purposely that the English might be massacred, and the Prince foiled, saying to those around him. Let us see what sport these English bull-dogs will make us." Ralph, vol. ii.

ered their lost ground. Their far-famed guards, with many princes and nobles at their head, were let loose, and in a bravado charged sword in hand. The Dutch and British sustained the shock with the greatest intrepidity. Deserted by their friends, they had nothing but their own bravery, and a sense of duty to animate them For four hours the combat raged with unabated fury, and scarcely was any victory ever more obstinately contested. The carnage on both sides was great; and never was the sword more impartial, for officers and soldiers fell without distinction, in one promiscuous heap of slaughter.

Notwithstanding the superiority of the French in numbers, have thirty battalions opposed to ten, the battle seemed to remain doubtful, until the arrival of Marshal Boufflers with his cavalry, which gave the fortune of the day a fatal turn. The brunt of the contest was sustained by the infantry, the horse being no farther engaged than merely covering the attack. The loss of both parties was extremely severe; above 10,000 men having fallen within the space of a few hours. The Scots and English alone, were said to have left 3000 dead upon the field. Many officers of rank on each side were slain or wounded; and here the Cameronians, who had been in the hottest of the action, lost their gallant Colonel, the Earl of Angus. He was succeeded in command by Lieutenant Colonel Monro.[13]

William conducted his retreat with the greatest order and coolness, while Luxembourg durst not stake the glory he had dearly won, by hazarding a pursuit. Satisfied with his escape, and unable to derive any advantage from his victory, he was content to remain quietly in his camp, and the allies returned unmolested to theirs.

The most extravagant joy was manifested at Paris, on the first news of this supposed overthrow. The young princes who returned from

---

13. Besides Lord angus, there were killed of British officers of note. Lieutenant General Mackay, Lieutenant General Sir John Lanier, Colonel Sir Robert Douglas, whose regiment drove four French battalions from their cannon. Colonel Roberts, Colonel Hodges, grandfather to the celebrated Colonel Gardiner, and several others, most of whom fell in the first attack on the hill. Mackay, according to Burnet, was sent on a post which he saw to be untenable, and gave his opinion accordingly, but the order being confirmed, he went on and met his fate, with resignation, only saying, *the will of the Lord be done.* "He was a man of such strict principles, that he would not have served in a war that he did not think lawful. He took great care of his soldiers' morals, and forced them to be both sober and just in their quarters. He spent all the time he was master of, in secret prayer, and in reading the Scriptures. The king often observed, that when he had full leisure for his devotions, he acted with a peculiar exaltation of courage."

the battle, were received with a veneration bordering on idolatry. The roads through which they passed, were lined with gazing multitudes who rent the air with their frantic acclamations. Any man who had been there was regarded with admiration. To commemorate this victory, fashion lent her aid; and Steinkirk had the honour of introducing a new mode of tying cravats, and giving name to every modish article of female attire. Jewels, hats, and handkerchiefs were named Steinkirks; and the populace vied with each other in the invention of flattering compliments.[14]

William, though vanquished and considerably shorn of his military glory, still continued a formidable enemy. After passing the winter in England, he opened the campaign of 1693, in the month of May. The allied armies which had been quartered about Ghent, Aeth, Bruges, and Oudenarde, were summoned to his majesty's camp at Park, near Louvain, where he was also joined by the Dutch and English Infantry. His first object was to cover such places as were most exposed and most likely to be attacked. For this purpose he ordered detachments to be posted at Liege, Huy, Maestricht, and Charleroi, himself remaining on the defensive in his camp, with about 40,000 foot, and 12,000 horse and dragoons. For above a month the two armies remained in this uncertainty, each ready to seize the first advantage.

On the 17th of July, the Duke of Wirtemberg gallantly forced the French lines between the Scheld and the Lys, in several places; and laid the whole country, as far as Lisle, under contribution. Louis had set out for the camp on the 2nd of June, with his ordinary equipage, where it was expected he would have achieved some mighty exploit; but to the great joy of the allies, after having reviewed his army, he returned with all his ladies to Versailles, leaving the prosecution of the war to Boufflers and Luxembourg. The latter took the town of Huy, and made a feint to invest Liege; but his real object was to surprise the allies, who had taken up a position at Nerwinden. And here was fought another of those disastrous battles, in which William saw himself forced to yield the palm of victory to his rival.

In this action, the Confederate Army had the advantage of the ground, but they were greatly inferior to the enemy in point of numbers, being much weakened by the detachments sent to Liege and other places. They were drawn up on a rising ground between the villages of Winden and Landen, distant about two miles; their right defended by the River Geete, their left by the brook of Landen. Their

---

14. Beaurain, Ralph, Burnet, and Voltaire's *Siecle, tom. i.*

front was covered by ninety pieces of cannon, planted along the ridge of the hill, and by a thick hedge which ran in the direction of their lines, to a considerable extent. The body of the infantry was posted on this eminence, with the cavalry in the rear. The Elector of Bavaria, with his division, in which were several battalions of Scots and English, occupied the village of Nerwinden on the right, which sustained the hottest of the action. On the 28th of July, in the afternoon, the French Army reached the plain of Landen, but Luxembourg, content with examining the position of the allies, deferred the attack until next day.

This delay gave William an opportunity of retiring behind the Geete, had he chosen to avoid an engagement, which he was advised to do, by the Electors and other Princes of the army: But he was resolved to give battle, hoping to make up for deficiency of numbers, by courage and perseverance. During night he cause, with incredible speed, a deep trench to be dug, from the one village to the other, which covered, as with a parapet, his whole front. By daybreak the works were finished; and between four and five in the morning, the cannonading on both sides began. The havoc became more terrible the nearer they approached, but without abating the resolution of either party.

About eight, the attack upon Nerwinden commenced. The carrying of this point was of the greatest importance to the enemy, as they could not approach the entrenched front of the allies, while their flank was exposed to the galling fire of this village. It was therefore vigorously assaulted, and carried in a short time. But the assailants were not long masters of it, until it was regained. The defendants in their turn, were again dislodged, and the enemy once more obtained possession of the place. In this manner, it was taken and retaken three or four times; and such were the desperate efforts made by William to retain this post, that after redoubled exertions, he had the pleasure of seeing it again recovered by the valour of the British Infantry, which he had twice led on to the attack in person.[15]

This obstinate and murderous contest was kept up until four in

---

15. Voltaire takes notice that in one of these attacks, was the regiment of Ruvigni, wholly composed of French refugees, all gentlemen, whom the terror of the dragoons, and the fatal revocation of the Edict of Nantz had forced to abandon and to hate their country. They had joined the ranks of the enemy, in the hope of being revenged for the intrigues of the Jesuit La Chaise, and the cruelties of Louvois. *Siecle de Louis XIV.* chap. xvi.

the afternoon. Both parties had continued to pour in torrents of fresh troops, which were swept away in whole battalions by the fire of their opponents. Each inch of ground was disputed to the last. The little mud-walls, about four feet high, which the inhabitants used instead of hedges to divide their gardens, served the purpose of entrenchments. The streets where they fought, were piled with heaps of slaughter, among which were many of the bravest troops in the French service, the Swiss and Royal Guard.

While the capture of Nerwinden was occupying the attention of Luxembourg, the centre of his army had remained almost in a state of inaction, exposed to the enemy's artillery, a part of his cavalry, however, finding between the village and the River Geete, a passage which the allies had been forced to abandon, took advantage of this, and fell upon the rear of the infantry that defended the trenches. William, who observed this, advanced with a part of the left wing, but being too distant, the line was forced and broken before he could approach.

The French dragoons poured in without opposition. The Spaniards and Hanoverians were charged and overthrown. The Dutch horse were put to flight before the English could form. Dismay and confusion became general; and as it was impossible to drive the enemy form their advantage, William gave orders to sound a retreat. The right wing being overpowered with numbers, was forced headlong into the Geete, where many, both men and horses, perished. The bridges were broken down by the pressure, and whole regiments were precipitated into the river, their dead bodies serving to facilitate the escape of their flying companions.

But the retreat which William conducted was managed with the greatest order, and was reckoned, even by his enemies, a masterpiece of good generalship. Luxembourg, however, was not in a capacity to profit by the advantages which fortune had put in his power; for though victory had declared in his favour, both parties were equally disabled.[16] In this bloody rencontre, above 20,000 men were slain, 8000 on the side of France, and 12,000 on that of the allies, besides 2000 prisoners, and a very great number of cannons, mortars, and colours which fell into the hands of the enemy. Here the Cameronian Regiment must again

---

16. Louis, who never failed to magnify his own glory, always caused Cathedral service to be performed for the entertainment of his good people of Paris, even when his triumphs were doubtful, for sometimes both parties were found celebrating the same victory at the same time. On this occasion it was remarked, that instead of *Te Deum*, he ought to have sung *De Profundis*. *Volt. Siecle, tom.* i.

have lost their brave Colonel Monro, for his name does not appear in the list of officers for the subsequent campaign.[17]

At Lew and Tirlemont, William collected the debris of his army, and though but a short distance from the field of battle, his antagonist durst not attack him weak and exhausted as he was, but retired back to his camp, near Liege. The conduct of the king during the whole action, showed the greatest courage and presence of mind. He visited every post in person, faced every danger, and undertook to remove every difficulty. He alighted not less than four times to head the infantry in their attacks, performing the office of subaltern, as well as of a general. He continued from the dawn on horseback, and had only taken two hours sleep in his coach, the preceding night. Several officers fell by his side; his own, and two led horses were killed. He had refused to put on his armour, that his movements might be more easy and expeditious. One musket ball went through his peruke, another through the sleeve of his coat, and a third passed through his sash, slightly grazing his body.[18]

The only other achievement of the French this campaign, was the reduction of Charleroi, which was taken in October—the allies finding it impossible to relieve the garrison, without forcing the lines of the besiegers.[19]

In the spring of 1694, the Confederates were again ready for action. Their misfortunes seemed only to redouble their efforts. The grand army was reassembled in the beginning of June, at Bethlehem Abbey, near Louvain, where William had his camp. The Scots and English battalions left their garrisons in Flanders, to join the main body. The Scots were reinforced by an accession of 7000 men: Of these, 3000 were new levies; and with such expedition were they raised, that although the proclamation for them was not issued until the 14th of March, by the 22nd of April, they were not only completed, but all

---

17. Beaurain *Ordre de Batt. des Allies,* 1694.
18. The escapes recorded of William are truly miraculous. He had the art of turning his faults to good account, and of making his rashness a matter of policy. The invulnerability of Dundee and Dalzell, was attributed to the possession of infernal spells: William's intrepidity was ascribed to his belief in Predestination, according to which, it was supposed, that swords and bullets had their commission, and their bounds set them, beyond which they could not pass. This opinion of him was confirmed the more by his frequent exposures and escapes in danger; and he even countenanced the belief, as he saw it made his troops more regardless of fear, and contributed to their courage and resolution.
19 Beaurain, Ralph, Burnet.

actually embarked in Leith Roads for Flanders.[20] France, enfeebled by success, and exhausted by her victories, was now forced to act upon the defensive. Neither money nor recruits could be procured, while the allies, like the fabulous hydra, seemed to multiply under the sword of the destroyer.

The enemy spent the summer in consuming the forage in the plains of St. Tron, Tongres, and Vignamont; and the only memorable action of this campaign was, the retaking of Huy, which surrendered to the Confederates on the 27th of September. About the middle of October, the armies again dispersed, and went into winter quarters.[21]

The campaign of 1695, was more disastrous to Louis than any of the preceding. His glory and greatness wee evidently verging towards a decline. His resources were exhausted with so many expensive wars, and Luxembourg, who had made France the terror and the scourge of Europe, was no more. These bereavements seemed to put an end to his rapid career of victories. Marshal Villeroi was placed at the head of the army in Flanders, while the second command was given to Marshal Boufflers. As they intended again to act on the defensive, Villeroi took his position behind the lines that ran from Menin on the Lys, to the Scheld; and Boufflers lay with his forces near Mons, to cover Namur in case of a siege.

The allies were superior in point of number, and formed into three divisions: One with the Elector of Bavaria was ordered to invest Namur. The king himself at the head of the main body, was encamped behind the Mehaigne, to sustain the siege, while Prince Vaudemont, with an army of observation, occupied a position between the Lys and the Mandel. The grand object of William was to retake Namur; but to amuse the enemy and conceal his real purpose, as well as to complete his preparations, he made a feint of attacking three different places at once. Having decamped suddenly from Rousselaer, he sat down (3rd of July) with his whole force before the town, which was already invested by a detachment, under the Earl of Athlone. Boufflers at the head of seven regiments of dragoons, followed by a large corps of engineers, miners, bombardiers, &c. had just time to throw himself into the place, before it was completely enclosed.

The garrison was computed at 15,000 men, well furnished with all sorts of stores and provision. The fortifications which Cohorn had left unfinished, were improved by Vauban. The citadel was deemed

---

20. Ralph, ii.
21. Beaurain, Ralph, *Volt. Siecle, Mem.* De Berwick.

impregnable;[22] and it was believed, the town itself could scarcely be carried. The trenches were opened immediately, and while the siege advanced with all imaginable success, Prince Vaudemont, with his division, executed one of the most masterly retreats recorded in history. While he lay encamped near Arsel, Villeroi with his whole army, instead of marching to the relief of Namur, thought it more advisable to leave the besiegers unmolested, and attack this separate body, which he doubted not would fall an easy prey to his overwhelming force.

About ten in the evening, he reached the prince's camp, who was taken by surprise, and kept his troops under arms all night. He caused entrenchments to be thrown up in case of assault. Finding next morning that he was in danger of being surrounded, and cut to pieces, he wisely altered his resolution from fighting to retreating. He ordered the infantry to file off in two columns, through the trenches, with their pikes and colours trailing. He had also a line of cavalry drawn up, behind which, the foot passed along, while their motion was concealed from the enemy. Nor was the deception perceived, until the horse quitted their post, which they did when the infantry were beyond the apprehension of pursuit.

The French were struck with amazement, to see a whole army vanish from before their eyes, as it were by magic; while the prince, who remained in the camp till the last, amused himself at their confusion. About 400 men were cut off, which happened by a stratagem of the enemy, a party of whom, speaking English, and having green boughs in their hats, a distinction which the allies used in the day of battle, were mistaken for friends, and had thus an opportunity of taking advantage by their disguise.

The Cameronian Regiment appear to have been in this famous retreat, as we find Lieutenant Blackader alluding in his diary, some years afterwards, to his narrow escape at Arsel on this occasion. [23] The same evening. Prince Vaudemont reached Deynse, next day he marched to Ghent, and some time after to Brussels, which Villeroi was preparing to bombard, in retaliation for the attacks of the English on the coasts of France. This was a piece of cruel and useless vengeance. Having mounted his batteries with mortars, and cannon loaded with red-hot balls, he began to play upon the city, continuing this process of devas-

---

22. So firmly were the holders possessed of this belief, that they caused the following inscription to be engraven over on of the gates of the castle: *Reddi quidam, sed vinci non potest.* "It may be restored, but can never be reduced." Ralph.
23. May 25, 1706.

tation for some days, without intermission. Churches, convents, public buildings, and above 1500 house were laid in ruins. The wind blowing strongly, the flames spread on all sides, presenting a scene of destruction at once sublime and terrific.[24] Prince Vaudemont was encamped on a neighbouring hill, and an eyewitness of this tragedy, but without the ability either to prevent or avenge it.

Meantime the siege was carried on with the most determined and invincible obstinacy on both sides. No contest since the beginning of the war had cost more labour and expense of lives. The natural bravery of the troops was aided and increased by the methods in which they were arranged, being often went to the assault in bodies composed of different nations, who vied with each other in feats of the most desperate courage. This national rivalry inflamed their resolutions to a sort of frenzy, and made them appear more like desperadoes and madmen than soldiers. The Scottish and English infantry, consisting of thirteen battalions, were detached from Prince Vaudemont's army to join the besiegers.

On the 12th of July, the batteries were opened, and continued for six days to ply without interruption. The fist exploit of any consequence was the storming of one of the outworks, on a hill near the Brussels' Gate. This was performed by five battalions of English, Scots, and Dutch, under Lord Cutts and General Ramsey, in presence of the king himself.[25] They faced the enemy's fire with great intrepidity, and after a sharp action of two hours, in which many brave men fell, they obliged them to abandon the fort. This attack was led by 120 fusiliers, armed, and carrying fascines before them. These advanced up to the very palisades, where, laying down their fascines, they discharged their muskets; the grenadiers then threw in their *granadoes*, and the rest marching close behind, presented over the palisades, and poured their whole fire upon the enemy. This success they followed up instantly by carrying the first counterscarp, which they did, though repulsed three several times, and left exposed to the shot from the bastion, their woolsacks and fascines having taken fire while endeavouring to effect a lodgement. The same day, the Elector of Bavaria reduced an impor-

---

24. The Duc de Berwick compares it to the burning of Troy, and estimates the loss at twenty millions. "*Jamais,*" says he, "*on ne vit un spectacle plus affreux, et rien ne ressembloit mieux a ce que l'on nou raconte de l'embrasement de Troye. On estime que le dommange causè par cet incendie, montoit a vingt million.*" Mem. tom. i.

25. During this assault, the king is said to have exclaimed repeatedly in a sort of rapture, "*See my brave English! See my brave English!*"

tant post on the opposite side of the town, with very little loss, and threw a bridge over the Sambre.

The next undertaking was to drive the defendants from their lines of communication between the Sambre and the Meuse, which would prevent them from annoying the besiegers in that quarter. This was reckoned a matter of difficult and almost hopeless execution, as they had a hill to climb planted with cannon, besides those that could be made to bear upon them from the fortifications. Yet with all these discouragements it was attempted. Wherever the officers led, the soldiers were ready to follow, as they had now forgotten what fear was. They made their assault with such hardihood, that they not only forced the besieged from their lines, but tuned their own artillery against themselves.

In order to effect a breach in the rampart of the town, the assailants plied their batteries, both of cannon and mortars, for two days incessantly. His Majesty went himself into the trenches to give the necessary orders. On the 2nd of August, the breach was deemed practicable, and Lord Cutts, with 400 grenadiers, entered, though several times repulsed, and made such slaughter of the enemy, who were now exposed on all sides to the fire of the besiegers, that they were glad, next day, to hang out their white flag as a signal of surrender.[26] The garrison were permitted two days to retire into the castle, against which the whole operations of the allies were now directed.

On the 12th of August, the siege of the castle commenced, and for several days the assailants continued their approaches with all possible diligence. As they had now possession of the town, they were in a condition to batter the citadel on all sides. On the 21st they had no less than 60 mortars, and 166 pieces of cannon pointed against it, s if they intended to level the walls, like those of Jericho, with one blast. A general discharge from all these batteries was made at the same moment, and with such effect, that the echo rebounded from the hills, and the whole circumference of the castle, with the rock on which it stood, seemed to reel under the shock Scarcely could the besiegers themselves support the horrors of their own experiment. For some time all was enveloped in one thick cloud of smoke and dust. In the interior of the castle, he scene of astonishment and confusion was indescribable. Every object wore the face of ruin.

Nothing was to be seen save bursting shells, fractured battlements, limbs of men blown to atoms and horses plunging headlong into the

---

26. *London Gazette*, Ralph.

trenches, or impaling themselves on the palisades in their ungovernable fright. Boufflers and the principal officers had found it necessary to retire to the vaults under ground, until the storm had abated; and even there they could scarcely believe themselves safe, as despair seemed to penetrate to their lowest caverns.

On the 29th, the garrison were summoned to capitulate, and time allowed to prepare their resolutions, but without success, and hostilities went on. A detachment of 10,000 men, divided into four parties among which were Mackay's, and other Scots regiments, were ordered to make four different attacks at once, with a view of taking the castle by one general storm. But this design, though the men, as usual, seemed to outrival each other in rashness and impetuosity, had only a partial success, owing to a mistake of the signals, and a miscalculation in timing the assault. The carnage within the citadel had become so great, that the defendants solicited a truce of one day, for the burial of their dead, which was granted. At the same time, they offered to surrender Fort Cohorn, and requested that the truce might be prolonged for ten days; neither of which the besiegers were disposed to listen to.

The garrison, finding no alternative between a total surrender and the hazard of another general assault, which they were less able to withstand, as the walls were broken down in some places to the extent of an English mile, proposed to capitulate, which they did on honourable terms; and on the 4th of September, the castle was evacuated; the whole siege having lasted nearly two months. This sanguinary contest cost the French nearly 10,000 lives, and the allies many more; although William gained by the recovery of Namur, more honour than he had lost during the three preceding campaigns.[27]

The following year produced nothing memorable, being entirely spent in feints and bravadoes, so ambiguous, that it was difficult to know whether they were intended to challenge or avoid an engagement. In 1697, the allies lost the town of Aeth: But France was no so much embarrassed and reduced, that she began to make advances towards a peace, to which the Princes of the Confederacy seemed equally disposed. Accordingly the peace of Ryswick, which was to suspend all hostilities in Europe, was concluded in October this year, although, as it often happens, the seeds of discord were planted in those very treaties which were designed to secure the general tranquillity.

---

27. *London Gazette*, Ralph, *Mem. de Berwick*.

Thus ended one of the most ruinous and expensive wars that this country had yet been engaged in. The enormous levies had exhausted the public treasures, left the fields uncultivated for want of hands, and the inhabitants in danger of starvation. [28] The military operations of this period might have been passed over in silence, but for the reasons mentioned in the beginning of this chapter. The subsequent part of our work, which is to be compiled from the *Diary and Letters of Colonel Blackader*, will necessarily be of a less general nature, and more restricted to his personal history.

---

28. Burnet's *History*. Dalrymple's *Memoirs*, b. v. Ralph.

CHAPTER 7

The Diary

After the peace of Ryswick, the regular forces in England were reduced to a standing army of 7000 men; 4000 of which were horse and dragoons, and 3000 infantry. This establishment was reckoned by William much too small, considering that France, by keeping up more than twenty-five times that number, was in a condition to recommence hostilities, as she had done at the peace of Nimeguen, whenever she might find it convenient to infringe the treaty.[1] The suspicious state of affairs abroad obliged him to declare his opinion, that the safety of Britain required a considerable land-force, and to strip it, from an ill-timed economy, of its military defences, was only giving their enemies an opportunity of effecting, under the notion of peace, that ruin which they could not accomplish by war. But the nation, jealous of their liberties, looked upon a standing army as the formidable engine of slavery and oppression. The parliament, with a resolution not to be shaken by the wishes or entreaties of the king, disbanded the troops, not excepting his favourite Dutch guards, who had been the companions of his glory and his toils, and the regiments of French Protestant refugees, who were attached to him in gratitude for their protection.

The Cameronian Regiment was not disbanded, but retained on the Peace Establishment. They appear to have continued in Holland in the Dutch pay, at least for some time, together with four other

---

1. The whole of the British standing forces, including those that continued on the Continent in foreign pay, amounted to nearly 60,000 men. The Peace Establishment of Scotland consisted of four regiments, viz. Royal Scots Guards, Row's Fusiliers, Hamilton's, Maitland's, and four companies in garrison; in all 4769 men. Ireland had a force of 12,000 and there were five Scots Regiments on the Dutch Establishment, amounting to 5568 men. *Vide Hist. of Standing Armies, State Tracts Temp. Gul.* vol. iii.

Scots Regiments, *viz*. Lauder's, Murray's, Collier's and Strathnaver's.[2] There was an express capitulation between William and the States General, by which the latter obliged themselves to send home the British troops, whenever the king should think proper to recall them. In virtue of this, three of the above regiments, known by the name of the Scots Brigade, were brought over to Scotland, where they were retained in the king's own pay, until the prospect of a rupture with France, in 1701, made their assistance necessary again in Holland.[3] Whether the Cameronian Regiment came over at the same time, I know not, nor is it material; they seem, however, to have been in Scotland in 1701-02, as we shall find, that in March that year, they were embarked for the Continent. They were stationed in garrison at Perth, as the writer of the diary mentions, who, by this time, was advanced to the rank of a captain.

At the commencement of the diary, October 1700, the writer was in London, where he continued a year, detained by business, partly relative to his promotion, and partly about regimental arrears; as all officers who had legal claims (among which his regiment was one) were required to state them to the commissioners of debts due to the army.[4] It does not appear that the above date was the original commencement of the diary. Most probably that journal extended to the preceding campaigns, or even to an earlier period; but those parts of it have been lost, and cannot now be recovered.

As the diary and letters are entirely personal, and relate almost exclusively to matters of private concern, the reader is not to expect from them much of historical or extraneous remark. His design was not to write commentaries on the military operations in which he was so long engaged, nor to treasure up for the entertainment of posterity, a boastful catalogue of his own achievements; for no man was ever more unambitious of renown, or less captivated by the frivolous glory of a name. His object was to keep a spiritual register of his experiences, to note down, day by day, the various phases of his own mind, that by comparing himself with himself, he might, from time to time, judge of his progress in Christian attainments. And this, I am persuaded, con-

---

2. The Cameronian Regiment, I take, to be that known at this time by the name of Ferguson's. It was so, at least, as we find a year or two after this, at the beginning of the next war. Colonel Ferguson most probably succeeded Monro, who fell at the Battle of Nerwinden, as his name appears on the list of new appointments for the subsequent campaign. *Vide Beaurain Ordre de Bataille*, 1694.
3. Tindal's *History*.
4. *London Gazette* 1700-1.

stitutes their peculiar value. The actions of warriors and statesmen, are matters of public history and of general notoriety. We know how battles have been lost or won, where valiant men have fought and fallen; but the religious annals of a soldier's life, the combats he sustains with enemies within himself, and the victories to be won over the corruptions of his own heart, are of comparatively rare occurrence.

As these papers were never intended to see the light, they may be reckoned to exhibit a faithful transcript of the writer's sentiments,—a fair unvarnished image of his thoughts. They present to our view a faith kept in lively and habitual exercise,—a devotion glowing with uncommon ardour and intensity, and engaging all the affections on the side of religion. They show us piety, flourishing under circumstances deemed the most hostile and unpropitious to its growth. They unfold a character, marked by a singular exemption from the prevailing immoralities,—a blamelessness of conduct, exemplary in any profession, but more remarkable when found in situation where moderation in vice may be accounted, in some degree, a mediocrity of virtue.

Though no outward condition, however adverse, can be reckoned altogether incompatible with the duties of religion and morality, yet some are more unfavourable to their cultivation than others. Of these, the army has always been held as one. There the mind has often little relish, and little vacancy for serious thoughts. The hurry and tumult of action, leave no room for their entertainment. The moments of interval are to apt to be filled up with levity, riot, or debaucher. The uncertainties and vicissitudes of events, distract and indispose men for calm and sober reflection. The pomp and parade of war, dazzle their imaginations with false charms, and misplace their affections on improper objects. The ambition of rising to fame or fortune,—of rivalling the glory of illustrious actions, while it excites them by more impetuous motives than those of religion, tends at the same time to inspire a certain disdain for the Christian character, as inadequate to these sublime and noble pursuits, and not calculated to make a figure on the stage of the world, by possessing so little to attract external notice.

Many thus argue themselves into a foolish and groundless contempt for religion, as if it were something mean and despicable, that checks the ardour of heroism, and chills every generous emotion of the soul. And hence it is, that the portraits of heathen conquerors, or even the achievements of a fabulous hero, will stand higher in their esteem and admiration, then all the magnanimity of Christian martyrs, or the most shining and sublime moral virtues that ever adorned human nature.

But perhaps the greatest enemy to piety, and the most formidable obstacle it has to encounter, are those criminal amusements and licentious pleasures to which a military life, more than any other, is exposed, and which are not attended in that profession with the same infamy and disgrace that public opinion has stamped upon them in civil society. Amidst all the rigour of military discipline, there is often a lamentable deficiency of moral control. And when the restraints of fear and shame are removed, the passions become more ungovernable. The contagion spreads by example; and many are carried away with the guilty crowd, from the dread of affected singularity, or the hopelessness of stemming the universal torrent of error and corruption. They are content to resign the glory of an honourable opposition, from the apprehension of incurring an ideal reproach,—to prefer the fleeting and frivolous satisfactions of a moment, to the more solid and durable felicities of a virtuous abstinence.

The extracts which we shall lay before the reader, will exhibit a character, in every respect the reverse of this general portraiture; the character of one who had the courage to be singular; whose principles were proof against the seduction of example,—the tyranny of custom,—and the terror of ridicule. So far from running himself into fashionable vices, or countenancing them in others, we find him, at all times, their avowed and determined enemy. If he did not always signify his disapprobation in formal reproofs, he shewed it by his example; his habitual seriousness and sobriety being a constant rebuke on the profligate and intemperate.

The prevailing cast of Colonel Blackader's mind was singularly devout and spiritual. His purest delights were in the duties and ordinances of religion, and he embraced every opportunity of being engaged in them. His intervals of business were generally filled up with useful reading, or company, when it could be procured, from which he could reap some improvement; and he dedicated a portion of every day to prayer and meditation. These duties he never allowed to be interrupted by the most urgent and pressing emergencies. On fatiguing marches, at the post of command, or in the head of action, he could snatch a moment to hold communion with the Father of Spirits. To him, no station seemed incompatible with maintaining this intercourse, and no circumstances so straitened, where the virtues and graces of the Christian life had not room for exercise.

Everywhere, his devotion could find for itself a temple and an altar;

in the camp, in the closet, or in the fields. It was his custom to spend an occasional hour in meditative retirement, and he would frequently steal from bustle and observation, to some sequestered walk, or the solitary banks of a river, where he could enjoy, unmolested, the benefits of contemplation and reflection. Sometimes he would visit the field of battle on the evening after an engagement, to moralise among heaps of slaughter, and "get a preaching," as he expresses it, "from the silent dead."

These habits and sentiments may probably be derided by some, and stigmatized as enthusiastical fancies, or the reveries of a gloomy and mistaken piety. To the gay, the thoughtless, and the dissipated, it may appear that he carried his abstinence from those amusements and recreations, which are thought harmless, because they are fashionable, to an unnecessary extreme; that he affected a strictness and precision, not only ridiculous in his profession, but apt to create errors and misconceptions of religion, as if it were an enemy to all cheerfulness, fit only for men of dark unsocial tempers, who shun companionship with the world, and betake themselves to melancholy solitudes, or the practice of rigid austerities. None, however, I am persuaded, will entertain such an opinion who have any relish for personal devotion, or have felt the pleasures which spring from piety and virtue,—pleasures which the world cannot give, and which strangers never intermeddle with.

Were they, who thus censure and condemn, more conversant with religion, and more deeply imbued with a sense of its importance, they could see abundant reason to think otherwise, and to judge more favourably, even of the pious excesses of good men, whose souls are purified, warmed, and inspired with heavenly affections. Profligates and *infidels* are not the persons best qualified to fix the just boundaries of morality,—to decide between sinful compliances on the one hand, and an overstrained scrupulosity on the other. They are not only unacquainted with its principles, but from their mode of life, have contracted habits and prejudices that unfit them for judging with candour, or drawing an impartial comparison. Hence all actions and pursuits, more rigid than their own, they brand with the name of enthusiasm, or some term denoting a stiff and puritanical cast of deportment.

This is very common practice, although the term is but vaguely understood, and often very erroneously applied. Many use the word *enthusiast* or *fanatic* as an epithet of reproach, without being able to attach to it any definite signification, or knowing what kind of people are comprehended in the aspersion; and if interrogated for an explanation, or to state their own ideas upon the subject, we would find them often ridiculously at a loss to give a determinate answer. They cannot tell exactly what ingredients must go to constitute an enthusiast, or what degree of precision will entitle a man to that appellation, but they fasten it in general, without troubling themselves to inquire into its meaning or applicability, on any who show an extraordinary veneration for religion, or who are distinguished for the strictness of their principles, and the severity of their manners.

If these are the odious characteristics of an enthusiast,—if he is obnoxious to that reproach, who fears an oath, and is offended at indecent speeches,—who reverences the laws of God, and strives to regulate his walk and conversation by them,—who acts at all times under a full and sensible impression of the Divine presence, aspiring after a nobler reputation than the esteem of men, and cherishing a contempt for the pleasures and vanities of the world, in proportion as faith reveals more nearly the pure and endless felicities of heaven; then it may be affirmed, more to his glory than his shame, the writer of the diary was an enthusiast.

His character, however, cannot be held up as a faultless model, worthy of indiscriminate praise, or unqualified imitation. He had infirmities that ought to be pitied; failings that cannot be too carefully avoided; and erroneous views that every sound judgement will mark with reprehension. Of his faults and infirmities, he was himself very sensible, and none could lament or condemn them more strongly than he has done. The restraints he imposed upon himself in conversation, made him, at times, appear deficient in cheerfulness and sociality. His constitutional proneness to melancholy or depression of spirits, gave a dark tinge to the current of his thoughts, and led him sometimes to form mistaken conclusions on the state of his own mind. Of the tendency of this disease, he was fully aware, though not sufficiently careful to distinguish its operation; hence he frequently mistook its effects as symptoms of spiritual desertion, or the hidings of his Father's countenance. But the liveliness of his faith, and the powerful influences of religion, tended, in a great measure, to correct the effects of this habitual dejection, which, in him, was a malady of the body, rather than of the mind.

With some who are of weaker faith, and less fortified by the aids and comforts of the Holy Spirit, this distemper rises to a most distressing height, and makes its unhappy victims truly miserable. It fills their terrified imagination with dismal images and apprehension, perplexes their reason with doubts and disquietudes, and overspreads the whole soul with clouds, and darkness, and tempest. It eclipses all their brightest hopes of futurity, and environs the throne of Mercy itself with a mist of discouraging fears. From these gloomy and desponding misgivings, the author of the diary was wholly exempt. In spite of his infirmity, he enjoyed the greatest peace and tranquillity of mind. It had no effect in darkening or deranging his views of Divine Providence, although it frequently made him querulous and dissatisfied with himself It is no doubt that characteristic of a true Christian, to strive after higher measures of perfection, and not to rest contented with present attainments; yet a fretful anxiety, a perpetual dissatisfaction with ourselves, is certainly culpable. If we exert our utmost, and make the best use of the means put in our power, there can be no reason for distressing apprehensions about the consequences.

But there is another mistake, (perhaps, however, an error of the times, as much as of the man) that runs through the papers of Colonel Blackader, and that is, his sentiments in regard to prayer,—the encouragements to it,—and the effects he expected to result from it. If at any time he felt in this duty a warmer edge upon his zeal,—a particular satisfaction and enlargement of mind, he seemed disposed to interpret it as a sure mark of the divine approbation, and the consequent acceptability of his petitions. On the contrary, if he felt any peculiar dejection or difficulty of expression, he was apt to attribute it to a withdrawing of the Divine aid—a temporary desertion of the Holy spirit.

This, to say the least, is a very fallible criterion. Frames and feelings alone, are no indication that our prayers are either rational or acceptable, and ought to be regarded with a salutary distrust. These accidental elevations and depressions have no necessary connexion with the operations of the Spirit; much less can they be construed into undoubted symptoms of favour or disapprobation. Encouragement and success are to be derived, exclusively, through the intercession of Christ, and the promises of Scripture, that if we ask anything, according to the will of God, he heareth us.

It is also an error to imagine, as the writer of the diary sometimes has done, that answers to our prayers will be returned either by secret intimations, or by visible and external expressions. There certainly is, and always has been, a very strong and general propensity in mankind, not only to solicit direction from heaven in cases of doubt and uncertainty, than which nothing can be more necessary and becoming to weak and erring mortals, but to expect or require some evidence a token symptomatical of their requests being granted; such were the fleeces of Gideon; the experiment of Abram's servant at the well of Nahor; and other instances recorded in the Old Testament. But they who would now entertain such expectations, seem to have forgot that the age of oracles and wonders has ceased; that signs and miracles made a part of the Jewish Economy, wherein men were indulged with supernatural directions and intimations, and permitted, for their special instruction, to hold immediate consultation with heaven, through the rude intercourse of visible and material symbols.

The Christian dispensation has introduced a communion altogether spiritual. It is manifestly wrong to hope that God will, on our account, or by the force of our importunities, reverse the established order of his providence, or cause a sudden and simultaneous concurrence of different events, in order to produce the effect we desire. Even those who think answers to prayer may be conveyed mentally, by secret impulses, or internal convictions, ought coolly and candidly to examine whether these impressions have any good foundation,— whether they are to be ascribed to the agency of the Spirit, or produced by the natural and ordinary operation of their own minds. The most sober and rational course we can pursue, is to refer the issue of our petitions entirely to the wisdom of the Divine Being. We are incompetent judges of what is most befitting to ourselves, and apt to mingle our follies and our passions with our wants. To have our wishes absolutely fulfilled, might often prove ruinous, or rashness in the extreme. This ought to teach us to moderate our anxieties about futurity, and to leave the issue of contingent events to Him who alone can know the propriety or the expediency of granting our requests.

There is also, in Colonel Blackader's papers, some other misconceptions in regard to interpreting certain promises and passages of Scripture; as if, in addition to their original and literal import, they had a secret and mysterious application to himself. Upon this slender, and it may be, erroneous analogy, he would sometimes build his hopes and consolations, or form his resolutions in difficult or particular steps of conduct. These, however, and some of the other misapprehensions into which he has fallen, are the less to be wondered at, considering the prevailing religious sentiments of the times in which he was educated. They were parts of a theological system, which many good men regarded with implicit veneration, and from which, it is not surprising, if his mind had not altogether emancipated itself: and it would be an invidious distinction, to censure in him those mistakes and imperfections which were systematical, and have been found in characters of the calmest temperament, and the most unaffected piety.

Those who may feel disposed to deride or reprimand, we would beg to keep in mind, that the papers now laid before them, were not originally intended for public inspection. They are the private registers of an individual, unfolding his mind without disguise or reserve drawing aside the curtain, as it were, and disclosing the inmost recesses of his thoughts. This consideration, while it does not preclude the liberty of pointing out errors, renders them an unfair subject of animadversion; and it would be ungenerous to drag forth the weaknesses of any man, for the single purpose of exposing them, or rake up his peaceful ashes in quest of food, for a captious and malevolent criticism. And notwithstanding these strictures, there are, in Colonel Blackader's papers, innumerable traits of manly independent thinking—of a mind rising above the prejudices of education, and disentangling itself from the trammels of peculiar creeds and systems.

His intercourse with others, and his opinions about religion, savoured extremely little of that intolerance, still prevalent in his time, and which continued to operate long after it had been proscribed, and put down by acts of the legislature. It is now time, however, to lay before the reader a few extracts from these papers, that he may be able to form his own sentiments; and it may safely be left to his own candid judgement to discriminate between what he ought to avoid, and what he should be emulous to imitate,—between what is according to pure undefiled religion, and what is inconsistent with it.

That part of the diary which refers to the writer's stay in London, and subsequently with his regiment in Scotland, before it was embarked a second time for Flanders, contains little allusion to political or public transaction. It is limited, chiefly, to his own feelings and experiences, and gives a fair undisguised representation of a humble and watchful Christian, lamenting the infirmities of his temper, and the mutability of his frame; sensible of the degeneracy of his heart, and struggling to be delivered form the bondage of corruption.

✶✶✶✶✶✶

October, 1700. I complain, that though well directed in business, better than could be expected, yet I am not thankful. Chagrined at my natural temper; my spirit too sensual, trifling, and carnal. Occasionally falling into temptation and ill company, then blaming my want of zeal and resolution. My life is a struggle, as it were, between faith and corrupt nature—a combat, in which sometimes strengthening grace prevails, sometimes earthly affections and sensual appetites gain ground, yet partly involuntary.

November. Dejected and dissatisfied with myself, the more from my retiredness and want of settled employment. I am sensible of this my infirmity. Solitude is the nursery of melancholy. Tried to divert it by amusement, and as a frolicsome experiment, went to see a *comedie.* More convinced of the folly and vanity of worldly pleasures. Faith is the best remedy, but too little used. The soul immersed in sense, looses its spiritual bias, and neglects to fetch new supplies of grace from Christ. My resolution is, to live more by faith, and converse less with carnal and worldly men. This places me, as it were, between Scylla and Charybdis; too much company dissipates the mind, and gives it any earthly sett; too much retirement from company and conversation, sours the temper, makes it morose, chagrined, unsocial. Melancholy is no friend to grace, and great enemy to religion.

December. Instead of a lively frame, I often feel a deadness and heaviness though unbelief. Though serious, I am not religious; though calm, not spiritual. Sensual appetites, and vain imaginations usurp the place of heavenly affections. Corruptions which I though subdued or extirpated, had only retreated into a corner of the heart, where they gather strength, and sally forth anew; but, through grace, they shall be conquered. I see if I could rely more on Christ, there would be more contentment, more peace and tranquillity of mind, even in outward troubles. On Sabbath, I was cheered and comforted by the joy which a sure interest in the Saviour gives: In the evening, I had one of the sweetest visits, the most sensible communion with him, I think, I every experienced.

I was admitted, as it were, to draw aside the veil, and look into heaven, and would have been content to have been dissolved that instant. O that I were in such circumstances in the world! wherein, free from the hurry of business, and the cares of this life, I might serve my God, and enjoy sweet communion with him. The world is not my element. I am like a stranger in a far country, an exile chained to his oar. I do not ask to be taken from the world, I only beg to be found in my duty, and that I may have counsel to conduct, and grace to devote myself to the service of God; and if he have any use for me either to act or suffer, here I am, but my warfare must be at his charges.

January, 1701. Resolution, at the commencement of a new year to improve my time more for the glory of God, and the working out of my own salvation. But, alas! soon forgot; time trifled away by foolish and idle amusements. I know I am censured by many as stingy and inconversible, because I keep so little company, and seldom mix in conversation. But when I do keep company, such as my business is with, ah! it is dear bought. A careless unthinking temper grows upon the soul. Grace wastes as water through a sieve, and as a spark of fire is stifled by throwing it into a river; so is grace by ill company. Let foolish men snarl and say what they will, I'll converse more with God, and less with the world. There the fancy and imagination are easily corrupted: and these are the door whereby most sin is let into the soul. They are the faculties wherein grace last enters, and is longest in sanctifying.

I am surprised at the odd composition of my own heart: Heaven, earth, and hell, seem to make up the mixture. In the renewed part, I delight in holiness; but I find another law in my members, warring against the law of my mind, and bringing me into captivity to sin. I know, in general, that I ought to make use of Jesus Christ, yet when it comes to the push, I neglect to employ him. When the Spirit of God shines upon his own work in the soul, then faith is the easiest thing in the world, and may rather be called sense; but when that light is withdrawn, then faith must tug against wind and tide, by pleading promises, remembering former experiences, and drawing consequences from them. Mine, I am afraid, is but a fresh weather belief, and has never yet been in any great storm. It is like a weak anchor, that slips in the least gale. Lord, increase and strengthen it, that anxiety, fear, and distrust may be excluded.

If under outward troubles, I might have inward peace and supplies of grace, proportionably as trouble is laid on, I should be so far from fretting, that I should pray for affliction; but my misery is, under outward distresses, faith gives way; and who can bear affliction without, and darkness within? I foresee storms are gathering, but I have a refuge to fly unto, where I shall be safe. Come death, come life, let him do with me what seemeth good. It is my request, that I may be found in a righteous cause, and out of all evil, and all appearance of evil, because of my profession, and because of wicked men. I bless God for all his providences, and that he keeps me out of temptation.

February. I observe, that as ill company stifles and dispels grace, so good company helps to refresh and revive it; and there is a blessing in the society of some; it tends to my spiritual improvement. But I have a weak side, and am often vexed at my easiness in yielding to silly temptations. And really it is very difficult for a man to live in this age, if he be not more or less double and knavish.. Hypocrisy is a kind of self-defence,—an armour which the world forces him reluctantly to put on. This keeps my mind in a prison, in straighter fetters than if my body were in irons; for what I hate in my soul, I am compelled to seem to like, for fear of being thought singular. I dare neither go along with the world, nor manfully oppose it.

My conscience hinders me from doing the one,—a timorous spirit a want of grace and courage, from doing the other. I think I know something of the way of the world, but for my life, I cannot practise it. When I retire from it, I am happy and full of comfort; when I enter it again, I am miserable. Lord, let my desires be singly and intensely after thee alone. Oh unite my hear to love thee, to delight more in thee. The whole stream of my affections is too weak; ah! why then do I divide it into earthly channels? I involve myself in other's sin, by my silence in not witnessing against it. Ill company is my greatest torment; and suppose there were neither loss nor pain in hell, I could not endure to live there for the sin and blasphemy in it. I am sure I love god, but alas! I want zeal to vindicate his honour when it is reviled and evil spoken of among men. And yet I know I could cheerfully venture my life against his enemies, and in giving a public testimony to his cause. Oh may he graciously pardon me and sanctify me, and restore to me the joy of his salvation.

March. Hindered all day by business, from retiring to seek communion with Christ, whereby I have missed my wonted supply and recruit of comfort, and in consequence, am dull, heavy, and dejected. About twelve at night, I got my liberty, and poured out my soul before him; the weight immediately fell off my back, and I was sensibly relieved. But, alas! I live with Christ as I live with mankind, reservedly, coldly, and too much like a stranger. I come to him by set and solemn approaches, but in the intervals I forget him. I neglect to depend and trust in him. Whatsoever one loves well he thinks often on it, and will not let it slip from his memory. I complain that the habit of my mind is not so spiritual as it ought to be; I should hunger and thirst more after righteousness, send up warmer desires, and more frequent longings for it. I know not how other Christians find it, who mingle in the world; but I must confess, the restraints I am obliged to put on myself destroy my comfort, and make life burdensome.

To me it appears that the world's way of living, and a Christian's living by faith, are directly at antipodes—diametrically opposite to each other. I cannot converse or do business in the world, without being a considerable loser in happiness and religion. This makes me often appear deficient in frankness and cheerfulness; it quite eats out and corrodes any thing that is agreeable or gay in my natural temper. My Sabbaths, I fear, are not rightly sanctified, ordinances not properly improven. Sensible of this during all the time of public worship. In the evening, I returned home sorrowful and dejected. I went to my knees, my soul filled with shame, humility, and contrition; then was I helped to cleave to Christ Jesus for pardon and for grace. Then the mountain of sin, sorrow, and desertion was removed, and joy began to flow in. Then it was but a little, and I found him whom my soul loved. I held him, and would not let him go, till the cloud had passed away, and peace made up firmer than ever.

April. It is my grief that I cannot more keep up a devotional frame and habit of soul through all my time and all my business, for there is no profession but may be adorned by the beauty of holiness—no turn of business so quick, but that I might send up an express about it, and receive an answer. My faith ebbs and flows, sensual desires sometimes prevailing. Gun-powder does not more suddenly flash up when a spark of fire falls upon it, than corruption, when Satan throws in his fiery darts. But I find to my unspeakable comfort, when I sin, I have an Advocate with the Father. I regret that my conversation and discourse is so idle, trifling, and unprofitable, it answers no solid purpose when the company is not made better by it. I should always be mixing something that may edify in my discourse, to make people fall in love with the ways of holiness.

May. what ups and downs I have in my life, just as God shines or hides his face. One day I lie grovelling in the earth; another, sunk in darkness and despondency; a third, my soul is lifted up to heaven, and dwells, as it were, on the mount with God. Though outwardly I may appear with a dark side to the world, yet I have much secret joy and sweet communion which they know not of, neither can they give. I dare not converse with, or haunt that company which the world calls good and genteel. I think no graceless, debauched company can be good or genteel, be they of ever so great quality. Perhaps this wrongs my reputation among fashionable people; but I value not their opinion. I think those men who are reckoned the best here in London, even ministers, are not so tender and circumspect in their walk as I could wish.

June. A believer should be an exact observer of the state of grace in his soul, whether it be making progress or decaying: He should be a careful observer of providences, and, like the bee, draw honey out of every dispensation. Alas! I am like a machine, that is moved by springs; when my soul is roused up, either by a powerful sermon, by good company, by a surprising mercy, or a cross Providence, then it acts for a while by that outward force, lively, brisk, and vigorously; but when this outward spring and weight is taken off, my spirits flag, I return to my natural state of indolence and dejectedness. I beg this natural temper may be changed into a cheerful, happy, spiritual lightness of heart. I have continual experience of this, that I must employ Christ daily if I would have grace daily. I find I must have a regular supply; my grace is like the children of Israel's manna in the wilderness, they that gathered much the day before, had nothing over the next: So must I gather for my daily sustenance. My corruptions need a constant check, they are like the flax to the least spark of temptation.—I find not the ministers of the word so powerful here, as I have found them in Scotland: But perhaps the fault lies in me, and not in them.

Oft times, on the Sabbath, I feel just such a frame as St. Paul complains of, Rom. vii. 15, &c. I converse much with good men, but I observe they have all their weak sides. I find men are generally bad, even ministers are swayed too much by a worldly interest. This stumbles me a little, to see a minister, in the pulpit, pressing us to live by faith; yet follow him into the world, perhaps you will see him crouching, fawning, and playing fast and loose to gain some paltry temporal interest. Such conduct and conversation does me more harm than any thing I know besides. I cannot, for my soul, flatter and wheedle men, I cannot insinuate into their affections, or work upon their passions by warm talking, or plausible speeches.

July. I will not conceal the goodness of God, who is the hearer of prayer. I fell down on my knees this morning, my soul full of anxiety and despondency. I was helped to employ Christ by faith, and sought a return of a particular suit I had put up in his hands, some time ago. He heard me, and answered me; comfort flowed in upon my soul; I came away rejoicing, and resolving to treat him more and more. This

I looked upon as a presage and good omen, concerning the circumstances which I was fearing. And so it was; for the same day I got notice that I am safe as to my employment; and I only beg, that I may be enabled to lay out myself more zealously for the glory and service of God. I believe, however, that people may sometimes be mistaken in their prayers about temporal things, *e.g.* a wife, or children, or estate. That which they reckon fervency, enlargedness, or freedom, is often only the strength of sensual appetites going out after earthly things; yet our condescending Advocate takes even their prayers, and fans away the chaff, and presents them to the Father, and solicits for us those things we want. But our safest way is to be very submissive and short; for while we enlarge, earthly affections and unmortified appetites take fire, and while we think the Spirit of God inflames our desires, we are mistaken, for its our lusts that are kindled. This is a strange unhallowed fire; love to the world furnishes fuel to it.

July. I have been in London just a twelve-month: I bless God it has been the sweetest time ever I had the kindest visits, the nearest sensible communion with God, lively faith and close dependence on Christ. I have not succeeded in the particular business I came up for; I bless God for it; it is better as it is; I have had an infinitely richer equivalent, (if I may call it so) pearls for pebbles, precious grace for worthless mammon and trash. I commit myself to him for counsel, conduct, and protection, on my return. Sailed on the 15th, and trust to Providence, we shall have a prosperous voyage.

July 20. A solitary Sabbath at sea; yet communion with God. In the afternoon, I went up to the cradle at the top of the mast, to be retired. We had been becalmed all day, and lay hulling on the water. I had not spent much time in prayer and meditation, when there arose a fresh gale, which obliged me to come down in great haste, and the seamen to handle their sails. So strong and fair was the wind, that we ran before it 140 miles.

July 23. This day I landed in Scotland; but company, business and drinking did so steal away my time, that I was not in a right thankful frame all day. I have trifled away eight days since I came home, and could wish them scraped out of the register of my life.

******

In August, Captain Blackader joined his regiment at Perth, where he appears to have exerted himself diligently for promoting their moral improvement. He says:—

> I pray that God would bless and countenance the endeavours I am using here for curbing vice, and furthering reformation: I hope he will, for I think I am upright, and have his glory singly before my eyes. I strive daily to do what good I can, by the example of a holy life.

About this time, he had resolved to change his "single and solitary life," as he expresses it, and fixed his affections on Miss Anne Callander, daughter of James Callander, Esq. of Craigforth, near Stirling. The habitual spirituality of his mind is remarkably evinced by his conduct on this occasion, which also illustrates some of those mistakes into which, as I have noticed, he was apt to fall with regard to having contingencies prognosticated or ascertained by special interpositions of Providence. He says:—

> I trust that in this affair, I shall be guided by the Spirit of God, for I hope I may appeal to him, I am single and upright in my intentions. I have examined my heart, and dare say there is no idol in it to draw me from the road of duty. I have not taken one step in it, without seriously asking counsel and direction of God. If it be for his glory, and the advancement of grace in me, let him prosper it; if any thing else, let him put a stop to it; I shall see afterwards, it was for my good that it succeeded not. I sought particularly that he would shew and determine me by some special providence, whether I should proceed or let it drop, and whether this should be the particular person or not. Happening within half-an-hour after, unexpectedly to fall into her company, I looked upon it as somewhat observable, and encouraging me to go on.

They were married on the 4th of February, 1702, and though their union was not blessed with any family, this circumstance seems to have in nothing abated their mutual affections. He cherished for her an ardent and steady attachment. She accompanied him to the Continent, and remained generally, during the campaigns, in some of the towns with the Dutch frontier.

******

September. I live much easier and happier here (Perth) than I did at Edinburgh. The reason is, I can retire and be alone as much as I please. I may be no longer or oftener in company than I choose. I like to withdraw in the intervals of business, and keep up fresh intercourse with heaven by faith. Here there is less bustle, and fewer temptations. My soul is making a voyage, as it were, to Emanuel's Land, through a stormy sea, like a frail bark on the wide ocean. There come flans and hurricanes that drive her fir out of her course; then a little easy weather, and she returns to her due course; she does not perhaps sail a watch, till another tempest drives her away again. Alas! at this rate, when shall I perfect my voyage, and gain my desired port. It is only fee grace and mercy that can prevent one from making shipwreck,— Awake, Oh north wind; come thou south and blow, that I may at last get an abundant entrance into my destined haven.

October. When I get not the morning to myself, I am not right all day. An earthly, sensual temper grows upon me. Vain fancies, and roving thoughts take possession of the mind. Satan being chased, as it were, out of all the rest of the faculties, seems to retire into the imagination, from whence, as from a garrisoned citadel, he makes war upon my soul. Lord, give me grace to be watchful, faith to be my anchor in storms and tempests.

November. I find my heart like the sluggard's garden, full of weeds if it be neglected but twenty-four hours. Worldly lusts, foolish thoughts, and trifling imaginations take root, and spring up in rank and rapid growth. My mind, in consequence, is disordered; my soul is inflamed, and takes in poison at my eyes, by viewing vanity.

December. Employing myself in the work of public reformation, and frequently in Society prayer.[5] O that God would make use of my poor endeavours, to kindle love to Christ in the hearts of others, how glad should I be. But I observe this, when I talk of assurance as that which should be pressed after, and that which may be attained, I am always snibbed; and Christians talk of it as a thing to be wished for, rather than attained; and they commend generally a frame and case of doubting and fears, as one of the best that is to be won to. But I main-

---

5. It is not improbable, that he is here alluding to, and was acting in co-operation with, the Society in Scotland for Propagating Christian Knowledge, which was formed at this very time. That Society, as is well known, had its origin in 1701, among a few private gentlemen, actuated by a laudable zeal for the reformation of their countrymen' and more especially for the abolition of ignorance and impiety in the Highlands and Islands of Scotland. Their usual place of meeting was Edinburgh. Whether Captain Blackader was an original member, I know not, but his name appeared sometime afterwards on the list.—*Vid. Account of the Rise, Constit. and Management of the Society.*

tain, assurance is to be had, and it is the sin of Christians, oft-times, that they get it not; for through an excess of mistaken humility, they dare not; they think it arrogance to act faith boldly on Christ. A bold assurance is quite consistent with a humble and needy reliance upon him. Lord, strengthen my faith more, and help me to improve my time better in future. Many years have now passed over my head: Oh to be so numbering my days, that I may apply my heart to wisdom.

★★★★★★

In the beginning of the next year, 1702, the Cameronian Regiment received orders to go abroad. We shall therefore suspend our extracts for a little, until we offer a few observations on the subject of the new war in which they were to be engaged, a war, distinguished by victories more brilliant, perhaps, than profitable, more illustrious to the military genius, than advantageous to the political interest of this country.

CHAPTER 8

War of the Succession

It often happens that treaties, destined to be permanent, and to allay for ever the feuds of rival powers, are the very source from which national hostilities spring. All those disputes that embroil states and empires in more implacable animosity, generally have their foundation laid in the intricacies or equivocal terms of those contracts. Contingencies happen for which there are no special provision. Advantages occur, either unforeseen or anticipated, which offer too powerful a temptation to be resisted. Leagues and bonds are then found to be but of slender obligation. The most solemn stipulations, when opposed to interest or ambition, are in danger of being disregarded, or considered as obsolete whenever they cease to be agreeable or convenient. Such was the fate which the peace of Ryswick experienced, which had professedly for its object, the amity and lasting repose of Europe. Several reasons contributed to this interruption, but we need only mention the two principal cause, *viz.* the disputed Succession of the Spanish Crown, and the recognition of the young Prince of Wales as titular King of Great Britain.

Charles II. of Spain, approaching his dissolution, and leaving no heirs of his own body, the settlement of his dominions became the primary object of attention and intrigue, in all the European Cabinets. The death-bed of the expiring monarch was surrounded with priests, nobles, and plenipotentiaries, each anxious to elicit symptoms of preference, or concessions favourable to their respective claimants. The three competitors who founded their pretensions on hereditary right, were, the Dauphin of France, the Emperor Leopold, and the Elector of Bavaria. Each had their several partisans. The Spanish nation favoured the claims of the House of Bourbon; the queen and the *grandees* declared for the emperor, while the general security and interests of Europe seemed to require the succession for the Prince of Bavaria. In this singular contest, His Britannic Majesty took a very lively interest. As he affected to hold in his own hands the balance of power, and to be the head of the Protestant cause, he deemed the accession of the Spanish monarchy too ponderous to be thrown, undivided, into either scale, especially into that of France, to which he was naturally an enemy, and whose aspiring ambition it had been the ruling passion of his whole life to humble and control.

A Treaty of Partition, as the best remedy against these apprehensions, was projected and signed by England, Holland, and France, by which the dominions of Charles were to be dismembered, and shared proportionably among the several competitors. But Louis, with his usual duplicity and finesse, while subscribing to this treaty, was secretly negotiating, through his ambassador at the Court of Madrid, for the whole succession, and had the address to get his grandson, the Duke of Anjou, nominated in the Royal Will as sole heir to the Spanish throne. The duke was second son of the *dauphin*, but this preference to a younger branch, was only a political manoeuvre; for while it secured the claims of the House of Bourbon, it tended to prevent any alarm which might be taken, had the two formidable monarchies of France and Spain been united in one person. Europe had thus the singular spectacle of witnessing a powerful nation choosing a king from the house of a rival and an enemy. The duke was accordingly proclaimed under the title of Philip V. and his accession notified to all the powers in Christendom.

This appointment placed Louis in a delicate situation. It was no doubt most flattering to his vanity, and a mighty acquisition to his empire, but contrary to his stipulations in the partition treaty, by which he renounced the entire succession of Spain. At first he affected to hesitate whether he should break his faith, or, by adhering to the treaty, deprive his grandson of a magnificent empire. But the feelings of nature, and the prospect of aggrandisement, speedily triumphed over all the obligations of leagues and alliances; and to satisfy his all-grasping ambition he was content to plunge his own subjects in new miseries, and deluge Europe with the blood of millions.[1]

The elevation of Philip, and the treacheries of France, excited a deeper and more general indignation than the treaty of partition had done. The emperor exclaimed against this preference as a piece of injustice to himself, and threatened to carry his resentment into execu-

---
1. Dalrymple, vol. ii. b. viii. *Voltaire Siecle*, chap. xvii.

tion by force of arms. Holland began to tremble, when she saw those towns and territories which had been the barrier of her security, put into the hands of her enemies, and planted with hostile garrisons. England, though equally indignant at the conduct of the French king, had less cause of apprehension, and therefore felt disinclined to involve herself in foreign connections, which might encumber her with additional losses and expenses, from which the country had not yet recovered. And it may be doubted whether she would have declared herself a party to the Grand Alliance, but for the information which arrived at his time, of the death of the late King James, and the acknowledgement of his son by the courts of France and Spain, under the title of James III. This was regarded as an insult by the nation, and a manifest violation of justice to the crown, since William had been solemnly acknowledged by the treaty of Ryswick, king of England, Scotland, and Ireland.

The whole country was set in a flame; party animosities, that had lately rent and convulsed the kingdom, seemed to be forgotten in one common resentment. The Jacobites held it as a national affront, that a foreign court should dictate a successor to the British throne: The Whigs spurned at the idea of owning the legitimacy, and much more of recognising the hereditary title, of a person reputed to be of spurious birth, and who had already been excluded and incapacitated by an act of the whole legislature. This indignation was heightened still more by an intercepted letter from the Earl of Melfort, governor to the pretended prince, purporting to support his claims by an invasion. Danger was now added to indignity, and the fears of the people cooperated with their resentment. Addresses to the throne were poured in from all quarters of the kingdom, filled with gratitude for the blessings of the Revolution, and breathing vengeance against this new aggressor of their peace and their liberties.

Nothing could have happened more opportunely for William, who was ready to seize every opportunity of humbling the grandeur of his ancient rival, and had now an abundant pretext from his violations of faith, and his interference with the British succession. His own conduct in the partition treaty had occasioned considerable displeasure, and incurred the reproaches of the parliament; but his popularity began to revive, and the clamours of discontent which had lately echoed through the kingdom, were exchanged for ardent professions of loyalty. William did not fail to take advantage of this accidental enthusiasm, and to improve it for the prosecution of his favourite schemes. The national ardour was fanned by an able and eloquent speech, wherein he set forth the danger that threatened their security, and the necessity of contributing their utmost to check the exorbitant power and the insolent usurpations of France.

The event answered his expectations. Parliament entered into all his views, and promised the necessary contributions for the war. another Grand alliance was negotiated and concluded at the Hague, between England, the emperor, and the States General. The object of this confederacy was, to defend themselves against the encroachments of Louis, who was now in a condition to possess the rest of Europe, and establish a universal monarchy; to put His Imperial Majesty in possession of those towns and dominions which had been assigned him by the partition treaty; and to attempt the recovery of the Spanish Netherlands out of the hands of France, as a necessary barrier on the Dutch frontier. The quota of troops to be supplied by each of the contracting powers was as follows: The emperor to furnish 90,000 men; the States 102,000; and Great Britain 40,000, to consist of 33,000 foot, and 7000 horse and dragoons.[2]

Military preparations commenced with the greatest activity. The towns in Flanders were garrisoned with French troops, and the Dutch forces who refused to surrender were made prisoners of war. The King of England, having completed his alliances abroad, and concerted the necessary operations for the campaign, returned home to put himself at the head of his army. But he did not live to see his schemes carried into execution. He fell from his horse, and fractured his collar bone, and the effects of this slight accident proved fatal to a constitution already enfeebled and decayed. He expired on the 8th of March, 1702. His successor. Queen Anne, adopted his measures without any great alteration, and resolved to prosecute them with the greatest vigour. The concurrence of the British court was absolutely necessary to unite and consolidate the Grand Alliance, and the resolution of the queen served to revive those hopes which the death of William seemed to have extinguished. On the 4th of May, war was declared against France, and the Earl of Marlborough appointed to the command of the confederate army.[3] After this short explanatory digression, we shall again resume our extracts from the diary.

The Cameronian Regiment, which had continued for some time in garrison at Perth, was again destined for foreign service. In the

---

2. *Dalrymple*, bb. ix. x. *Ralph*.
3. Somerville's *History of Queen Anne*. Burnet.

month of February, 1702, they received orders to repair to Holland, and join the confederate army. Captain Blackader remained in Scotland with a recruiting party until the middle of July, when he rejoined his regiment on the Continent. His observations and reflections on this occasion, we shall record in his own words.

******

February 1. Going to church in the forenoon, I first got the news of our going abroad. I bless God I have a sweet complacency in his will on this point; go or stay, the earth is the Lord's. As to all temporal things, I resign the disposal into his hands; his will is, that I should depend implicitly and frankly upon himself, and through grace I will depend upon him, and trust him cheerfully. He does all things well and wisely.

February 20. This morning I employed in pouring out my soul before God, to implore his blessing and ask more grace of him, now when I have more need of it; and to beg, that if he send me out of Scotland at this time, he will let his presence accompany me, (and if that go with me, all the world's alike to me.) I laid out before him the snares and temptations my employment is subject to; the grief it would be to leave the gospel behind me, and launch out again among the trials, and vices, and perils of camps and armies. But I resign myself into his hands, to carry me wheresoever he will: And I am persuaded, wherever he orders my lot—in whatever service he employs me, I shall not be sent on a warfare at my own charges. His grace will be sufficient for me, and keep me from the pollutions of a wicked world I bless him for all his mercies, and for the good appearances of reformation in this place (Perth) with which he has favoured my poor endeavours.

March 5. This important crisis of my life is approaching near, and I am again to mingle in the troubles, dangers, and toils of a new war. This morning I took a solitary walk, and went up to the craig at Craigforth, and there I renewed my covenant with Christ, and ratified whatever I had done before. I implored him for such measures of grace as I should, from time to time, stand in need of; and that he would supply sufficient strength and furniture, and order all my ways and actions aright.

March 7. This day our regiment embarked, and it has been a sad day for me, for from five in the morning till late at night, I have not had a serious composed thought; all has been noise, bustle, and confusion. This is not the element I delight to breathe in.

March 11. The clouds are gathering thicker and blacker, and a gloomy storm is coming on. Happy they who are compassed about with the shield of Divine favour. My comfort, in general, as to our church and nation is this, God sits at the helm, and rules and disposes all for his own glory and his people's good. As to my own particular, he who guides the universe, is my God and my Father. Let the world be turned upside down—let the kings of the earth combine, and the nations rage tumultuously,—I am safe, I have a city of refuge to flee to.

March 12. This is a doleful day; we have just got the common table news of the death of the best of kings. Our dear Deliverer is taken from us. Alas! our cup of iniquity is full it appears, and we seem to be a people prepared and fitted for ruin. But the same God who raised up for us a Moses to bring us out of Egypt and the house of bondage, sits at the helm still, and can, after him, raise up a Joshua to perfect the deliverance, and lead his people into the promised land. Gracious Lord! be thou our strong tower of defence. Cast the arms of thy protection around the church and work of reformation h Scotland. Be our hiding-place in the evil day, our fortress in times of trouble. Disappoint the expectations of our enemies, and raise up the faith and the fallen hopes of they people desponding under this mournful dispensation.

★★★★★★

During Captain Blackader's stay in Scotland, the diary continues to run on in the same devotional strain; every line breathing sentiments of piety, resignation, and humility. Wherever he was stationed on duty, he regularly attended the public ordinances of religion. He let slip no opportunity of paying his vows before the people, at the stated solemnities of the sacrament; and his deportment at a communion table, is said to have been peculiarly grave, serious, and becoming. His self-denial and abasement were very remarkable: if prosperous in any of his undertakings, he never ascribes his success to his own prudence or dexterity, but to the blessing and guidance of heaven. Though never backward or remiss in his military duties, he frequently admits that a military life is his aversion, and regrets had had not preferred a situation wherein he could have done God more service, and employed his own talents to more advantage.

His greatest horror was be compelled to listen to their impure or profane conversation. He would rather have marched up to the enemies' batteries, than have sat at mess or remained in the company of such associates. The cannon's mouth was not so terrible to him, as the artillery of oaths and obscenities with which his ears were often assailed. And to this cause is to be ascribed his predilection for solitude and retirement in the intervals of duty, as well as those expressions of peevish and fretful discontent, which threw a dark shade even over his happiest moments, and gave the semblance of morosity and dejection, to a temper naturally mild and cheerful.

The vice of swearing was then become shockingly fashionable, and by the troops in Flanders carried to a shameless and execrable height. This must have been offensive to every man of common delicacy, but peculiarly distressing and painful to a mind such as Captain Blackader's, naturally sensitive, and seasoned with the most lively impressions of religion. And it is rather surprising, that among military men, where the sense of honour and courtesy is so acute, and resentment of affronts so keen, that his practice should be tolerated or treated with impunity. The swearer commits a breach, not only of morality and religion, but of modesty and good-breeding. He wounds the feelings of his hearers without cause or provocation. It may be true, that he offers no violence to their persons or their reputation, but he inflicts a pang which bleeds inwardly, and is more excruciating than mere bodily injury.

And surely the man who needlessly and insolently tramples upon our conscience and our feelings,—who trespasses against all that we are accustomed to hold most sacred, ought to be reputed as culpable and unworthy of our society as he who is guilty of an incivility, or perhaps undesignedly, or in the heat of passion, casts an imaginary stain on our professional character. This vice, though one of the most common, appears to be one of the most absurd and indefensible. It cannot, like many others, plead motives of interest, of sensuality, or any natural propensity. Destitute of these aids and encouragements, it springs up, as it were, the rank and spontaneous growth of a superabundant corruption.

In his political opinions. Captain Blackader implicitly adhered to neither party. He says:—

> My temper does not incline me to be zealous for any party or faction. I only wish to be zealous against sin; on that side let me always be found.

For some time, he had been employed about Stirling, Edinburgh and Leith, in levying the necessary complement of men, in which he was very successful, notwithstanding his disdain of the usual alluring and plausible arts of a recruiting officer. He had also to provide a chaplain for the regiment in lieu of Mr. Shields, who had one on the Darien expedition, and died in the West Indies.

******

June 12—24. I bless God who guides me by his Spirit and his providence: If I would but trust him and have patience, I would see all my concerns well managed, and all turn to the best. I have reason to be grateful for his mercies in regard to my employment and recruiting, and that instead of bringing myself into snares by unwarrantable practices, my men are brought to my hand, and I have only to lay out the money. Everything is ordered and disposed of well, though I know it not, and be ignorant which is the right way; I see it was best for me that I went not away with the last convoy. I stayed partly on a spiritual account, and God has followed me with a temporal blessing also, for I have since got more men than I got in three months before. The one that run away some time ago, came back after wandering up and down several weeks, and says he could have no peace until he returned to me again.

How true do I find that Scripture: *Be careful about nothing, but in every thing, by prayer and supplication with thanksgiving, make your desires known to God.* When I was anxious and solicitous about getting of men and recruiting my company, I got few or none: But when I came to a composure of mind, and trusted to Providence (still in the use of means), men, as it were, came to may hand. At first I had very little hopes of getting my company made up; but now that He has provided for me, I find I shall not be behind others. O that he would give me grace to serve him in this and every station he puts me in. I have been taking some steps about getting a minister. Lord, direct and guide, and if this be the man, send him to us in *the fullness of the blessing of the Gospel of Christ.*

July 6. I am glad of the account I have just got from Holland of Mr. P. coming to be our chaplain; may God give him a commission to do us good. I was not expecting it, but it is a pleasing surprise, for Lord, thou knowest it was one of the greatest griefs I had to leave the gospel behind, and go where I could not enjoy it. O let me always enjoy thy precious gospel, though my worldly circumstances should be the meaner. I find help and delight in godly society, were it but in the company of four or five private Christians; and I would rather have the fervent prayers of the righteous on my side, than the whole Scottish army. The world may think this folly or hypocrisy, but I am not much anxious what people's opinion of me is, or what they think; though I desire to possess the goodwill and esteem of all good men. But there is a day coming when everybody must appear in their own colours, without any disguise; then it well be known who are sincere, and who are hypocrites.

******

Having obtained his full complement of men, he set sail from Leith on the 13th of July.

******

I bless God who directs and disposes of all my business well, and makes every thing fall right without disappointments or cross providences; I look to him for conduct and protection, and commit myself and family to him in this voyage: And it is a great comfort to me, that there are several worthy Christians interested for us, and plying the throne of grace on our behalf; and I am persuaded it will not fare the worse with us for their sakes.

July 17. This day we had several fears and troubles from contrary winds and storms, hi the afternoon a French privateer appeared at a distance, but came not near us.

July 23. We landed (in the Maese.) I bless God who has brought our voyage to a happy issue, who has preserved us from sea-hazards, from enemies, and under sickness and indisposition.

July 25. Our voyage up the river appeared to be tedious, but it fell out otherwise, and we came to our journey's end safe and well. And now I commit my way to God's providence, and beg more grace as I need. I entreat his blessing for my employment,—for this place, and the people I live among.

July 26, Sabbath. I am now obliged to do many things that are not the proper work of a Sabbath; I was on the guard, and in hurry, noise, and company all day. This makes me look back and think, with pleasure and melancholy, on the sweet intercourse and ordinances I enjoyed in Scotland. Here every thing is the reverse with me; the means of grace are fewer; quickening influences more rare; and snares strewn thicker. This makes me tremble to think how I shall get through, for I find temptations in every company,—in every step of my life,—in every minute of my time.

August 23, Sabbath. I complain of the deadness and formality of worship in the French church. I hear preaching, but it excites in my soul no earnest longings and desires. The edge of my affection continues blunted and dull. Here I am not so earnest for spiritual supplies, nor so sensible of the want of them.

August 31. I often find in the morning when I awake, the world standing ready, as it were, at the door of my hear, importuning for admittance, and whenever the door opens, it is sure to thrust itself in under some specious pretext: This makes prayer the more necessary. I wish to have the world under my feet, trampling upon its vanities, and not usurping the throne of my heart or reigning over my affections.

******

About this time. Captain Blackader appears to have got some considerable accession to his fortune, though he does not mention through what channel. His generosity, on this occasion, was very commendable, and he speaks with extreme disinterestedness regarding the possession of earthly treasures.

******

September 11. God is giving me, at this time, some means in the world, and more than I expected of it; and I take it as a token for good that he gives his blessing with it, because he has now put an occasion in my hand of laying out £100, a-year, for the relief of a relation dear to himself, that needs it. (This relation, most probably, was his sister, Mrs. Young, then residing in Edinburgh, a widow with seven children, and in narrow circumstances. A few years afterwards, he made the same affectionate application of another legacy, which fell to him by the death of his eldest brother, generously renouncing his claims and his share of that bequest, in favour of his sister and her family.)

September 30. I have been much taken up about my temporal affairs, and was afraid and jealous of myself, that my affections were too much going out after the world. But I pray God to keep earthly cares out of my heart; to let me have no riches or estates, but what he will give me his blessing with; that I may use them all with a holy carelessness and indifference, without losing a hairbreadth, or abating a grain-weight of my desires after a better treasure in heaven.

★★★★★★

It does not appear that the captain was engaged in any of the sieges or actions of this campaign, at least, he mentions none of them in his diary. Most probably he was employed on some of the detachments that were ordered to garrison such towns as it was supposed the enemy might attack. It is therefore unnecessary to take any retrospective notice of this year, further than is requisite for preserving a connection in the order of events.

This new war, which was to humble the power of France, and reflect so much lustre on the British arms, commenced auspiciously on the side of the allies; notwithstanding various advantage which fortune had now thrown into the scale of the enemy. The present confederacy was inferior in strength and numbers, to that formerly headed by King William, a great proportion of the forces and treasure which they then commanded, was now in the hands of Louis. He had at his disposal the fleets and armies of Spain, besides her gold and silver mines. The Netherlands, Sicily, Sardinia, Milan, and Naples, were accessions which added vastly to his resources. The Duke of Savoy was now united to the House of Bourbon by a double affinity, one of his daughters being married to the King of Spain, and another to the Duke of Burgundy. The electors of Cologne and Bavaria had revolted from the alliance, and admitted French troops into their territories. Louis had, besides, a vast advantage in having all the barrier towns in the Netherlands in his possession, and all the fortresses garrisoned with his own troops, so that, to all appearance, the allies were completely overmatched.

But these acquisitions did not secure to France that superiority or success which might have been anticipated. Though her power seemed then at the zenith, it had, in reality, begun to decline. An internal change had imperceptibly taken place in her court and her councils, the effect of which soon became visible in her military operations. The age of her renowned generals and ministers was passed away, and her glory had departed with them. The exchequer and the war-office were no longer conducted by the policy of Colbert and Louvois. Condé, Turenne, and Luxembourg, who had led her armies through a splendid career of victories, were dead; and no successor had risen with talents or genius to supply their place.

Military honours and promotions were bestowed on young men of rank, rather than veteran officers; as if nobility of blood could supply the want of knowledge and experience. The troops thus lost all confidence in commanders whose only qualification was the lustre of their birth, and whom they saw elevated at once to preferments which are often the reward of twenty years service. Such was the situation in which the affairs of Louis were placed at the commencement of the war, a situation which rendered all his advantages unavailing. All his resources in talents and treasure were feeble and inefficient, when opposed to the financial strength of Britain, and the capacity of Marlborough and Prince Eugene, who, in military genius, perhaps surpassed the most celebrated generals ever France produced.[4]

The rapid successes of the allies at the opening of the campaign, shewed to the world that the fortune of war had changed sides; and Louis, instead of overrunning the enemy's country with his victorious arms, was forced to retire within his own lines, and act upon the defensive. The French Army in the Netherlands was commanded by Marshal Boufflers, or rather the young Duke of Burgundy who had come to study the art of war under his directions: that of the Confederates, by the Earl of Marlborough, who arrived in the camp about the end of June.

Previous to that date, the allies had made considerable progress, and gained several advantages over the enemy. Their first conquest was the small town of Keyserswaert.—It belonged to the Elector of Cologne, who, being in alliance with Louis, had admitted a French garrison into it. The trenches were opened on the 10th of April, by a detachment under the Prince of Nassau, and after an obstinate siege of two months, the town capitulated, and was reduced to a heap of ruins.

Another division of the Confederate Army, under General Cohorn, broke into Flanders, forced and demolished the whole line of fortifications between St. Donet and Isabella, which the enemy had been many months in raising with great labour and expense; and at the same time, laid the castellany of Bruges under contribution. In June, Marshal Boufflers made an attempt on the city of Nimeguen, but his design was completely frustrated by the Earl of Athlone, who commanded the third grand division of the Allied Army.

On the arrival of Lord Marlborough, it was resolved to bring the enemy to a decisive action. But Marshal Boufflers, whose peculiar talent lay in commanding a flying camp, preferred a retreat to a pitched battle; and the Duke of Burgundy who had come to study military tactics, thinking flight unbecoming his dignity, quitted the campaign

---

4. *Dalrymple*, vol. ii. part iv. *Voltaire Siecle,* chap, xviii.

in disgust, having learned nothing but how to avoid an engagement. The allies followed up their successes, and took several places with little or no resistance. The Castle of Wert was taken; the towns of Venlo, Ruremonde, and Stevenswert surrendered; Marshal Boufflers all the while remaining in his camp, without offering to annoy the allies, or making any motion to relieve the besieged.

With these conquests, the Deputies of the States were willing to have closed the campaign, but Lord Marlborough[5] resolved to attempt the reduction of Liege which the Elector of Bavaria had delivered into the hands of the French; foreseeing of what advantage it would be for winter quarters to a part of his army, and the glory that would redound to the Confederates from this important acquisition. This rich and populous city lies in a pleasant valley environed with hills, the Meuse entering it in two branches, which with several smaller streams, form many delightful islands. The castle, which stood on the brow of a hill, was of great strength, and commanded the whole city. The Allied Army sat down before the place on the 12th of October; on the 14th three English Regiments of horse, and as many battalions of foot under Lord Cutts, took possession of the town.

On the 18th the batteries were opened against the citadel, and on the 29th the garrison capitulated. The French were thus obliged to abandon Spanish Guelderland, and resign to the Allies the command of the country between the Meuse and the Scheldt, while the reduction of Keyserswaert and Landau opened a communication between the armies on the Meuse and the Rhine. Such was the termination of this prosperous campaign. The Earl of Marlborough, by his good conduct, had established himself in the affection of the army. He was complimented by the States, and created a duke by Queen Anne, in reward for his eminent services. The army broke up, and retired to quarters in November.[6]

---

5. *Marlborough's Wars 1* (1702-1707) and *Marlborough's Wars 2* (1707-1709) by Frank Taylor are also published by Leonaur.
6. Lediard's *Life of Marlborough*.

CHAPTER 9

Campaign Second, 1703

The Duke of Marlborough arrived at the Hague on the 17th of March, to open the campaign of 1703. Ten days afterwards he reviewed the English forces which were garrisoned in the country about Liege, and ordered all the troops to be in readiness to take the field. Operations commenced (14th of April) with the siege of Bonn, a very ancient and strong city in the circle of the Lower Rhine, within the Archbishoprick of Cologne. The siege was carried on with vigour and success, and on the 15th of May the city surrendered. On this service. Captain Blackader was not employed, being then at Meastricht; in the neighbourhood of which, a number of the Confederates lay.[1]

As he was not engaged in any particular action, for little of importance was transacted in course of the campaign, his diary for this year, is rather uninteresting. While in quarters he laments, as usual, his want of opportunities frequently to attend religious ordinances, and that the discourses he heard, were not calculated to make that impression on his mind he could have wished.

******

February 21. Sabbath. I heard a Dutch sermon in the forenoon, and a French one in the afternoon, but felt little the better for either of them. They had not that quickening and reviving influence to put an edge and fervour on my mind. In the evening, I retired to pray to God for more tender meltings of heart, and more intenseness of desires towards him; and when I had poured out my soul, I came away easy and cheerful.

******

---

1. Lediard, vol. i.

The following passage refers to the death of his brother's wife in Edinburgh, which affected him very sensibly.

******

March 24. This day I got the sad account of the death of a near and dear relation. I bless the Lord she has died in the full assurance of faith. Her soul is now wafted beyond this boisterous sea of afflictions and crosses, into a delightful haven of rest and happiness. May the Lord be a comfort to the disconsolate, solitary husband, and a parent to his poor small children. I trust to him, and cast upon his care these five motherless children, with my sister's five fatherless children; his goodness can supply their loss. May he sanctify this providence to us all, and make us submissive when his rod speaks to us.

******

Most of this, and the subsequent month, he complains of fatiguing marches; want of repose; and danger of being surprised by the enemy. His arrival at Meastricht, which he now visited after an interval of many years, brought to his recollection a very memorable and fatal accident of which he had been the innocent occasion, but for which he ever entertained the sincerest regret. This refers to a duel which he fought with a brother officer, the son of a noble family in this country, and in which he was unhappily instrumental in depriving him of his life.

The affair took place in 1691, when he was a very young man: It is said to have originated in some trifling verbal dispute with a Captain S——, while over their wine, in a company after dinner. Captain S. it appears, had taken offence at some expressions dropt by his friend in conversation, as if intended to call in question his veracity. Meeting with him some time afterwards, he reminded him of the alleged insult, and insisted upon having immediate satisfaction. His friend, astonished and unconscious of giving offence, asserted his innocence, as he could recollect of nothing he had said that could have the least tendency to asperse or injure his character. In vain, however, did he attempt to justify himself, and to shew him that the words he had used were on a trifling occasion, and not capable of the construction he put upon them.

In vain did he assure him, that if he had given him just provocation, he was ready to make any proper apology, or any concession or reparation he had a right to demand. In a paroxysm of rage, and incapable of listening to reason. Captain S. drew his sword, and rushed on Lieutenant Blackader, who, for some time, kept retreating and expostulating; willing to terminate the dispute in some more amicable way. At length, finding all his remonstrances ineffectual, and perceiving his own life in danger, he saw himself obliged, in self-defence, to close with his antagonist. An unfortunate thrust soon laid the captain lifeless at his feet.

The consequences of this rash misadventure might have proved fatal to himself, but fortunately the whole contest was seen from the ramparts of the town, by several soldiers who bore witness to the necessity under which he was laid to defend his life. The matter was speedily adjusted; and after a regimental trial, the lieutenant was honourably acquitted. The event, however, was too solemn, and made too deep an impression on his mind ever to be forgotten; and it is said, as long as he lived, he observed the anniversary of it as a day of mourning, of penitence, and prayer.

******

April 28. Marching all this day. We came to Maestricht in the evening, but things here have a bad aspect; the enemy preventing us, and disappointing our designs: although, I bless God, I am not anxious about events; he keeps me in perfect peace, I have nothing to fear. At night I went alone to visit that spot of ground, as near as I could find it, where, twelve years ago, I committed that unhappy action: There I fell down on my knees, and prayed as I had done several times throughout the day, that God would deliver me from blood-guiltiness; that the blood of the Lamb might purify the stain, and wash away the crimson dye of the poor man's blood. I hope the Lord heard my prayer, and cleansed my heart as well as my hands from that pollution.

May 2. This night I went again to the same place, where I had serious thoughts, and some assurance of my sin's being pardoned.

******

When upon this subject, we may notice another occurrence of a similar nature, that took place at a subsequent period of his military life. The precise date cannot now be ascertained, but it must evidently have happened during some of the campaigns, either in Germany or the Netherlands. He is said, upon what occasion we know not, to have received a challenge, which he refused to accept; as he did not see sufficient cause to justify so desperate a resource. His adversary, in consequence of this refusal, threatened to post him as a coward, to which he replied coolly, "That he was not afraid of his reputation being impaired, even if the threat were carried into execution." It happened at this time, that an attempt was determined on against the enemy, of a kind so desperate, that the Duke of Marlborough hesitated to what officer he should assign the command, and had resolved to decide the matter by throwing the dice. Captain Blackader went immediately to him, and offered to undertake the duty. His offer was accepted; and by the Providence of God, he came off with great loss of men, but without any personal injury; and with the complete establishment of his character, not only as a brave man, and an able officer, but also with general estimation as a consistent Christian.

These anecdotes exhibit Captain Blackader's character in a very interesting and instructive point of view. Though persuaded that the profession of arms is not, in principle, incompatible with the profession of religion; yet when the laws of the one were found to be directly at variance with the laws of the other; he had no hesitation in deciding which of the two ought to regulate his conduct. Though a soldier, he did not forget that he was a Christian; and he has shewn, that while he served with zeal and fidelity under the standard of an earthly sovereign, he could maintain an allegiance no less inviolable to the sacred banner of the cross. He had too much regard for the sanction of the Divine Law, and the express declaration of Scripture against murder and revenge, to shed innocent blood from the caprice of fashion; or submit to be regulated in his actions by the fanciful and arbitrary enactments of human authority.

In the first unhappy accident related above, he drew his weapon with reluctance, and not until self-defence had made it absolutely necessary. If he had injured his antagonist, he was willing to repair the injustice. If he had been betrayed into any inadvertence of speech, from levity or want of due circumspection, (for he disclaimed all intentional offence,) he was ready to apologize or offer any reasonable satisfaction. He considered it no humiliation—nothing derogatory to his reputation as an officer or a gentleman, to acknowledge his imprudence or his error. But the unfortunate victim, deaf to every remonstrance, rushed headlong on destruction, and paid with his blood the price of his folly.

In the *second* instance. Captain Blackader prevented the repetition of a similar tragedy, at the fearful risk of committing a trespass against the omnipotent laws of military honour. He was threatened with the odious and appalling imputation of a coward, because he refused to expose his life to the fury of a madman, or become himself a deliberate murderer. This refusal was not made from any want of courage, or on any ground of fear, which the most pusillanimous are always the most reluctant to acknowledge; but from his conviction, that no law of *honour*, though enforced by all the penalties of infamy and disgrace among men, and sanctioned by the patronage and example of the highest military authorities, could possibly impart to any human being a right to shed the blood of his fellow-creature. He would have been content to relinquish his friends and his commission, sooner that be in any way a willing accomplice in an affair so repugnant to his conscience and his feelings, so utterly in violation of every principle he had been accustomed to venerate as sacred.

To purchase the esteem of the world on these terms, would be to incur an indelible disgrace, to establish an idle reputation on the ruins of his own peace and innocence. Having expressed his contrition for the undesigned offence, and tendered overtures of reconciliation, he may be considered as having done enough to acquit himself—not perhaps according to the refined maxims of his profession, but certainly in the judgement of every candid and sober mind.

As to the charge of cowardice, he might perhaps have repelled it by an appeal to his former rencontre—to the many dangers he had already faced—and the unimpeachable honour of his military reputation. In the general tenor of his character for meekness, forbearance, and aversion to stir up strife, he had a moral armour that might have blunted the shafts of calumny, and made the false or petty accusations of his adversary recoil upon his own head. He might have rebutted the charge with the truly noble reply of his celebrated countryman and companion in arms, "I fear sinning, though you know I do not fear fighting."[2] But he went a step farther. He retrieved his honour without violating his principles.

He made his sword cancel the imputation of cowardice—not by plunging it, without provocation, into the bosom of his friend—not by depriving the service, it may be, of a brave officer—or involving perhaps, in sorrow and disgrace, a widow and orphan family; but by signalizing his courage against the enemies of his country—by venturing fearlessly, and of his own accord, on a desperate expedition of chance, where neither duty nor necessity called him. Here he displayed his bravery where alone it could be most honourably and most advantageously displayed. And how much more creditable does this conduct appear, I may venture to say, even in the eye of his own profession, than if he had come off with the heroism of running his

2. *Life of Colonel Gardiner.*

antagonist through the body, or fallen himself a victim to this imaginary test of valour.

It has been matter of just and frequent astonishment, how this detestable practice of duelling, should not only be tolerated as an indispensible evil, but meet with advocates and defenders, who would retain it either from motives of *virtue*,—as if this barbarous and Gothic custom were of a more polishing and civilizing influence than the spirit of Christianity; or of *necessity*,—as if no other principle on earth were powerful enough to maintain order and propriety among men. The laws of murder and assassination they have exalted into a study, and a science which must be cultivated as an accomplishment by every pretender to genteel education; which forms the cabalistic charm of admittance into the company of *honourable* men or the circle of *polite* society. A few such instances, however, as the one recorded above, would go far to alter the prevailing taste, and direct the current of public opinion against these absurd and erroneous maxims

We know well what unbounded efficacy the patronage and example of official or leading characters exert over matters of fashion or amusement. Places of public resort sink rapidly into discredit and decay, the moment they cease to frequent them. Manners or opinions that may have held long and undisputed sway over the human mind, whenever they cease to be honoured by their countenance and support, are proscribed the circles of politeness, and abandoned as the relics of a vulgar and antiquated age. In short, even pleasures and dissipations that have all the advantages of secrecy, and may plead the desires of nature, no sooner lose the magic attraction of fashionable names, than the general taste instantly declares against them. Examples of this kind, therefore, would operate as a salutary antidote against the epidemic contagion of single combat, and furnish a more successful weapon than all the argument and raillery that has been employed against it, for attacking and putting down a custom, which is contrary to the principles of reason and justice—repugnant to the feelings of humanity,—and condemned by the laws of God and man.

While the allies were besieging Bonn, the Marshals Villeroi and Boufflers conceived the project of attacking Liege, and with this design had provided 15,000 pioneers, 3000 waggons, and other necessaries. In the beginning of May they advanced unexpectedly with an army of 40,000 men, to Tongres, 13 miles from Liege. This obliged the confederate troops in that place to retreat with all possible speed, under the cannon of Maestricht, eight miles off. The enemy fell upon the small garrison of Tongres, and compelled them to surrender at discretion, after a brave defence of 28 hours. This delay gave he rest of the forces about Maestricht time to draw together; and when the enemy approached they found, to their surprise and disappointment, the Confederates drawn up in order of battle, under General D'Auverquerque, and prepared for an engagement, though much inferior in number. An opposition so unexpected staggered the resolution of the two marshals. From ten in the morning until three in the afternoon, the two armies stood gazing at each other, within cannon reach; when the enemy, not daring to attack, returned back to Tongres, leaving to the Allies an unstained victory.

★★★★★★

May 1. Now there is some appearance of action. I bless God, I need not be afraid to face death or go to fight, for the Lord of armies is my covenanted God, and I commit myself cheerfully to him.

May 3. This has been a remarkable day. In the morning, the whole French army advanced to attack us: Our army drew out, and there was all the appearance could be of a battle. Their lines came so near us, that our cannon played upon them. For myself, I had a serious spiritual composed frame through the day; was in no hurry or fear, and not anxious about the event. I did not depend on any stock of courage within myself, but sought it from God, and he gave it me. Towards evening the enemy retired, and we returned to our camp.

May 15. Marching from four in the morning till eleven: much fatigued. I was surprised a little with passion, and spake a rash ill-chosen word, for which I was sorry, and implored Christ for pardon. Lying now near Tongres, which brings to my mind a providence of twelve years old, and stirs me up to bless God and be thankful.

★★★★★★

The whole month of June was spent in pursuing the enemy from place to place, and endeavouring to draw them to a battle, which they carefully avoided. The Duke of Marlborough, who had proceeded to Maestricht after the siege of Bonn, pressed them so hard, that they were obliged to continue at arms night and day, retreating before him with great precipitation. Finding it impossible to provoke them to an engagement, the duke resolved to force their entrenchments, which was done in two different places by General Cohorn and Baron Spar.

★★★★★★

June 9. This day we were reviewed.

June 15. On command this and the three following days, which discomposes me, as I am never right unless I have quiet retirement in the intervals of business.

June 18. Marching all this week, often both night and day. It has been the hardest for fatigue I ever marched in. Yet I bless God, I was serene and contented. Though a slave in the galleys, I should think it heaven to enjoy communion with him. With His presence, all places of the earth are alike to me. I see from the ill company around me, that the peace of conscience, satisfaction and tranquillity of soul, flowing from the reflection of having employed time well, far surpasses all the sensual pleasures that earthly men are capable of relishing in this world.

******

Speaking of the decline of morality in the regiment, and contrasting the general conduct of the military with what it used to be, he observes:—

This is a sad corps I am engaged in; vice raging openly and impudently. They speak just such language as devils would do. I find this ill in our trade, that there is now so much tyranny and knavery in the army, that it is a wonder how a man of a straight, generous, honest soul can live in it. I own I am, on many accounts, unfit for it, or for any business or dealing that requires a suppleness and dexterity of temper to play and manage every body according to their various humours and passions. Armies which used to be full of men of great and noble souls, are now turned to a parcel of mercenary, fawning, lewd, dissipated creatures; the dregs and scum of mankind: And those who will not fawn and crouch, are made the butt of malice, and oppressed by the joint conspiracy of wicked men.

On the last day of June, the Battle of Eckeren was fought between General Obdam, with a few battalions of the Dutch, not exceeding 10,000 men, and Marshal Boufflers, who was detached from the main army, with a body of about 30,000 troops, and came upon the Allies, by surprise, at the village of Eckeren, four miles north of Antwerp. In this action, the marshal had the advantage, though he lost more than double the number of men, and was obliged to abandon the field of battle by night, without beat of drum. That part of the army, under the Duke of Marlborough, was not present at this engagement; but in order to repair the disadvantages they had sustained, his Grace, on the 27th of July, again attempted to draw Marshal Villeroi to a battle, which the latter avoided, setting fire to his camp, and retiring within his lines.

Of these operations, the diary for this month, takes no notice. The only passage worth extracting, is one which gives, very distinctly, the writer's notions on his favourite, though somewhat fanciful theory of prayer.

******

July 6. I met with something very remarkable this morning. I was praying for sanctification, and for more grace, without thinking on any temporal mercy. The Spirit of God impressed me, of a sudden, to seek a temporal blessing, which I did; and I found such access and enlargement, and faith so lively and strong, that I had reason to think he heard me; and I believed in the performance of it. Now, ordinarily I do not seek temporal mercies peremptorily or positively, but with submission to his will and Providence; nor do I think I am inclined to enthusiasm; but I think I should slight and neglect the motions of God's Spirit, which certainly impress the soul sensibly on frequent occasions, if I should not take special notice of these impulses, when I find so many concurring marks. I wait therefore patiently for the accomplishment; and am also well satisfied to want it, if the Lord please; but I think it was sealed to me, and his Spirit never seals a lie.

I have this uptaking of prayer, and the hearing of prayer: When Christ, who has purchased all good things for us, has a mind to give us a particular mercy, he intercedes with the Father as our Advocate, and having detained it, the Spirit, who being God equal with the Father and Son, and is witness to what Christ intercedes for and obtains for us, comes down, or is sent down, and suggests to the believer's soul; impressing it strongly to put up that very suit, and ask the same mercy he heard granted to Christ's intercession in heaven. The believer entertains and cherishes the motion, and puts up the suit in Christ's hand. The Spirit intercedes boldly with us, because he knows Christ has obtained it. The believer begs boldly, because Christ having a mind to give, does always give faith the honour of it, by setting it to work; and whenever faith interposes, he sees the business is done. When faith draws, Christ lets go the hold to us; and when it stops, he stops.

August 26. We had a design of fighting, the enemy making as if they intended action, but it was again put off.

August 27. Riding all this day. In the afternoon, I retired all alone to the fields to offer my grateful remembrance of God's goodness to me and mine through this campaign.

******

On the 17th of this month Huy was invested by a detachment from the grand army, and in ten days the town and castle surrendered; the allies having not lost above twenty men. At this siege Captain Blackader was not present, Colonel Frederick Hamilton being the only English brigadier in that service.[3]

The siege of Limburg was next determined upon. This, though a small, was a very strong city, and capital of the Dukedom or territory of that name. The Duke of Marlborough took the command in person. On the 10th of September the town was invested, and on the 27th it capitulated. The city of Guelders was bombarded in December by a detachment of Prussians, and reduced to a heap of ruins, and with these achievements ended the campaign for this year. The allies thus quitted the field with honour, having made themselves masters of the Duchy of Limburg, and the whole Spanish Guelderland; and secured the country of Liege and the Electorate of Cologne from the incursions of the enemy. In October, orders were issued for the necessary disposition of the troops in their quarters, and the Duke of Marlborough soon after returned to England.

Captain Blackader immediately repaired to Rotterdam where his lady usually remained during the campaign.

******

October 11. This afternoon I arrived at Tongres. Next day I came to a place where I might well set up my Ebenezer; mercy was on all hands: on the right was that place, where, twelve years ago, that ever to be regretted and mournful business fell out; but God, I trust, has delivered me from blood-guiltiness, and pardoned my sin. On the left was that place where the enemy thought to have surprised us, and cut us off; and where I had a merciful deliverance the beginning of this same campaign, about half a-year ago.

October 19. Marching towards Breda.

October 23. Travelling still, sometimes by land, sometimes by water,

---

3. Lediard, vol. i.

and with good company. Came at night to Dort, where we have likewise reason to set up our Ebenezer, and remember God's vast goodness and mercy in this same place.

November 20. My lot is full of mercy, but like a spoiled child, except I have that which I am most fond of, I cannot relish any other mercy. After a long and weary march we came into Rotterdam. O what shall I render unto God for all his goodness to me; now he has brought me home, after a long campaign, to the same place I went from. I beg grace to pay my vows, and mind those engagements I entered into when I went out. The Lord has mercifully preserved me, amongst the hazards of a camp, kept me from the infection of ill company—let no evil befall me—no plague come near my dwelling. But ah! what shall I say; I am not pleased with myself since I came into garrison. I see I cannot carry right either under the want of enjoyments, or under the possession of them; I have too much complacency and satisfaction in them; I am ready to turn secure and fall asleep, and forget that this is not my home.

December 9. I am learning, and to learn to know myself every day; and since I came here I have made a discovery of myself I knew not before. There is the half of religion, and the best half too, that I am a great stranger too, *viz.* submission and resignation to God's will and a giving up of my own will. I see that strong affections with weak grace, is like a sword in a madman's hand. When the inferior passions, appetites, and desires, come to get the sway and command, we resemble a crazy vessel manned by drunk slaves, who run it among rocks and shelves, in storms and hurricanes, and in danger of shipwreck every moment. But when the Spirit of God, (the true pilot of the soul,) calm reason and grace take the helm, and clap these unruly slaves under hatches again, then all goes well; the soul glides smoothly under the gentle gales and breeze of the Spirit, and pursues its steady course to the desired haven of everlasting rest and happiness.

Chapter 10

Campaign Third, 1704

This year has become memorable in the annals of British history, being signalised by more brilliant victories, and more remarkable success than had hitherto attended the Confederate arms. The Duke of Marlborough, no more distinguished as an intrepid warrior, than as a skilful general, resolved to make the experiment of transferring the seat of war from the Netherlands to Germany. The state of the Imperial dominions rendered the interposition of the Allies, in that quarter, absolutely necessary. The Elector of Bavaria, now in the interest of France, had carried hostilities into the very centre of the empire. He had taken Neuberg, Ratisbon, and Passua; and having joined Marshal Villars, they defeated the Imperialists on the plains of Hochstet, a place which was soon to become renowned by one of the most signal victories of the Allies.

The emperor was struck with consternation at these disasters, and reduced to the last extremity. His territories were overrun by the French and Bavarians, who had penetrated beyond the Danube, and threatened to besiege him in his own capital.

The insurgents in Hungary menaced him on the opposite quarter, and nothing but immediate succours seemed capable of preserving all Germany from revolution, and the House of Austria from total subversion. Count Wratislau, the emperor's Envoy Extraordinary, presented a memorial to the Queen of Great Britain, soliciting speedy succour, which Her Majesty was pleased to grant, by ordering the Duke of Marlborough and a part of the Confederate troops, to be sent to rescue the empire from its imminent danger.

These subsidies could be the better spared, since the frontiers of Holland were now tolerably secured against the invasion of the enemy, being strongly defended by rivers, forts, and entrenchments. A small army, under the command of Mons. D'Auverquerque, was to be stationed in Flanders, to act on the defensive; while the main body with the Duke of Marlborough, were to march upon the Rhine, (which, by the taking of Bonn, was laid open as far as Coblentz) with the design, as was given out, of penetrating into France, but in reality, to carry the war to the very confines of Austria. All matters relating to the operations of the campaign being happily adjusted, the duke set out, having orders to the British troops, and the rest of the forces, to direct their march towards Coblentz and the Moselle. We now recur to our subject.

******

January 1. Resolution to spend my time better, so as I may have peace in it; to serve God more cheerfully, to trust him, and cast all my burdens upon him; not to be anxious or careful about any thing, but by faith and prayer, to interest him in it. Lord, give me grace to live so.

January 2. Sabbath. On guard this day; and by company, kept from retirement for spiritual thoughts.

January 4. My judgement sees the emptiness and vanity of things here below, yet my affections, for all that, will be doting upon them. Blessed Jesus, raise my affections, and fix them upon thyself.

January 6. This day, from morning till night, my spirits sour and chagrined: there is still, as it were, weight upon me; a melancholy temper, inclined to discontent, poisons all my comforts. Satan also works by it, and the least accident is fuel to it. If this grows upon me, my life, which has been made sweet and comfortable by a long track of singular mercies, will become miserable. At night, I found help in prayer by faith, believing firmly that God will help me to serve him more cheerfully and pleasantly.

January 15. I bless God, who keeps me so out of temptation—keeps me easy, contented, serene: It is his goodness alone, for if he should leave me to myself, my own corruptions would rise in rebellion against me, and make me miserable.

January 20. I find great difference in my frame. Some days I am serene, cheerful, contented; others, without any outward cause, quite the reverse; every thing ready to become a temptation.

January 21. This day business went on well. I find the best way to get through business is, to commit all to God.

February 3. I keep too fast a hold of earthly enjoyments: I shall never be well, until I come to that, *viz.* to rejoice that I am a stranger in the world, that this is not my home,—to rejoice that the world is vain and unsatisfying, and all its comforts temporal and perishing.

February 4. If I could live by faith, I might have a sweet life; for I find the very moments in which I believe, that my thoughts and temper are only pleasant and cheerful.

February 8. This morning access to God in prayer; faith lively; trusting in God; putting all my interests, my wife and family in his hands, believing firmly that he will give a good account of all that mercy and goodness shall follow me and her this campaign, as it did the last; for besides the promises of God I had last year to trust to, I have also the sweet experiences of the last campaign to encourage me, how he gave his angels charge over us, that no plague came nigh our dwelling—no evil befell us. We saw a peculiar care of Providence about us. Oh then, I desire cheerfully to trust a covenanted God still, and pleasantly to put a blank in a kind Father's hand, who, I am assured, will give me a good account of all, and once more put songs of praise and deliverance in our mouths. Lord Jesus, strengthen our faith. It is only by faith we can live. When that fails, all fails.

After writing this sweet experience, and praying it over alone, I called my wife, and she and I prayed it over jointly, blessing and rejoicing in God for his mercies last campaign; trusting in him, and casting ourselves upon him this campaign; believing firmly that he will follow us with mercy and goodness still—that he will give his angels charge over us,—that he will protect, preserve, guide, and direct by his Spirit and Providence,—and that all shall be well if we trust and rely upon him.

February 18. Sabbath. Oh how much do I stand in need of reviving, quickening ordinances. I complain that I am here infected by the people, the country, and the company I live in; grace wastes away, and I become dry as a parched and thirsty land wherein no water is. *Woe is me, that I sojourn so long in Mesech, that I dwell in the tents of Kedar.* I long to be under a refreshing gospel ministry, where I have felt the sweet influences of his Spirit and grace upon my heart, like *Dew upon the tender grass. One day, Oh Lord, in thy courts is worth a thousand.*

February 17. Again set apart this morning and forenoon, with my wife, for prayer, to humble ourselves in prospect of a new campaign, and to depend upon him for grace and strength.—I prayed over the ninety-first Psalm, believing the sure performance of every particular promise in it. I resolved to depend more upon Christ, and to employ him in every circumstance of my life.

February 20. A melancholy Sabbath, dejected and desponding. Oh how much I long for those rousing and quickening ordinances I once enjoyed, wherein I have felt the spirit of God powerfully reviving and refreshing a dead soul. The longer I stay in this country, I think I am the worse. Oh Lord, carry me wherever thou wild give me most of they presence, for I take no comfort in a life absent from thee.

February 24. Deeply affected with my condition, both as to the sin and the misery of it. I looked to Christ for comfort, and especially to that promise. *Come unto me all ye that labour, and are heavy laden, and I will give you rest.*

February 25. Concerned in an affair this day. Blessed Jesus, thou who art the truth, teach me what I should believe and own as truth; and let me receive nothing as current, but what thy Spirit stamps thy image upon; and then, be it never so small a truth, I desire grace to own and adhere to it at my utmost hazard. Give me. Lord, in my own cause, a meek and quiet spirit; but in thine, give me zeal, courage, and boldness.

March 2. This morning and forenoon again set apart for prayer, for the presence and blessing of God this campaign, in the view of launching out into new storms and temptation.

March 9. On guard this day, but kept out of temptation. Taken up all the morning about the regulations of our employment. I bless God for his Providence, that he keeps me in garrison here, when others are going out. I went out before when they were kept in. I know I did get good of that, and shall do of this likewise.

March 12. Sabbath. Still I have not here that heavenly, spiritual frame that I used to have in Scotland. This country is infected with an air of formality. *Oh that I might again behold the beauty of the Lord in his temple, and sit under his shadow with great delight.*

March 17. The day soberly spent at home; company in the evening. I see the world to be a theatre, and human life to be a downright farce, a stage—play of folly, vanity, and pageantry. My judgement, in its cool reasonings, despises and sees through this vanity and emptiness, but alas, my foolish affections refuse to answer the helm, and will run out fondly after earthly trifles; though, in the meantime, I see their insufficiency, that they cannot make me happy.

March 20. On guard this day; but not watchful enough over my own spirit, and apt to sin through hastiness of temper. There are two things that frighten me most in the campaign. The ill company I may be engaged in, that I cannot shun; and too much occupation with the world, that withdraws me from the service of God. I have put up my suit to Christ against these two.

March 31. On command, and marching all this day. My frame serene and spiritual. Singing hymns and psalms, and yet alas, sinning between hands by passion of hastiness of spirit. When I consider my way of religion, I think it is this: As to internals, my thoughts, meditations, and secret outgoings of my soul, the spirit of God seems to guide and influence them; but when it comes to words or actions, then the weak man appears, and I seem to act by my natural temper, and do not so sensibly feel the conduct of the Spirit, as in the motions of the heart. This makes me shun company, public posts and appearances, and choose solitude and retirement; for I cannot get my words and actions so ordered, as to be the true mirror of my mind. This employment also exposes me to ill company which I hate, and cannot live with. My soul is weary of the tents of sin.

April 22. In company all this day; yet easy, serene and cheerful. I dare not say but I have made escapes in company, and I complain much I have not the talent or dexterity of bringing in edifying discourse, but rather join in their trifles.

April 24. In the evening got accounts of our making the campaign far up the country. Serious and fervent in joint prayer, casting ourselves upon a covenanted God, and trusting in him. *The earth is the Lord's, and the fullness thereof.* I care not where I go, if he go with me. His presence will make even a camp pleasant. But if thou go not with me. Lord carry me not out of the Busse. We were helped to believe that he will conduct us well through.

April 25. Serious, easy and cheerful. In the winter, I was more frightened for the snares, temptations, and discouragements of a campaign, upon a distant view of it, than now when it approaches nearer. I bless God who makes me so serene and cheerful at my going out to the camp, and for the faith that I believe firmly I shall have the blessing and presence of God with me wherever I go.

April 28. This day we marched out of the Busse to the camp. I admire the goodness of God, that I am so easy and comfortable, for I was frightened in the prospect of a campaign, for snares and evil company, but now as it approaches, these fears are dissipated.

April 30. Sabbath. Marching all day, but alas, involved in sin by company and idle discourse. A sad place to be in an army on Sabbath, where nothing is to be heard but oaths and profane language.

May 1. On command this day, yet spiritual thoughts between hands. I am daily getting fresh instances of God's goodness to me.

May 2. Marching all day; retiring occasionally for prayer. I have company the world knows not of; and were it not for thy presence, Lord, I would sink under discouragement; and could not live among the scum and dregs of mankind, who seem like devils broke loose from hell. I protest, I seek no higher post or preferment in this army; I rather seek to be fairly quit of it; I see it is not my element. I desire also to have a spirit above the foolish pageantry, and false notions of honour which the world admires.

May 3-7. Marching every day. This not a proper work for a Sabbath. Met with a merciful Providence, my horse falling upon me, yet not hurt; this stirred me up to thankfulness. Joining the rest of the regiment in the afternoon, where I got accounts of two or three particulars that were like to make me uneasy; but I retired to prayer, and there I cast all my cares,—all my burdens upon God. He lets me see this world is but a stormy sea,—a vale of misery and tears, one blast after another.

May 8-15. Marching every day a merciful and remarkable Providence happened to me this day. Lord, give me grace never to forget it. I had almost been drowned in the Moselle at Coblentz, if it had not been the goodness of God that sent me help. This I think remarkable, that I have been serious since ever I heard of our coming to the Moselle, praying for the blessing and presence of God; and yet at my very first sight of it, I was like to be lost in it. God deals frequently so with me; when he promises me anything, he gives it such a turn by contrary providences, as may make the thing seem impracticable and past belief; and then in that difficulty, he tries faith by the event, for faith would not be faith, but sense, if all things went smoothly on without cross providences; but to believe when the thing seems impossible, is faith; like Abraham sacrificing his son Isaac. Lord, let the impression of this sink deep into my soul, and make me holy and thankful. I take it as a pledge of yet greater mercies to come in this journey.

May 17. At night I got a warning that I am a frail creature; but, O Lord, thou art the God of my health. I trust to thee that thou wilt keep me in health, and prevent sickness in this expedition, for how ad would it be here among strangers! Thou art my Physician for soul and body. Lord, I tremble to think on the profanity and wickedness of this army that I am in, and what judgements we are like to pull down upon our own heads; for the English army are sinners exceedingly before the Lord, and I have no hopes of success, or that this expedition shall prove to our honour. Howsoever much we may think of ourselves, thou wilt humble us; but for my own part, I am not anxious, thou keepest me in perfect peace; and whatever thou do with the English Army, I am persuaded, that by the mercy of God, I shall set up my Ebenezers through Germany. Wherever thou lead me, I shall be still and see the salvation of our God, while thou exaltest thyself among the heathen; be thou exalted very high, and work with they outstretched arm, and let not an arm of flesh have the glory.

May 18. Resting this day, not designedly, but by reason of the roads. This is like to be a campaign of great fatigue and trouble. I know not where they are leading us, but. Lord do thou lead me in thy way. I will not trust to General's leading; thou who leadest the blind by a way they know not, I trust to thee alone, and put myself, and all I am concerned in under they conduct. I see the kind hand of a Father still about me.

May 19-22. Marching every day. Arrived at Mentz after a long journey.

May 27. Army resting this day. I went into Heydelberg in company and hurry, and have no time for retirement.

May 28. Sabbath. Army marching. By being in town I had retirement, for I shook off all company, and retired alone upon the banks of the Neckar the whole forenoon. I hope I had communion with God; my covenant with Christ ratified; my Ebenezer here set up; his presence implored: And this I beg, dear Lord, if this be an unlawful expedition, that thou wouldst yet turn me back; if thou go not with me, carry me no farther. When I consider this, that we are here assisting those oppressors that have wasted the church and people of God, persecuted and oppressed them, it makes me afraid the quarrel is not right, and that we shall not prosper; that I be satisfied that our quarrel against France is a very just one. O Lord, I commit all to thee; let me be found strictly in they way, in the road of duty, fighting thy quarrel against thine enemies. It is a sad thing to be in an army where one has not confidence to pray for success, and dare not seek it with faith.

Take, Lord, the honour and glory to thyself; work so that the arm of flesh may not boast, but that the finger of God may appear. When thy judgements are abroad on the earth, then the inhabitants thereof will learn righteousness. When the carcases of the one half of us are dung on the earth in Germany; the, perhaps, the other half will bethink themselves. Be it as thou wilt; I flee to the chambers of mercy thou hast provided in Christ; there I shall be safe, and may be, I shall be hid from the outward stroke also. I bless thee I have such sweet minutes in this army, they are as cordials which keep up my fainting spirits. At the writing hereof, I am sitting under a great rock, (it being a scorching hot day) cool and refreshed: Even so, Lord Jesus, be thou the shadow of a great rock in this weary land to me.

June 1-12. Marching every day, except resting occasionally from great fatigue, or from bad weather and bad roads.

June 13. Marching; frequent in ejaculatory prayer. I think this the great secret of Christianity, whereby a spiritual heat and edge of soul is kept up; communion with God and his Spirit, cherished and entertained. I live as retiredly as possible, though I know this retired way is condemned by the gay world; but I care not, it is the safest way of living, to be kept free from the filth and pollution of the world. I value not their opinion; nay, it is rather a happiness to be hated and ill spoken of by them, for in all ages, the seed of the serpent has spit venom at serious Christians. They hate holiness and the image of God; and when they love any good people, it is a strong presumption that they are too like themselves.

June 14. Marching and on command.

June 15. Marching and in fatigue until midnight.

June 16. This day we joined Prince Lewis' army.

June 17-21. Marching and expecting to come to action.

★★★★★★

Thus, by rapid and fatiguing journeys, in little more two months, the Confederate forces had penetrated to the banks of the Danube, and reached the scene of action. Their difficulties were not a little augmented by the frequent bad weather they encountered, and the almost impassable state of the roads, which in those days were often little better than foot-tracks. Yet the writer of the diary has few or no complaints on the score of bodily fatigue, and not one anxiety about facing the dangers that were now gathering round him on ever side. These were not the objects that occupied or discomposed his thoughts. The irritability of mind he sometimes betrays, though it may have been increased by lassitude, was always occasioned by the impiety or profane discourse of the company he was obliged to mingle with.

We find him, amidst hurry and confusion, constant in the exercise of private devotion, and embracing every opportunity of retirement for religious mediation. It was from these sources he drew not only his comfort, but his courage; and to this secret spring must be traced up that calm and resigned fortitude which could render him superior to fear. Some can be bold on the prospect, or in the midst of danger, from a constant familiarity with it. Some have the faculty, as it were, of averting their thoughts from disagreeable images, of dismissing those timorous apprehensions that always create uneasiness or concern, and become daring from mere carelessness or insensibility. Others must have their nerves fortified by artificial stimulants, or their minds wrought up into unnatural frenzy.

The Christian acts upon principles totally different. His composure rests on a better foundation than a thoughtless levity of heart, or a reluctance to contemplate his own situation. To exclude from his thoughts what he cannot prevent, or rush on destruction with his eyes shut, he regards as the foolish and despicable shift of a madman or a coward; and calculated rather to increase and multiply his fears. He is never overtaken by surprise, because he is prepared for every vicissitude that can befall him; and in the day of danger he is uniformly seen more tranquil and consistent, and not less intrepid in his conduct, than those whose courage depends upon the temperature of their blood, or the artificial heat of their minds. And the reason of this conduct is obvious.

Vice debilitates the mind as well as the body: while virtue warms and elevates the soul to great and noble actions; for can anything be bolder than truth, or more fearless than conscious innocence? No conviction can be more animating that that which the Christian entertains, that all the contingencies of his life are in the hands of Omniscience; that the Divine presence, go were he will, compasses him about as with a shield; that it draws, as it were, a sacred fence around his person, and furnishes a surer protection against *the arrow that flieth by day*, than all the defences of art or of nature.

The action alluded to above, was that which took place at Schellenberg, in the immediate neighbourhood of Donawert, in which the enemy's entrenchments were forced, after a most obstinate and bloody contest. The Duke of Marlborough had conducted his march with such secrecy and despatch, that he was on the borders of Suabia before the enemy were apprised of his real destination. Their belief was, that he intended to lay siege to Traerbach, and penetrate into France along the Moselle. His purpose was originally communicated only to three persons, and was long kept a mystery to many of his own officers; some allusion to this uncertainty is made in the diary for the 18th of May.

Being joined by the Imperial Army under the Prince of Baden, it was agreed to proceed without delay to the Danube; a resolution which greatly surprised the enemy, who now saw, for the first time, how far they were mistaken in their conjectures. The French and Bavarians had effected a junction, and a strong detachment of their best troops, under Count D'Arco, was posted on a rising ground at Schellenberg, where some thousands of pioneers had been employed several days, in casting up entrenchments and perfecting other works of defence. Notwithstanding these advantages and preparations, the Duke was resolved to drive them from their position. On the 2nd of July, at three in the morning, he set out at the head of 6000 foot, and 30 squadrons of horse. About noon he reached the small River Wernitz, within a short distance of the enemy; but having to construct bridges for transporting his troops and artillery, it was six in the evening before all was ready for the attack.

The action commenced with the Dutch and British infantry, who attacked with their accustomed valour and intrepidity. An hour elapsed before the Imperialists could come up to their assistance, in consequence of which some of the English regiments suffered very severely. In half-an-hour after, the cavalry broke into the entrenchments, followed by the infantry, when a terrible slaughter ensued, the soldiers appearing to forget the weariness of a tedious and fatiguing march. The enemy fled with precipitation on all sides, leaving 6000 men dead on the field of battle. They were pursued to Donawert, and the very brink of the Danube, into which hundreds threw themselves, imitating the example of Count D'Arco and other general officers who saved themselves by swimming. In this contest Captain Blackader was not called into action; for although Brigadier Ferguson headed the infantry in the first attack, it appears that only a small proportion of his own regiment was actually engaged.

******

June 21.[1] Easy and serene all day; cheerfully committing myself and all that concerns me into the hands of God; fetching all my supplies of courage, and strength, and furniture, for going through the duties of my function, from him alone; for indeed I pretend to no stock of my own either of courage or conduct. In the evening I witnessed one of the hottest actions I have seen. It continued from six to eight o'clock. We gained our point, and beat the enemy from their post, and yet we have no reason to boast or think highly of ourselves. The British value themselves too much, and think nothing can stand before them. We have suffered considerably on this occasion, and have no cause to be proud.

During the action I was straitened in praying for success and victory to our people, and had not enlargement to seek anything but that God would get the praise to himself, and work so as the arm of flesh might not rob him of his glory. Oh that God might reform this army, that good men might have some pleasure in it. When we see what an uncertain thing our life is now in health, and the next moment in eternity, it is wonderful we are not more affected by it. I see also that the smallest accidents give a turn to the greatest actions, either to prosper or defeat them: that human wisdom, courage, or any thing else we value ourselves upon, is but weak and fallible. There was only a detachment of 130 of our regiment engaged in this battle.

June 22. In the evening I went alone into the field of battle, and there got a preaching from the dead. The carcases were very thick strewed upon the ground, naked and corrupting; yet all this works no impression or reformation upon us, seeing the bodies of our comrades and friends lying as dung upon the face of the earth. Lord, make me humble and thankful! I trusted in thee that I should set up many Ebenezers through Germany, and here in the field of the slain do I set up my memorial. *Hitherto thou hast helped me.*

---

1. The dates in the diary are given according to the old style of reckoning, *viz.* with a variation of eleven days. The battle was fought July 3rd.

June 24. Passing the Danube, the effect of our victory the other day.

July 4. Marching every day. O may I be found in the way of duty, for, like wisdom's, her ways are ways of pleasantness, and her paths peace. In our *King's* highway there are lights set up for direction, and a voice behind, saying. *Walk ye in it.* In our *King's* highway are cordials for the weary fainting traveller, streams of refreshment and of comfort. In our *King's* highway are magazines and storehouses of grace, that the traveller may go on from strength to strength.

July 5-10. Marching. Things begin now in this country to take another aspect. Nothing is talked of here but accommodation and peace; but perhaps we count without our host too hastily. I know not how it will be; only do thou. Lord, direct and overrule all for they glory.

July 11-30. Marching almost every day, and sometimes on command. We are now divided and detached into three or four armies. I know not what Providence is about to do with us; but this I know, that wherever or with whatever army I may be, I shall set up my stone of deliverance as I do here at Rain,[2] for we have marched back again to the Danube.

July 31. This day, after a fatiguing march, we repassed the Danube and joined three of our armies together.

August 1. Resting till far on of the day, then drawing out our lines as making ready to be attacked by the Duke of Bavaria and the French. I bless God I was stayed and composed, very easy and indifferent about fighting, recollecting my interest in him.

★★★★★★

These preparations were the harbingers of the ever memorable Battle of Blenheim or Hochstet. After taking possession of Schellenberg the Allies seized Donawert, which had been abandoned by the Bavarian garrison. The Elector had retired with the shattered remains of his army under the cannon of Augsburg. Finding it impossible to dislodge him from this strong position, the Duke of Marlborough, eager to profit by his recent victory, resolved to cut him off from all supplies. He entered the Bavarian territory and took several places by storm. He ravaged the whole country, as far as Munich, with fire and

---

2. A small town in the circle of Bavaria, about six miles east of Donawert. It was besieged at this time, and taken by the Allies.

sword, in order to compel the Elector to sue for peace or relinquish his connections with France. A negotiation was begun, but without sincerity on the part of the Elector, who only wished to prolong the truce until the French Army should march to his assistance.

On the 4th of August, Marshal Tallard joined him with 22,000 horse and foot. Reinforced by these new auxiliaries he left Augsburg, with the intention of surprising Prince Eugene, who, with one of the Confederate armies, lay encamped on the plain of Hochstet. The Duke of Marlborough, with his accustomed vigilance, soon penetrated the design of the enemy, and on the 12th he formed a junction with Prince Eugene. Being now in a condition to cope with their adversaries, who by this time had encamped very near them, the two Confederate Generals proposed to attack them, though they were advantageously posted, their right flank being covered with the Danube and the village of Blenheim, and their whole front defended by a rivulet.

This resolution being adopted, preparations were made with the utmost diligence. The drum beat about midnight, and by two in the morning, the whole army was in motion; but it was seven before they could be drawn up in order of battle. About noon, orders were given for the general attack, which was begun on the left, at the village of Blenheim, by the British infantry and four battalions of Hessians, who boldly advanced to the muzzles of the enemy's muskets, some of the officers exchanging sword-thrusts with the French through the palisades. But the tremendous fire made such havoc among them, that they were forced to retreat, leaving nearly one third of their number dead on the spot. A second assault, in which Captain Blackader was wounded, was made by Brigadier Ferguson, but with no better success, though they had returned three or four times to the charge, and were as often repulsed. In this action, the Cameronian Regiment suffered severely, having about twenty officers either killed or wounded. While the infantry were thus occupied, the cavalry passed the rivulet advanced up the hill where the enemy's horse were posted, and put them to the rout, notwithstanding they rallied several times.

It is not requisite here to enter into the particulars of this celebrated battle; suffice it to say, that after an engagement of five hours, victory declared for the Allies, although they attacked with a visible disadvantage, and after a march of ten hours in an extremely hot day. The loss of the French was computed at 30,000, and that of the Allies about 12,000, killed, wounded, and prisoners.

Thirty battalions of the enemy threw themselves into the Danube to escape, and perished before the eyes of the conquerors. Twenty-eight battalions, and twelve squadrons of horse surrendered to the British, who, after the fatigues of the day, were obliged to continue on their arms all night to guard the prisoners, as there was no place of security in the country where they could be put. They were kept enclosed in a lane or hollow square, formed by the troops at the village of Blenheim. On this duty, Captain Blackader mentions himself as one of the officers on command.

★★★★★★

August 2. Many deliverances I have met with, but this day I have had the greatest ever I experienced. We fought a bloody battle, and, by the mercy of God, have obtained one of the greatest and completest victories the age can boast of. In the morning, while marching towards the enemy, I was enabled to exercise a lively faith, relying and encouraging myself in God, whereupon I was easy, sedate, and cheerful. I believed firmly that his angels had me in charge, and that not a bone should be broken. During all the little intervals of action, I kept looking to God for strength and courage, and had a plentiful through-bearing, both to keep up my own heart, and help to discharge my duty well in my station.

My faith was so lively during the action, that I sometimes said within myself, Lord, it were easy for thee to cause thy angels to lay all these men dead on the place where they stand, or bring them in all prisoners to us. And for encouraging our regiment, I spoke it aloud. That we should either chase them from their post, or take them prisoners; and I cannot but observe the event at seven—'clock at night, when they laid down their arms to us. Twenty-six regiments (some say thirty) surrendered themselves prisoners at discretion, to the Duke of Marlborough, and our regiment was one of those that guarded them.

This victory has indeed cost a great deal of blood, especially to the English. I was always of opinion that the English would pay for it in this country; and when I consider, how, on all occasions, we conquer, yet with much blood spilt, I am at a loss to know what the reason may be. Perhaps it is that our cause is good, and therefore God gives us success in our enterprises, but our persons very wicked, and therefore our carcases are strewed like dung upon the earth in Germany. Among the rest I have also got a small touch of a wound in the throat;[3] but this,

---

3. *Vid. List of Killed and Wounded.* Lediard, vol. i.

so far from making me doubt of the care of Providence, is really to me a great confirmation, and a remarkable instance of his protection; for the wound is so gently and mercifully directed, that there is no danger; whereas, if it had been half an inch either to one side or other, it might have proved mortal or dangerous.

The Lord is a shield and buckler to me. We have all indeed good cause to rejoice; but Oh, shall nothing work upon us—shall nothing be blest to reform us, when so many of us are cut off—shall not the rest bethink themselves and turn unto thee. If they will not, thou wilt yet break us more and more, for thou canst waste us with victories, as well as with defeats. Oh Lord, thou hast assisted me, and given such liberal supplies during the action, that I was helped to discharge my duty, even with credit and reputation. Dear Lord, I lay down all at thy feet. I have no reason to be lifted up. It was not my own strength that carried me through, it was a borrowed stock, so the praise is thine, and not mine; for hadst thou withheld thy support, I had behaved scandalously.

※※※※※※

Such are the humble and modest reflections he makes on his own conduct, although, on this occasion, it appears to have been highly courageous. His confidence and composure in the heat of action, are thus expressed by himself, in a letter written on the field of battle to Lady Campbell at Stirling:—

> I am just now retired from the noise of drums, of oaths, and dying groans. I am to return in a few minutes to the field of battle, and, wrapping myself up in the arms of Omnipotence, I believe myself no less safe, as to every valuable purpose, than if sitting in your Ladyship's chamber.

※※※※※※

August 3. Worn for want of rest and refreshment; yet in the morning I went back to the place of our attack, where we were posted, and there among the dead, I again blessed God for my wonderful deliverance.

※※※※※※

The Allies were much embarrassed by the great number of prisoners, as they had no proper depot to secure them in, and little to subsist them. The duke resolved to send his proportion, amounting to 5678 by water, to Holland, that they might be distributed among the garrisons in the United Provinces. Brigadier Ferguson, with five battalions of British foot, were ordered to guard them to their destination. With this convoy. Captain Blackader also returned; we shall therefore follow him down the Rhine from Mentz, where the prisoners were to embark.

※※※※※※

August 4. Riding all day alone into Norlingen, and pleasantly employed in thinking over the ninety-first Psalm. At night, thankful for my good accommodation, and how happily I am sent in here among the kindest of my friends.

August 5. Well all day; but in the evening a little uneasy, my wound beginning to grow painful; but why should I be exempt from trouble more than others? I bless God I am not groaning with broken bones, or bullets in my body, as many are.

August 9. This day busy going though and visiting the wounded and dying officers. I see the vanity and emptiness of all things here below. Many who last week thought themselves brave and healthy men, are groaning and sinking down to the dust again.

August 12. Somewhat uneasy that my time has been encroached upon by company too long, when I had no mind for them. At night seeing officers in pain and torment with their wounds, makes me thankful I am not so severely handled.

August 13. Sabbath. Taken up all day in the house of mourning, burying a friend. Oh I wonder at the sottish stupidity of men of our trade. They see their comrades with whom they used to drink and debauch, plucked out of the world in a moment, yet they have not so much as a thought that they have a soul, or what will become of it when they die. I look upon this impiety as the greatest madness a rational creature can be guilty of. The longer I live, I see the greater necessity for holiness. To see a poor creature on a death-bed, on the brink of eternity forced to quit the hold of all earthly comforts,—nothing but horror—nothing comfortable to look to in the other world, surrounded with jolly companions, miserable comforters, is very affecting. Then a view of Christ is precious, an interest in him is worth a thousand worlds.

August 25-29. Travelling by water (down the Mayn.) Arrived safe at Frankfort. I bless God for his goodness, in restoring me to health and strength, while others are pained with their wounds, and some dead.

September 1. Travelling this day, and coming to the baths at Wysbaden.

✶✶✶✶✶✶

From this place is dated a letter to his wife, containing some reflections on his present situation, which we shall insert.

Wysbaden, September 9

I have at last received a letter from you, the one you wrote to the care of Major Lawson at Frankfort. I suppose all you wrote to me at Norlingen have been missent. This is the only one of yours that has come to my hand since the battle. I desire in all things to fall in with the designs of Providence, and am grieved at heart to think I have so much love to the world, and so little to God, who, though he had never done any thing for me before, yet the experience of what he has done for me this campaign, the wonderful deliverances, preservations, signal mercies, and loving kindnesses he has heaped upon me, might shame me out of all other love, and make me cry out. *He and He only is altogether lovely.*

I used to wish for solitude and retirement, yet I must tell you, that though I have been in good company since I came from Norlingen, and had a pleasant voyage, and abundance of retirement and quietness, yet such has been my inward feeling, my want of peace and serenity of soul, that I have often wished to be in the midst of the army again, and in the brunt of the hottest battle. It has been ill with me these twenty days bygone; but it is not always so. I have consolation when I get access to the throne of grace with my petitions, and am enabled to pour out my soul there. I write the more plainly to you: knowing that I open my case to a tendered-heart sympathiser, who has a fellow feeling for my infirmities, and will remember me at the throne of our compassionate High Priest, who has bowels of mercy for tempted souls.

But we need such trials and troubles to keep us humble and sensible of our needy dependence; especially after such mercies as I have experienced the whole of this campaign. I beg of you not to be discouraged with my complaints, for the Lord will deal bountifully with me.

I know not whether I shall return to the regiment, or remain here till they come down. Our brigadier is on his way with five regiments that suffered most, (ours is not with him.) He is to be at Mentz tomorrow. I deign to wait on him there, to see what Providence will order. Perhaps I may be sent for Scotland this winter, for recruits. I would rather it came from himself, then that I should ask it; and if it do so, then I shall come down to Holland with him to get myself ready. If this do not happen, then I may be desired to return to the regiment.

But I am indifferent about all these things; let Providence work for me. If I come, the Lord will perhaps be gracious to me, and send me down to Rotterdam before the sacrament there, which I believe is about the beginning of October; and it would be a very desirable mercy to us both, if we might go into His house together, to take the cup of salvation in our hands, and pay our vows in the presence of his people. The Lord's blessing be with you, and give you grace to walk suitably to our great mercies,— to devote the rest of our lives to his service; and may the love of Christ be the tie and bond of love between us, that we may be more and more blessed in each other.

I am thine.   J. B.

Mrs. Blackader, Mr. Montier's,
Merchand, Scots Dyke, Rotterdam.

★★★★★★

September 14. Still on our journey, and sometimes in none of the best company. Passing by Coblentz, and at the writing hereof, just upon the place in the Rhine where I had almost been drowned in going up the country. This stirred up a sweet thankful frame. I looked upon it now as an earnest and pledge of his goodness to me in the campaign.

September 15. Came safe to Cologne. When I am passing though towns or places I have been in before, it always awakes in me a tender remembrance of my past mercies and deliverances.

September 18. I am brought back again in safety to Holland. Coming to Dort at night, I recorded the goodness of God in the same room where I had done it before, when I arrived this time twelvemonth from the last campaign.

September 19. Arrived at Rotterdam. My soul humbled before God under a sense of the deadness and unthankfulness of my heart, after such signal favours as I have experienced.

September 24. Sabbath. Enjoying the ordinances of the gospel, yet I could not have believed my heart would be so hard and insensible. *It is deceitful above all things, and desperately wicked.*

September 30. Upon the wing, and in hurry all day; leaving Rotterdam the very day before the sacrament, when I expected to have taken the cup of salvation, and paid my vows. I do not understand the language of this Providence; perhaps it is that my heart is not filled enough with love to Christ.

October 1. Sabbath. Went on board.

October 5. Pleasant passage; fair wind, and calm sea.

October 7. After a prosperous and speedy voyage, we landed in Scotland safe and well.

October 8. Enjoying ordinances which my soul delights in, and which was my principal reason for coming to Scotland at this time. I find also that I am the first that has yet reached Edinburgh, of any that were at the battles in Germany.

★★★★★★

While in Edinburgh, he complains of being too much exposed to company, and occupied with visitors that he could get no leisure for retirement. In a short time he set out to Craigforth with his wife, where they spent several months.

The remainder of the campaign in Germany was marked by a series of successes. Ingolstadt, Augsburg, Ulm, Landau, (see note at end of chapter), Treves, Traerbach, and several other towns, surrendered to the Allies. The whole of Bavaria was abandoned to their possession, and they were masters of all the country from the Danube to the Rhine. The victory at Blenheim was the key to all these successes. Its consequences were most important. But for that, the emperor must have been stripped of his dominions, and forced from his capital, for the Bavarians had penetrated into Upper Austria; and the Hungarians, on the other side, were broken out into open rebellion, and wanted nothing but artillery and ammunition to have taken all the fortresses in the empire. Such were the effects and the conclusion of this splendid and celebrated campaign, which terminated after an uninterrupted prosperity of seven months, without experiencing a single reverse of fortune.

★★★★★★

Note:—Few sieges ever witnessed a more heroic intrepidity than that of the Governor of Landau, Mons. Laubanie. The besiegers summoned him by a trumpet to surrender the place, before he was buried under its ruins. He replied with a noble scorn of their proposal and their threats, "that such an honourable funeral was to him an object of ambition, and not of terror; and that the love he bore to his country, would not permit him to surrender, until he was compelled by force." He kept his word; resolved to dispute it to the last. But while going round giving orders to his men, he was struck blind with the gravel thrown into his eyes, by the bursting of a bomb near where he stood; while, at the same time, a splinter of wood wounded him in the body. His spirit, however, was invulnerable; and he was led about the walls groping with his hands, and measuring the breaches made by the enemies' batteries, that he might give his directions accordingly. He continued to defend the town with the same firmness and resolution; his soldiers admiring his fortitude, and lamenting his misfortunes, but obeying his orders without murmuring. In this situation, he prolonged the siege for several weeks, and at last obtained an honourable capitulation.

CHAPTER 11

Campaign Fourth, 1705

The exploits of Marlborough and Prince Eugene were now the theme of universal admiration. They were regarded as twin constellations in glory, and all Europe resounded with their applauses. On his arrival in England, the duke was complimented in the most flattering terms, and received the thanks of both Houses of Parliament. The memory of his distinguished services was perpetuated by the most substantial marks of royal favour. The manor of Woodstock was bestowed upon him, where a magnificent palace was built, and named in honour of his great victory at Blenheim. Foreigners were not less grateful than his own country. He was created, by Leopold, a Prince of the Empire; the territory of Mindelheim being, for that purpose, erected into a Principality.

But these splendid conquests were not productive of all the advantages that might have been expected to result from them. France, though impoverished and discontented, was not yet exhausted. The despotism of Louis, in a great degree, rendered him superior to his straits and embarrassments. By arbitrary compulsions, he was enabled to overcome the reluctance of his subjects, and replenish the coffers of his treasury; and to the astonishment of Britain and her Allies, he again entered the field with armies as numerous and well equipped as they had been in any year since the commencement of the war. Marshal Villars, with 70,000 men, lay encamped on the Moselle; while Villeroi, with a smaller force, commanded in Flanders.

The Duke of Marlborough's plan was to open the campaign, of this year, on the Moselle, by attacking Villars, and pushing the war into the interior of France. D'Auverquerque, as formerly, was to carry on operations in the Netherlands. On the 26th of March, the duke departed for Holland; and having concerted measures at the Hague, he marched his army towards the Moselle, which he reached on the 30th of June. In a few days he was within sight of the enemy, who were encamped on the same river, near Syrk. Magazines of ammunition, and stores of all sorts were formed at Triers. The Prince of Baden was expected to join the Confederate Army, and to co-operate with them in the same plan.

Various events, however, concurred to disconcert the duke's projects, and render his schemes abortive. He was mortified with disappointments from the quarter where he had looked for succour, and at the very time when he hoped to reap unfading laurels, by giving a final blow to the power of France. The Prince of Baden failed to perform his engagement. In a fit of pretended sickness, which was supposed to be at the reputation of his illustrious colleague, he quitted his army; and neither expresses nor expostulations could prevail with them to hasten their approach. Villars was too advantageously posted, and too strongly fortified, to be attacked by an inferior force. He had swept the country of forage and provisions, and thus rendered it impossible for a large army to subsist in his neighbourhood.

By the treachery and tardiness of his friends, and the masterly arrangements of his foes, the duke saw himself constrained to relinquish his designs of offensive hostilities on the French frontier. Under these mortifying circumstances, he was compelled to march back to the Maese, where the state of the war demanded his assistance. The enemy, in that quarter, had not failed to profit by his absence, having retaken Huy, and attempted the reduction of Liege. He left Triers on the 19th of June, and with incredible expedition, arrived before Liege, in time to save the citadel; for upon his approach, Villeroi caused his artillery to be drawn off, and sent back to Namur. This changed the whole face of affairs in the Netherlands, and enabled the Allies to become the assailants in their turn.

In order to retrieve his misfortunes on the Moselle, and make atonement for the misconduct of Prince Lewis, he resolved to attack the French within their own lines, and force them from their entrenchments, which was immediately accomplished, the enemy being repulsed with great slaughter. This, with some successes, under Baron Spar, closed the operations for this year; but from the sluggishness of the Germans, and an envious opposition on the part of some of the Dutch officers, it was far deficient in military glory to the preceding campaign. We now return to Captain Blackader, who was on a recruiting party in Scotland; and this short sketch will prepare the reader for the extracts we are to lay before him.

******

January 5. Hearing a sermon this day, on a subject I was much delighted with—how the angels were employed in taking care of the saints, and the many offices of kindness they do us, and how we are given in charge to them to look after us. It reminded me how wonderfully I was delivered last campaign—the angels encamping about me, and putting a hedge of security around me and all that I had.

January 6. This morning set apart for secret and joint prayer. I hope we had access to God, and were accepted.

January 12. My mind harassed all day with business. In the evening taken up with company, and involved in sin by idle, foolish conversation, which defiles the soul.

January 14. Taking great pleasure in hearing a sermon on the Providence of God directing and disposing all things. This is a comfortable doctrine to me, who am as great an instance of the care and kind conduct of Providence as any in the world.

******

Some proposals for his advancement being made about this time, he remarks with his characteristic diffidence and humility:—

******

January 18. I am so far from seeking preferments or great things for myself, that I am really afraid of higher posts in the world, and sincerely think I am unfit for what I have already. Lord, teach me in every thing to be humble, and to seek thy council and conduct, even in the smallest particulars.

January 26. Easy and cheerful. In the evening I designed to go abroad, but was kept at home by Providence; and I bless God for it. I was alone all the evening, which I employed in reading, meditation and prayer. I had access to the throne of grace, and one of the kindest visits that I have had since I came to Scotland. I poured out my soul to God, and told him every thing in my heart without reserve. My former petitions that I had put up were answered, and I had that word fulfilled, *I have heard thee in an accepted time.* My doubts and fears that seemed before like great mountains, were now cast into the sea, and I saw, as it were, this promise written. *Be it unto thee, even as thou wilt.*

February 15. This vexing trade of recruiting, depresses my mind. I am the unfittest for it of any man in the army, and have the least talent that way. Sobriety itself is here a bar to success. I see the greatest rakes are the best recruiters. I cannot ramble, and rove, and drink, and tell stories, and wheedle, and insinuate, if my life were lying at stake. I saw all this before I came home, and could have avoided coming; but it was the hopes of enjoying the blessing of the gospel that brought me to Scotland, more than recruiting; though I do not deny that I had an eye to that also.

February 20. Hearing of our going abroad, and much encourage by that promise, Exod. xxxui. 14. *My presence shall go with thee, and I will give thee rest.*

February 25. I complain of disappointments in Scotland. I have not got that good of gospel ordinances that I wished and expected. I experience also vexation in other things about the business of the regiment. But I shall wait and have patience. I hope to have reason to praise God before I leave the country. That his way is the best, and that he orders all things well.

******

At this time he expresses an inclination to have left the army, intending to purchase a property, that he might reside in Scotland; but was dissuaded by his friends.

******

March 10. I see the hand of Providence appearing about our going abroad. Oh Lord, do as seemeth good to thee, either by stopping or furthering us; thou only canst direct our ways. I desire to be resigned.

March 23. Toiling all the morning embarking men. business prospering and going on well. I see Providence orders every thing better than I could do myself.

March 25. Sabbath. Heard a sermon upon that subject, Exod. xiv. 15. the passage of the Israelites through the Red Sea. It was lively and suitable, and came home to me with power and life. I hope it is by the Lord's command I go forward, and having his orders, I trust I shall have his presence and conduct; and though they had the Red Sea in their way, and insuperable difficulties, yet they obeyed, and this engaged Omnipotence to work miraculously on their behalf. He can do the same still to those who trust in him.

March 31. Embarking this day at Kirkaldy; committing myself, my wife and family, tot he conduct and care of a kind God and Father, who must be our convoy and safe-guard.

April 1. Weather blowing and tempestuous.

April 4. Alarmed this morning by the motions of some French privateers appearing and coming close to us, and waiting on us most of the day. In the afternoon the ships retired, but appeared again and came up to us in the evening, and followed us all the night. I bless God I was easy and composed.

April 5. Disordered by stormy weather, contrary winds, and fears of a tedious voyage. Privateers hovering about us all the day. A life at sea is the true emblem of a Christian's life, tossed up and down while here; *But there remains a rest.*

April 7. Landed this day, but not at the port designed; being chased in here by fear of enemies and storms.

April 8. Reached Rotterdam.

April 12. Leaving Rotterdam and going up to the regiment; at night came into the Busse.

April 17. Taken up all day in preparations for marching. More easy and composed this year in going out to the camp than last.

April 20. Marching out of the Busse. I trust God will accompany me, and keep me from the infection of bad company, which is the greatest discouragement I have in the army.

April 22. Sabbath. Marching all day. This is what I hate most. Nothing but cursing, swearing, and profaneness, as if hell itself had broken loose about me.

April 23-30. Marching every day.

May 1. Arrived at Maestricht.

May 2. Got account this day that we are to march to the Moselle. I will not fear any evil, for God is a tried God to me there already. I remember the 15th of May last year, one of the most notable deliverances I have met with.

******

The same day he wrote to his wife at Rotterdam, giving her a farther account of his destination, of which he had till then been uncertain.

Maestricht, May 2

You see I neglect no opportunity of letting you hear from me. We are come up this length, though I could not give you any account in my last, how we were to be disposed of; but now I can tell you. We are to be reviewed tomorrow by the duke, and we are to march on Friday straight up the country to the Moselle. I commit myself to the same God who has hitherto dealt so bountifully with us, and wrought such great deliverances for me. I bless his name that I am every way well as I could wish, hearty and cheerful. I hope to hear the same account of you. Live by faith and you shall not want comfort. I know not where this shall find you, for the colonel tells me his lady is not at the Busse, so I think you are probably all gone to Rotterdam together. I have not seen William Young, (my nephew,) his regiment is just now marching to join the camp. You see I have altered my seal and chosen another motto, *Separez de corps et non de coeurs*. I write in haste, as I have many things to do in this town before marching. The Lord's blessing rest with you.

I am thine. J.B.

To Mrs. Blackader, Mr. Montier's,
Merchand, Scots Dyke, Rotterdam.

From Maestricht the army marched to Treves, which they reached on the 17th of May. From the camp near this place he wrote again the following letter to his wife:

Near Treves, May 15.

We are now come within two days march of Treves, and are resting this day, which gives me the opportunity of writing. It is said we are to join Prince Lewis' army on the other side of the Moselle, and what we are to do next I do not pretend to tell you. Perhaps the French will be so strong that we will not think it advisable to attack their lines; and you know Prince Lewis is not thought rash of fighting. But all this is but poor comfort, and not to trust to I confess, so I recommend you to go for support where you have already had it, and where all needy humble believers should always have it. The name of the Lord is a strong tower, the righteous flee to it and are safe. I told you before, that I in particular, beyond many others, need not fear to go to the Moselle, for God is a tried God to me, and I have the experience of a remarkable preservation there already.

I bless God I am well, easy, and cheerful, more than I have been since I went to Scotland,—and now, except my being absent from my dearest joy on earth, there is almost nothing else that troubles me; but in that as in all things else, I desire to trust God cheerfully, hoping a comfortable meeting in God's own time. All things about me have been right and well ordered. My company is very well, and my horses hold out well upon this long journey. At writing this we have the worst weather I have seen at this time of the year. It is just now showering snow and hail, and so cold that I am forced to lay aside the pen to draw on my boots. The Lord's blessing rest with you.

I am, &c.   J. B.

To Mrs. Blackader,
Scots Dyke, Rotterdam.

The march still continuing, he reached Treves on the 17th. A letter to his friend Mrs. Balderstone, in Edinburgh, is dated from this place, two days after his arrival.

Treves, May 19

I have never had time, before now, to salute you and your kind husband by a line; for we were not well in our garrison till we had orders to march out, and we have been marching now this month almost every day. The Lord was merciful to us on our voyage; for though we had the French privateers about us almost every day, and sometimes within cannon shot, yet by the goodness of God they did us no harm. Dear friend, I invite you to extol the Lord with me, and let us exalt his name together. He has in mercy removed much of that melancholy and chagrin that I was sometimes troubled with in Scotland, and helps me to trust in him cheerfully: the sweet experience of the last campaign, and the wonderful deliverances I met with, do help much to strengthen and bear me up, and I am no way afraid of going into Germany again this year.

We have indeed a very wicked army, which is a great discouragement; and I am weary of dwelling in the tents of sin. I see not how good people can pray with confidence for success to it, only that we have a good and just cause, though we be foul-fingered hands that manage it; and we see by our last year's success, that God in his sovereignty use any instruments he pleases for carrying on his own work, and I doubt not but he shall get glory by us, either one way or other. We know not well yet where we are going, or what we are to do. I know I need not bid you mind me, for, as you tell me, I am laid on you as a charge, that you must mind me; and pray, go on, for you are well paid for your pains. You serve a good master, and get something for yourself when you ply the throne of grace for your friends. The Lord's blessing rest with you and your family.

    I am, &c.   J.B

Mrs. Balderstone,
Edinburgh

The following is another letter to his wife, of the date of the 20th:

           Camp near Treves, Sabbath

I wrote to you from Treves on Friday last. The same night, when I came home to the regiment, I found a letter from you, dated May 5-8, wherein you tell me of the colonel's lady going to Coblentz, and the inclination you had of going with her, if you had orders from me; and that you think I consult your ease more than my own inclination. I answer, you need not doubt but my inclination would lead me to have you always near me, and if both of us had our wills and wishes, we would never be parted at all. But you must consider, it is not by inclinations we are to be led, but by duty,—and I am persuaded it is your duty to stay still at Rotterdam; considering that you have the gospel there, good company, edifying conversations, time and opportunity to serve God, advantage of living by faith, and trusting him with a husband who is far from you.

On the other hand, you will find no solidity or weight in reasons for coming up the country, but the fond inclination of seeing that which we love. There is no pleasure in living in a Popish country without the gospel Make good use of it; it is a mercy not to be slighted. You know you are not fitted for travelling, and should you meet with any accident by the way, you would not have peace. But I need not use many words, when I know you would obey the very thoughts of my heart if you knew them; and I hope you shall be no loser by being in your duty. You will remember last campaign, how Providence gave us a comfortable meeting several months sooner than others who travelled many miles to see their husbands.—We are lying still here near Treves, and what we are to undertake I know not, nor care not. There is no great probability of fighting this summer, that I can see; but this is not to make you secure. It is all one for God to preserve from danger, or in the midst of danger. The Lord's blessing rest with you.

      I am, &c.   J.B.
Mrs. Blackader, Rotterdam.

       ******

May 20-24. Marching every day. Walking alone, and meditating along the banks of the Moselle. Drawing near the enemy, and in prospect of fighting.

June 2. Resting this day; quietly reading over the 126th Psalm, and applying the promises to myself.

       ******

The army at this time was encamped near Syrk; and form this place he dates another letter to his wife.

          Camp near Syrk, June 2.
I received your letter with the enclosed to Captain Lawson. You have no reason to quarrel, for I have taken all occasion upon the march to write; and sometimes after fatiguing marches, when others lay down to sleep, I sat up and wrote to you. Many of my fellow-officers write their wives only once in two months. I ought, both as a soldier and a Christian, to wish that I loved earthly enjoyments less, and that I kept a looser hold of them. I think I could part with all other comforts pretty easily, without much regret, except thyself. I wish I may not provoke a holy God who seeketh the whole heart, and ought to have it all.

There is no news since my last. We are still lying here, expecting more troops to join us. But we must look above all human help, to that God who hath hitherto covered my head in the day of battle; he only is my sure defence. We hear the French are making progress in Flanders, and besieging Huy. Brigadier Hamilton's Regiment is in it.

Let me know what you are at present reading. I find Mr. Rutherford's book very sweet and comfortable. May the experience of God's goodness to us both, make you cheerful and easy; and trust in him generously without fear or doubting. You will always find that God bestows mercies on his people, proportionably as they believe on Him, and according to the trust they put in him. Let us not then bind up his hand, nor stop the course of our own mercies by misgiving fears, unbelief, or narrowness of heart. My love to all who are kind to you.

I am thine.

J.B.

To Mrs. Blackader,
Mr. Montier's, Rotterdam.

******

June 5. Getting account this day that we are to march back again, just down the same way we came up. Travelling all night, yet easy, and committing my way to God.

******

Camp near Treves, June 7.

When I wrote to you last, I had no news; but now this is to acquaint you with news which, I believe, will not be displeasing to you. We are upon our march back, down to Holland, the French are so strong there, and making such progress; and measures here being a little disconcerted, appear to be the reasons of this march. We are to go towards Liege or Maestricht, but it is all one to me, up the country or down; for *the earth is the Lord's,* and wherever he gives his presence, I care not what place it be. I just now received your letter, wherein you beg a thousand pardons, for quarrelling me without reason. I take your submission, and pardoned you before you sought it. You know I have that in my breast, that you need never fear my resentment; though indeed I take it ill to be quarrelled with on these two very heads that I piqued myself most upon—writing often, and writing kindly.

But I see I should not make an idol of anything I do. There is always most ease and satisfaction, when we are found precisely in the way of duty. Then we are kept in perfect peace, or else the being sure that we are in the road of duty, makes trouble easy. I am very thankful to God I have such a wife, who needs no commands or authority to oblige to duty, and needs no more but to have duty pointed out, and to be advised to it; and I do you but justice to say, that I have always found that duty, and the sense of duty, pleasantly determines both your judgement and your will, to whatever side it calls, though inclination should murmur against it. May the Lord prepare you for the approaching solemn occasion, and doubt not but I shall mind you. Have exalted noble thoughts, by faith, of the Master of the feast, of his liberality and bounty, then shall you *Taste and see that God is good.*

I am thine. J.B.

To Mrs. Blackader

******

June 10. Still marching down the country. Being Sabbath, I retired much of the day, and rode alone, to be out of the hearing of such company and such language.

June 19. Coming back to Maestricht again. I bless God for his preservation of me all this long march up and down. Wherever we set up our standards, there have I some memorial of his mercy to set up. If we encamp on the banks of the Maese, there I had my Ebenezers fourteen years ago, and also great deliverances two years ago. If we encamp on the Moselle, I had my preservations there last year. If on the banks of the Danube, I have Schellenberg and Hochstet. Wherever I go, I meet with some remembrancer to stir me up to gratitude and thankfulness, and to beget confidence and trust for the time to come.

June 21. Crossing the Maese. This day has been a fatiguing long march, continuing from three in the morning, till eleven at night. A great many of the army fell by with weariness, and some died, it being a scorching hot day. I bless God for his mercies to me, for my health and strength, and the good accommodation I have in a camp, which make me live easy and well, while others (better than I) are miserable, and serve in bitterness of soul.

June 23. Marching all day. Uneasy with hot weather. A soldier's life is an odd unaccountable way of living. One day too much heat, another too cold. Sometimes we want sleep, meat, and drink; again, we are surfeited with too much. A bad irregular way of living.

June 26. Short march. Lying near the enemy (at Liege.) I commit myself to thee, Oh Lord, and put my trust in thee. I will not be afraid, though an host encamp against me. Through thee I shall do valiantly. I fetch all my supplies from thee.

June 27. Taken up during the day, judging of criminals in a court martial. Seeking the conduct of the Spirit of God to judge uprightly and righteously.

July 2. On command these three days. I had the charge of about 1500 artillery horses, which made me somewhat uneasy, as fifty men might easily have come and taken hundreds of them. I have just got notice from the officer who succeeded me in that post, that the enemy fell in and carried off 100 of them. I own it was neither my care, nor prudence, nor conduct that prevented this misfortune, but purely the goodness of Providence to me, who watches over me continually. Employed again this day in a court martial; well guided and directed; I bless God I was there as a judge, and not as a criminal. It is only his grace that makes me differ from the worst of men.

July 4. This morning putting my hand to a small affair before prayer, it went wrong. I checked myself that I should undertake any thing before prayer, so I went to my knees; and after prayer I set about tie same affair, and went through it with ease. I observe this, that I may be encouraged, the first thing I do in the morning, to commit myself and all my ways to God; and put all I have within the hedge of his protection.

July 6. The day quietly spent. In the evening I went out to meditate in the fields, and I observe it as a mark of the Spirit of God guiding and influencing me, I had more access and enlargement in prayer than ordinary, and was helped to act faith very strong, trusting in God, and believing that if he were with me, I durst attack the French lines alone; and that a straw in the hand of Omnipotence, is better than Goliah's spear. In returning home, it came into my mind to ask a sign; but I immediately checked the thought as sinful, saying to myself, "I'll trust the Lord's work and promise without any sign." I had no sooner said this, than a bullet came whistling close by my head, shot at random by a soldier cleaning his piece. I wist not what to think of it; but I said within myself, this is the promise accomplished, Psalm xci. *He will give his angels charge over thee; thou shalt not be afraid of the arrow* (or bullet) *that flieth by day.*

All this while I knew nothing of what was doing in the army; but when I came home, I found that our regiment and the whole army had orders to march immediately. We guessed it was to attack the French lines; accordingly we marched at nine o'clock at night in great silence, and marched all night. It was one of the sweetest nights I ever had in my life. Faith lively; access to God, and communion with him; trusting him, and securing myself in the chambers of his grace and mercy, so that I had no manner of fear or concern of any danger that might be before me; the stock of strength and courage being in Christ's hands, and not in my own. Sensible of my weakness, I was determined to come every moment, as the occasions of the day might require, to draw fresh supplies out of Christ's fullness.

I did so, and he was a liberal master, he supplied me bountifully with courage to do my duty creditably in the functions of my post. Oh Lord, I give thee all the praise and glory; none of it belongs to me, for I trade but with a borrowed stock. I desire to allow myself in no other ambition, but of serving thee, and laying out myself and all thou givest me for thy glory and service; and if thou give me any credit in this army, I desire to lay it down at thy feet. If it make me more capable of serving thee in the army, I seek no other advantage of it. I find that a good exhortation. *Be careful about nothing*; for though I am far from a pushing ambitious temper as others are, yet Providence takes care and gives me occasions, like this, of acting honourably, and puts me in posts that I was neither expecting nor seeking; and when these occasions are over, I can return to my own way again with contentment.

July 7. We attacked the French lines this morning, and got in much easier and cheaper than we expected. The lines were partly forced and partly surprised, for the French had a part of their army there, but not sufficient to make head against us; not knowing that we were to attack them at that place; for there was a feint made to attack them in another part, which made them draw their forces that way. Our horse had some action with them, and beat them wherever they encountered them. Our foot had nothing to do, for the enemy fled before they came up. As I said before, the Lord assisted me, and gave grace and strength as I needed. Through the day, and in the intervals of action, I plied the throne of grace by prayer, and he carried me through well.

July 8. Sabbath. Marching all day. We seem to have committed a great error, neglecting the opportunity of pushing our victory my marching straight on between them and Louvain. The French, by marching all night, have prevented us, and got before us, and stopped us. This shews us men are but men; that there are flaws and weaknesses in the wisest mens' prudence. One day a great heroic action, and the next, perhaps, a great blunder. We seemed also, by too much wariness, to have neglected a fair opportunity of attacking them on their march, or in their camp. But let God alone have the glory, and all flesh be grass.

It was confessedly an oversight in the Allies to allow the enemy, when they were driven from their lines, and might have been attacked a second time with advantage, to possess themselves, without molestation, of the strong camp at Parck, whereby they secured Louvain, Brussels, and Antwerp. But this error is not to be imputed to the Duke of Marlborough, who had projected a second attack before they had time to recover from their consternation, and was preparing to put it into execution. In this scheme, he was supported by M. D'Auverquerque, but opposed by the other generals of the States, especially by Schlangenburg, who, it is said, had a personal pique against the duke, he persuaded some others of the Dutch commanders to join him, representing the enterprise as neither advisable nor practicable.

The duke, in consequence, was obliged to submit, though with great reluctance, and much mortified that his sanguine hopes should be disappointed of closing the campaign with distinguished glory. He mentions himself, in a letter, that he had formed the troops in order of battle; but that the deputies of the States having consulted their other generals, would not consent to it, so that he was compelled to abandon a project which promised all imaginable success. The deputies themselves appear to have become sensible of their mistake, and approved of the duke's conduct, so far as to remove Schlangenburg from the army.[1]

July 9. Resting this day over against the enemy. The town (Louvain) between us, which is firing upon us, and some of the bullets coming in among our tents; but little hurt done.

July 10-11. The firing still continuing briskly, but no hurt done: that promise was made good, Psalm iii; *I laid me down, and slept; I awaked, for the Lord sustained me. I will not fear though ten thousand were against me round about.* I lay at my post two days; and just as I was writing this, some cannon balls, shot from the town, came close over my tent, and lighted among those in the rear, but did me no harm. We are all fretting and uneasy about this mismanagement and blunder, that we have not improven our victory as we ought to have done; and I am fretting among the rest.

July 12. Removing our camp this day out of the reach of the town's cannon. Tomorrow is appointed by the general to be observed through the army in thanksgiving for our success, and prayer. God grant that

---

1. Lediard, vol. i. Sommerville's *Hist. Queen Anne*, App. No. v.

we be not found mocking him in this exercise, when these mouths come to His service hot from cursing and swearing, pretending to thank God for mercies they have no sense of; and when the work is over, return to their trade of swearing and blasphemy. But, Lord, whatever the army do, make me single, and fervent, and tune my heart to praise and gratitude.

I see plainly the race is not to the swift, nor the battle to the strong. Providence laughs at men's projects, and often works by disappointments, and contrary to their expectations. Our passing the lines was a pleasant disappointment, for we were far from expecting such success, a victory so cheap. But then again, here was a gallant army, that (humanly speaking) might have carried all before them, beat the enemy, and possessed all this country; yet Providence steps in and again disappoints us, for we stopped short by blundering in the midst of so fine a career. It is the Lord's doings, and wondrous in our eyes; he says to the purposes of men, as to the raging waves. *Hitherto shall ye come and no farther.*

******

There is a letter to his wife, of this date, from the camp near Louvain, in which he makes a recapitulation of some things already taken notice of.

Thursday, July 12.

I wrote you the good news of our having passed the lines, and I now write you again in an advanced post, near the enemy. Yesterday we had a bickering with them, but the water was between us, and it was only the picquets of regiments that were engaged. Lieutenant Dalrymple was wounded in the head, but not badly. We have not lost one man in the regiment as yet. We are all fretting that we have made such a mistake—as we might probably have been masters of this country.

I believe you will be pretty much concerned for me at present, considering the circumstances we are in, and the news you will be hearing daily; but be not afraid for me, be not concerned, I am in good hands.—The Lord is my defence, I shall not be moved; he is my fortress, my shield and buckler, and my strong tower.—Continue you to trust him cheerfully. You must not only believe when all goes fair before the wind; then any body may believe; but you must believe when all is in hazard; and there must be a time between the promise and the accomplishment; and this is the season of the trial of faith.—My best advice to you is, to be humble, watchful, circumspect, and self-denied.

I was on command some days ago, and had the charge of 1500 artillery horses: it was an alert post, and parties thick about me, &c. I can give you no account of our operations, or what we are to undertake next; probably we must try to make some farther progress, and to reap some fruits of our passing the lines. Be not you anxious about it. Take no notice of reports of news or stories flying about. You are too much impressed with these. Providence often works against all our probabilities, and it signifies not what people, even the wisest of them, either think or say.

I am thine.   J. B.

To Mrs. Blackader, Mr. Montier's,
Merchand, Scots Dyke, Rotterdam.

******

July 18. Here (near Louvain) have we been stopped these ten days; but we are now going to march again, towards the enemy I believe. If the Lord would lead us on as the captain of our host, then we would do great things; but without his presence the smallest obstacle will stop us. Marching all night to attack the enemy: it has been a pleasant night to me. I rely on the divine promises, and cast the weight of my soul upon the well-ordered Convenant. Acting again in an honourable post, wherein I was well assisted to go through it creditably. In all the intervals of business and of action, I was sensible of the goodness of God. Our army got another check and mortification this day, (19) for we did not succeed in passing the water, (the Dyle) and dislodging the French. They did not beat us, nor did we lose any men; but our general, it seems, found the thing in prudence not practicable, and that we could not pass at that place. Such of our troops as did pass, beat the enemy from their posts.

I observe this throughout the campaign, that in all our encounters with the French, Providence lets us see we are fully masters of them, and can easily beat them, for they appear in our hands like a cur matched against a mastiff. But at the same time we are prevented, and kept, as it were, in a chain from giving them a total rout: For either we let occasions slip when they are put in our power, or we greedily pursue occasions when it is not the will of Providence to favour us. But I hope our chain shall yet be loosed, and we shall be successful.

Arise, Oh Lord, let thy enemies be scattered; for they are thy enemies as well as ours. I am very much fatigued with our march, for we were twenty-two hours under arms, and so my spirits are not lively, especially for want of sleep. The enemy cannonaded us on our march, but did us no harm, for we came safe to our camp at night.

The skirmish here referred to, was that which took place on the 30th of July, between Louvain, and the village of Neer-ysche. The Duke being informed that several posts on the Dyle, between these places, were but slightly guarded, resolved to force them, in order to pass the river. The Duke of Wirtemberg, and Count Oxenstiern, with a part of the troops, were ordered on this service. They decamped about eleven at night, and reached the enemy's posts by three next morning, some battalions of grenadiers crossed the river on bridges, and repulsed the French Guards with great vigour; but not being timely supported, they were obliged to retire with the loss of a few officers, and about fifty privates.[2] On whom the blame of this misadventure rests, is not well explained. Captain Blackader merely says, their commanding officer judged it impracticable, yet he was himself plainly of a different opinion; and was evidently dissatisfied at losing so many opportunities of fighting. For the first time we find him here differing in opinion with his superiors, and venturing a short military critique on the operation of the army since their action on the 7th.

July 25. As to public affairs, when I think upon our conduct this campaign, we seem, in my weak judgement, to have committed several mistakes and weaknesses since we attacked the lines. I say not this to reflect in the least on generals or their conduct, but only I would be a narrow observer of providences; which rules the successes and victories of armies as it pleases. First when we attacked the lines in the morning, they were surprised; and we easily beat all the troops that made head against us. Their army was coming up, but in no great order; and if we had pushed the attack vigorously with the troops we had over, or kept them in play with our horse till the foot had come up, in all probability we had routed them. But instead of that, we suffered them quietly to retire, and stood and looked on. Then in the next place, if we had but posted our army so as the right had run to Judoigne, and the left to Tirlemount, we had lain just across their way, that they could hardly have got by us; whereas, we camped about Tirlemont, and so gave them a passage clear to get before us again.

---

2. Lediard, vol. i.

Then again, if we had but marched on three hours farther that night, and had taken up the pass and strong camp of Parck, we had been betwixt them and Louvain, and all that country: But instead of that, we lay still at Tirlemont, and the French, by marching all night, got before us, and stopped us at Louvain. Then again, though we had rested all night, if we had but marched next morning at daybreak, we had fallen upon them in their march, weary and unawares. But we lay still till nine o'clock; and, as it was, our army came in sight of them, while their foot was passing the Dyle in great haste and confusion; and if we had attacked them even then, in all human appearance we had beat them. But we suffered them to pass quietly, and then cut off their bridges.

Then the next day after we had encamped at Louvain, our pickets and some regiments marched to the right, to the water side, and fired upon them. Our men had no cover, but the French had breastworks along the river side; and so we got a great many men wounded, and some killed, foolishly and to no purpose. Then on the 18th we marched all night, designing to pass the water, and surprise the enemy as we had done at their lines, and had over ten or twelve battalions who took post on a village on the other side, which they beat the French from. It is true our horse could not pass there; but it is granted by all, that our foot might have passed, and taken their posts, and kept them in spite of all the French Army; because we were reckoned superior to them by 25 or 30,000 men. But instead of that, those that were over were ordered to come back, and take off our bridges; and so we marched off. The French, by their mein, did not look as if they would stand to it, but came up stragglingly and hovering off at a distance, that they might retire in case we pushed over the water: *But the battle is not always to the strong*: Providence laughs at man's projects.

※※※※※※

Such were Captain Blackader's sentiments with regard to the operations and lost opportunities of the army; and there can be no doubt, this indecision would not have happened, had the Duke of Marlborough not been thwarted in his measures by the tardiness or timidity of the States' deputies and their generals.

While near Tirlemont he writes again to his wife, to relive her anxiety after the recent engagement.

Camp near Tirlemont. Monday, July 23.
I believe you have been pretty uneasy these four or five days

bygone, by not hearing from me since our late action with the French; though I comfort myself in the hopes of this, that the manifold experience you have of my preservation and deliverances, makes you trust God more fixedly than before, without unbelieving fears. I could not possibly write to you on Thursday, the post day, for that was the day of our action; and we were in arms from Wednesday night at ten, marching all night, till Thursday at eight at night. We were to have attacked the French by passing the water that is between us and them; so we marched silently all Wednesday night to the left above Louvain; and by break of day our detachments were at the waterside, where we were to pass, and laid on bridges without opposition; for the French were surprised in the same manner as before at the lines, and made no head against the regiments that crossed. But unluckily, it seems there was a mistake as to the place, for when the general came up he found it was not practicable for the horse, as the place was marsh ground. In the meantime, the foot were still passing the bridges, and had taken post on the other side, and had beat some brigades of the French from their posts; but the General, finding the horse could not pass, sent orders for the foot to come back, which they did without any loss; for the French never charged them, only they brought down a battery of some cannon to the waterside, and played upon our lines as they were marching, but did very little harm, and so we got safe to our camp.

This action is variously talked of; commended and censured according to men's various humours. Some are of opinion, if we had gone over with our foot only, that we had beat them; for when we observed their motions first in the morning, they seemed to be irresolute and wavering whether they should come up to defend the passage or retire towards Brussels. Others think it was prudently done, not to risk our army to an affront, when our horse could not act. But whatever it be to the army, I look upon all God's ways of dealing with me to be mercy and goodness,—and I believe myself to be as sound and safe in the chambers of his Omnipotence, faithfulness, and love, in time of action, as if I were with you at Rotterdam.

Our whole army seemed to be mighty keen and eager to be at the French, and were uneasy and out of humour when ordered to retire. I do believe, by the blessing of God, we would have beat them if we had gone over. For I observe this, all this campaign, that in all skirmishes between us and them, it appears we are masters of them, and could beat them as easy as a mastiff worries a cur-dog; but at the same time I observe that we are, as it were, chained down, and cannot get them soundly beat. It is currently believed here, that both at the lines and now, it is the States and their generals that hinder us to fight, and to improve our advantages as we might. So that if you have a value for my safety and preservation, you should go and thank the States for it.

I hope this letter will come seasonably to your hand; though I flatter myself that you are quite another woman, for a masculine and strong heart, than you were the first or second campaign. You have more reason, more experience of God's goodness, and I hope more grace. You will excuse me if I add a fourth cause; that you begin now to be an old married wife, and should be settled and calm.

I am thine.   J.B

Mrs. Blackader, Rotterdam.

★★★★★★

July 27. My mind is getting becalmed again with lying idle, and I now begin to wish for action, because it rouses the spirits into activity. This day, three of my men were taken prisoners, and the other day two of them deserted. This is a providence that I do not well understand. Most captains of the army know nothing but to curse and swear at their men. I ordinarily every day put them, by prayer, within the circle of God's protection. But I believe every dispensation to me is fraught with mercy and kindness.

August 2. The very morning of this day is an Ebenezer. The day of Hochstet,—a day much to be remembered for the wonderful mercy and deliverance I got. The Lord wrought a great salvation for us that day; he delivered my soul in peace from the battle that was against me. A thousand fell at my side, and ten thousand at my right hand, but it came not near to me, but in a way of remarkable mercy and favour; for though the ball was at my throat, the angel of the Lord held it as he did the knife in Abraham's hand. I cried unto the Lord, and he answered me. I employed this day in meditating on these things; and there was a thanksgiving appointed by the general for commemorating that great day.

August 3-6. Marching every day, but very uneasy; scorching hot weather my horse sick and my servant in the hospital.

August 7. This day there was a great preparation, and all the appearances and dispositions for a battle. We were to attack the enemy (twenty battalions of us) through the wood (of Soignies.) The action threatened to be a bloody one, for they were well fortified, and occupied a strong post at Waterloo. The time we were lying in the wood, I retired frequently for mediation. The enemy was so strongly posted, that it was thought impracticable to attack them, so we were ordered to draw off at one o'clock, having marched at nine in the morning. I observed at our coming off, what a poor weak creature man is of himself. There came a panic fear, and surprise among the soldiers at the head of the line, that before they knew what they were doing, they rolled and turned back one upon another, from one regiment to another, and knew not what hand to turn them to. I thought upon that Scripture, *One man shall chase a thousand.* It was over in two minutes; they came to themselves and were ashamed. Late at night we came to our camp, and lay on the bare ground all night for want of our tents, for we thought they were all taken by the French, and indeed they were very near it.

August 8-16. Marching back to the camp at Tirlemont.

★★★★★★

These operations are more enlarged upon in his letters, of this date, from which we shall make one or two selections.

Wavre, August 9. Thursday

I believe you may be somewhat anxious by not hearing from me these eight days; for we have been marching since Friday last, still courting the occasion of falling upon the French; but Providence still disappoints us, and balks our projects. On Tuesday there was all the preparation, and dispositions, and appearance of a pitched battle; and if it had come to a battle, in all probability it had been one of the bloodiest most of us ever saw. But when we came up to them, we found them so strongly posted and fortified, that it would have been a butchering to have attacked them in their camp. There was also a stratagem to be used, which, if it had taken effect, would probably have decided the battle in our favour. There were twenty battalions, (ours was one,) and horse conform, that were to march through a wood and post ourselves quietly in the wood till we should hear that the battle was fully joined. Then we were to come out and attack them in the rear. Accordingly we marched at three in the morning, and posted ourselves in the wood, where we stayed till three, afternoon. General Churchill commanded us; but the duke finding it impossible to attack them, as I said, we came off.

I have still reason to say, that times of fighting and action, and prospects of danger, are the pleasantest times I have; and I should be well satisfied to have every day the same prospect of danger, to have the same supplies and furniture of faith in Christ, relying upon the well ordered Covenant. I trusted much to that promise. Josh. i. 9, which was strongly impressed upon me.

We are now drawn off farther from the enemy, and there is no more talk of attacking them; and in all probability there is but little appearance of any more action this campaign. I will not say what Providence may do, which ordinarily works by disappointment of expectations. You may thank your friends the Hollanders again, for it is said generally, that we owe it most to them, our sleeping a sound skin on this occasion; and that they were positively against fighting there. However it be, it seems Providence will not work by these means; not this time at least. It has been a fatiguing march this week bygone, and we have had very little rest. I lost five men in that camp, two by desertion, and three taken prisoners. The Lord's presence and blessing be with you.

    I am thine.   J.B

Mrs. Blackader, Rotterdam.

                 Monday, August 13.

We are marched yesterday still farther from the enemy, so that the appearance of actions grows less, and we scarcely expect to see the *Messieurs* this campaign again. But let me warn you, as thoughts of action wear out, not to let castles in the air come in their place; for at the very time you wrote of coming to Aix-la-Chapelle, we seemed to be upon the brink of a battle, where probably ten thousand had lain on the spot. For my part, I dare not allow myself in wishing earnestly to be in garrison, (though I be weary enough of the camp,) or to wish that it were peace; for without God's presence and blessing, the garrison and winter would be but a melancholy time. Comforts and enjoyments, when we expect much satisfaction from them, may be blasted, and a time of peace may be more troublesome than war. I have cause to bless God while I live, for the bountiful supplies of his grace and spirit that he gives me in times of war; and if he should withhold these from me in peace, I should wish to be back to the camp, and in action every day. It is his presence alone that can make any place, any lot, any condition happy.

The campaign is slipping away, and I hope God will give us a comfortable meeting at the end of it. We are going to take St. Lewe; and our regiment having been on command when we expected to fight on Tuesday, we do not think it will be our tour to be on the siege. About your coming to Aix, I do not think it safe or convenient. If I thought it would benefit your health, I would order you there; but I may say in jest, it is because you are promised a temporal blessing, and as Papists go to our Lady of Loretto to get favours, so you would go to Aix; but with this difference, they expect their favours by way of miracle, you would have it by means.

They begin now to talk of peace, and that proposals are making; I know nothing of them, only if we had improven our success at the passing of the lines, as we might have done, and if we had got Brabant, it might perhaps have procured a peace very soon: but we must look to a higher hand, and the scourge of war must continue till God have wrought his purposes by it. Let him be exalted in the earth. Remember me to all kind friends.

     I am thine.   J.B.
Mrs. Blackader, Rotterdam.

            St. Lewe, August 20.

We are now marched back to the lines, and are lying covering the siege of St. Lewe. It is observable that we have been these six weeks marching and countermarching, and seeking all occasions of coming at the enemy, yet our prospects have been blasted, and we have been kept as a lion in chains, and cannot get out. There seems also to be a spirit of division sown among our generals, and as long as it continues I never expect we shall do any great things. I confess I begin to turn more dull than when the prospects of danger and death were more frequent. God gives the charges suitable to the errands he sends us on.

If he sends us among snares and temptation, he gives the more grace; if he do not send difficult errands, we need the less expenses. Blessed be God who has borne us both so well through. O that we may have grace to pay our vows when he deals so bountifully with us, and to walk before him in all holy circumspect tenderness, as becomes the children of so many mercies. The Lord's rich blessing be with you.

I am thine.   J.B.

Mrs. Blackader, Rotterdam.

P.S.—August 27. St. Lewe is over when we thought it was but beginning; which gives us a new proof, that the French, if they be well holden to, are no formidable enemy. We are now demolishing the lines hereabout, after which I believe we shall march. These three men of mine that were taken, I have got again, they were exchanged.

******

Early in September he left the army to return to Rotterdam.

******

September 7. Travelling this day, but not so serene, being continually in company. I slipped off from the party on pretence of hunting, and retired alone where I had sweet and spiritual meditation. I look upon it as a great mercy that I have left the camp so soon; for I wearied more these twenty days bygone, than I had done all the campaign.

September 8. Coming in to the Busse this day. Next day set out for Rotterdam: we were very late upon the water.

September 11. Here have I reason to be grateful; after a campaign of fatigues, hazards, and dangers, the Lord has brought me back safe to this place, and given me a comfortable meeting with my wife. He has compassed me about with songs of deliverance.

******

He continued in Rotterdam for some time, enjoying the ordinances of the gospel, and the fellowship of religious people, which was always his greatest happiness. He says:—

I am always cheerful and merry in good and innocent company. Perhaps I am now too much so, but I would wish to commend religion by a cheerful conversation, to convince the world that religion does not make people sour and morose.

About the middle of October he returned again to the Busse, where he got the melancholy news of Brigadier Ferguson's death.

******

September 13. I got the surprising account of our brigadier's death, with which I was greatly affected. *Man's breath goeth out, to earth he turns, that day his thoughts perish.* Oh the vanity of human grandeur! He was just come from court, where he was sent for that he might be raised a step higher for his services.

September 15. This day we were employed in the funeral of our brigadier.

November 1. This day our regiment came in to the Busse, and I went out to meet them.

******

Several promotions were at this time to take place, and his among the rest, as appears by the following letter to Mrs. Balderstone, Edinburgh:—

Busse, November 7. 1705

I received the kind letter you wrote to me in summer, and I cannot but observe how seasonably it came first to my wife's hand just at the communion of Rotterdam, and then to my hand. It came just upon our march, when we were going to attack the French, and the army was halting in sight of the enemy. This gave me an opportunity to retire for an hour or two alone in the fields, at a hedge side; and there I looked over all the Scriptures that you had sent me, and was helped to act faith, leaning on those sweet promises. But I thought some of them gave such high titles, that I blushed to take them; though, as to the spiritual part and accomplishment of a promise, I think no promise so large or great, but the believer, though mean otherwise, may lay hold of it.

I wrote you to rejoice that another campaign was brought to a happy issue. I was never better borne through or supported, particularly when there was any appearance of fighting or action; and I could have wished all the campaign to have been made up of those days, to have had such liberal allowances of grace. I must confess at other times, when we were idle, I was, as it were, becalmed, and grace at a stand; but still new providences, especially surprise and danger, stirred me up to more vigorous acting.

Our brigadier is dead. Lieutenant Colonel Borthwick is putting in for the regiment; Major Cranston to be lieutenant colonel, and I, as oldest captain, to be major. I know not how it will go, but I desire to be very easy, go as it may. I must confess I am grown weary of living in the tents of wickedness, in a place of so much profanity as an army is, especially now that I am growing grey-headed in following the regiment. I would desire a quiet retreat out of the noise of drums and oaths, but a wise God knows best what is good for me. I desire to trust him cheerfully with all that concerns me. Remember us kindly to your husband, and pray let me hear from you soon.

Yours, &c.   J.B.

Mrs. Balderstone, Edinburgh.

In the beginning of December, he went to the Hague on the business of his promotion, and had a conference with the Duke of Marlborough, who was there on his way to England.

******

December 12. At court here for several days, where I have but little to say, and no body to speak well for me. I talked this forenoon with the duke about my business, and got a good answer, (for none ever get ill words from him.) But I lay no stress upon these things, I look above them. I am incapable of making my court to great men, though I know how to make moyen with Him who is greater than all. He will dispose of things the way that shall be best for me. If He smile upon me, I envy not the Duke of Marlborough in his own post.

December 15. Got my major's commission this day. I wish it may not be burden too heavy for my weak shoulders. I see Providence brings about my affairs, as well as theirs who have dexterity to manage them.

December 17. Coming back to the Hague from Rotterdam. We have a proverb, *Meat and mess never hindered any man.* I lost nothing by going away, all my business went on well and smoothly. I found more friendship and credit at Rotterdam than I expected; and when I came to the Hague, my affair had taken such a good turn, that it has saved me 2000 *merks* I thought to have been out of pocket. I met with far more generosity and kindness than I could ever have looked for from that quarter.

CHAPTER 12

Campaign Fifth, 1706

Until the opening of the campaign, Major Blackader continued at Rotterdam, happy in the society of his friends, and more cheerful, because more occupied in the duties of his new commission, and enjoying regularly the ordinances of the gospel. He mingled also more in diversions and company, to which his post necessarily more exposed him; still, however, he was on his guard against being misled by their seductions; and at the same time he speaks of his compliances in a strain of self-accusation, resolving not to let his respect for the opinions of the world betray him into a conformity with its vices and follies.

******

January 26. I often stay out in company too late at night. But I must keep at a greater distance from the world, and not be so conform to it. I must rise above its opinion and applause, else I can never serve God aright, or be at ease in my own mind. I cannot serve two masters; if I cleave to him, I am sure to be hated and reproached by the other. I could easily change my conduct, and overcome my natural reserve of temper, and live more freely and gaily; but I dare not do it for fear of involving myself in sin, especially in the army among vicious men. So I think the safest and wisest course is to take rather the hatred and reproach of men, than to wound my conscience, or offend my God. I have been better carried through and provided for, than many others who have turned themselves into all shapes in conformity to a wicked world. Therefore I'll keep my old way, and study holiness and strictness of life, let the world laugh or think as it will.

March 11, 12, 28. Sitting in a court martial these three days; putting up short requests for counsel and direction. I see men are ready to flatter themselves—to judge and determine things according to the rules of gentlemanly breeding and honour. I believe things will go in a far different way at Christ's tribunal.

March 29. This forenoon set apart for prayer, and imploring God's presence and blessing with us this campaign. I desire, as formerly, to go out, trusting him,—hoping in his mercy,—depending upon his promises, that he will go with me, to *be a present help in time of trouble; that his grace will be sufficient for me; that he will perfect strength in my weakness, and never leave me nor forsake me.* So I hope I shall be well carried through.

April 23. Making court to some great men. I am like a speckled bird among them. *If ye were of the world, the world would love its own, but I have chosen you out of the world, &c.* I know my post requires that I should keep more company than I did, and live more open and sociable with my acquaintance; but then the conversation of the men of the army puts a lock and continual restraint upon me. I fear the snares and poison of bad example.

April 24. This day is kept by the authority of this country as a fast and humiliation before the army go out. I kept it also in my family by secret and joint prayer.

April 29. In confusion and business all day, in order to marching.

April 30. Marched out of the Busse this day. Now my life of hurry and noise begins.

May 1. This day we had a long fatiguing march. These was a great eclipse of the sun about ten o'clock.[1]

May 2-6. Marching every day. In the afternoon, when our regiment came to their ground (at Bilsen,) I met with a signal mercy. My horse had very near fallen above me, plunging and rearing, being frightened with the colours and drums.

May 8. We joined the great army today (near Tongres.)

May 9. Marching. One of the worst days and roads we ever travelled in. I pitied the poor soldiers, though very well myself. Now we begin to talk of action, and that very quickly. Oh Lord, here I am, do

---

1. This eclipse happened the very day on which the siege of Barcelona was raised; and according to Burnet, (*Hist.* vol. ii.) was total in those parts. It was regarded by the vulgar as portentous of the declining glory of Louis, who had chosen the Sun for his Device, with the motto, *Nec pluribus impar.*

with me what seems good unto thee, for thou art my God. I trust in thee, and hope in thy mercy. I flee to the chambers of thine Omnipotence, love, and faithfulness; there I shall be safe. Help me to discharge my duty as a man, as a Christian, and as a soldier.

May 11. Advancing this day toward the enemy. I observe, to the praise of free grace and mercy, that the nearer I come to action, the more cheerful and vigorous I am , and grace more lively. Faith in exercise through the day; fleeing to the well-ordered covenant, and resting on the promises of God.

******

Camp, St. Tron. Friday, May 10.

I wrote you on Tuesday last, when we lay within two leagues of Maestricht. I thought when we had joined the great army, I should have got time to go in and see the colonel's lady; but we did not so much rest one day, but marched immediately after we had joined. I never saw the roads and the weather worse. It is generally thought we are marching straight toward the enemy, to do something before they be joined by Marshal Marsin who is coming in all haste. They are lying near Tirlemont, but we flatter ourselves they will retire behind their lines when we march up that way. For my share, I wish with all my heart they could stand where they are, and give us a fair day of it, and fair play for our lives; for though I am no way fond of fighting for fighting's sake, yet I wish to see the war at an end; and before I marched such another day as yesterday was, I would rather fight them tomorrow; for I hate fatigue above all the business of our employment.

Be not the least concerned for me, for I am in the hands of a merciful God, who only makes me to dwell in safety. You must excuse me for not writing long letters. I hope you have consideration enough to think that I have now a great deal of business more than I had, and I rather choose to write short letters than to write none at all. Remember me to your kind host Mr. Montier, and all friends at Rotterdam. I mean to see Colonel Borthwick this afternoon if I have time.

I am thine, &c. J.B.

To Mrs. Blackader. Mr. Montier's
On the Scots Dyke, Rotterdam.

The action they were now upon the eve of, was the famous Battle of Ramillies, the consequences of which were as important in the Netherlands, as those of Blenheim had been in Germany. The campaign of this year opened with the most brilliant success on the side of the Allies; and proved in its termination one of the most calamitous and disgraceful that France had yet experienced. The disasters of 1704 were forgotten, and partly repaired by the temporary advantages of last year; and Louis had recruited his ranks with such astonishing celerity, that an army of 70,000 men was again equipped and ready to take the field. It was commanded by Marshal Villeroi and the Elector of Bavaria.

The magazines were replenished with all necessary stores, and the most extraordinary exertions were to be made to retrieve the glory of their nation, and call back fortune, which seemed to have deserted their arms. During the preceding campaigns, they had generally acted upon the defensive, and left the Allies to become the assailants. Yet victory seemed to declare against them, though they had often the superiority in numbers and the advantages of the ground.

This year the French cabinet changed their mode of tactics, and determined to try the event of active hostilities. Their generals were instructed to become the aggressors, in the fond hope of becoming conquerors. But these sanguine expectations, as will appear, became their ruin, by betraying them into rash and precipitate measures.

The Confederates were no less eager for an engagement, but they scarcely anticipated so early an opportunity for it. Louis, who had in vain employed all the arts of his intriguing court to create jealousies and division among them, now resolved to attack them before the Danes and Prussians could effect a junction with the main army. But the expedition of these troops disappointed his expectations, for they joined the duke on the very morning of the battle. Both armies met on the 23rd of May, N. S. at Ramillies, about eleven miles north of Namur. This place, though but a paltry village surrounded with a ditch, has been rendered famous to all posterity, by one of the most celebrated battles that took place in the whole course of the Confederate War.

The particulars of this memorable engagement are too well known to be here recapitulated. I shall, however, transcribe the account of it which Major Blackader gives, in a letter to his wife, two days after the battle.

Camp Vilvoord, May 15.

Every campaign produces new and greater mercies to me. I has pleased the Lord to give us a signal victory, on Sabbath last, over the French army; and, in particular, he has mercifully covered my head in the day of battle, and compassed me about with songs of deliverance. We had marched every day almost without intermission since we came from the Busse, and the duke was resolved to come to action with the French as soon as possible. But we were surprised to find that they were camped without their lines; and expected whenever we should advance, they would retire. But we have heard since, that they were as forward to fight as we were, and had positive orders to fight; and if we had not attacked them, they would have attacked us; for they had more battalions than we had, and all the best troops.

On Sabbath about eleven o'clock, we and they being both on our march, came in view of one another. They possessed themselves of some villages that were strong and not easy to be forced. We advanced and made our dispositions to attack, and whenever we came near enough, they cannonaded us furiously all the time we were advancing. We had here about twenty men killed and wounded. Poor Harry Borthwick was the first, and had his leg shot off by a cannon ball.

The English had the right, and when we were just beginning to attack a village opposite to us, the duke sent his orders not to attack there, but to march to the left, were the Dutch were, and push on the affair: but the Dutch had forced it ere we came up. It is said the French thought themselves very sure of the day, for they had made the dispositions so that all their *gens d'armes*, and best troops, should sustain the attack upon the left, where they knew the Dutch were; thinking so to beat the Dutch first, and then they would afterwards beat the English.

It was very hot work for above two hours. None of the English came to close action but Mordaunt's and Churchill's regiments; and all we lost was by cannonading. There were about 4000 prisoners taken, with most of their cannon and ammunition, and bread, waggons, and horses, and most of the generals' and officers' baggage. The battle began on our wing between four and five o'clock, and we pursued them till midnight. We did not think the action at first so considerable, but the effects of it are very remarkable and surprising, for there is like to be a revolution of the whole country.[2]

The hand of God was visibly to be seen, and his judgement, in sending a panic fear among the enemy; for they retired in such disorder, that their soldiers flung away their arms: Their muskets, scabbards, &c. were scattered up and down the whole country.

We marched all Monday, and came near Louvain, expecting assuredly that they would stop us at the Dyle, where they stopped us last year. But we got account on our march that they had quitted Louvain and retreated towards Brussels; and the people of Louvain told us, that their army marched through there in such a pitiful hurry, that they could hardly keep in a body at all, and most of them were without arms. So we took possession of Louvain, and marched next day (for the duke does not sit his time this year) towards Brussels; and on our march we heard that they had abandoned that also, and in short the whole country, for Colonel Durell is gone with 200 horse to take possession of Mechlin. They have also quitted Antwerp, and this letter is written within a league of Brussels, which we are in possession of.

There is a spirit of division among them, for the Spaniards refuse to join with the French, and seem inclined to submit all to the House of Austria; and the Bavarian troops that are here say, they came to assist their duke, and have no business with the French.

In this surprising turn of affairs there is much of the hand of God to be seen; and indeed we are like men in a dream, to see ourselves so suddenly possessed of so many places. I hope there are greater things to be done yet. The Lord make us thankful, and Oh grant that his mercies may reform us. I have particular reason to be grateful; but what puts water in my wine-cup is, that poor Colonel Borthwick was killed that day, behaving like

---

2. It was in this battle, as the reader will recollect, that the brave Colonel Gardiner, then an ensign, was shot through the head by a musket-ball, which entered his mouth, and passed through without killing him. The character of these two officers, destined to become an honour to their country, and an ornament to religion, presented at this time a singular contrast; the one, the unreclaimed devotee of every wild principle and wayward passion; the other, pursuing the steady paths of virtue, from which he had never deviated, and combining the sanctity of religion with the reputation of a soldier. *Vid. Life of Colonel Gardiner, Baynes' Improved and Enlarged Edition.*

a gallant man. We buried him yesterday at his colours. Captain Denoon is killed.

Do not fear fighting, for we think to see only Frenchmens' backs all this campaign. I hope you will offer up the sacrifice of praise for the public and for me.

I am thine, &c.   J.B.

To Mrs. Blackader. Rotterdam.

******

From the above it appears that Major Blackader's regiment was posted on the right wing, which sustained the smallest share in the contest. The Duke of Marlborough had ordered the attack to commence on that side, but it was entirely a manoeuvre to deceive the enemy; for while they were misled to detach their best troops to support the left wing, where it was supposed the attack would be made, they unguardedly left their centre and their right exposed, against which the Duke intended to direct the main efforts of his army. The stratagem succeeded; Villeroi and the Elector were completely outwitted. The greatest slaughter was made by the Dutch and Danes on the enemy's right, near the villages of Franquenies and Ramillies. The French, both generals and troops, never shewed less conduct or courage than on this occasion. At Hochstet they fought for eight hours, and killed or wounded nearly 11,000 of the Allies. At Ramillies all was flight and consternation in two hours; while the victors did not lose above 3000 men.[3]

The Duke of Marlborough displayed no less talent in improving this victory, than he had shewn in achieving it. The rapidity with which he pursued the vanquished army, prevented them entirely from drawing together into a body, so as to form any obstruction to his future progress. As no former battle had been more disastrous to the enemy, so none was more extensively beneficial to the Allies. The submission of Brabant, and almost the whole Spanish Netherlands, followed in the space of fifteen days: Louvain, Brussels, Antwerp, Ghent, Oudenard, Mechlin, and other towns surrendered at discretion. Ostend, Menin, Dendermond and Aeth, were reduced by force, the garrisons making some opposition, but the French not daring to attempt their relief. At several of these sieges Major Blackader was present, as we shall find in course of the diary.

******

---

3. *Volt. Siecle*, chap. xx.

May 12. Sabbath. Day of the battle; and here I have one of the most remarkable Ebenezers of my life to set up. This day we fought with the French, and by the great mercy of God did beat them. The battle was not general, but it was hot to those that were engaged. Our regiment was no farther engaged, but that we were cannonaded for some hours, and had several men killed and wounded. I was not near the duke; but upon our wing we had great want of generals and distinct orders; and some of those we had, seemed somewhat confused: So it was not our conduct, but kind Providence. I observe also that the English had but small part in this victory. They are the boldest sinners in our army, therefore God will choose other instruments. Also the English have got a great vogue and reputation for courage, and are perhaps puffed up upon it; and so God humbles their pride, as it were, by throwing them by. I was easy, and helped to discharge my duty well. We were very much fatigued with the pursuit, and lay all the night in the open fields without cover. Give me grace, O Lord, never to forget this great and glorious day at Ramillies.

May 13. Marching this day to improve our victory; but we are stopped, for the enemy has retired over the Dyle, and is there posted and strongly fortified. Probably we may attack them tomorrow, and if they stand to it, the action is likely to be very bloody.

May 14. The ways of God are wonderful, and past finding out. A disappointment this day that was not unpleasant; for instead of meeting with a vigorous resistance, as we expected, the enemy is gone, and we have got possession of Louvain. The effects of this battle are much greater than we expected. The Lord has sent a panic fear among the French Army, and they are so shattered, that they can hardly get them kept together. They seem not resolved to stand any where.

May 15. Marching to Brussels, Still more and more of the surprising consequences of this victory. They have abandoned Brussels and all Brabant. The Lord is taken heart, and hand, and spirit from our enemies. He has sent a spirit of division, an unaccountable consternation among their generals, and among the sundry troops they are made up of.

May 16. Passing the canal at Vilvoord. No resistance from the enemy, though we thought, happen what might, they would have defended the canal.

May 19. A fatiguing march this Sabbath. All day I met with what

I fear and hate in this trade, *viz.* cursing, swearing, filthy language, &c. yet though it was a hell around me, I bless the Lord there was a heaven within. We are still pursuing our victory, and they are still fleeing before us. There is certainly something in this affair beyond human working, for our beating them merely could not have such wonderful effects. They called themselves 70,000 men before they fought; eighty battalions of foot. I do not believe there were 3000 of them killed,[4] and yet their army is mouldering away, so that they have almost no foot in any body together. This is the finger of God, and not the doing of man.

May 20. We advanced this day towards Ghent, and still the French give way and retire. They have now quitted the Scheldt, and we are masters of Ghent peaceably.

May 21. This day is appointed by the general as a thanksgiving through the army for our victory and success, and all the chaplains are to preach.

May 23. Effects of our victory still more surprising; towns that we thought would have endured a long siege, are giving up and yielding without a stroke. Even the thoughtless creatures in the army observe the hand of Providence in this rapid success; but they laugh at these things.

May 24. Marching still forward; crossing the Lys above Ghent. Still no enemy to be seen. Bruges, Antwerp, and in short all Brabant and Flanders almost yielded. What the French got in a night by stealth at the King of Spain's death, they have lost again in a day. That old tyrant who wasted God's church, is about to be wasted himself. Last war, and for a long time while God was using him for a scourge to the earth, there was conduct in his generals,—strength and courage in his armies. They were a warlike people which their enemies were forced, at their sad expense, to confess: But now these is a sensible change, they are not like the men they were. I heard one of their own colonels who is now killed say, "the only thing he regretted was, that he could not live till he should tell the king that he had his armies composed of generals without heads, and soldiers without hands." Our ordinary regiments beat their best troops, wherever we meet them in any equality of numbers.

May 25. Marching this day to Arsel, a place famous for the retreat

---

4. Their loss was computed altogether at 20,000, of which 3000 were killed.

of Prince Vaudemont, made here in 1695, in presence of the French army, who were thrice as strong as ours. And at this place I have a monument set up of thankfulness and praise for merciful deliverance from men who were ready to swallow us up. Now we are got in again to Cambray, where we were in the last war. I hope to have comfortable remembrancers of the mercy and goodness of God to me in several places.

May 27. Our success and good news come thick upon us from all airts: We had this night a *feu-de-joi* for the French raising the siege of Barcelona.

June 5. Going on command; and I observe with thankfulness, the goodness of God to me. I sought of him (and always do seek) to give me such commands and parties as I may be kept free of ill company; and this day I was threatened with such, but Providence turned them another way. It was lot and chance apparently that did it by the dice, but I look above these things to an overruling power.

July 10. We are now advanced farther into the country than ever we were able to penetrate last war. Most of this day, like many others, spent in idle company, foolish jesting and conversation. At night I rode the round through the second line.

July 16. Diverting myself this day, riding abroad hunting all the forenoon. I was surprised when I came home by an unhappy accident (a duel) in the regiment. What a mercy it is to be kept out of temptation.

July 21. Sabbath. In the house of mourning, where I was called to see an acquaintance die, the effect of that unlucky accident I spoke of. Oh that men would be wise, and learn at other men's cost. Drunkenness and gaming was the occasion of this tragedy.

August 2. Hochstet; a day which I will remember as long as I live, &c.

August 3. I went this day to see the siege of Menin, and was in the trenches four or five hours; and I observe this of myself, (and I set it down that I may be humble,) I own freely that any measure of courage and resolution I can pretend to is allenarly the free gift of God, and not owing to natural temper, or constitution, or blood, or anything of that sort; for I find if God were to withdraw his grace from me, I would be one of the most timid creatures in the army. I own too, that whenever I have clearness that I am in my duty, or called to such a post, be there ever so much danger, I can go cheerfully, for I know that my charges are borne. But my spirits fail always in proportion as I am doubtful or unsatisfied.

******

Menin, which the Allies were now besieging, is situated on the Lys, nine miles north of Lisle, and five south-west of Courtray. It was on of the most regular fortifications in Flanders, and nothing that art could invent was wanting to render it impregnable. It was built under the immediate direction of Vauban, and was reckoned the master-piece of that celebrated engineer. It was defended by a garrison of 6000 men, with abundant stores of all warlike provisions. Being a place of such importance, and reckoned a key to the French conquests in the Netherlands, the Duke of Marlborough resolved to besiege it instantly, although it was reckoned by many too bold an undertaking. The troops to be employed on this occasion were those who had shared least in the previous services of the campaign. The trenches were opened on the 4th of august, and on the 23rd the town capitulated, much sooner than might have been augured from the strength of the place.

******

August 7-12. Going towards Menin. Marching most of the night, and mistaking our way in the dark. But what is all mankind but a mass of confusion, wandering in the dark. I was serious, and tolerably helped to do my duty. I was concerned at seeing the poor soldiers snatched in a moment into eternity, and many, perhaps, not well prepared. On the night of the 8th we were alarmed, and our regiment was drawn out by three next morning; but it proved only a feint of the enemy. On the 12th I rode again in to Menin, which surrendered that day. The evening I spent in secret prayer to God, earnestly begging that his presence may go with me wherever we go next, whether to fight or besiege. On the 14th I witnessed the whole garrison of Menin march out.

******

The next place the Allies besieged was Dendermond, a strong town at the confluence of the Rivers Scheldt and Dender, which had been under blockade ever since the Battle of Ramillies. It was situated among morasses, and had formerly baffled the whole army of the French King, who commanded in person. General Churchill had the direction of this undertaking, and took the place after a siege of seven days.

✶✶✶✶✶✶

August 13—26. We marched out here this day, and are going to the siege of Dendermond; and how things may go, or what may befall us there, the Lord only knows. On the 16th we were on our journey by three o'clock in the morning, and marched till five at night; a sore day for the poor soldiers. We had good quarters, and good accommodation. I observe the goodness of the Lord to us; for on the 19th our regiment was ordered to take post at a place near the town, where we would have been continually exposed, even lying in our tents, to the enemy's fire; and it was also a very unwholesome place, by reason of water and marsh-ground. But just as we were marching to it, we were countermanded, and ordered to lie and cover the general's quarters. As we marched, we were almost within musket shot of the town, and we wondered they did not ply their cannon at us. As we retired they fired some pieces at us, but they did us no hurt.

The kindness of Providence to us at this siege is remarkable in other respects, in withholding of rain for so long a time, whereby the marsh-ground is dried up, and the water, which is the strength of the place, is now of no use to it. Even the people of this country say that God fights for us; for old men of seventy years observe, they never saw such a drought, or the waters so low about the town as they are now. On the 24th I expected to go into the trenches, or command an attack on some part of the town. I should not be afraid to go alone in the strength of God, for he is able to lay the walls as low as those of Jericho. *His arm is not shortened*; he can keep me safe, though all the bombs of France were raging over my head, and all their cannon arrayed in a battery against me.

Next day (Sabbath) we attacked a redoubt, and soon carried it; and upon this, the place did immediately capitulate. On the 26th I spent all the forenoon visiting the works and the town; it is a very important place, and we have go it very easily. The Providence of God is very observable, for now that the town is ours, there are great rains come on. If this weather had come a few days sooner, I know not what might have been the consequences. I bless God for the good accommodation I have had at this siege, which has been so gentle and cheap to us.

August 29. This day an easy march. I was obliged to be in company all the afternoon, where there was too much drinking. There was no body drunk, but a great deal of time trifled away. I hate myself when my head is in the least heated, or when a cool-thinking distinct temper is in the least marred, though it should be far from drunkenness. And I bless God that my heart never warms, nor my soul mixes so with any company, as to steal me off my feet. The longer I stay, the more uneasy I am; and the worse the company is, the more I am upon my guard.

September 5. Now we are ordered to the siege of Aeth. We were surprised at this, for we expected, after our taking of Dendermond, that our regiment should not have been concerned in any more sieges this campaign; and indeed we are wronged and imposed upon. For my part I am very well satisfied at our coming to this siege. It is thou, Oh Lord, that sendest me here; I look above generals. It is in mercy thou bringest me here, for all they dealings with me are mercy. Thy presence will go with me, whether I go to trenches, attacks, or batteries. It was a fatiguing march this day, and very late before we got to our camp. At three next morning I went the round through all the English regiments.

******

Aeth is a frontier town of Hainault, situate on the Dender, twenty-four miles south of Ghent. The fortifications were in good repair, and there was every provision necessary for a long and vigorous defence, except men, the garrison consisting only of 2000. The campaign of this year was sufficiently glorious, and might have ended with the reduction of Dendermond. The troops also appear to have been satisfied with their successes, and rather discontented at the prospect of embarking again in another siege; but the Duke of Marlborough was determined to follow the current of victory, which now ran so strong in his favour. On the 17th the besiegers began their line of circumvallation; the trenches were opened in a few days after, and on the 2nd of October the place surrendered.

In this siege the Cameronian Regiment had their due proportion of fatigue and danger, being in the trenches, with little intermission, night and day; although they did not suffer very severely.

******

September 6-21. I am lodged in a house pretty near the town, and exposed to the fire of the batteries; but I can lay me down in peace, and sleep, for the Lord makes me to dwell in safety. On the 9th we got orders that we were to mount the trenches tomorrow. I was taken up all the afternoon in getting necessary preparations and viewing the posts. Our regiment entered the trenches at night, and though there was a great deal of firing all night, we had not a man either killed or wounded. I had not the distinctness of faith that I would, but I was fervently plying the throne of grace for strength to do my duty. The 11th we continued in the trenches all day. There was a great deal of firing, both cannon, bombs, and small shot, yet we lost only two men. I have new experiences of God's goodness in preserving and defending me. Others may take it for chance or random, but I look to a higher hand. On the 15th we had a respite, that day being appointed a thanksgiving for the great victory obtained in Italy. At night there was a *feu-de-joi* through all the army, trenches, and batteries. The Lord is doing great things for us, and humbling the proud tyrant of France. On the 17th I went into the trenches again to join our colonel, who was then on command. In the afternoon I was ordered myself to take command of the workmen, where we continued the whole night. We pushed our trenches very near the counterscarp; there was a brisk fire kept up, and seven or eight of my workmen wounded, yet it pleased the Lord to protect me.

Next day our whole regiment was ordered to the siege, and a very bad rainy day it was. Our trenches where we were posted, ran close to the counterscarp; and at twelve at night we took post and made a lodgement in the counterscarp with eighteen men and an Ensign. Cannon balls, bombs, grenades, and small shot, were flying thick yet we lost not a man the whole night. The 19th was a day of particular providence to me, that I shall not forget as long as I live. Judgement and mercy were mixed together. We continued in the trenches the whole day, and lost several men, having seventeen killed and wounded. We were beat out of that lodgement in the counterscarp at two o'clock in the afternoon, and we retook it again at six. I fell into a mistake of about a quarter of an hour in timing the attack.

I cannot tell what influence this had, or whether the same consequence might not have fallen out had it happened otherwise. But my conscience smote me about it, and I thought the surest way for me was to flee to the blood of Jesus for pardon. At night, coming out of the trenches I was in great confusion of spirit. I had only a servant with me, for the regiment was gone off before. Being very dark and wet, and on foot, we wandered and mistook the way; I had a water to cross, and my servant durst not venture to bring my horses over, as it was a very bad bridge. I got a horse of the colonel's, and coming to the bridge, it fell, and both horse and I were thrown into the water; I was in danger of being drowned, the horse falling on his side, and my foot sticking in the stirrup. I got clear, and got out, but could not get out the horse for near a quarter of an hour, so that he was almost drowned. At last I got him out, and presently my own horses came to me: so I came home blessing God for his merciful deliverances, and in the meantime trembling at his judgments. On the 21st the town surrendered. The Lord has put new songs of praise in my mouth. May he give me grace to pay my vows, and walk humbly with him all the days of my life.

******

The siege of Aeth closed the campaign of this year. On the 1st of October Major Blackader marched with his regiment from the town. They were ordered to Courtray to superintend the repairs of the fortification under Major-General Murray, a service which appears to have created some murmuring among the exhausted troops.

******

October 22. We are disappointed this day, for instead of marching into our garrison as we expected, we are ordered to march to Courtray tomorrow, which has put us all out of humour.

******

In November they returned to winter-quarters at Bruges.

Chapter 13

Campaign Sixth, 1707

The campaign of this year is very barren of military exploits. The Duke of Marlborough shone more as a diplomatic character in foreign Cabinets, than in the field of victory. From a warrior, he had become a negotiator. The only memorable transactions with which our subject is concerned, were the overtures for peace, and the attempt to force the French army to an engagement which, however, they avoided; retiring with precipitation behind their lines near Lisle. But of these we shall speak in their order; meantime we return to Bruges where we left Major Blackader with his regiment.

While in winter-quarters, the major occupied himself most assiduously in his official duties. Scarcely a day passed in which he was not employed in regimental affairs—in examining accounts, or exercising the men on drill and parade. He seems to have taken a special care of their moral conduct, as well as of their military training; and set himself to correct their vices, as well as to punish their faults. His discipline extended to offences which are too seldom brought under the cognizance and control of military law; yet his punishments were always tempered with the greatest mildness; and if at any time he had been influenced by a hasty and irritable temper, he was the first to censure and condemn his own weakness.

> In punishing faults in the regiment, I am sometimes inclined to hastiness. This day I had rather a violent, but short sally of passion; but I must say the occasion of it was just; for it was against a sin I am always angry at, that of swearing. It was soon over, and I was sorry I had shewn so much of it. I was so vexed that I went to my knees, and implored Christ for pardon, for mixing with my zeal, too much of the wildfire of passion. Lord, give

me a meek and quiet spirit; for shame and confusion of face is my due.

Notwithstanding his strictness, he appears to have had in his nature a great deal of tenderness and benevolence, and was always ready to exert his influence in saving the lives of such culprits, as he considered proper objects of mercy and compassion. Of this we have an instance in the case of one of the recruits he had brought from Scotland.

> I was taken up all day in a court-martial, and much concerned to save a poor creature's life, that I had some interest in. I was earnest to have him spared, but could not get it, for the whole court agreed to have him hanged; nor would they recommend him to mercy after they had sentenced him. I dealt with the general, and it pleased the Lord to incline his heart to mercy, for in a few days a pardon came down, which was read at the head of the regiment. I confess the *fault* deserved death, but there were circumstances that helped to exculpate the *offender*, and I think extremes of severity should never be used when the example is not like to serve any good end.

He continued in Bruges with the regiment until the month of May; and such was the happy result of his good discipline, that at a grand review, after they had joined the main army, the major was complimented by the general, and publicly thanked at the head of his own regiment, for their correct conduct and the masterly manner with which they acquitted themselves in their several exercises.

While in quarters, his greatest complaint was, as usual, too much exposure to company, and the little improvement to be derived from the ordinary topics of conversation.

> I am too often and too long tied to companies, wearied and dissipated with dinings and diversions. I cannot live without short breathings and intervals of retirement. It makes me tremble to think, that in this employment of mine, I am always walking upon the very brink and precipice of temptation. I rejoice indeed that the grace of God is sufficient for me, and keeps me out of snares. It makes me unacceptable to the world; but I desire to be above the opinions of men. I esteem the reproach of Christ greater honour than the approbation of the whole world. I am generally dissatisfied with the most part of conversation I hear, even the best; for though their be nothing ill in it,

yet there is little solid or edifying,—little savouring of grace, or ministering to the improvement of the hearers.

✶✶✶✶✶✶

March 14. All this morning abroad exercising the regiment. In the afternoon going through some of the churches here, it being a great holiday, seeing their idolatries. I desire more and more to be thankful for the purity of the gospel; and pray for the downfall of Antichrist.

March 20. Employed in private and joint prayer, imploring the blessing of God this campaign; confessing my sins and short-comings; seeking grace, counsel, and direction. I was helped to depend on his power, to hope and trust in his mercy.

March 23. They begin now to talk warmly of peace. I will seek nothing, or wish for nothing, though I be weary enough of campaigns, but what is for thy glory, O Lord. Camps have been sweet places to me; my choicest mercies have been in them. Though I hate the ill company that prevails in camps, yet by the presence of God with me, and the providences of war, I have never been better, as to grace, than in campaigns.

✶✶✶✶✶✶

The peace, warmly talked of, unfortunately did not take effect, although Louis, harassed and depressed by his misfortunes, had solicited a truce; and during last campaign, had presented, through his minister, a memorial to the States on the subject; yet no attention had been paid to his overtures, because they were believed to be insincere. Nevertheless he solemnly disavowed all sinister or insidious designs, and proposed that a conference should be opened by the ministers of all the Confederate powers. This proposal was rejected by England and the States; but whether they were actuated by honest motives, or grounded their rejection upon sufficient reasons, is a matter which has been thought questionable. France had certainly very pressing reasons to sue for peace. Her treasury was exhausted, and her troops defeated, not only in Flanders, but in Spain, where the siege of Barcelona was raised; and in Italy, where her army was totally routed under the walls of Turin, by the Duke of Savoy and Prince Eugene.

But these necessities, though they might excite suspicions that Louis only wanted time to strengthen his own hands, or sow dissension among the Allies, were certainly neither inconsistent nor incompatible with sincerity. The truth is, both the Dutch and the English acted in such a manner, as leads to suspect that the charge of duplicity and insincerity rests more with them than with their overpressed adversary. They rejected the offers of pacification abruptly, and without due deliberation. They discovered an anxiety to conceal from public investigation, every thing relative to the business, and would not allow the preliminaries of France to be inserted in the common newspapers. War had become, to the ruling faction, a source of patronage and emolument, which they were unwilling to resign; and it is to be lamented, that the delusions of ambition, and the flatteries of admirers, should so far blind mens' eyes to the miseries they are unavoidably entailing on their country, by the expenditure of her revenues, and the wanton destruction of so may thousands of her subjects.[1]

Notwithstanding the eagerness of the Allies to continue hostilities until they could extort more advantageous terms, the campaign of this year was not only unproductive of success, but more unfortunate than any of the preceding. The military strength of France had suffered only a temporary diminution; and the expedients of uncontrolled despotism, aided by the supplies of an abundant harvest, were capable of repairing the immense losses she had sustained. New armies appeared on the frontiers, equal in numbers and appointments to any that had been levied since the commencement of the war. They adopted again the system of defensive operations, and the Duke of Marlborough resolved to become the assailant. But though he pursued them through all Brabant, from camp to camp, in the hope of bringing them to a decisive engagement, they contrived, by their vigilance and the celerity of their movements, to elude his pursuit.

******

April 6. Making preparations for the campaign. I have been looking over my diary of this time twelvemonth. I find just the same frame I feel now. I went out with no other stock but this,—trusting in God, and hoping in his mercy. And indeed I shall never desire to go out to a campaign in a better frame. What was last year at this time a matter of faith to me, is now a matter of praise. Ramillies, Dendermond, and Aeth, are to me at present just as Hochstet was the year before; and so I hope this campaign, which is now a matter of faith, will prove in the end a matter of praise and thankfulness.

April 29. Going up and down among our great men here, and getting orders for marching. I waited on a petty court all the forenoon.—

---

1. Somerville, *Hist.* ch. xi. Lediard, vol. i.

Vanity and pageantry. I hate these ways of living; and indeed what is it all but a vain show. I saw those same persons who were attending the great man in the forenoon with the most sycophantic behaviour, in the afternoon when he was gone, ridiculing him, and laughing at him for a———.

May 5. Marched this morning out of Bruges.

May 10. Arrived near Ghent. I came out of that town in the morning, and I bless God that brought me safe back to the regiment. I ran the risk of being taken prisoner; there having been French parties between the town and the camp, which was two leagues off. This was the first night of setting up my tent and lying in it. And now, Oh Lord, make it a Bethel, a place where thou delightest to dwell. Thou hast given me much of thy presence in camps and tents, aid I again devote myself to thee. I go forth in thy might, and win fight under they banner.

*May 11. Sabba*th. Marching a long march and joined the great army (near Brussels.) But, Oh such a spent Sabbath, and such company! This is one of the greatest hardships of my employment, to be tied to such things. In the marching I had almost forgot it was Sabbath, but recollected myself, and retired from company, (I mean in my thoughts,) and strove to keep up a spiritual habit of mind by meditation. But I have less leisure for retirement, having a great deal to do as major, looking after the business of the regiment. They are now beginning to talk of action speedily.

★★★★★★

The French at this time were lying quietly within their lines. They had given out that they were ready to offer battle to the Allies, and threatened, if they declined, to lay siege either to Mons or Charleroi. Upon this intelligence, the Duke of Marlborough resolved to meet them halfway. In two days, he was informed that the enemy had quitted their lines, and encamped on the plain of Fleurus, but in a position so strong, that it was deemed imprudent to venture an attack. The Allies posted themselves at Meldert; while the French, seeing their design frustrated, advanced to Gemblours, without daring, in their turn, to hazard an engagement, though greatly superior in numbers. In this situation both armies continued above two months, nothing but slight skirmishing being attempted on either side.

★★★★★★

May 15. A long march; a scorching hot day, very annoying to the poor soldiers. The French Army is now without their lines, and we are advancing up to them.

May 16. We hear the enemy have retired within their lines again, and probably we shall attack them.

Yesternight we marched from the army for a convoy to the baggage; and everybody believed the duke was to march up to the enemy, and that there would be a battle. I was tranquil, believing that Providence orders all well. Our regiment had indeed left the army to go on the convoy. But Providence frequently works by disappointing our expectations, for this night the whole measures were altered. The French, who we thought within their lines, are without them, and threatening Brussels, and the open country, so that we were obliged to decamp to cover our own country. It was a fatiguing march, for we travelled all night until two o'clock next day.

May 18. Marching. The scheme of this campaign is turned out otherwise than we expected. The French are in no pain about defending their lines, but marching up and down, giving us a great deal of trouble and fatigue. I believe they will shun fighting too, except at our disadvantage.

May 24. Employed in the functions of my post. Well assisted and carried through. I got a compliment from the general, and thanks upon the head of the regiment, that they exercised so well. But all this is the goodness of God alone, that gives me favour in the sight of any man.

May 25. Sabbath. I was invited to dine abroad with a great man; but I shunned it, fearing temptation, company, and conversation unsuitable to a Sabbath. I wish to live tenderly and circumspectly in this army. Next day I dined, but staid too long in company.

May 30. Employed all the morning in the show and parade of our employment, reviewing and exercising my men before the general. All things went on well and smoothly.

June 4. In the evening we had one of the severest storms I have ever seen, of hail, rain, and wind. Most of our tents were beat down and torn, and the hollow ways running like rivers. I observed what a poor shiftless creature man is. If any of the elements were let loose upon us, or any accident, how soon would we be reduced to our first nothing, what a comfort to have the God of nature to be our protector,—then though the earth be removed—though the mountains shake, and the waters roar, we need not be afraid.

******

Nothing particular occurred to him while the army continued in their stationary camp. He says:—

> I reckon our lying so long here a great mercy, for I get living in a more sober and regular way than in constant marching and hurry.

******

July 30. We left our camp here, this afternoon at three o'clock, and marched all night, a tedious and wearisome march. We continued our journey till three afternoon next day, so that we have been twenty-four hours under arms. It has been a sad march for the poor soldiers.

August 1. Marching in the afternoon, and coming close to the enemy, so that there is all appearance of an action tomorrow.

August 2. The day of Hochstet, a day never to be forgotten by me. This same day Providence gave us the opportunity to make it as glorious a day as that was, but we had not the hearts to improve it. We had crept up pretty near to the enemy last night by stealing a day's march upon them, so that they could not easily get off without a battle, if we had pushed them. But we contented ourselves with making a bravado of attacking their rearguard, with the grenadiers, and mismanaged that too; so that they got off scot free to our shame, but it is fit that men commit mistakes, and blunders, and weakness, that they may see themselves but men. We know of no other way of working here but by great armies. Omnipotence needs none of these. An army of frogs or flies is as good to him, and can do more with him than we can without him. This is the finest army just now in the world, and yet does the least. Perhaps the reason is this, we adore the arm of flesh always, and God will have men humbled.

I was chagrined and uneasy all day, for the neglect of this opportunity; for through God's assistance I was very eager to come to hand with them, and to have had a battle. The very day encouraged me. And I am of opinion, that we second Providence very ill this year, for the French seems to be a cowed, frightened army; and I have no doubt, but if we attacked them briskly, we should beat them; but instead of that, we seem afraid of them. This makes them pluck up their drooping spirits. Their time is not yet fully come it seems; and there is but one Prince Eugene in the world, and he is not everywhere.

August 3. Sabbath. Marching; and the worst day for the poor soldiers I have seen. It poured down a heavy rain, and the cavalry had so broken the ways, that the men marched in clay and dirt to the knees, almost the whole day, for four leagues. There was hardly a hundred men of a regiment with the colours at night. It seemed to be heaven contending with us, for I never saw the army so harassed. We came late to our camp. I set up my tent and rested sweetly.

August 4. Resting this day, not out of choice, but necessity, for a great part of the army is not come up yet by reason of yesterday's fatigue; and for all the diligence we make, yet these vermin, the French, are still before us. Providence has taken away much of their heads they had last war, but I think he has left them their heels.

August 6. For two days we have not been able to stir out of our tents for bad weather. We are lying among mire and dirt. Raining from morn till night, so that the artillery cannot be brought forward.

August 8. Hearing of a friend that died the other day at Brussels. He regretted that he had misspent and trifled away so much precious time, and that he had been so drawn away by company to tippling and drinkings. O that others would learn and take warning; and all of us so learn *to number our days, as to apply our hearts unto wisdom; and to redeem the time.*

August 10. A Sabbath of rest, which is a great mercy in a camp; for this day-week was a sad day, liker a hell than a Sabbath. Came to my knees this morning with a sense of sin, and pollution of heart and nature. My heart was enlarged by faith, to flee to Christ for pardon and washing; seeing in him an infinite fullness as a complete Saviour. I was helped also to trust him cheerfully for the events, dangers, and actions of this campaign which are yet to come.

August 19. Got the bad news of the Duke of Savoy's raising the siege of Toulon, which is very mortifying; for our hopes were raised high, and probably the taking of it might have hastened a peace. But Providence will not be tied to our little projects: He can work his ends by ways and means which we think contrary.

******

The attack upon Toulon was a project concerted between England and the States. Its design was to weaken the maritime power of France, and disable her for maintaining the war, by cutting off her commerce with the Spanish West Indies, which furnished her with the principal resources. Prince Eugene and the Duke of Savoy, at the head of the Italian Army, were to enter Provence by way of the Alps, and co-operate with the British fleet, under Sir Cloudesly Shovel, who had instructions to invest Toulon. The latter part of the plan was executed in the most gallant manner by the British seamen. But owing to the remissness of the Duke of Savoy, and especially the obstinacy of the emperor in employing his troops in the conquest of Naples instead of aiding the expedition, the French gained time to throw in provisions and reinforcements. The Allies, after carrying several considerable posts, destroying a number of ships and magazines, &c. were compelled to desist from their attempt. They struck their tents under cover of night, and marched off with all possible speed.[2]

******

August 20. Marching this day; the French marched also; so we hardly expect to see their faces this campaign, but we know not what may be. Now here is the best army in the world, and have made the idlest campaign, and done nothing at all. This French tyrant has been a dark riddle of Providence; for a long time we thought he was falling before us, and that the scourge was to be thrown into the fire. But it seems their cup is not full yet; for Providence is putting a defence about them, and blasting our designs.

August 21,22. Resting. I went in to Aeth, and viewed all our last year's attacks; and with thankfulness remembered the deliverances I had at the siege. I went round the town where our trenches had been, and particularly that part in the counterscarp where I was the 19th of September, and had exercises of spirit, and met with such providences as I shall never forget.

September 3. In town (Courtray) all day. At night my wife arrived, and we had a comfortable meeting, with the blessing of God I hope, and mercy to us both.

September 4. We got an alarm of part of the army marching, and of some appearance of action. I went out to the camp, easy and trusting in God. The French did not meddle with our foragers or escort, and so there was no action.

September 5. I returned again to town, and in the afternoon, brought

---

2. Sommerville's *History*, chap. xi.

out my wife to my cottage here in the camp. Lord, let they blessing and presence by with us, and our cottage shall be a palace.

October 20. This day we marched into our garrison (at Ghent.) The Lord has preserved me in my outgoings and incomings, and followed me with mercy and goodness through this campaign, and brought me in safety back. Here I am resolved to be still more spiritual, and to have more intercourse with heaven in the midst of my business.

★★★★★★

On the 2nd of December, Major Blackader and his lady left Ghent, and after a speedy passage arrived at Rotterdam, where they spent the winter quietly and comfortably, remote from many snares and temptations to which they would have been exposed in the garrison.

CHAPTER 14

Campaign Seventh, 1708

The fortune of war seemed to delight in alternatives. The balance of success, which last year inclined to the side of France, now preponderated visibly in favour of the Allies. The selfish and mercenary views of some, and the secret jealousies of others, had weakened the hands of the Confederacy, and introduced discord into their councils; circumstances which Louis resolved to avail himself of, and hoped to turn to his advantage. He had two grand projects in view, the one to make a descent on the eastern coast of Scotland, to reinstate in his ancient kingdom the young Pretender, who he had already acknowledged by the title of James III. For this the extraordinary tumult and discontent which the Union had excited, seemed to offer a favourable opportunity; and from the symptoms of general disaffection, he augured the speedy reduction of the whole British Empire. His next scheme was to push the war with vigour in the Spanish Netherlands, expecting that the recall of the English troops to defend their own territories, would lay the whole country at the mercy of his victorious arms.

Had these views been carried into effect with the same wisdom and resolution with which they were formed, they must have placed Britain and her Allies in a critical and perilous situation. Happily, however, by the activity and address of Marlborough and Prince Eugene, the plans of Louis were rendered visionary and abortive. The Allies augmented their forces by drafting as many of the Imperial troops as could be spared from the service on the Upper Rhine, to reinforce the army in Flanders, where their principal operations were to be carried on. Preparations being ready for opening the campaign, the two armies took the field towards the end of May. We now return to the diary, leaving any other explanatory remarks to be made in the order of events.

✶✶✶✶✶✶

February 8. Sabbath. Composed and serious, enjoying ordinances; but I observe this difference in myself now, from what I was in my younger years; it was then an act of the affections and the heart; now it is more an act of the mind; the understanding has cooled the ardour of the affections.

February 16. The afternoon taken up in innocent diversion; at night in good company. I bless God for his mercy to us here, that gives us such respect and favour in this place.

February 19. Leaving Rotterdam. Praying for the blessing of God with us on our voyage back to our garrison.

February 22. Contrary winds for two days: But now we are free of them. We came ashore this day at eleven o'clock.

February 25. Going through paying my duty to the general and superior officers. I have been so long down in Holland in good and quiet company, that I find myself, as it were, a stranger here.

March 8. Hearing of several providences. Black clouds seem hanging over our heads.

March 10. Getting orders to be in readiness to march for embarking for Scotland, in consequence of hearing that the French fleet have sailed, notwithstanding of our fleet being so strong. But armies and fleets are but broken reeds when we trust too much to them.

March 18. This day spent in reading, prayer, and meditation. Concerned for the public affairs, and the work of God in Scotland. I trust their confusions and troubles shall ultimately turn out for their good, and the disappointment of their enemies.

✶✶✶✶✶✶

The fleet, with the Pretender on board, known by the romantic title of the Chevalier St. George, set sail from Dunkirk on the 6th of March, with above 5000 soldiers, 10,000 muskets, and a supply of other war-like stores. The most sanguine hopes of success were entertained. The Jacobites in Scotland were all in arms. Many, who had hitherto been enemies to the Pretender, declared themselves ready to join his standard, so soon as any insurrection should be attempted in his favour. (See note following).

✶✶✶✶✶✶

Note:—Men of all ranks and persuasions were at this time so exasperated against the Union, which they regarded as the loss of their independence and the irretrievable ruin of their country, that they were persuaded nothing could recover their ancient rights, but the restoration of the Stuart Family. Thousands took to arms, and mobs paraded the country, insulting all that refused to declare against the Union. The articles were publicly burnt at the cross of Dumfries, and all the Southern shires were ready to start into rebellion. The fiery zeal of the Cameronians burst forth on this occasion, and with equal intensity, though in a less honourable and important cause than the Revolution. They embodied themselves into regiments, chose officers, and provided themselves with horses and arms. They were so far reconciled to religious differences, that they were willing to join the Episcopal heretics to forgive their old oppressors the Highlanders, and even to overlook the objection of the king's being a Papist, trusting to the possibility of his conversion, or his having Protestant children. In this state of affairs, had the chevalier effected a landing, he might have set himself at the head of thirty or forty thousand men. Lockhart's *Memoirs*.

✶✶✶✶✶✶

The intention of the invaders was to land at Dunbar or Leith, and on the 13th they reached the mouth of the Frith; but providentially they outsailed their port, and were carried several leagues to the northward. Their appearance struck Edinburgh with alarm, and spread consternation over the whole kingdom. All the troops in England were ordered to march to the North, and several battalions in Flanders were in readiness to embark at Ostend. But fortunately, their mistake gave the English admiral, Sir George Byng, full time to overtake them; and ere they could rectify their error, he had, with a superior fleet, come to anchor in the Frith. The French refused to venture an engagement, and stood out to sea, followed by Byng, who made all the sail he could in pursuit. After being tossed a whole month in tempestuous weather, they reached Dunkirk with the loss of a single ship, which was taken without resistance; and about 4000 men who perished by sickness and other accidents. This gave a death blow to the hopes of the Pretender and his party, both in Scotland and France, and left the Allies at liberty to concentrate their efforts for prosecuting the war on the continent.[1]

---

1. Burnet, vol. ii. Lockhart's *Memoirs*. M'Pherson's *State Papers*, vol. ii.

✶✶✶✶✶✶

March 20. Hearing great and good news this day, that our fleet has beat, and totally ruined the French fleet upon the coast of Scotland. If this be true, I confess I am in a wide mistake about this providence, and the design of it. I did not at all think it likely that Providence had sent out the Prince of Wales and the French fleet, and taken all rubs out of their way, and blasted all attempts on our side to oppose them; and thus to bring them to the coast of Scotland to be immediately beaten there. I was of opinion that he might be sent there to be a scourge for a while to that island. But we are blind creatures, and know nothing. When we are expecting God to come one way, he comes in another. He acts in his sovereignty, often disappointing our expectations. When we expect him in a way of mercy, he comes in a way of judgement; and when we look for judgements, he often comes in mercy. I am very glad to be disappointed this way. But unless the Lord gives a spirit of grace and repentance, all these mercies will be lost upon us; for we frequently use his own mercies to fight against himself. They swell us with pride and insolent boasting, for we put too much confidence in fleets and armies. Oh Lord, get glory to thyself, and let not man rob thee of it.

March 22. By this day's news our great hopes are vanished into smoke. The great victory which we thought so sure, amounts only to the taking of one ship. I suspected we were triumphing before the victory, and always thought there was more in this providence than our rational reasoners would see; who can never be brought to look above probabilities and second causes.

March 23. Getting better confirmation of our good news, and the French king's design being broke, which I look upon as a surprising act of the divine mercy.

March 24. Most people are of opinion the danger is now over; I wish it may be so, and hope it is so. I confess I was expecting confusion and war in Britain; perhaps a melancholy cast of mind leads farther into such thoughts than I am aware. But several good men who walk close with God, and observe his providences, believe that troubles are awaiting Britain, and these by the French. *But God's ways are not our ways, nor his thoughts our thoughts.*

April 14. This day being appointed by the States to be kept a fast-day through the Seven Provinces, to implore the blessing of God upon their arms this campaign, I was resolved to spend the morning and forenoon in secret prayer at home, but was diverted from it by business I could not shun. Oh Lord, pity, and accept of the will instead of the form.

April 18. This Sabbath employed in seeking the blessing and presence of God to go with me. I ask not great things. I am seeking no advancement, nor making court to any man for favours and posts, I only beg *grace to help in time of need.*

April 20. Well directed in business; getting my horses and equipage provided.

April 21. I am sure I am one of those men in the world that owe least to my own conduct and management, and most to the goodness and kind Providence of God. Lard, make me thankful, and give me thy blessing with all my enjoyments.

April 29. Got orders in the morning to go upon command for a week. Somewhat troubled at this, for it is the most terrible to me of all my employment, to be chained, as it were, in hell so long. I could cheerfully undergo the fatigues and dangers of our trade, to be free of that shocking company, the dregs and scum of the earth. But I am not to choose my own lot. *Thy will be done.*

Going out to my post in the afternoon, I found that which I feared was come upon me; for I had the off-scourings of the garrison along with me, both officers and soldiers, most abominable vermin whom my soul abhors. Oh Lord, how long shall I dwell among men whose tongues are set on fire of hell! Oh when wilt thou deliver me out of this horrid and noisome company. All night in hurry and confusion.

April 30. Marching all day, on command; and troubled with several occurrences, not knowing what course to take. In such junctures, I find my mind is so confused that I cannot apply to a throne of grace with any distinct thought or serene mind.

May 1. One of the worst days I ever had in this employment. My mind chafed and vexed the whole day with villainy and abominations of all sorts, both against the laws of God and man. Cursing, swearing, drunkenness, robbing, thieving, mutiny, &c. I made some severe examples of punishment, but was ill assisted by some officers, who rather encouraged the villains; so that I believe I shall not be so well liked among many of the English; but I shall be glad to be hated by such.

It should be bad enough before such beings would love me. O Lord, thou who knowest my heart, knowest that a battle would not be so terrible to me as this day has been; but thou seest this trial needful for me. Arrived at Willebrook in the afternoon; and there I was somewhat relieved of this sad company, by getting conveniency to live by myself in peace and quietness.

May 3. Marching, and making some more exemplary punishments. Retiring, in thought, from the world, between hands, to converse with God. I was pretty serene, and well secured with what I had the charge of.

May 4. Marching homeward (to Ghent,) my mind more tranquil than it has been since I came out. Riding frequently on before the party out of the noise of their tongues.

May 9. I bless the Lord for this Sabbath of rest before we set out. I know not when I shall get another. I go to the campaign, trusting in thee, Oh Lord, and hoping in thy mercy. I am free from all despondency and ill-boding fears. I am not afraid of dangers or battle; through grace I shall do valiantly. I am more afraid of the snares and sin of the wretched company I must be chained to; but thy grace can make me escape that pollution also. I cheerfully leave my dearest concern upon thee, trusting thou wilt again compass us about with songs of deliverance. Thou has done great things for us, and thou canst do still greater. If we believe, all things are possible.

May 10. I never went out of the garrison more serene.

May 11. We had an easy march, and reached the camp at night.

May 12. Pretty severe march. The day of Ramillies, a day well to be remembered by me.

May 15. Marching all day. This irregular, camp-way of living is a pleasure to many, but it is a most unpleasant, hateful life to me; and only because of ill company. Otherwise I should like it very well, for, I bless God, I keep good health, and am no way afraid of the dangers to which this way of living exposes me. Nay, I would with pleasure fight a battle tomorrow, if I though it would put an end to this war, and this sad way of living.

May 19. Resting this day, and busy with the affairs of the regiment. There are orders tonight, that this day-week there shall be preaching and prayer through the army to implore the blessing of heaven upon our arms. Tomorrow we are going to march, for we hear the French are in motion some way.

May 22. Orders coming unexpectedly for marching to the enemy. We are observing the motions of the French, and must take our measures from them; whereas, before we came out, we thought ourselves so far superior to them, that we expected to find them behind their lines.

May 23. A sad Sabbath both by fatigue and ill company. Marching all day in the middle of an English army. I need say no more to give a notion what a hell on earth it is. It was also a sore day for fatigue, for we marched all yesterday, all night, and all this day. There was a constant heavy rain most if the time, which made the roads very bad, and the march very tedious. We were sometimes four hours in marching half-a-mile. I was thirty hours on horseback, which is the longest time ever I was in my life, either the last war or this. I know not how things will turn, but I think there are appearances of a battle; for the French seem not to shun it much, if we be very keen in courting the occasion, as we still pretend to be. Lord, I commit myself and all to thee, and, through grace, will be very easy, come what may.

May 26. Resting these two days. This day kept by public orders through the army for preaching and prayers. Grant, Oh Lord, the English army be not found mocking thee, and aggravating their own guilt on such occasions, when there is not so much as the appearance of seriousness, or a belief that there is a God who either can give or mar our success. We had sermon, and I retired as much as possible from company. Oh Lard, let me be among the Lots that are in this Sodom, whom thou wilt spare in the day of they wrath.

May 28. Taken up the whole fore-day in reviewing the regiment. Well guided and directed; I cannot but see the kindness of Providence in every thing. Last winter I nearly lost all my horses; yet I have got all made up again, and better provided than ever I was; and equipage better than most of my station in the army. May I have grace to lay myself out for his service who takes such care of me and all that concerns me.

May 29. Diverting myself with seeing the troops reviewed. We are here a huge army if God be with us; but if he be not, we are only so many ciphers.

May 30. Sabbath. I kept in my tent till four o'clock in the afternoon, and in the evening heard sermon.

June 1. Attending a court-martial, a very unpleasant part of my duty; prosecuting a deserter for his life. Yet I have peace of mind in this affair, for I pardoned this same man once before for desertion, and recommended him to mercy. Now Providence has cast him in the way again. I know not what is in it, but all God's ways are holy and just. He brings mens' sins to light, and malefactors to punishment, when they are least thinking on it; and when men punish for one crime, he often discovers other crimes in them for which sentence of death has passed against them in heaven.

June 2. This day about some means to advance a titulary step in my employment. I bless God I am very easy whether it succeed or not. I have enough, and far more than I deserve.

June 4. Awake most of the night. I could not sleep; my thoughts being taken up about that poor wretch in my company, who is to die tomorrow by the hand of public justice. Serious with God for the welfare of his soul.

June 5. I attended the poor creature at his death. He seemed penitent; and I am not without hopes of him.

June 8-12. On command these four days. Very stormy, bad weather. I am never easy among a club of English officers; but I have got all the English sent from me to other parts, and I keep the Germans; for they are not such bold profane sinners, and do not swear so much; and when they do, it does not make my flesh creep, or sound in my ears with that hellish ringing echo that English oaths do.

June 15. This day I was with the duke in his quarters on business.

June 16. In the forenoon the Electoral Prince of Hanover (afterwards King George II.) came along the line; we drew out without arms.

June 20. Sabbath. No sermon. We are here a great army; but what do we signify, we are chained and fettered as it were, that we cannot stir to the right or the left, backward or forward, without disadvantage.

June 22. We have accounts that Prince Eugene is to join us in two days.

June 24. We marched at two o'clock this morning, the enemy also being upon their march. Between four and five in the evening we came within sight of them; and they advanced as if they designed a battle. We took post, as the generals thought, to the best advantage, and lay at our arms all night, having orders to be ready in the morning for the attack. I committed myself to God, believing he can keep me as safe in a battle as in my chamber in a garrison.

June 25. But when the light appeared, we found the enemy were marched off; and that their design was not to fight, but to give us the go-by, and possess themselves of Ghent, which they have done. I commit my dear concern there to thee, Oh Lord. Keep her in perfect peace, for I trust we shall yet praise thee.

June 26. There is great appearance of action suddenly.

June 27. Concerned for the present posture of our affairs, and somewhat anxious about the surprisal of Ghent.

June 28. Marched at two in the morning, a tedious march. We camped about thee times in the evening for a feint, and then marched all night, which was great fatigue to the army. Our mistakes and weakness give us trouble. What a vain thing is man, and the wisdom and courage of man! He who, one day, performs great actions and is extolled as more than man, the next is as much decried and guilty of great blunders. We have still a prospect of sudden action if the enemy defend what they have got.

June 29. A fatiguing march to retrieve our past mistake. Passed the Dender. In all probability it well be retrieved, and the French will quit what they have taken. It seems to be little else than a piece of vanity and gasconade.

June 30. This is another great Ebenezer of my life, to be added to Hochstet, Ramillies, &c. We fought the French, and, by the great mercy of God, beat them. I was liberally supplied with courage, resolution, and a calm mind. *All is the gift of God.*

★★★★★★

The losses and fatigues of the Allies were compensated by the decisive Battle of Oudenard, to which the diary alludes. The town from which this victory takes its name, stands on the Scheldt, thirteen miles south of Ghent. Being the only pass on that river which was left to the Allies, the French had the vanity to suppose they could reduce or take it by surprise, as they had done Ghent and Bruges; and thus completely intercept a very important line of communication. But these projects were defeated by the diligence and extraordinary expedition of the Confederates, who came upon them on the 30th so unexpectedly, that they hesitated much whether to retire or venture an engagement. The commanders-in-chief, the Dukes of Burgundy and Vendome, differed in their opinions. Both were inclined to retreat; but the ardour of the younger officers, who had more fire than prudence, induced the former to declare for battle, and the latter to submit with reluctance. This irresolution, which continued until three in the afternoon, the Allies did not fail to turn to their advantage.

The attack commenced with the cavalry, before most of the infantry had time to form or reach the place. It was obstinately contested by both sides; and about seven o'clock the action became general throughout the whole line. The enemy finding themselves charged so determinedly, fled in the utmost confusion, having lost above 14,000 men. The slaughter would have been much greater, and few perhaps would have escaped, had not night put an end to the carnage, and prevented all pursuit; the darkness rendering it impossible to distinguish friends from foes. The fugitives made a scattered retreat to Ghent, which they reached early next morning. The Confederates remained on the spot all night under arms, ignorant as yet of the extent of their victory. Their loss was very inconsiderable, scarcely exceeding in all 2000 men. The share Major Blackader's regiment had in this victory, and his reflections on the occasion, we shall continue in his own words.

******

June 30. The battle began about five in the afternoon, and lasted till night put a screen of darkness between us and them; and thereby saved them, in all probability, from as great a defeat as every they got. The battle came by surprise, for we had no thought of fighting through the day. My frame was more serene and spiritual than ordinary. My thoughts were much upon the 103rd Psalm, which I sung (in my heart) frequently upon the march. Our regiment, properly speaking, was not engaged in the attack; but what was worse, we were obliged to stand in cold blood, exposed to the enemy's shot, by which we had several killed and wounded, for there was heavy firing for about two hours. Throughout the whole course of it I was constantly engaged, sometimes in prayer, sometimes in praise, sometimes for the public, sometimes for myself.

We lay all night upon the field of battle, where the bed of honour was both hard and cold; but we passed the night as well as the groans of dying men would allow us; being thankful for our own preservation. I was mercifully supplied with the comforts of life, and wanted nothing good for me. We marched again by daybreak, and formed our lines, the enemy making still some appearance; but it was only their rearguard, which was easily repulsed; so we returned to our camp. I went again through the field of battle, getting a lecture on mortality from the dead. I observe this of the French, that they are the most easily beat and cowed of any people in the world, did we but second Providence in pushing them when the opportunity is put in our had. Arise, Oh Lord, and let thine enemies be scattered. Let the fruits of our victories be the advancement of Christ's kingdom on the earth.

July 3. Marching to Tournay.

July 4. Marching towards Lisle. We are got within the enemy's lines, and they seem to have shut themselves up so, that their army runs the risk of being lost if we act vigorously.

July 5. Employed in demolishing the French lines.

******

This was in accordance with the resolution taken immediately after the battle, that the Duke of Marlborough's army should pass the Lys, and level the enemy's lines between Ypres and Warneton, to intercept the retreat of the French in that direction. Meantime the Dukes of Burgundy and Vendome, being somewhat recovered from their late consternation, sent a detachment of 10,000 men on a foraging expedition into Dutch Flanders, to burn and plunder the country by way of reprisals.

******

July 6. I went in the afternoon to take a view of the French lines. There are strange turns of Providence this campaign. The French are got into our country, and we are in theirs. They are closed up by the canal (between Bruges and Ghent,) so that by remaining there, they run the risk of losing their army. But yet, so long as they stay, we can get nothing done here. Oh Lord, guide and direct our general, and thy presence be with us; then canals, ramparts, walls, &c. shall be levelled like the walls of Jericho. Give us courage and conduct, as thou has sent upon them a spirit of terror and panic fear. Let this be the time, in they wise and holy dispensations, for unriddling that dark providence, the French tyrant. Waste him, as he has wasted thy church; get glory upon him as thou didst upon Pharaoh. For this cause, I trust, thou hast raised him up.

July 7. My dearest concern is now in the midst of the enemy (at Ghent;) yet she is kept safe and in peace. They are fettered and restrained as the lions in Daniel's den, that they can do no harm: Yea they are made to befriend and protect, when we expected they would plunder. Let others take this for chance or for their generosity; I take all as mercies from thee, Oh Lord. Thy promise is accomplished. That when a man's ways please the Lord, he maketh even his enemies to be at peace with him, and who shall harm you, if ye be the followers of that which is good? Praying for the downfall of the French tyrant and of Antichrist. Oh let the time come when thou wilt avenge the blood of thy servants. Let the cry of the souls under the altar come up and be heard by thee (Rev. vi. 9.) Let all this great assembly know that the battle is the Lord's, and that he saves not by sword or by spear.

July 8. This day kept by public orders through the army, a thanksgiving for our victory, and a *feu-de-joi* at night.

July 11. Anxious about my wife, how she may be disposed of. Though enemies have been restrained from doing harm; yet I know not but it is her duty to leave the place, and go back to Holland where she may enjoy the gospel and kind friends.

July 14. Got orders to march from the army. We decamped at three in the afternoon, and marched all night. We have had more fatigue and night marches this campaign already, then we had all the last war.

July 15. We have been full twenty-four hours under arms marching, and the horses as long under their loads. There was an appearance of action too, and of an advantage on our side of taking a place and a body of their troops in it, but it turned to small account. Whether we acted prudently or not, I shall not say: It does not become me to blame generals, but to obey.

July 17. After a day's rest, we marched again at twelve at night, and came at six next morning to Leuse. We are much farther advanced into the enemy's country than ever we were, either last war or this. It appears, now when we are upon the spot, that we might have attacked the enemy here the other day with success: but men are wisest behind hand, and human prudence cannot foresee all things. We are kept very busy in preventing the town from being plundered.

July 18. Sabbath. Dining abroad, and too long engaged in company. I wish I had dined on bread and water, rather than been in conversation so foreign to a Sabbath.

July 23. Marched this day back to our camp, and so our expedition ends. It is certain we might have done more than we have done; but all things are ordered by an overruling providence. The French save themselves often by our weakness and mistakes. Since I returned, I have got accounts that my wife is gone for Holland, to her friends at Rotterdam.

★★★★★★

This expedition was commanded by Count Tilly, who had orders to penetrate into the French territories, and lay the country under contribution. The body of troops they attacked, was a detachment of 800 cavalry of the Duke of Berwick's army, of which a considerable number was either killed or taken. There were 1400 infantry in Leuse who made their escape; but in Major Blackader's opinion, they might have been all cut off or made prisoners.

★★★★★★

August 1. Sabbath. But we are so far from knowing it, or seeing any marks of it here, that it is more like hell than any other day. Oh how is grace wasted in this dry barren land of Popery, and idolatry, and wickedness. How long shall I be banished from the gospel and Christian conversation.

August 8. The army was drawn out in the morning to review before the Prince of Hesse-Cassel, and King Augustus of Poland; and this is the first time I recollect of our reviewing on a Sabbath these twenty years bygone. Lord, pardon our sin, that we regard the day so little. I kept in my tent all the afternoon, and shunned company.

August 12. Short march over the Scheldt. There will be an action again if the enemy attempt to relieve Lisle.

August 15. Sabbath. At night, hearing of some immorality in the regiment among the officers, I went to bring them to order. They thought I was unreasonably passionate and severe in the matter. I will not say but my own fiery spirit mixes itself with my reproofs on these occasions. But I was provoked, and I hope it was zeal against sin, for I had no self-interest in being angry, or prejudiced against any of them.

Their abominable practices vex me, (the officers I mean) for I think they grow daily worse, and more impudently shameless in vice.

August 21. Marching forward to cover Lisle, which is under siege.

August 23. I went this day into the trenches and batteries. The French are come up this night close to us, and give out that they will fight us, and relieve the town; so that there is all appearance of a battle, and like to be the most deliberate one we have ever fought. May the Lord of Hosts be upon our side, and go before us as our captain. Let the fruit of all this be the advancement of his honour and glory.

August 24. The army drew out and formed the line of battle, and made all the necessary dispositions to receive the enemy, whom we expected to attack us; but they came not. They were lying close by us, and we were alarmed twice or thrice by them. They do not think fit to attack us, for Prince Eugene has joined us from the siege.

August 27. At night there was an attack made upon the counter-scarp of Lisle. I went up to the top of a windmill to see it at a distance. Serious all the time in prayer for success. We know not how it has gone, but we hope all is well. The close firing lasted about two hours. I went back after all the company was gone to the top of the mill, and sat alone some time in meditation. Next morning we heard that the counterscarp was taken, and the loss not very great.

August 31. Employed all this forenoon in perfecting our trenches. At two o'clock the enemy appeared behind our retrenchments. About four the French had raised a battery of twenty-six pieces of small cannon, and played upon our lines, but with little effect.

September 1. We lay at our arms all night, expecting they would attack us by break of day. But we were disappointed, for they only continued to cannonade us as the day before, and to as little purpose.

September 2. We had no disturbance from them this day, and we are persuaded they have no mind to attack us here if they can do any thing else. It is the Lord that gives us a spirit of firmness and resolution, and takes it from them that they dare not venture a battle.

September 7. The siege proves very tedious and troublesome. The French army have now got between us and Brussels.

★★★★★★

The siege of Lisle was by far the most remarkable that had happened since the reduction of Namur. This city was the capital of French Flanders, and second to Paris in wealth and importance. Its situation amidst pools and marshes—its immense merchandise and extensive maritime power, made it the Venice of the Netherlands. Art and nature had done every thing to render it impregnable. There Louis had expended the vast resources of his treasury, and the engineer Vauban exerted his utmost skill. Marshal Boufflers was the governor, and it was filled with troops that composed an army instead of a garrison.

A more than ordinary value was set upon the place, and the possessors made corresponding preparations to defend it. They looked upon any attempt to reduce it as a rash and hopeless enterprise, and boasted they would compel the Allies to abandon the siege without striking a blow. But the Allies were not to be deterred by these threatening predictions; and on the 13th of August the city was invested, on one side by Prince Eugene, and on the other by the Prince of Orange-Nassau. The Duke of Marlborough with the main army covered the siege. Both parties, in expectation of the greatest obstinacy and resolution, had concentrated upon Lisle all the strength and talent of their armies. The fame of the siege attracted illustrious strangers to the spot, among whom were the King of Poland, and the Landgrave of Hesse, to share in the dangers and the glory of so bold an enterprise.

On the 22nd N.S. the trenches were opened, and for sixteen days the besiegers continued to batter the town with 100 pieces of cannon. A large breach in the wall was effected, and the ditch almost filled with the ruins. On the 7th of September preparations were made for storming the counterscarp, which was carried, but with considerable loss; the enemy having kept up a tremendous fire, and destroyed great numbers by the springing of mines. During all this time, as the writer of the diary has already informed us, the French continued to amuse the covering army of the allies with marches and counter-marches, and feints of attack. But they had no real intention to engage; their object was to fatigue the troops, and retard the siege.

Perceiving this, the Duke of Marlborough caused entrenchments to be thrown up in front of the army, which secured them against any sudden surprise; and permitted detachments to be sent occasionally to the camp before Lisle. One of these parties was sent under Major Blackader, who had the honour to command at the attack on the Tenaille, the 12th of September, O.S. Of this assault he has given a more than ordinary interesting and lively account.

★★★★★★

September 11. Ordered on command this afternoon with 400 grenadiers, to go upon some attack at the siege. I was easy and calm, committing myself to God. This is no surprise to me, for I have been laying my account with it; for since the commencement of the siege, (though our regiment was not there,) I have had constant impressions that I should have share of some attack or other before it ended. So it is God that commands me there. I take the order from him, and not the brigade-major. We were so late in arriving, that the attack is deferred till tomorrow, and we are sent to Marquett Cloyster to lodge all night. We lay down upon the beds prepared for the soldiers that my be wounded upon the attack; and probably, by tomorrow at this time, may of us may be lying here groaning with wounds and broken bones.

In the morning (Sabbath) I was serious, in view of the hot and dangerous service we are to be employed on at night. Yet I was very easy still, supplicating grace to do my duty every way, and believing I may be as safe as in my own chamber. We got orders that we are to attack the counterscarp. I went into one of the chambers of the Cloister alone, and took out my Bible and read over several comfortable promises, such as Joshua i. 9. 2 Samuel vui. 6. 14. 1 Chron. v. 20. Psalm xviii. xxxii. 7, 8. Ix. 24. Isaiah xl. 29, 30, 31. xli. 10. 13, 14. xlii. to the 5th verse. I sung the 91st Psalm, when I had done, and was walking up and down, I cast my eyes upon the chimney-piece. There was a coat-of-arms, and the motto *deus fortitudo mea,* (God is my strength.) I laid hold of that, and was strengthened, and encouraged myself in the Lord.

We marched into the trenches about twelve o'clock. There my thoughts were not so distinct, being fatigued, and my spirits dissipated. I went up and down to see where our attack was to be. Prince Alexander of Wirtemberg came in about four, made the dispositions, and gave us our orders. When he posted me, he bade me speak to the grenadiers, and tell them that the Duke of Marlborough and Prince Eugene expected they would do as they had always done—chase the French; and that it was better to die there, than to make a false step. I answered, "I hope we shall all do our duty;" so he shook hands with me, and went away.

Near seven, the signals being given by all our cannon and bombs going off together, I gave the word upon the right. *Grenadiers, in the name of God attack!* Immediately they sprung over the trenches, and threw their grenades into the counterscarp; but they fell into some confusion. I then ordered out fifty more to sustain them, and went out myself, and in a little time I got a shot in the arm. I felt that the bone was not broken; and all the other officers being wounded, I thought it my duty to stay still awhile, and encourage the grenadiers to keep their warm post. About a quarter of an hour afterwards, the fire continuing very hot, I got another shot in the head. I then thought it was time to come off. Both these shots were so mercifully directed, that there is not a bone broken; and I still say, notwithstanding these two wounds, that God put a hedge round about me, and gave his angels charge over me. The nice ordering of the bullets to touch there, and go no deeper, is to me a clear proof of it; and that he only wounds to make me a greater monument of mercy and kindness. I had a great deal of trouble to get out of the trenches in three hours space. I was mercifully provided for at night with a good bed, a house, and good company. I rested well, although my wounds broke out and bled in the night.

September 13. Most of this day was taken up with visits; our kind officers coming to see me. I wrote to my wife; the Lord support and comfort her, and make her thankful for his goodness to me. Next day I rode to Menin in very good health, and very easy. I am well provided with good quarters, an excellent physician, and expert surgeon. Lord, be thou my physician; they mercies are great to me; for most of the other officers that were with me, are now lying groaning *with broken bones.*

September 15. Our regiment marched through this town. Still visited by our kind officers, and my wounds easy.

September 17. I was sent for to see an officer who was on the attack with me, who is very weak, and lying in great torment. Oh how thankful should I be that I am so tenderly dealt with. Next day I was sent for again to see the same gentleman, but ere I got there he was dead. May the Lord be a father to his poor wife and children.

September 20. There are more of our officers come in wounded at this late action down the country, where God's goodness has been very great to us in giving us victory, though they were more than two to one. He has been peculiarly merciful to our regiment; there is not a man killed or wounded that was with it, except one officer who had his finger shot through.

✶✶✶✶✶✶

The action here alluded to was the battle and victory of Wynendale, gained on the 17th O.S. by a detachment from the duke's army.

In this action was Colonel Preston, with a detachment of the Cameronian Regiment.[2] Its object was to hinder the enemy from intercepting a convoy of ammunition and British troops which were landed at Ostend for the use of the siege. To prevent this communication, the French had laid the greater part of the country between Ostend and Nieuport under water, by cutting the dykes at Leffinghen. All their arts, however, proved fruitless; and during the action at Wynendale the convoy marched undisturbed, and in a few days reached the camp before Lisle. In this engagement, the Confederates had not more than 6000 men, while the enemy was computed at nearly 24,000. The loss of the former was about 900, and of the latter above 6000.

******

September 21. My wound is not at all painful, considering the place where it is, the elbow, where the roots of the tendons and ligaments of the hand and fingers are collected.

September 22-25. Continuing quiet and easy; though this day I have had more pain in my wound than for several days. They have made a small incision, and enlarged the wound in my head lest matter should lodge about it; and because it runs more than they would have it.

September 26. Sabbath. All night and all this day there is nothing but noise and hurry of marching. The army is going through this town, down the country again towards Bruges, (to repulse the French who were making another attempt to cut off communication with Ostend.) Probably there may be another action in a few days. This campaign has still a strange drumly aspect; our enemies are compassing us about, while we are wasting ourselves before the town. Oh Lord, be upon our side; let our extremity be thy opportunity. My wounds are mending well, and I have still many people coming to visit me.

October 2. My condition is less sad than many others that I see in this town. Lord, sanctify thy providence to those poor creatures, officers and soldiers, who are lying here under thy hand wounded. I cannot be thankful enough that I recover so well and have so little pain, considering that, by the wound in my arm, several tendons are broken and bruised; yet I have the use of my hand and fingers as well as I could desire. An unhappy accident has fallen out in the regiment.

October 5. I was calm and serene through the day, but at night put

---

2. Lediard, vol. ii.

out of order by a dismal melancholy object in the same house with me—a poor gentleman who is wounded, and has gone perfectly mad and furious, and is forced to be tied. He blasphemes God in his fits, and is a most terrible instance of the judgement of God.

October 6. The poor creature is growing worse and worse; he tears open all his wounds, continues to blaspheme, and is likely to die so. It is a dreadful and heart-rending spectacle.

October 19. God is the hearer of prayer. He heals the diseases and distempers both of soul and body. I have had sweet experience of both. He sweetens my temper by his grace into a thankful contented frame, and he eases the pains of my body also, for I have been in trouble by the toothache. I was directed to the use of means, and I take this as much from God as if he had healed me with his hand, or as Christ did to poor sinners in the days of his flesh on earth.

★★★★★★

While the major continued at Menin he was attacked by a malignant fever with inflammation, which however did not prove dangerous. His wounds being perfectly cured, he began to think of rejoining the regiment, and on the 13th of November he returned to Lisle. He says:—

> Should I be afraid to go back, where I have one of the greatest preservations of my life? It is my duty; and I will go, trusting to that promise, *I will never leave thee nor forsake thee.* The very sight of Lisle, instead of fear, should stir me up to songs of praise to my great Deliverer.

By this time Lisle had surrendered, having sustained an obstinate siege of two months, and presented difficulties which nothing but the greatest intrepidity and perseverance could have overcome. The citadel, however, held out two months longer, and did not capitulate until the 10th of December. While these operations were going on, the enemy began to annoy the Confederates in a different quarter: finding it impossible to intercept convoys from Ostend, they laid siege to Brussels, which was invested by the Elector of Bavaria, and resolutely defended by General Pascal the Commandant, who compelled the Elector to abandon the siege with the loss of 3000 men. This sudden retreat of the besiegers was unexpected, but occasioned by the intelligence that the Duke of Marlborough and Prince Eugene had passed the Scheldt, and were on their march to relieve the city.

The passage of the Scheldt was deemed an extraordinary feat, the banks being strongly fortified with lines which had cost the enemy nearly three months in erecting. But the Allies conducted their march with such secrecy and expedition, that they crossed the river in a moonlight night, while the French were sleeping securely in their entrenchments. When the alarm was given in the morning, their only thought was to provide for their safety, and setting fire to their huts and barracks they fled with precipitation. The Confederates hung upon their rear, and pursued them till dark, dispersing and killing vast numbers of them. The duke went to Brussels, and Prince Eugene returned to the siege, which he had the honour to conclude by the capitulation of the citadel. The surrender of Lisle was speedily followed by the reduction of Ghent, the abandonment of Bruges, and the retreat of the enemy within their own territories, which closed the important transactions of this campaign. Major Blackader's regiment, it appears, was on the expedition to the Scheldt, though he himself was not with them, being yet unable to undergo much fatigue.

★★★★★★

October 14. Things look rather with a dark and melancholy aspect at present, and we know not well what hand to turn to. Our regiment got sudden orders to march away, and there is great appearance of action quickly.

October 16. I went out in the afternoon and viewed the breach in this town, and the place where I got my wounds. The goodness of God to me is very great. It was by his mercy that I was not killed or wounded this day by a cannon-ball from the citadel, while walking in a street where I did not apprehend danger. The bullet came hard by, and battered upon the wall close beside me. They mark expressly at officers. Oh Lord, let me not forget thy mercies. I would have had no peace to have been wounded in this manner, where I had no call. We have got the agreeable news this afternoon that we have beat the French from the Scheldt, though we have not yet the particulars.

October 17. Our good news is confirmed. The French have made but very little opposition to us in passing the Scheldt. Help us, Lord, to improve this victory to better purpose than we have done several others, both as Christians and as soldiers, for we have failed in both. Thou lettest not our foes triumph over us, though they compassed us about like bees, and boasted they would famish and starve us here.

October 18. Our regiment came into the town this evening. This success that we have got is the Lord's doing, and wonderful in our eyes. The French have been fortifying these posts on the Scheldt these two months, and made them so strong that they boasted they would starve us; yet the Lord hath so taken heart and hand from them, that they suffered us to pass at all the places we attempted, without opposition.

October 20. In the afternoon, I went out alone to the place where I got my wound, and desired to offer up the sacrifice of praise to God for my merciful deliverance, with a thankful heart.

October 24. Kept as a day of thanksgiving and joy for beating the French from the Scheldt, and relieving Brussels. The duke never fails to give thanks after victory and success. But these things are mocked and ridiculed in our army. I usually observe, that the greatest Atheists among us despond most, and are most sunk when things go cross.

October 26. I took a resolution to go down the country with the first escort I can get, and made all ready accordingly. On the morrow we were surprised with the agreeable accounts that the citadel had hung out the white flag, and they are capitulating. We did not expect it so soon. God is very kind to us, and his Providence has been wonderfully favourable to us this campaign, so as to be taken notice of even by the gracious creatures in the army. On the 29th I went into the citadel, and saw the interview between two great men. Prince Eugene and Marshal Boufflers. I thought it all ceremony and compliment, and no reality.

October 30. I left Lisle; desiring to be very thankful for the goodness and mercy I have met with.

★★★★★★

The major was now on his return to Holland, by way of Oudenard, Dendermond, and Antwerp. On the 1st of December he left Courtray, and came to Oudenard. Here he reviewed with emotions of gratitude the field of battle. Next day he continued his journey to Alost, where he arrived very late. The town was so full, that he and his escort were almost obliged to lie in the streets, and could get no other accommodation than "a sort of a lodging among the canaille in a soldier's house." On the 3rd he arrived at Dendermond; and in two days came to Antwerp. On the 6th he set out by water to Rotterdam, which he reached on the 8th, and was cordially welcomed by all his friends.

Chapter 15

Campaign Eighth, 1709

The most distinguished achievements of the Allies this year were the reduction of Tournay one of the strongest towns in Flanders; the Battle of Malplaquet or Blaregnies; and the recovery of Mons. The campaign did not open until the summer was far advanced, owing to the extreme backwardness of the season and the negotiations for peace, which proved ineffectual.

Major Blackader did not leave Rotterdam until the middle of March. He was in the covering army at the siege of Tournay, and present at the Battle of Malplaquet; and from the great loss of officers sustained at this latter place, he was promoted to the rank of lieutenant colonel. Proposals for his advancement, it would appear, were made before the opening of the campaign, but more by the instigation of friends than his own desire; for his honours were urged upon him, and always shunned rather than sought. In reference to this he observes:—

★★★★★★

January 4. I went to court this morning, and spoke to the duke about *something* that others rather push me to, than I have any great bensel for myself. I bless God who makes me so easy. I have more already than I deserve. I am never troubled with ambitious thoughts of rising and growing great. I should be very unthankful if I were not well content with my lot. I leave all to the disposal of Providence. *Man's heart deviseth his ways, but the Lord directeth his steps.*

January 9. Extremely cold weather. Thankful for so many of the comforts and accommodations of life which I have this severe season.

February 9. Now the time is coming about that I must be thinking on another campaign, to launch out again into new dangers—new fatigues and difficulties. If I look to them upon this side. That now I am growing old, strength and natural endowments not so vigorous as before, this would make me melancholy, but I look, by faith, to the other side; God is the strength of my life, he is my shield and buckler, my fortress and my high tower. When young men *faint and fail, they that wait upon the Lord shall renew their strength.* His grace is still sufficient; I trust to this as my only refuge, my prop and plight-anchor.

February 28. The severity of the storm still hinders our going up to Ghent. Here we enjoy every comfort, while others are pinched with excessive cold and want. Lord pity them, and make us grateful. [1]

March 12. Making ready to go away. I observe Providence seemed to point out several ways of our going up to Flanders, and has still disappointed these again and stopped us.

March 14. This day we left Rotterdam. Good accommodation in the yacht.

March 16. We came safe to Sas, and next night arrived at Ghent. No sooner were we come off the water, than a great storm came on which continued all night. Here I joined the regiment; and was busy going about making visits.

March 26. I dined with the general; but I find there are temptations in great men's company that much overbalance all the advantage we can get from their goodwill.

April 15. I went upon command this day, and got pretty well through. I was well accommodated at night, considering circumstances, for the poor soldiers had nothing but the heavens above them, and it was a very cold night.

May 11. There was a talk of peace, but now we hear it is all blown up, and we are making ready for a vigorous campaign. I was employed all the morning, from five o'clock, in exercising the regiment.

---

1. This is said to have been the severest winter then remembered. The frost was so intense, that in less than twenty-four hours, rivers were congealed so as to bear loaded waggons; the horses feet were frozen to the ground; most of the cattle, sheep, and birds perished. Great quantities of snow fell, and the storm continued for three months. A backward season, and a general scarcity was the consequence. *Somerville's History.*

May 15. Sabbath. Taking a review of my last campaign. God has been the hearer of prayer to me, both for the public and for myself. The hopes of peace increase again. Lord, send peace and truth together.

May 25. All the news this day say that the peace is blown up: That the French king refuses to sign the preliminaries. This makes me thoughtful and dejected. Yet I hope it shall be for the confusion of that tyrant, if God harden his heart to reject peace. It is also talked that he is plagued, as Herod was, with vermin, (Acts xii. 23.) and it will be a just judgement, for he has permitted divine attributes to be asserted to him on several occasions. I had entertained some hopes that I should not dwell any more in the tents of wickedness; but now that peace is set aside, it makes me serious in the view of launching out again into new storms. The will of the Lord be done.

June 6. I have been busy about the regiment, and going among several of our generals. This morning we marched out of the garrison.

******

The Confederate Army, to the number of 110,000 men, had now assembled between Courtray and Menin. As the French were strongly posted in their neighbourhood, some detachments, in which Major Blackader's Regiment appears to have been, were sent out to reconnoitre and examine the enemy's camp. The position being deemed too advantageous to render an attack practicable, the siege of Tournay was instantly resolved upon. The troops decamped at night without beat of drum, and as the resolution had been kept secret, they were surprised to find themselves, next day, under the walls of Tournay, which they invested without giving the enemy time to reinforce the garrison.

******

June 10. We have here the best army that ever we had in this country; and if God be the Captain of our host, it will give us weight, and strength, and success. We have two, perhaps, the best generals in the world; but we ought not to trust in prince's nor in men's sons. We had a fatiguing march which continued from five in the morning till five at night, and very bad roads.

June 16. We marched yesternight at eight o'clock, all night; a wearisome fatiguing march till four o'clock this day. We are also much surprised and disappointed, for we believed all the night that we were marching straight up to attack the French army, or to take some pass upon them, so as to oblige them to move and quit their strong retrenchments. But instead of that, we are marching straight to Tournay, and investing it to besiege it. For my own share I would more heartily have gone to attack the enemy, and was hopeful God would have delivered them into our hands. I wish our generals had seconded Providence, when he gave us such favourable opportunity. We boast of 170 battalions, and 280 squadrons. It my be as in Gideon's case, this is too many for God to work by, lest we be proud and say. Our great army brought us deliverance. I got very good accommodation at night in a cottage.

June 20. This morning again vexed with the immorality and scandals committed by some in our society. I immediately punished them so far as military law allows. I know I get ill-will among many of the officers for this way of dealing; but I will glory in it. I bless God I hate no man's person, it is only their vices. Lord, give me zeal for thee, and let not passion, or humour, or any thing of self mix with it. I went in the afternoon to view Tournay with some company, pretty near their guards, and they fired some cannon at us.

June 28. Taken up about securing ourselves here in our post, wherein I thought I observed too much anxiety and care. I would not neglect any necessary care or means; only I would keep my mind easy. If the Lord watch not over us, all our guards are vain; and we have this promise. That his angel encamps round about those that fear him. I was busy, and abroad late at night posting guards. It is really unnatural judgementlike weather; heaven frowning upon us, threatening famine. I rode out in the afternoon with company to see the siege. They fired some cannon at us, and one of their bullets lighted within a few yards of me: but I look upon nothing as coming by chance.

June 30. This day twelvemonth was the battle of Oudenard, a day never to be forgotten by me. I kept at home all day, serious and meditating on the goodness of God.

July 1. Quietly employed about the regiment. Too late in company, and falling hot in debate and dispute. Oh where shall I enjoy the benefit of good company, that may do me good and not evil I desire now in every debate to be found on the side of truth, religion, and virtue. Long ago I used to dispute *pro* and *con.*, for argument's sake; but it is not right. By taking always the side against sin, vice, and error, zeal is strengthened.

July 8. I went this evening through the trenches. I bless God who preserves me in my outgoings and incomings. On the one hand, I desire not to value my life more, or to think dangers greater than they are; but, on the other hand, I would not let mercies and deliverances, even the smallest, pass stupidly without taking notice of them, as the most part do. Involved all night in a multitude of promiscuous company. But they put the conversation on such a footing, either by swearing, profane talking, bantering, or some impiety or other, that I can take little part in it. To reprove would be needless, and to join them is sinful.

July 17. There has been an attack made on the town these two nights; and this morning (Sabbath) we got an alarm just before our sermon began, at the time of singing the psalm. It came to nothing; but we had no sermon all day.

July 19. Yesterday our recruits and officers from Scotland came up; and this day I was busy in dividing them, which prospered well. I am always glad when my companions are kept from kindling and clashing together from selfishness, for self-interest, as the proverb says, makes *Homo Homini lupus.*

July 20. This day I have taken home an old servant who had been wandering through Spain, Portugal, and France, these five years; and Providence has at last brought him back to my hand like the prodigal. We are now masters of Tournay, (the town,) and they are going to put on new regiments to the siege of the citadel, which probably will bring the next siege of a town to our door. But I am not anxious about any of these things. No general can send me till Providence sign the order.

July 24. Day appointed by public orders as a thanksgiving for the reduction of Tournay. I went into the town and had another preservation, for a cannon-ball grazed just before me; but fortunately I saw it bounding ere it came my length; so I stopped and it passed close by me.

August 9. We were reviewed by these two great men, the Duke of Marlborough and Prince Eugene. All went very well. Our regiment appeared in good order and full.

August 18. Our siege (he observes in a letter, of this date,) goes on slowly, and in the dark underground. I have not yet been near it, and need not wish it over except for the sake of the public; for when it is over our fatigue will probably begin, if a cessation of arms prevent not. But I cannot with any ground flatter you with that, for indeed I know nothing of the matter, either for or against; and they that are much more conversant with great men than I, and think they know their secrets know as little. I pray the Lord send it in his own good time; for these countries have much need of it. There is a great mortality among the boors through the country, occasioned, no doubt, by the famine, and scarcity, and unwholesome food they are forced to eat. And as pestilence often treads upon the heels of famine, so we are getting melancholy, and alarming accounts of the plague being in several places in Germany, and some say in France.

August 19. On command these two days, but easy. My time was divided between my duty and charitable offices, for there are in this castle above fifty poor boors sick, and starving for hunger. I assisted them as much as I could, and I bless God who gives me a heart to do it.

******

These charitable offices, and the nature of his command, are explained more at large in a letter.

Sabbath, August 21.

I went out upon command on Thursday last. It is the first I have had since the business of Lisle, which is now very near a twelvemonth. It was an easy post. I was in a castle guarding the horses of the army grazing, and stayed there two days. I had not a British man with me, which I was very well pleased with; for, indeed, I think them, generally speaking, the worst company in the army. They have a heaven-daring boldness and effrontery in sin beyond other men, without any shame; and that impudent pertness in wickedness, and boasting of it, is the humour I most abhor of any thing. I lived very pleasantly and quietly with two Prussian captains. But there I had melancholy spectacles of misery before my eyes every moment. The boors, about a hundred of them, had retired in there for shelter and protection; and of these there were between fifty and sixty lying sick, by reason of the unwholesome food they are obliged to use. The want of bread is alarming. I assisted them what I could; I caused buy bread about a *pistole's* worth, and distributed among them; and I gave my little bottle of orange-water to some that were worst. I thought it the best bestowed of all that I have made use of yet. There is great reason to fear a plague in this country. War, famine, and pestilence do frequently follow each other. But for all these things, we are wickedly hardened in sin, and will keep back nothing which our vanity and lusts crave, to relive our fellow-creatures. The great ones of the earth will set themselves to fight against Providence, and against nature, and when the had of God is lifted up they will not see it. But when his judgements are on the earth, the inhabitants therof shall learn righteousness.

The Lord preserve and bless you.

I am thine.

J.B.

To Madam Blackader, care of Sergeant J. Reid, of Colonel Preston's Regiment, Ghent.

******

August 23. The citadel capitulated this morning.

******

The siege of the town, as we have seen, lasted about three weeks, but the citadel stood out a month longer. From the regularity of its fortifications, and the strength of its outworks, it was reckoned one of the strongest in Europe. The progress of the besiegers was much retarded by being obliged to adopt the slow and laborious method of sapping; the enemy having wrought all the ground into mines, which rendered it unsafe to approach from the hazard of explosion. Every step they took was under the apprehension of being blown into the air. Hostilities were carried on chiefly under ground, and in total darkness. In countermining, it frequently happened that adverse parties met and fought with their shovels, spades, and pickaxes. In these subterraneous attacks, the besiegers had to contend with new and appalling dangers. They were sometimes crushed by the falling in of the earth, or destroyed by the springing of the mine.

Great numbers perished in this manner. Above 400 were killed in a single explosion. Sometimes they were inundated with water which the garrison let in upon them, or suffocated with the smoke of straw or hemp and gunpowder. Yet nothing could repress the gallantry and perseverance of the assailants. They confronted these hidden terrors with the greatest resolution, and made themselves masters of the citadel although they had lost, during the siege, above 4000 men.

In the reduction of the town Major Blackader was not employed, though occasionally a spectator. He was stationed with his regiment in the neighbourhood, where they had remained peaceably in their camp above two months. They were soon, however, to be called into activity, and sustain a part in one of the most obstinate and bloody battles that had occurred in the whole course of the war.

Upon the surrender of Tournay, the next deliberation was, either to besiege Mons, or force the enemy to an engagement; both of which took place, and in both the Allies were successful. Marshal Villars, suspecting their design, had advanced with the French army as far as Malplaquet in the vicinity of Mons, where he had chosen a camp of great natural strength which was augmented by several lines and trenches. Each of his wings was defended in front by a deep hickwood, the left being covered by the wood of Sart, and the right by that of Lagniere. The centre was posted on the open ground in the middle, with the cavalry behind. This position was so advantageous, that to hazard an attack was reckoned a very rash and dubious enterprise. The Allies, however, made the attempt, and after an engagement which lasted nearly six hours, they purchased the name of victory at the expense of 18,000 men; the loss of both sides being nearly equal. The two armies lay for two days in their camps, adjoining each other; the Duke of Marlborough having deferred the attack, in expectation of some detachments which he had ordered from Tournay, and the blockade of Mons. These joined him on the morning of the battle. We now return to the narrative in the diary, which is given at some length, and shews with what ardour and animation, troops inured to conquest will face the most discouraging obstacles.

✶✶✶✶✶✶

August 24. We marched (from the camp near Tournay) this morning at three o'clock. We know not where we are going; some say to besiege Mons, some say to the French lines. Go where we will, I commit all to God. We had a bad march by reason of the rainy weather. It was a bad night, and I was ill accommodated, lying in a soldier's tent wet and cold. But I have no cause to complain, considering the good accommodation I have had hitherto all this campaign. In two days, and after a long march, we encamped near Mons. We expected to have rested a day, and prepared ourselves for the siege; but we have got sudden orders to march, the French Army appearing near to us on their march, so we expect to come to action. I pray for strength and courage to discharge my duty in my post. We lay at our arms all this night.

August 27. Expecting a battle tomorrow. I am no way afraid; I trust not to my own strength or parts, but the Lord of hosts; through him I shall do valiantly. Next morning we marched in line and order of battle. But about ten o'clock, we got notice that the French were gone off again, and that their design was not to fight. I was uneasy at this as a disappointment. This was not out of vanity to shew myself, for God knows I have no reason to boast of self.

August 29. The enemy being now near, we marched suddenly. In the afternoon they came in view, and our line of battle was formed and posted. They are in strong ground. They raised batteries, and played upon us with their cannon. There was not a place in the whole line so much exposed as where our regiment, aid two or three more stood; and we had considerable loss. Many a cannon-ball came very near, but He gave his angels charge over me. *Thou art my shield and buckler.* This I trusted in, and repeated several times when I saw the cannonballs coming straight towards me, as I thought; but the goodness of God let none of them touch me. This night was an unpleasant uneasy night to our regiment, for they have wanted bread these five days, and are faint. It was a cold wet night, and we lay at our arms. I laid me down and slept sound, for God sustained me; and I am not afraid of ten thousands that set themselves against us round about.

August 30. Next morning we expected to have been saluted by break of day with their batteries, as last night; and we laid our account, if we stayed upon the same spot of ground, with having a third of our regiment killed and wounded, for the general would not allow us to draw back our men a little way behind a rising ground that covered us. But God in mercy prevented us; for the enemy had drawn off their cannon from that place, and did not trouble us all the day. In the afternoon an extraordinary thing happened. The French officers and ours, as if it had been concerted between them, went out between the two camps, and conversed with one another, and called for their acquaintances, and talked together as friends, as if there had been a cessation of arms; but it was broken off by the generals on both sides. I was unwell all night by reason of the cold, and bad diet I had got these days bygone.

We have got an order this night, that we are to attack the enemy tomorrow by break of day. I will both lay me down in peace, and sleep, for thou, Lord, only makest me to dwell in safety. I never was more serene and easy. Early in the morning, (the 31st) we attacked the enemy in their camp, a strong camp, and strongly entrenched by two days working. We fought, and by the mercy and goodness of God, have obtained a great and glorious victory. The battle began about seven o'clock and continued till near three in the afternoon. It was the most deliberate, solemn, and well ordered battle that ever I saw,—a noble and fine disposition, and as nobly executed. Every man was at his post; and I never saw troops engage with more cheerfulness, boldness, and resolution. In all the soldiers' faces appeared a brisk and lively gaiety which presaged victory. The Lord of Hosts went forth at our head as Captain of our host, and the army followed with a daring cheerful boldness, for we never doubted but we would beat them.

Providence ordered it so, that our regiment was no farther engaged than by being cannonaded, which was, indeed, the most severe that ever our regiment suffered, and by which we had considerable loss. But the soldiers endured it without shrinking, very patiently, and with great courage. For my own part I was nobly and richly supplied, as I have always been on such occasions, with liberal supplies of grace and strength, as the exigencies of the day called for. I never had a more pleasant day in my life. I was kept in perfect peace; my mind stayed, trusting in God. All went well with me; and not being in hurry and hot action, I had time for plying the throne of grace, sometimes by prayer, sometimes by praise, as the various turns of Providence gave occasion; sometimes for the public, sometimes for myself I did not seek any assurance of protection for my life; I thought it enough to believe in general, to depend with resignation, and hang about his hand.

Our regiment with some others, were honoured in particular to do some very good service, by marching up, and manning a retrenchment which the enemy had left. And there we sustained our own horse, which were pushed by the French horse, and might have been of dangerous consequence, had not the foot sustained them. Not unto us, Oh Lord, be thy glory, but to thyself. It was not our sword or our bow, but it was the Lord's doing.

The French foot did not behave themselves well. They soon quitted their retrenchments; but the horse stood more stiffly to it. I did not expect to see a cowed army fight so well. I believe the loss may be about equal on both sides. It was as bloody a battle as has been fought, either this war or the last. God is working his holy ends, sweeping off sinners in both armies from the face of the earth. But God be blessed for this, that though he be angry with us, and mowing down our carcases thick on the fields, yet he is not with our enemies; he is angry with them too, and laying their carcases upon the face of the earth. He is staining their pride, for they are a vainglorious nation. How would they insult and boast if they were suffered to beat us as we do them. The earth could not bear them.

September 1. This morning I went to view the field of battle to get a preaching from the dead, which might have been very edifying, for in all my life, I have not seen the dead bodies lie so thick as they were in some places about the retrenchments, particularly at the battery where the Dutch Guards attacked. For a good way I could not go among them, lest my horse should tread on the carcases that were lying, as it were, heaped on one another. I was also surprised to see how strong they had made their camp. They had a breastwork before them, round about like the rampart of a town, to fire over. The Dutch have suffered most in this battle of any. Their infantry is quite shattered; so that it is a dear victory. The potsherds of the earth are dashed together, and God makes the nations a scourge to each other to work his holy ends, by sweeping sinners off the face of the earth.

It is a wonder to me the British escape so cheap, who are the most heaven-daring sinners in this army. But God's judgements are a great depth. He has many arrows in his quiver, and is not tied to our times and ways. We marched back at night to our camp which we left on the 29th. I bless the Lord who brings me back in peace, while the carcases of others are left as a prey in the fields to the beasts and birds. *A thousand shall fall at thy side, and ten thousand at thy right hand, but it shall not once come near to thee.* That Psalm has many times been made out to me literally, every promise in it; and shall be, I trust in God.

★★★★★★

In a letter to his wife, written the day after the battle, he gives some account of the loss the regiment sustained in officers, and mentions some others of the English Regiments that had suffered.

September 1, Thursday.
I doubt not but this has been a time of great anxiety to you, but now I send you a new Ebenezer, and one of the greatest of my whole life. Yesterday we fought a battle, and by the great goodness of God have obtained a great victory.—It has

not been a cheap battle to the army, especially the Dutch foot, who have suffered much. We attacked them in strong entrenchments. The most that we suffered was by their cannon. Our loss is considerable, but the greatest is poor Colonel Cranston. He was killed by a cannon-ball, (sitting at the head of the regiment,) shot in at the left breast, and out at the back: He spoke not a word. Captain Shaw also is killed, his thigh-bone being broken; and also Ensign Inglis. You will have heard that Captain Lawson, and Lieutenant Simpson were wounded two days ago at another cannonading, when we came up first to this camp; for our regiment happened to be posted in a place which was most exposed to their cannon of any in the army. Lawson's is very slight. It is a contusion on the chin, but no bones broken. Simpson's is in the body, but not dangerous.

Ensign Burnet also got a more dangerous wound in the neck, which I am afraid of; and Lieutenant Cockburn is shot though the body. Sergeant Wilson is wounded in the arm. I have three men killed. We buried the Colonel, Captain Shaw and Inglis yesternight at the colours. It is put upon you to prepare Mrs. Cranston, and to give her the doleful news. Everybody sympathises tenderly with her, and none, I am sure, more than myself. None is more universally regretted than he.

My dearest, what reason have we to adore the divine goodness who puts such songs of praise in our mouths, while others are employed in mournful lamentations and sorrow. Go as soon to her as you can, for she will be suspicious at not getting a letter with the first. We found a letter to her in his pocket, which he wrote that same morning I wrote the enclosed, but none of us could send it away. You are almost the only wife in the regiment who will not be in tears and anxiety, either of grief or concern about their friends and husbands. Let us have our hearts the more filled with thankfulness, and our mouths with praise to the God of our mercies, who gives us such signal and frequent deliverances.

For as busy a day as it was, and hot action, I never had a pleasanter in my life, for all was well with me.—The French stood stiffly to it, especially their horse, (they behaved well,) and repulsed ours several times; but our foot sustained our horse. Brigadier Lalo is killed, and poor Captain Monro. Argyle's and theirs have suffered most of the English, and the Guards. Lord

Tullibardin is killed, and Colonel Swinton, Colonel Holborn and his Lieutenant Colonel Hamilton, and their regiments are almost mined. Brigadier Douglas is ill wounded. In short, it has been a very dear victory, but it was a glorious day. The Lord of hosts went at our head as Captain of our host, and all the army followed with courage and resolution.

I never saw troops go on with more hearty briskness in my life. I cannot tell you what will be the fruit of our victory: I hope a lasting peace. We are now lying in the field of battle, and I have been this morning riding thorough the entrenchments, getting a very edifying preaching from the dead. In some places they are lying so thick that we cannot, for a good way, pass through without treading on them. We are going to march back this afternoon to our camp near Mons, from which we came before the battle. The Lord be with you, and make you thankful, and give you grace never to forget the last of August.

    I am thine.   J. B.

To Madam Blackader, care of Sergeant J. Reid,
of Colonel Preston's Regiment, Ghent.

The death of Colonel Cranston having opened a way for promotion, the major immediately waited upon the duke for that purpose, expressing himself, however, in his usual terms of indifference as to the success of his application.

******

September 2. I went this day to court to put in my claims for advancement in my turn. I commit all to God. I know promotion comes not from the east or the west. I leave myself in they hands, Oh Lord, to dispose of me as thou seest fit; Thou knowest what is best for me. If it be for they honour and glory, and my good, to keep me in this employment, and to raise me higher in it, no man will have leave to keep me from it. If thou hast ordered it otherwise, and if it be better for me to leave this trade, let them distribute their places among them as they please; I shall not seek them. Only guide me by thy counsel, and direct me what I should do. I depend upon thee, and through grace am very easy.

September 3. I went to court again, and found the generals and every body more favourable and friendly than I could have expected, who am not much in the practice of going to courts. It is God that gives me favour, and makes my ways prosperous.

September 4. This Sabbath is appointed to be kept a thanksgiving through the army for our victory. Alas, I fear it may be said of us as of Israel of old. *They sang his praise, but they soon forgot his mighty works, and tempted him.*

******

There is another letter to his wife of this date, written from Mons, which they were then preparing to invest.

> Sabbath, September 4.
>
> I hope by this time you have received mine of Thursday, the day after the battle, which, I trust, will turn your melancholy and anxiety into songs of praise, while many others are sobbing in the anguish of their spirits, with tears and lamentation.—I never had more reason to bless God, or was more signally delivered. He carefully kept all my bones, while the cannon-balls came so thick among us and swept away whole files of men, crushing them as one would crush a worm. I heartily sympathise with poor Mrs. Cranston. The Lord support and comfort her, and be *a father to the fatherless, and a husband to the widow.* That day has made many widows.
>
> I pray God, the fruit of all this may be his honour and glory, and a good peace. I believe our campaign may end with the siege of this town. We lay our account to be one of the besieging regiments, so that there is nothing in the world but one wave upon the back of the other. The just must live by faith. The Lord of Hosts is the God of battles, and has preserved me many a time there. He is also the God of sieges, and has preserved me as wonderfully there. I desire to put my trust in him. When you grow anxious and thoughtful, take my riddled hat and hang it up before you, and trust in God who hath delivered and doth daily deliver.
>
> As to my advancement, I shall say but little about it. I bless God I am very easy, go as it win. I am using the ordinary means, and have promises enough. If it be good for me, and for God's glory, I shall get it; if it be not so, I do not seek it, I have no business with it. It is a crisis in my life, as I hinted in mine before the battle; though I did not know how it would be, yet I had impressions that the campaign would take another turn, and would not be idle. This day was appointed to be a thanksgiving. We had sermon, and *feu-de-joie* at night. The Lord's peace rest

with thee.

I am thine, &c.					J.B.
To Madam Blackader, care of Sergeant J. Reid,
of Colonel Preston's Regiment, Ghent.

Notwithstanding his want of talents "in making his court to great men," his prospects of advancement were becoming more favourable. Several of his illustrious countrymen acted with great friendship towards him, and took an interest in his promotion; among others the gallant Earl of Orkney, as appears in the following letter.

Friday, September 9.
I have received yours of the 4th. The Lord has been very gracious both to you and me,—and you see it is not in vain to trust in him, *for in the Lord Jehovah is everlasting strength; there is none ashamed that trust in him.* What a mercy is it that providence did not pitch upon you to be the melancholy widow as others are, who stand so much in need of the sympathy of their friends, and that you are serving God cheerfully, lifted up in his ways, while others are sitting disconsolate and desolate.—Every day we have new funerals of some friend or other. Major Row died yesterday, who was a kind friend to me.

Lord Orkney told me today, that he had spoken in my favour about my advancement; I praise God I am kept very easy about this matter. My inclination stands in a kind of poise or balance, either as to my staying in, or leaving the army. What is most for God's glory and my good, let him do it. I trust that mercy and goodness, as it has done, shall follow me either the one way or the other. Give my humble service to poor Mrs. Cranston; if there be any thing she would have done, let her signify her mind to Captain Dickson. The Lord's presence, blessing and peace rest with you.

I am, &c.					J.B.
To Madam Blackader, care of Sergeant J. Reid,
of Colonel Preston's Regiment, Ghent.

He appears to have taken a kindly concern, and felt much sympathy for Mrs. Cranston in her melancholy situation, and wrote her about this time a very affectionate letter of condolence and consolation. And it is a most amiable trait of his character, that instead of a callous spectator of the sorrows of others, or forgetting their bereavements in the selfish contemplation of his own happy escape, he could thus own kindred with the unfortunate, and appropriate their distresses to himself. The letter itself is not preserved, but we have the reflections it suggested to his mind in the following to his wife.

Sabbath, September 11.

I have complied with your desire, with my own duty and charitable office, to write poor Mrs. Cranston. The Lord bless and sanctify the rod to her. And Oh what songs of praise have we to sing in extolling the Lord for his mercy to us, that he deals with us in quite another manner. He brings us in by mercy and goodness, and singular providences; working great salvation and signal deliverances for us, while he is scourging others with sharp rods. Oh let us be as a towardly kindly child, that needs not to be whipped into his duty; but that seeing the rod upon others, and shaking it over our heads, may be sufficient to bring us in to him. O let us serve him cheerfully, and have our hearts lifted up in his ways. Let us not be like the children of Israel who sung his praise, but soon forgot his wondrous works. But his grace must be sufficient for us, his strength must be perfected in our weakness. Through him we can do all things: Without him, nothing.

We have still the hopes of being free of the siege, by these regiments coming out of the garrison. The Providence of God is kinder to us than we could have expected, for we laid our accounts so firmly for the siege, that we thought nothing could put us by it. But kind Providence has fallen upon a way to prevent it. I can give you no farther information yet about my affair, but I am no way solicitous about it. I proposed to Colonel Preston, who is very much concerned for Mrs. Cranston, about advancement for her son, and he told me he had been thinking of the same thing, and that he resolves to propose it to the duke. But do not speak of this. I do not like to puff up anybody with empty promises; I had far rather do a favour, and speak nothing of it till it were done. I have had many letters from Scotland, from Dean of Guild Brown, Mrs. Balderstone, Mr. Carstairs, &c. The Lord's blessing and peace rest with you.

I am, &c.   J. B.

To Madam Blackader, care of Sergeant J. Reid,
of Colonel Preston's Regiment, Ghent.

Their expectations of being upon the siege of Mons were fortunately disappointed, other regiments being draughted from the garrison for that service. They were however employed in covering it.

******

September 9. How great is the goodness of God to us unworthy sinners! We laid our account to be on this siege; we thought we could not miss it; but kind Providence has found out a way to put it by us, by bringing so many regiments out of the garrisons. I desire to observe all these things, and see the loving-kindness of the Lord. We this day marched back to our post in the army for covering the siege.

******

While they continued in this camp, he wrote several letters to his wife, which we shall insert in their order, as the diary for this period contains nothing particularly interesting.

Wednesday, September 14.

I have no news since my last. I spoke to the duke yesterday about my advancement, and told him I did not like to importune his grace, for I depended entirely upon his word. He told me that I might do so. There is no help for these delays but patience. I am ready either to stay or go as Providence shall see best for me. I dare hardly own it in a public company that I am so easy; for they do not think a man deserves any post in the army, who either gives himself rest or any other about him, general or other, till he get what he is seeking. But as I do not look upon ambition to be any Christian virtue, so neither do I look upon that carking anxious care to be any greatness of mind, rather the contrary.

Faith is a grace to be exercised at all times, and on all occasions. It keeps the soul in its seat, in a sedate composed temper. The mind stayed on God is in peace; it makes no haste, but is patient.

Our regiment does not go to the siege unless new regiments are called for. This is a mercy we were not expecting, and God presents us daily with his mercies. But detachments may go from the army. I do not say this to frighten you, but the contrary, that we should humbly depend and trust on God, and rejoice that he puts us in a necessity of dependence; for we would gladly have all our enjoyments out of the reach of hazards and dangers. But it is not good for us that they be so; we may easily see, that when they are so we turn secure.

The weather begins now to be somewhat cold. I lie in my tent, for houses are difficult to be got; but I am very well, and lie very warm. This is my birthday, as I think; but the 12th is a day I remember more, and ought never to forget.

      I am thine.   J.B.

To Madam Blackader, care of Sergeant J. Reid,
of Colonel Preston's Regiment, Ghent.

           Monday, September 19.

Nothing new has occurred since my last, nor can I give you any further account of my affair. Let Providence work its work for me. I am satisfied that it is not greatness, nor any thing else in the world that can make us more happy. That gentleman, as you observe, may give us an edifying lesson on the vanity of ambition—how, in a moment, our designs and prospects may be extinguished, and vanish away. Happy they who have God for the portion of their inheritance and cup; they have a goodly heritage, and the lines fall to them in pleasant places.

The four garrison regiments are now yoked to this siege, and we give no more detachments from the army. The rainy weather makes the trenches a very uncomfortable post; yea, I find a tent begins to be a cold lodging. But I have reason to be very thankful for the good accommodation I have had all this campaign. I must change the day of writing, for we lie a day's journey from the duke's quarters. I am just now at his quarters, but only to make my bow. The Lord's peace rest with you.

      I am thine.   J. B.

To Madam Blackader, care of Sergeant J.Reid,
of Colonel Preston's Regiment, Ghent.

           Wednesday, September 21.

I received yours of the 16th. It troubles me much to find you are so indisposed, and that melancholy preys so much upon your spirits. I know you are more reasonable than to indulge yourself in it. But such is the composition of our machine, that these things do not depend upon us. We cannot keep our spirits in that temper and frame they should be in, or as we would have them. You are very sensible that none in the world have less reason than we to be melancholy. None have more reason to be cheerful, and to have their hearts lifted up in the ways of

God; for while he is writing bitter things to others, and giving them occasions of mournful and melancholy lamentation, he is compassing us about with new songs of deliverance. To that great deliverance he gave me at the battle, he has added this other, which indeed we could not have expected, *viz.* to keep us free from this siege, which I would have looked upon as ten times worse than the battle, for that is my nature.

Danger, though it be great, yet being soon over, and nothing in it to occasion anxiety of mind, seems to me a small thing in comparison of a constant tract of fatigue either of body or mind. The former rouses the spirits, the other sinks them. It is very probable that your room may be partly the occasion of it. But I am very well pleased, and desire you earnestly to change it if you can get a better, and get a more cheerful and heartsome lodging. Do as you please; you know I never was nice about these things, and indeed I have no very fashionable fancy about them. You will get the colonel's rooms, when we come into garrison, for 300 *gilders* in the winter. I think of keeping three horses in the garrison if I stay.

Our affair here begins to weary our patience. The duke seems to be uneasy at the pressing him to fill up the commissions, as if it were taking something from him; and he was never better trysted upon this head with any body than with me, for I hate as much to importune as he does to be importuned; and except when my friends push me and hector me to go, I never incline to go near the court; for I had always that bashfulness of nature, that I cannot endure to be where I think I am troublesome. Let others whose talent it is get places and posts by assurance and forwardness, I shall have mine by modesty or want them, for I cannot force nature. I know promotion comes not from the east nor from the west. It is He who has the disposing of our lot, who has promised, that neither *Grace, nor glory, nor any good thing, will be withheld from them that fear him.*

This winter probably will make you either a lieutenant-colonel's lady, or a farmer's wife; and I must say in your commendation, you are fit for either of them, which is more than I can say of myself. I hope Providence shall give a comfortable close to this campaign, and that there is not much of it now before our hand; and that he will give us a joyful meeting, with hearts filled with thankfulness and love to our kind benefactor. Remember me kindly to Mrs. Cranston. The colonel has spoken to the duke, and given in her son's name to be an ensign, and hope the duke will do it. Her friends are advising her rather to seek a pension from the queen than to take the widow's gratuity; but I humbly differ from them. The gratuity is a certain thing; she comes to it of course, and without any trouble. The other is uncertain, and depends upon interest and friends. Let her once enter herself into the first, and afterwards, if she can procure a better pension it is well; but a bird in hand is worth two in the bush.

I am thine.   J.B.

To Madam Blackader, care of Sergeant J. Reid,
of Colonel Preston's Regiment, Ghent.

Sabbath, September 25.

I received yours, and bless the Lord you are no worse. I entreat you not to give way to melancholy. Neither of us have reason for it, but much the contrary; and if grace were stronger, and sanctification more deeply rooted, it would be more our element to serve God with delight, aid more natural to us. We have great cause to be thankful that we missed this siege, for such judgement-like weather I have hardly seen in a camp. Just now it rains and blows so hard, that it is like to blow down all our tents about our ears. I have got the shelter of a house, which I reckon no small mercy in such weather; though it be but a sad house, for I am sitting in water at the fireside, which blows in; the soldiers having unthatched one side of it. However, I am very thankful for what I have.

If I can get time I shall answer Mrs. Cranston's letter. There seems to be a work upon her spirit—a sense of sin, and of the wrath of God contending for sin, and great doubting and fears as to mercy and pardon. I pray the Lord may carry it on with his spirit to be a saving work of grace, and make her flee to Christ.

Let me know as soon as you can what you design about a lodging. As yet it is not altogether certain whether Ghent will be our garrison. Some speak of Brussels; but it is more than a month to garrison time yet. We do not know how things will be. I have seen much of the vanity of far forethought projects, how they are ordinarily disappointed; so that as we are directed to seek our daily bread from day to day only, so I seek direction from day to day without grasping at long tracts of time. Now that the weather is broken, and the roads become very bad, and our horses harassed with foraging five or six miles, every thing looks like garrison, and every body longs for it. But the great ones of the earth will fight against Providence. I pray God to give a comfortable close to the campaign, and send peace and truth upon the earth. The Lord's presence be with you.

     I am thine.   J.B.

To Madam Blackader, care of Sergeant J. Reid,
of Colonel Preston's Regiment, Ghent.

           Wednesday, September 29.

I received yours yesterday. I am here in a village close by the rear of the army, on command guarding the train horses. I go home tomorrow, and I hope to have no more command this campaign. Now that you are in Mrs. Hamilton's lodgings, I hope your mutual company will divert each other. Give my humble service to her. I ordered you to drink our healths in a glass of wine as often as we do yours, which is twice a-day at least. It is a shame and a sin both that you should look lean after such a great campaign as this has been, when we in particular have been so mercifully dealt with. How would you look if the battle had been lost and your husband killed, when you grow lean upon victories and deliverances. I must shame you out of it. Do you want, or need you want any thing that may be for your good. I told you long ago that no detachments were to go from our army, and that I had got a cottage to lodge in. So all your grievances are redressed; pray grow fat again.

We have a report this morning (Friday) that the town is capitulating; and indeed we have not heard any firing all the night since yesterday afternoon. I know not what truth is in it, till I go to the army to hear farther. We hardly wish it to be over so soon, for fear we be employed at another siege. But I am glad for the sake of the public interest, and let Providence dispose of our particular concerns as seems good.

     I am thine.   J.B.

To Madam Blackader, care of Sergeant J. Reid,
of Colonel Preston's Regiment, Ghent.

******

This report of the surrender of Mons was rather premature, as it did not take place until the 12th of October. The siege lasted about a month, but the enemy were so much haunted by the terrors of Malplaquet, that they made no attempts to relieve it.

★★★★★★

September 12. Coming off command where I had the charge of 1200 horses. While in the fields I met with one of the greatest storms of hail and rain I have seen. Was surprised when I came home with the account of my Ensign's being killed this morning by another officer who is also ill wounded; they were both very drunk. God's judgements are just and righteous. Oh that men would take example when they see their comrades hung up in chains as terrible monuments of the divine displeasure against sin!

October 4. There is a report today that the French design to pay us another visit here. I do not believe it. Yet God may harden their hearts as he did Pharaoh's and his host to follow Israel into the Red Sea, that they might perish there. Be it as it will, Oh Lord, I put my trust still in thee.

October 7. Again we have got intelligence that the French are coming to attack us. The Lord plucked them out of our hand last day at the Battle of Tannier, and they are grown vain and insolent upon it; but he can humble their pride, and bring them down like the mire of the streets.

I was at court in the morning, and got promises, but I see nothing but delays in this affair. I know not how Providence will order it. I cannot cringe at a court, neither is it decent or becoming for a child of the house to be fawning upon the servants for a favour. A child of God should have a nobler spirit, and carry their suit straight to their Father in heaven, and make their court there; and then they need not cringe to any creature. Our heavenly Father knows what we stand in need of. I seldom go to court, (says he in a letter of this date) for I see it is to no purpose to importune; the duke stands impregnable against the solicitations of generals and colonels to fill up the vacancies, so what can such as I a poor obscure fellow do. Besides, I find that a constant plying and working about court and among generals, would but create an uneasiness and anxiety in my mind about these things; and I esteem serenity and contentedness to be a far greater blessing than all the posts they can bestow upon me.

October 12. Our alarm has turned to nothing, the town has capitulated. It is good news; Providence is very kind to us. I went to see the garrison march out, and Lord be blessed, that we have such a sight to see, and that sooner than we expected. They were a parcel of poor miserable creatures.

Thursday, October 13.

The French marched out of Mons yesterday. We are going to march, they say, on Monday, and I hope it shall not be long ere it please God to give us a comfortable meeting. Everybody is now leaving the army. The colonel goes away tomorrow. The duke has given him new promises this morning, that we shall get justice; but he has not signed the commissions yet, and perhaps it will cost a journey to the Hague ere it be done, which I shall be very unwilling to undertake, if I be not obliged to it. I think you had best go into the colonel's house now, as we may be down towards the end of next week. Cause provide forage, corn, and hay for my horses. I am busy now at the colonel's going away, about the regiment, and the recruiting officers, &c. I make no apology for my short letter, for you may be thankful you hear at all from a man of so much business.

I am thine. J.B.

To Madam Blackader, care of Sergeant J. Reid,
of Colonel Preston's Regiment, Ghent.

October 16. Sabbath. Yesterday we marched. Blessed be God that has put a comfortable close to this campaign. This day is appointed by the duke a thanksgiving for our taking of Mons, and the success of the campaign. I hope the Lord will bless the duke for his piety and gratitude. Some laugh at these things and many have taken this opportunity to leave the army. I believe indeed that God will be mocked by the generality of us. I beg grace to praise and magnify his name for the great things he has done me. With a heart filled with gratitude and love, let me never forget his goodness. We have all cause to bless him for his mercies, for it has been a very great campaign—two such strong considerable towns as Tournay and Mons taken, and a great victory; and with all this, it is a shorter campaign than any we have had this war.

Our fears have also been mercifully disappointed. For my part, I laid my account we should be hard put to it for scarcity, both for man and horse. I expected little less than famine. On the contrary, we had abundance of provisions. Neither my horses nor myself ever had so little fatigue. I have been but twice upon command, and have likewise had quarters in houses almost the whole time; so that I did not lie more than three weeks in my tent all the summer; whereby I got living more retiredly out of ill company. It is also to be remembered with great thankfulness, that we were also threatened with pestilence; for in all the villages the poor boors were lying starving and dying with the bad nourishment, and victuals they were obliged to eat. Yet God in mercy kept this infection out of the army.

October 17. I have now got my commission, and the charge of the regiment. I pray the Lord to take charge both of me and them, otherwise they will be very ill ordered. After three days march, we reached Ghent, where I had a happy meeting with my dear concern here. The Lord has brought me back in peace and safety, may he give us his presence and blessing.

October 24. Kept in continual hurry with business, and people about me. I am sure greatness must be a troublesome thing, when this small shadow of command I have is so troublesome.

November 1. My time almost wholly spent with company and business. I am so afraid of neglecting my duty, that I fear it will make me contract a carking careful temper. Company come thronging in upon me in the morning before I get retiring alone. I must rise earlier; for if my heart get a right set in the morning it possesses it all day, and keeps the world out.

Being now in winter-quarters, and much occupied with regimental affairs, the colonel passed the winter cheerful in his own mind, and prosperous in all his concerns.

Chapter 16

Campaign Ninth, 1710

The three months which the colonel passed in Ghent, previous to the regiment's leaving that garrison, were spent very agreeably, but without any remarkable occurrence. He was much in society, which he found here to be more gay, and less edifying than what he had been accustomed to at Rotterdam, and seems occasionally to have mingled in the fashionable amusements of the place; not however without regret, and reflections on his misspent time.

★★★★★8

January 31. The day soberly spent; but in the evening I went to hear a famous musician, where I was kept too late, and neglected better exercise. This made me somewhat uneasy; but I bless God that he keeps me from falling often into these snares.

★★★★★★

While in garrison he had several occasions to sit in the court-martial. This was always a melancholy duty. He expresses the greatest anxiety to *judge righteous judgement*, and if possible, to temper justice with mercy.

★★★★★★

February 14. In a court-martial all the afternoon, and I hope well directed in judgement. I sought light and guidance, for indeed in many cases we know not the right side from the wrong. Oh that my sentence may be such as thou dost approve, and such as would come from they righteous tribunal of equity!

March 15. This day is appointed to be kept by our garrison, as it is in England, for fasting and humiliation. I was in a serious composed frame, relying upon God for strength, courage, and every thing else that I need to furnish me out for a new campaign.

March 23. We had expectations of a peace; but these hopes grow less. Busy all the forenoon, in going up and down among our generals. I trust it shall be well with me, peace or war; and that God will turn all to his own glory.

March 27. In company most part of the day. Now my time of hurry begins again to disturb the quiet and peaceable life I have had all winter. Lord, fit me for launching out into new storms.—I go to this campaign, upon the one side weary of the war, (woes me that I am forced to dwell so long in the tents of wickedness; Lord, scatter those that delight in war.) But on the other side, I go out cheerfully, trusting in God, hoping to see him arise and scatter his enemies, and do great things.

★★★★★★

In the campaign of this year, the Allies still continued to have the advantage, although it was not so distinguished as the last, either in the importance, or in the variety of its events. Overtures of peace were again renewed by France with larger concessions, and greater sincerity than ever; and it appeared she was really anxious to put a period to that expensive warfare which had exhausted her treasury, and desolated her provinces. The offers of Louis went much farther than any he had made in his former conferences, and approached so near to the demands of the Confederates, that a single article formed the only exception.

The advantage he was willing to forego, discover the necessitous abasement into which he had sunk, and form a striking contrast to the domineering language and lofty pretensions which he arrogated to himself, in the meridian of his grandeur. They leave little room to doubt the sincerity of his professions. The exhausted state of his finances,—the miseries of his subjects, and the universal wretchedness of the country, are evidence enough that his overtures flowed from a genuine solicitude for terminating hostilities.

There is too much reason to believe that artifice and duplicity had changed sides. The general conduct of the deputies and plenipotentiaries of the Allies shewed they had no anxiety, perhaps no intention of coming to any agreement or accommodation with the French Court. They studied rather by their ambiguity and indecision to throw difficulties in the way, to perplex and entangle the proceedings. Marlborough and Prince Eugene were paramount in the Confederate Assembly, and their views and sentiments were implicitly adopted. To these the continuation of war was essentially beneficial, both in point of character and emolument. It was only in the field of battle, where Prince Eugene was most calculated to shine, that he could hope to maintain his reputation and his importance. The cessation of arms, it was evident, would not only strip the duke of a great part of his military revenue, but terminate his despotic sway in the English Cabinet;—since his supporters were daily declining in the royal favour, and could only hope to retain their offices so long as his services were deemed essential to the country. The rejection of peace, whatever party writers may have said on the subject, if candidly considered, will be attributed, not to the insincerity of Louis, but to the interested views of those who had manifest advantages to reap from the protraction of the war.[1]

But however enormous may be the guilt of those who shed innocent blood for the purposes of ambition and aggrandisement—who seek merely to gratify their own avarice, under the pretext of humbling a rival power, or providing for the national security; that guilt must be charged, not on those who are the dupes of their artifice, or the unconscious instruments of their designs, but on those who misinformed and misled them. Though the war must now be regarded as conducted upon different principles from those of necessity, or even those motives from which it was undertaken, there is no evidence in the subsequent papers to shew that the writer of the diary was apprised of this alteration, or that he had changed his original persuasion of the scared justice of the cause in which he had been so long engaged. The intrigues and mercenary arts of statesmen came not within the scope of his observation or intelligence. These are the discovery of subsequent investigation being hid from the eyes of contemporaries by the false glosses of party writers, or varnished over with the colouring of truth, by the advocates and partisans of the existing administration.

The negotiations for peace did not suspend or retard the operations of the campaign. Forage and other necessaries were provided, and on the 15th of April, the troops from the garrison of Flanders and Brabant were ordered to march for Tournay, the place of rendezvous. Their first exploit was the successful attack of the French lines on the

---

1. *Somerville's History*, chap. xvi.

Dyle. This was followed by the surrender of Douay, after an obstinate siege. Bethune, St.Venant, and Aire were afterwards reduced; and with these conquests, the transactions of the year terminated.

✶✶✶✶✶✶

April 2. Sabbath. Obliged by the hurry of having to march tomorrow, to be about things foreign to a Sabbath. O Lord pity and pardon. Now I must launch out again into new difficulties and confusions. I put my confidence in thee alone. I bless thee that I am not given up to melancholy, despondency or anxious fears, as I have sometimes too much been. I go out in thy name, and thy presence must go with me. I cast all my care upon thee. Furnish me out in this new post according to the occasions of it, and the service thou callest for. I bless thee for the mercies of the winter and leave my dear concern upon thy care.

April 3. This day we marched out of garrison. O Lord, get glory to thyself, and go forth at the head of our army as the captain of our host, and let thine enemies be scattered. Direct and guide me, and those under my charge. I put myself and them under thy protection.

April 4-8. Marching every day. We made a movement this day by a mistake, for though the army marched, we, having the artillery, were not to have moved.

April 9. Sabbath. Lying at arms from morning till two o'clock, ready to march. I retired as much as I could for prayer and reading; applying several promises with comfort and joy, both for myself and the public, Deut. xxxii. to the xliii. Josh. i. 9. v. 13, 14. Isaiah ii. 11. 17. 19. iii. 10. v. 4, 5, 6. viii. 9. 10. I trust God shall do great things this campaign, and be exalted in the earth, and work salvation and deliverance to his church and people. We marched at three o'clock , and marched all night with a design, as we hear, to attack the French lines tomorrow.

April 10. This morning we got within an hour of the lines; but we hear the French have quitted them and retired. Last year these lines were a bug-bear to us; we durst not go near them. God's time was not come then. Now he had given us them without stroke of sword. This is the doing of the Lord, and should be wonderful in our eyes. When I saw the pass and bridge where we were to have attacked them, I could not but admire his goodness; for it was so strong a morass, that we could hardly have made ahead to attack it. But he sent a terror and consternation among our enemies, that made them quit them. I hope this is a presage of more and greater successes to follow. Lord make us humble, and let there be no vain-boasting among us, in trusting to an arm of flesh.

******

In a letter to his lady, which appears to be the first this campaign, the taking of the lines and some other particulars are mentioned.

Lens, April 10.

Now I begin my old employment again, and indeed it is one of the most agreeable that I have in the camp, that of writing to you, and receiving your letters. I bless the Lord all has gone very well since we came out; Providence lets no troublesome or cross accidents come in our way. The weather has also mightily favoured us, and we are all hearty. The army assembled between Lisle and Tournay; and the garrison of Courtray has joined us. We have begun the campaign well, blessed be God; for St. Amand and Mortaign, two considerable forts, are taken we hear.

This is a good omen. I am glad I can now give you better news, for it has pleased God we have passed the French lines this morning, in several places, without the least opposition. The boors here tell us the French are in no condition to oppose us; their army is not assembled. The Lord works far above, and contrary to man's expectations. We marched all day yesterday, and all night, from near Tournay; there were several attacks to be made if the enemy had stood.

Our regiment has been upon the artillery these four days, and this keeps me in constant hurry. I can tell yet nothing what we are to do; but trust God cheerfully. I hope, by his blessing, this campaign shall prove so much to the advantage of the common causes, as to procure us such a happy peace as has hitherto been unattainable. I never know about the plenipotentiaries, nor what they are doing; perhaps peace will come another way. And now that they have put us to the trouble of coming out to the camp, we ought to push the war with vigour; and appealing to the great decision of heaven, say with Jephthah, *The Lord the judge, be judge this day between us and our enemies.* I have had very good accommodation every night. The pillow of my camp-mattress was forgot; but I made a very good shift without it; I took a bundle of hay, which did even as well; so do not scold the servant about it. I bless the Lord I am very easy, and no way anxious about events; I commit myself and all my concerns to him who does every thing well for me. His blessing and peace rest with you.

I am thine.   J.B.

Madame Blackader, *chez* Madam Penieman,
St. Michael, a Gand.

******

April 11. We have still the guard of the artillery. Another instance of the goodness of God to us, for we expected the French, who had retired behind the River Scarp, would make a stand and defend the river; but upon the appearance of the front of our army, they quitted that too, and retired farther into the country; by which we have free access to besiege Douay. We marched on and encamped near it. This town is a nest of rogues of Jesuits, and seminaries of idolatry. It would be but a just judgement to set it on a flame.[2]

April 12. This day we came off the guard of the artillery and joined the army, which made a movement nearer the town.

April 19. Here I have good accommodation, a quiet cottage in the midst of a wicked army, where I can retire and hold communion and fellowship with God. My neighbours here envy me this poor cottage, but they are not permitted to wrong me. *Who shall harm you if you be followers of that which is good?* I bless God for my peace and quietness: here I have just as much business as diverts me, no so much as to be troublesome.

April 20. A new instance of the Lord's goodness to us in disappointing our expectations of going upon this siege. We laid our account with it; but other regiments have been brought out of the garrison.

******

This was only a temporary respite; for they were shortly after ordered to the siege as a substitute for one of the other regiments.

---

2. Douay had a famous university, where many English Papists were educated, by whom a translation of the Old Testament and Apocrypha, from the Latin Vulgate, was published in 1610, about the same time with our present established version of the Scriptures. They added notes, with a view to pervert those passages which are opposed to the doctrines and practices of the Church of Rome. The Duke of Marlborough granted leave to the rector of the English College, and his students, about sixty in number, to retire to Lisle, where they remained during the siege.

Near Douay, April 24.

The regiments are now named and gone to the siege, and Providence has yet spared us. There are seven gone, and it stopped just at ours; and now we are the first. I take it from the hand of God as a mercy and a kind dispensation, come after what will; and when he does send us any such errand, I trust it will be in mercy also, and to give us more signal experiences of his goodness to us. We broke ground yesternight at this town, and it is hoped the siege will not be tedious. It is probable Colonel Preston may arrive at Ghent this week, or Major Aikman with our recruits; they are about 85 in number, and were to sail upon the 10th.

I bless the Lord I was never better in health. I am about half a mile from the regiment, and walk up twice a-day, and return at night. I regret I had not brought Dr. Tillotson's sermons with me, for I have no good books here to read. The Lord's peace be with you.

J. B.

Madam Blackader, *chez* Madam Penieman,
St. Michael, a Gand.

******

April 25. I trust we shall see the tyrant of France humbled and mortified in another manner than we have yet seen. I only wish we had a fair and full stroke at them. At the two last Battles of Tainiers and Oudenard we were held back, as by a chain, from pursuing them. But the day of their calamity is at hand. The Lord can open to us a wide and effectual door into France through this town, that no man shall be able to shut it. We have begun our approaches and are raising our batteries.

April 27. Yesternight the enemy made a sally out of the town, and one of our regiments (Sutton's) gave way; most part of the officers are either killed or wounded.[3] This in all appearance will bring our regiment to the siege. This is the Lord's doing, and not blind chance. It is he who orders us, and where he sends us we will cheerfully go. I will depend upon thee for suitable grace and furniture, according to the posts thou puttest us upon: and this regiment that I have the charge of, I commit the charge and direction of it to thee. What shall we say when our regiments give way and turn their back before the enemy?

---

3. Lediard's *Life of Marlborough*, vol. ii.

But, I do not wonder at it; for every word that our British soldiers speak is a damning of their own blood, and impious swearing by God's blood and wounds. It will be no wonder to see them wallowing in their own blood and wounds. God is just, he can work his own purposes by us, and yet lay our carcases as dung on the face of the earth.

April 30. We have got notice this morning that we are to go upon the siege tomorrow.

May 1. This morning our regiment went into the trenches, and blessed be God, we had a very good day, and had no a man killed or wounded, though the enemy continued a very smart firing all night with cannon, bombs, and small shot. Oh Lord, I commit myself and all to thee. Give me courage, strength, and conduct, as I need it. Without thee, I find I have neither head, heart, nor hand, but through thee I shall do valiantly. We were in the trenches all night, and came out next morning about ten o'clock, and had only one man hurt. The power and kind providence of the Almighty, can make the trenches or the hottest attack of a breach to be s safe as our houses in garrison are. *The name of the Lord is a strong tower; the righteous flee into it and are safe.* I am much fatigued by want of sleep, and running up and down seeing to get everything right

Doay, May 3.

I wrote to you yesterday, being desirous that you should hear of our being at the siege, rather from myself than from any other hand. But trust still in God and hope in his mercy; for we shall yet praise him; and new trials shall produce new deliverances. Every campaign adds new links to that long golden chain of our rich experiences. Let us be always found in the way of duty. We were very lucky in the trenches yesterday, for we had not a man hurt all the time; only in the coming out Sergeant Allan got a shot somewhat like mine at Hochstet. We go in on Friday or Saturday next, and all I hope shall go well. Our regiment having marched into the besieging army, Sutton's has taken our post in the line. Our batteries begin tomorrow, and it is hoped the siege will not be long.

I shall not fail to make you easy by writing as frequently as I can, especially when we come out of the trenches. You should think us well out of the covering army, for the French give out that they will come and relieve the town. You have no reason to be alarmed about us, for though that misfortune happened to our predecessors, yet we that come in their place are in no more danger that way, than any of the forty battalions that are here; and, indeed, now our trenches and works are so advanced, that the French cannot now make any *sorties* as they did at the beginning. Providence disposes of us and of our lot as is best for us; time of thoughtfulness and a rod above our heads, are much better than a constant tract of sunshine.

Our natures and our graces do require a sharp winter as well as a warm summer, to nip and kill our corruptions and lusts, which otherwise would spoil and quite eat out all the power of religion and grace. I am altogether persuaded of this, and therefore bless God for my lot, that I am obliged to a life of faith, and a humble needy dependence upon a complete Saviour; for it is a wonder to see, when we are without rods and crosses, how dead, careless, and unwatchful we grow; our hearts how vain, earthly, and light. The Lord's peace and blessing be with you.

     I am thine.   J. B.

Madame Blackader, *chez* Madam Penieman,
St. Michael, a Gand.

May 4. We have lost four or five men last night in the trenches. I bless God for the rest and sleep I had after my fatigue.

May 5. This morning went into the trenches again, and got one of the best posts there for safety from the cannon and bombs of the town. I desire to observe all to the praise of God's mercy and goodness. The weather is good; and we had not a man hurt all this day.

May 6. This day is one of the greatest Ebenezers of my life. In the morning the French made a sally from the town upon that post where our regiment was. It was a little before break of day. They came on silently, expecting to surprise us; but by the goodness of Providence we were ready. Our sentinels gave us warning, and we put ourselves in a posture, and received them so warmly, that they immediately retired in confusion without firing a shot. It is observable that it was so ordered, that this second sally of theirs should happen to be only upon us, who were brought in to relieve that regiment upon whom the enemy fell at the first sortie, and used so ill. *Not to us, Oh Lord, not to us, but to thy name be the praise and glory.* It was thou who madest our enemies faintly to turn their backs without attacking us,—for if they had attacked us briskly, we have no reason to believe, as to our own behaviour, courage, or conduct, but that there would have been as bad an account of us, as of those who were there before us.

For, indeed, I did see among several of our soldiers manifest signs of fear and confusion; but the goodness of God hides our failings; and not only so, but makes those actions, which our own hearts know to be mixed with great weakness, to turn to our honour and reputation. I have often observed this since I have been a soldier, and now it holds good as to me and the regiment, that our actions, though in themselves not worth a button—no better than other peoples—yea not so good—often-times more weakness and defects; yet God is sometimes pleased so to distinguish them with such circumstances of reputations, and to place them in such a light, as gives them a peculiar lustre in the eyes of the world. I am sure this should make us humble and thankful. I acknowledge for my own part, if the Lord, by his grace, did not very powerfully supply and furnish me with courage and fortitude, I would behave very ill.

I would have neither heart nor hand. I am not ashamed to own that I have no fund of my own, neither courage, nor wisdom, nor conduct, but what I get from God. I find him in straits a present aid; he gives most liberally and abundantly as occasions require. Therefore I shall rejoice in my own emptiness, and weakness, and fear, because it leads me to an infinite inexhaustible fountain and magazine of all sorts of spiritual supplies. I shall be distrustful of myself; but in God I will boast all the day long. He makes true my motto to me every day, *Deus Fortitudo mea*.[4]

May 7. Sabbath. I bless God for sleep and sweet rest after fatigue. The most of the world, by not knowing the want of them, do not enjoy the pleasures of the most common mercies. Many poor soldiers at this siege are exposed night and day to fatigue and danger, and get not sleep one night in a week.

May 8. Serious through this day, and seeking new supplies. This is a thoughtful time; many poor souls are hurried into eternity ever night at this town, where bombs, cannon and musket bullets are flying like hailstones all the night over.

May 10. Our regiment went again into the trenches this morning.

---

4. This sortie of the enemy is mentioned by the historian of Marlborough. "On the 17th of May, the besieged made another sally with nine companies of grenadiers; but Colonel Preston gave them so warm a reception, that upon the first firing of his men, the enemy retired in great confusion, and left above 100 men prisoners." Led. *Life of Marlborough*, vol. ii.

Our post was not so exposed to sorties as the last; but more to the bombs, &c. and most to our own, which, falling short of the town, did incommode us; but we had no loss. The British this night got several things to humble them. There was 100 grenadiers commanded out to sustain the workmen that were to go out and make a lodgement on the other side of the *avant-fosse*. The French came out with a great noise, perhaps but a small number, and they all gave way, and quitted the lodgement; several being killed and wounded.

May 12. This night I had the command in the trenches, to sustain the workmen to make up that same lodgement. Our workmen were in great disorder this night also, and did not do their duty as they ought. I could not help it. There was hot firing all night; I came off at sunrising, and had some lest. We have made a lodgement on the other side of the fosse.

✶✶✶✶✶✶

On this subject he remarks in a letter to his wife:—

I find the command far less troublesome when the regiment is in, than with the workers; there is always a great deal of confusion at any business of that nature, in the night; and so it was yesternight. We were to make up the lodgement on the other side of the outer fosse, which we had been put from the night before; and indeed our workmen did their business very ill, for the French came out several times with great noise on purpose to frighten the workmen; and it had the effect, for they ran away so that it was impossible to get the third part of them kept together. However there was lodgement made. These commands are exceedingly troublesome, because of the vexation it gives an officer when his men do not do their duty.

In another letter, dated the 14th, he observes:—

Our siege goes on well; somewhat more slowly than at the beginning. We are now near the counterscarp. The covering army marched yesterday, advancing a little way to the front to meet Marshal Villars, in case he have a mind to come and pay them a visit, which most believe he will not. We are to be in the trenches tomorrow; we go there every fifth day.—We expect our recruits on Tuesday or Wednesday; if they came away on Saturday, they may be useful to us yet this siege.

******

May 15. Our regiment marched into the trenches this morning. We had a good day. Providence is favourable to us; we were bombarded pretty smartly from the town, yet by the goodness of God, we had very little loss. As for myself I see distinguishing marks of his favour toward me.

May 16. We came out this morning. The firing from cannon, bombs, and small shot continued on us all night. We hear the French army were upon their march yesterday to Arras. They and our army were encamped pretty near each other last night. There are four regiments to be sent for from the siege, in case they come to attack us; and it is said ours will be one.

May 17. This day the enemy being in motion towards us we expect a battle tomorrow. All my hope and comfort is, that the Lord of hosts is on our side, and when he is the General of the army, what have we to fear?

Tuesday, May 16.
We are come from the trenches this morning; and blessed be God all well. Hitherto, the days that the regiment has been in the trenches, are the best and safest. We have less loss then than when detachments go to work. The siege goes on well enough, though perhaps not so quick as the people in the coffee-houses imagine it should do. We are now sapping and mining close to the palisades of the counterscarp. The imperial attack is not quite so far advanced yet, and both must be carried on together. My dearest, trust still in God, and possess our soul in patience, living by faith. For there would be no occasion for faith, may there would be no such thing as faith, if we had all our wishes and desires accomplished just in the very way and time that we carve out to ourselves. But these various dispensations of Providence do bring forth the peaceable fruits of righteousness to those that are exercised thereby.

Our covering army moved three days ago to take up their post in the line of battle; and we hear that the French army were upon their march towards Arras. It is altogether uncertain (to me at least it is) whether they have a mind to come and offer battle to our army or not: Most believe they will not. In case they do, four of the British Regiments here are to join the army; what four it may be I cannot tell you. All things are to left to the disposal of Providence; we cannot do better.

We expected our recruits to be here this day, and that they would have made greater haste, considering our circumstances here. The colonel is not very well pleased about it, for there are between forty or fifty of our regiment killed and wounded already. I wrote you the day after we came out of the trenches, and after I had been there on command next night. It is true that our workmen were frightened from their work several times, but the work was done at last; and now most of our labour is sapping, which is a sure and a slow work; and therefore do not grudge the siege lasting eight or ten days longer. The saving of men will recompense the loss of time, though we will still be losing men every day at working. My service to all friends.

Thine, &c.   J. B.

Madam Blackader, *chez* Madam Penieman,
St. Michael, a Gand.

May 19. This day the enemy advanced towards us. There are four regiments sent for from the siege, whereof ours is one. We marched up to the army in the evening, and were put into one of the entrenchments which are cast up along the line. It is expected they win attack us tomorrow.

May 20. Our army wrought all night entrenching themselves. The enemy do not think fit to attack us in this post. Our four regiments were sent back to the siege, and we marched straight into the trenches. I was detached upon command into the sap, to command the grenadiers and those who were to fire all night. I was surprised at this, because I was not near command; but it was the pure decision of Providence, being done by lot; so I went cheerfully, being assured that it was not blind chance, but God who sent me there. I was very well carried through, for he lets me see that the hottest post at the siege, is as safe as my own chamber. I see also that he sends me upon these posts, on purpose to make me an instance and monument of his goodness,—of his protecting, defending, and delivering mercy, and to put new songs of praise in my mouth; new links added to that golden chain of sweet experiences.

We had an alarm in the night from a magazine of the enemy's grenades blowing up on the counterscarp, which we took to be a sortie. We had no harm by it, though it was hard by us. *Thou shalt not be afraid of the terrors by night.* Going through the saps and bridges where the bombs, small-shot, and grenades were flying pretty thick; I believed I was even as safe there, under the protection of God, as if I had been at home. *Thou art my shield and buckler.* I shall never attribute my deliverances to blind destiny.

May 21. In the morning I came off the advanced post, and joined the regiment in the trenches; we had a good night, only one man killed by a bomb. *Sabbath.* This is two nights we have been at arms. I came home, lay down and slept from ten till two o'clock. I bless God who gives me rest after fatigue, and sleep after long watching. I was sent for to sup abroad, where we had much idle conversation. Lord, cleanse my soul from the filth and sin I contract in evil company. I endeavoured also to testify my dislike at vice, and abominable things, as they came to be the subject of conversation.

May 23. Unwell and feverish. I sent for a surgeon, and took blood, and grew better. I was preparing for my post, but the colonel would not permit me to go into the trenches with the regiment, because the night air might do me hurt.

******

By this temporary malady, he probably made an escape from an unforeseen danger; for, as it appears in the following letter, an accident happened, by the blowing up of some grenades, which killed or hurt several of his men.

******

Wednesday, May 24.

There is nothing extraordinary among us since I last wrote you. The siege goes slowly on. It is a very great mercy we have had such fair weather all along, for otherwise it would have been sad working in the trenches. There is no appearance of the enemy's coming near us to relieve the town.—Yesternight we had sixteen men wounded and burnt by an accident of the blowing up of some powder and grenades. Two of them are dead. Lieutenant Graham is hurt, and Sergeant Davidson. We have but little loss now, except by these accidents that cannot be foreseen.—Our regiment goes in again to the trenches tomorrow, and I hope the Divine care and protection will be around us as it has been. The Lord keep and preserve you.

J.B.

Madam Blackader, *chez* Madam Penieman,
St. Michael, a Gand.

May 30. We went into the trenches again this morning. The goodness of God puts a hedge round me; he is also gracious to the regiment in sparing them.

Thursday, June 1.

We came out of the trenches yesterday, where Providence is still kind to us, and brings us out with little loss. No doubt you are wearying of this siege, and think it lasts very long: so are we too. But we must be patient, and wait God's time which is the best. Let it be our work to profit under all these dispensations, by a true solid Christian growth, laying aside every weight, and running with patience the race set before us, looking unto Jesus. I bless God I am as well as ever I was in my life, as to my health, and every way else. Providence makes me easy, and I should be very ungrateful if I were not fully content.

We are transacting about Brown's commission, (the Dean of Guild's son.) I know not yet what he has to pay; if it be more that 500 *gilders*, (which I believe it will not,) I must engage for it myself till I draw upon his father. I wrote to Colonel Cunningham the other day, as we had a design upon Ypres lately, but it has mislucked. We must leave it to the French to take towns by trick and treachery; we never get any that way. We get all we win very honourably, with our blood and the sweat of our brow.

Let me know who are kind to you, and give them thanks in my name. That God may bless you with every rich blessing is the constant prayer of thine.

J.B.

Madam Blackader, chez Madam Penieman,
St. Michael, a Gand.

June 4. Sabbath. We went into the trenches, and Providence has been kind to us as it hath always been. The Lord was very gracious to me in particular, and put a new song of praise into my mouth: While I was looking to our batteries firing, there came a musket-ball from the town and shot through my hat, slanting close by my head. Thou, O Lord, coverest my head in time of danger. Oh make me careful to treasure up these experiences in my heart. We came out of the trenches next day with small loss.

June 6. This morning I was hurried out by company ere I got time for retirement; and was led away to a place in the trenches, where we were needlessly exposed to great and small shot from the town. I have no peace in these needless exposings of myself. When I have a call that it is my duty to go into danger, then I depend upon God for suitable through-bearing. But where I have no call, I have no such promise. Riding abroad in the afternoon I went to our hospital, where was a melancholy sight of wounded men. May it please God in his mercy to put an end to this tedious troublesome siege.

June 8. I went through all the imperial attack in the forenoon. In the evening there was an attack upon the two ravelines of the town. I went up and saw it. It was hot work for a while; but we know not yet how it has gone. But many poor souls, no doubt, by this time are hurried into eternity.

June 9. This morning we went into the trenches. We see that our attack did not succeed so well as we could have wished, for we were beat back and got not full possession of the ravelines; yet we made a lodgement in them both. This attack has cost us dear. Many were killed and wounded, as we may guess by our own regiment, for of thirty-nine that were there, we have thirty-two killed and wounded. I observe the goodness of God to me also on this occasion. I was the first upon command, of the field officers of the besieging army, yesterday when the attack was ordered; but our regiment being to go next day into the trenches, the custom is, that that regiment gives no men or officers on command the night before. In this way it missed me, and the next officer on command was taken. *Whoso is wise will consider these things, and see the loving kindness of the Lord.* I have occasions every day of observing this. I would have blessed God also if he had sent me, for I trust he would have borne my charges, and carried me through to the praise of his grace. The Lord is merciful to our regiment, for we have not had a man either killed or wounded in the trenches these twenty-four hours.

June 10. We came safe out of the trenches this morning. I went to bed and slept till the evening, and it was well I did so, for I was ordered in again at night with 200 grenadiers to sustain our lodgements.

And here again I observe the kindness of God towards me; for about an hour before I came into the trenches, the enemy sprung a mine upon that raveline where my post was to be, and overturned all our lodgement, and killed and blew up a good many men. We soon recovered our lodgement, and made up our works. We expected it would be a troublesome night, and that the enemy would dispute every foot of ground with us, as indeed they have hitherto done; but we were mercifully disappointed, for they quitted all the ravelines entirely to us, and we had not a more quiet and peaceable night since the siege began, for they threw not so much as a bomb or a stone all the night. We were expecting also to have our lodgement on the left hand blown up; but in that also we were agreeably disappointed. Oh how many mercies have I had in this siege! new songs of praise every day! Lord, make me thankful, and humble, and holy.

June 11. In the evening I came off my command in the trenches. The Lord makes the most dangerous posts a safe habitation to me. Just before I came out, the enemy began to throw bombs, grenades, and stones, from the town, and all the night following have plied our trenches very hot with these, especially stones, whereby many of our men are wounded. The Lord restrains my enemies from doing me hurt. Let these things sink deep into my heart, never to forget his goodness. The Sabbath, but not spent like a Sabbath.

June 14. Resting these two days. This morning we went into the trenches. At two o'clock they beat the *chamade*, and hung out a white flag to capitulate, which was a very acceptable sight to us all; for this has been a very toilsome, long, and bloody siege. I bless the Lord for the bountiful supplies he has given me during the siege, and for his protecting, preserving mercy.

June 15. They have not yet relieved us out of the trenches. We are much fatigued by being two days in them. We hear we are to get Fort Scarp also, which we were hardly expecting. This is a great mercy, for it would have proved troublesome, and perhaps taken up much of our precious time.

June 16. We were not relieved till twelve o'clock this day. We have got possession of a post, and of the fort also. Blessed be God who has brought this troublesome siege at length to a happy issue.

June 18. Sabbath. The garrison of Douay marched out, and we were under arms all day on that account. I was invited to dine with a general, but I had rather fasted. Oh Lord, wash and cleanse me from the filth I contract among wicked men, by filthy, idle conversation. I flee to the mercy of God in Christ, and to the blood of Christ for repentance and remission of sin. Deliver me out of these snares. Sanctify my soul.

June 25. Yesterday I went in to Douay and viewed all our works, and the French works. There I erect new monuments of gratitude; for mercy and goodness have followed me remarkably all this siege. This day is kept by orders in our army, a thanksgiving for the reduction of the town. None have more cause to keep it with a grateful, cheerful heart than I have. None have experienced more signal deliverances, or been attended with more distinguishing marks of the Divine care. After spending the day at home, I walked again, in the evening, to the trenches, and went through all the works where I had been during the siege. At every post I met with fresh remembrances and monuments of mercy.

★★★★★★

Thus, after a siege of two months, maintained with the most obstinate resolution and defence on the part of the garrison, the large and well-fortified city of Douay surrendered. In addition to the resistance from within, the besiegers were greatly retarded by other obstacles, such as the difficulties of the ground, and the menaces of Marshal Villars, who made several efforts to attack the covering army. The garrison was reduced to nearly one—half of their original number, but the Allies suffered much more severely, having in killed and wounded above 8000 men. The loss of Colonel Preston's Regiment was comparatively small, amounting to 50 killed, and about 200 wounded. This service seems to have been the last in which the regiment was employed this campaign. They joined the army under the Duke of Marlborough who was marching after Villars, in the hope of provoking him to an engagement which he declined, having retired within his new lines near Arras, which rendered it impracticable for the Allies either to attack him, or invest that town as they wished.

★★★★★★

June 26. Now we are going to march again. The Lord direct us what is next to be done. Thy presence go with us. I depend upon thee alone, come battles, or sieges, or what else thou pleasest. Being near the French, I went to view the army close at hand, and mercifully escaped a trap that was laid.

July 2. Sabbath, But forced to do many things foreign to a Sabbath, by preparing for a review tomorrow. This is a sad way of living. How is the mind defiled and the edge of zeal against sin blunted. Sin becomes common and familiar. The spirit of God is forced away. Grace withers. The heart grows hard and dead. I earnestly besought the Lord to deliver me out of the tents of wickedness. How long shall we hear the sound of the trumpet and the alarms of war. Woe's me that I sojourn so long among them. I am in a dry, barren, thirsty land, where I want the means and influences of spiritual communion. O that thou wouldest in mercy restore me again to the tabernacles of they grace; and let me see the beauty of the Lord, as I have seen thee in they sanctuary. In meditating upon the present state of affairs, I found my temper too ready to fret and grow melancholy, by seeing our army, which we have reason to esteem the best ever was in this country, stopped from making progress, by an enemy which we flattered ourselves could not well make head against us; and that now we are obliged to turn away from them, and march another way.

But in reading the Scriptures in my ordinary, I got both reproof and instruction. The first was I Chron. xiii. 10. to teach me not to be solicitously or sinfully anxious about the ark of God: He will take care of his own ark. The second was in the 14th chapter, 14th verse, where we may see that God sometimes takes a plain direct way as in the 10th verse; and sometimes works by contrary and improbable means. Providence is never at a loss, though we may be ignorant and in the dark as to its operations. We are patiently to follow and not to limit, or prescribe rules.

July 3. This day we were reviewed, all going well; and tomorrow we march from the army I know not whither.

July 6. Our order for marching is countermanded, so we stay still.

July 15. Hearing from my wife that she is not well. I went to Courtray, where my fears were prevented, for we had a comfortable meeting.

July 21. There is a report that both armies are marched in prospect of a battle. I was somewhat uneasy that I should be here at Courtray absent from my post.

July 24. Heard again that there is no action, nor any appearance of it.

August 3. This day I left Courtray, and at night came to Lisle. Next day I returned to the camp. The weather is now stormy, and I have lost my little cottage by the army's removing.

August 17. We had a *feu-de-joie* for our victory in Spain.

August 18. We went to see Bethune, which is capitulating. The Lord be praised for it. Let him direct us what we are to do next.

August 20. Walking in the fields in sight of the French army. I have great boldness in praying they may be defeated. Their master is the great supporter of Satan's and Antichrist's kingdom, the plight-anchor of all that are haters of true religion and the liberties of mankind. I live in the faith to see his power yet more humbled, broken, and confounded.

August 21. Very much troubled and vexed with the folly and madness of an acquaintance, who seems to be abandoned of God and left to himself. Lord, touch his heart with a sense of his miscarriages, stop him in the career he is now running, and reclaim him as the prodigal son. I was serious with him, laying his duty home to his conscience as he will answer at the great day upon his peril. May the Lord render it effectual to him.

August 26. At court; but only to hear the news, as I had nothing to ask. Abroad at dinner, where we drank no more than what all the company thought very moderate and sober, yet I thought it too much: not that reason was disturbed thereby, but I cannot endure to have my head the least warmed, or that coolness of thinking marred which I would always be master of.

September 4. Left the camp yesterday and had a long journey. This day I have again a comfortable meeting with my wife and friends. Lord, make us thankful and give us grace to pay our vows. Let us rejoice in thee, and in thy goodness, and let not the enjoyments of the world steal our hearts away from thee.

September 8. We have been alarmed here all day by the enemy being near us, apprehending that perhaps they might have a design upon this place. But about twelve o'clock we found that their design was upon the convoy. We went out in the afternoon with the few men that could be spared here, to try if we could give any help, but when we came within half an hour of the place, we were informed that the convoy was beat, and they are burning and blowing up the ships. This is a very great loss, and great affront. Next day we went out to view the field of battle, and saw a melancholy sight of near 200 men lying drowned on the river sides. There seems to have been great mismanagement and bad behaviour in this affair. When God is not with us, we have neither courage nor conduct.

✶✶✶✶✶✶

This disastrous action took place at St. Eloy-Vive, a short distance from Courtray. The Confederates were obliged to fetch their provisions and ammunition from Ghent, Tournay, and Lisle. A convoy of forty boats, laden with powder, bombs, hay, &c., with a guard of 1200 men, commanded by Colonel Ginkel, while coming up the Lys, was surprised and attacked by a party of the enemy about 4000 strong. This superior force must have been more than an overmatch for the convoy, notwithstanding the strictures of Colonel Blackader. Besides the 200 killed, about 600 were taken prisoners, among whom was the commander himself. Some of the boats were sunk to stop the navigation of the river, others were blown up, and so tremendous was the shock that the village of St. Eloy-Vive was laid in ruins; the country for miles round was shaken, and windows broken as by an earthquake. The Lys was diverted from its channel, and divided into tow currents. This misfortune retarded the sieges of St. Venant and Aire, in which the Allies were now engaged.

******

October 4. My time passes here very agreeably. I have good company. May it be blest for our mutual edification. Sometimes too keen in dispute. Lord, make me always zealous for thee and thy truth.

October 21. This morning I left Courtray, and next day came to the camp, through eight leagues of the worst road I ever travelled; but blessed be God we came all safe without any accident. I find all quiet and peaceable here as when I left it, so that I hope no inconvenience has arisen from my long absence. All this is the goodness of God.

October 28. The weather has now become unpleasant; and it is very uncomfortable for the poor soldiers to live now in a camp. This night about nine o'clock the town (Aire) began to capitulate. Lord be blessed that we have carried it at last, after many errors and mistakes. Providence frequently humbles us in the details and the execution, but it favours our undertakings in the main.

November 1. I went down to visit the town and the trenches, and saw the French garrison march out. We have drawn lots for our garrisons, and we are to go to Ghent.

November 4. I have to praise the Lord for bringing this campaign to so comfortable an issue; for having preserved and protected me in the midst of dangers and fatigues.

November 18. We arrived at Courtray, and (12th) came into garrison.

CHAPTER 17

Campaign Tenth, 1711

Advances were still making towards peace, and the British Cabinet was much inclined for pacific measures, but the mutual jealousies of the Allied Powers prevented them from acting with decision or unanimity: These divisions abroad, and the party contentions among the ministry at home, emboldened the French king to renew his exertions in the Netherlands; and Marshal Villars, as commander of forces, opened the campaign with a more numerous army than any that had taken the field since the commencement of the war. The Duke of Marlborough, notwithstanding his friends had lost their influence in the queen's councils, continued to preside over the Confederate arms, and this year gave fresh proofs of his extraordinary talents, and military capacity. The two most remarkable of his exploits were the passing of the French lines by stratagem, and the reduction of Bouchain. This was his last campaign, for such is the instability of human greatness, that on his return to England, he was prosecuted by the attorney-general for the dishonest application of the public money, in consequence of a petition from the House of Commons to the queen, and was by her removed from the command of the army, and from all his public offices.

This was also the last of Colonel Blackader's campaigns, having quitted his regiment in the month of October, during the siege of Bouchain; and in course of next year, disposed of his commission. He never had any delight in the society of the army; and now that he was, from his office, unavoidably more exposed to it than he could wish, he became anxious to resign his post, and contemplated every new campaign with terror and aversion. He had begun, while in garrison, to negotiate about this affair, but the early summons to take the field, prevented the matter from coming to any conclusion.

✶✶✶✶✶✶

January 6. I have this day been making a proposal that may be a crisis of my life, in quitting this employment. I commit it to thee, Oh Lord. I have only proposed, do thou dispose, and prosper it as far as thou seest fit for thy glory and my good. Let me have no wrong bias, or leaning to any selfish or worldly interest, but have thy glory singly before my eyes in every thing I do.

February 26. Got orders to be ready to march, which is likely to make me begin my campaign very early. Serious and thoughtful about it. I see that most men of the world keep up their hearts by vain imaginations, and make themselves easy and cheerful; is it not a sad thought, that religion and reason should not have a like effect upon them? Oh to live by faith! That would do it. That would make us rejoice in infirmities, in temptations, in losses and sufferings. Oh for grace to practise more what we profess.

March 10. We marched out of Ghent. This is an early commencement of the campaign. I have been uneasy about this command, as it chains me too much to ill company, which is not my element. The care about doing my duty properly, and other things, trouble me, which ought not; for I should commit all to God by faith. I have that unhappiness of temper which forms melancholy ideas of things before hand, that vanish away when it comes to the acting part.

March 13. Marching yesterday, and this morning I went upon command to take possession of a post which we were apprehensive the enemy designed to possess, but it fell out well, for we took peaceable possession of it. We posted our men the best way we could. I committed myself and my charge to him who is a fortress and a high tower to all that put their trust in him. I remembered and applied that promise in Josh. i. 9. and I observe Providence has ordered it so, that I am the first this campaign that has begun hostilities, and taken post in the enemy's country. In they name, Oh Lord, will we set up our banners.

March 15. We have been busily employed and much fatigued in fortifying ourselves, and guarding this post; but unless the Lord do keep it, the watchmen watch in vain.

March 26. Going abroad early to St. Amand, where I dined with the general. I committed all my way to God, for I find business never goes on well till I do this. An affair committed to God by prayer, is as good as done.

April 10. Went into Douay, and took a view of our attack at the siege. I had a serene, thankful frame of mind. Sitting alone in my chaise by the way, I meditated on the goodness of God, and his singular mercies to me. My business went well and smoothly on, and I had the same serene frame coming back at night. But Providence lets me see that all our earthly enjoyments are like Jonah's gourd. There is a worm at the root of them. I observe that no sooner do I begin to rest any pleasure or satisfaction in any earthly comfort, than Providence gives some check, and lets me see there is nothing but vanity and emptiness in all; for when I arrived at home, the chaise going in at the coachhouse gate, by some accident startling the horses, they took fright, and broke it in pieces. I should learn from this the unsatisfactoriness of earthly enjoyments, for at the very time we are hugging ourselves in our conveniences and pleasures, the Lord may be preparing a worm to gnaw and eat out the comfort of them.

April 17. Now the armies are taking the field on both sides, and probably will enter soon into action. I flee to thee, Oh Lord, to hide me under the shadow of thy wings, to enter into those chambers which thou hast provided for thy people in a day of trouble. This is my refuge. I received orders from Douay, to be ready to march in case the enemy make any attempt that way as they threaten to do. All the rest of the cantonment are marched.

April 19. This has been a quiet retreat these five weeks past, but now that all the British cantonment is come here—a hundred men of each of twenty regiments it is become, as it were, a hell—nothing about me but cursing, blasphemy, violence, &c. All this while I was glad to stay here, now I would gladly march to get free of such company.

May 9. Was at the duke's quarters all the forenoon. Hearing of my brother's death in Scotland, I took the resolution to go to Courtray to communicate the melancholy news to my wife. I arrived on the 11th and bless the Lord who has given us a comfortable meeting with each other again.

May 15. We had a great alarm here this day, expecting the French were on their way to attack this town; but their design was not here.

May 23. Left Courtray, and came to Tournay at night. Next day I came safe home to the army to my cottage. I praise thee, O Lord, who preservest my outgoings and my incomings, and lets no evil befall me—no plague come nigh my dwelling.

May 28. Taken up all day in reviewing before the duke. All going well. I dined at a great man's table, where others fell into snares by drinking, while I escaped. It is thy goodness, Oh Lord, and nothing in me.

June 3. Sabbath. Marched this day, (from the camp near Douay,) which was one of the severest I ever saw, by excessive heat. Several men marching in the ranks, fell down and died upon the very spot. The whole fields were like a field of battle, men lying panting and fainting. Most of the regiments did not bring above sixty or seventy men to the camp with their colours. I bless the Lord for his mercies to me. I have got the accommodation here of a cottage, though it is like to be pulled down about my ears by the soldiers searching for wood and straw. If we would look more to those who are below us, and compare their condition with ours, it would make us more thankful and contented with our lot; for what makes us to differ? It is only the goodness of God that makes our circumstances better—the men are every whit as good as we.

June 22. In the afternoon I went out upon command, where I continued for two days, doing my best to keep things in order upon my post. I came home at night, and bless God I have been kept out of snares and temptation.

June 26. Dining with company. This is a great folly in the army, that when a friend dines with another, they are pressed to drink too much. I am always uneasy on these occasions. It is really an admiration to see men endowed with reason, and with immortal souls, so degrade themselves of that dignity, and lead such poor, animal, sensual lives as they do. Oh what fools,—what brutes,—what fiends has sin made man!

All this, I know, would sound harsh with the genteel world, whose example has dignified these customs, and given them the reputation of virtues. But that does not change the nature of the thing. Make me, Oh Lord, to escape the pollution that is in the world through sin. Most people think there can be no good company, or welcome without drinking; and many, even good sober men, have too warm a side to this custom. It is a great thing to get above the opinion of the world. This ruins many.

✶✶✶✶✶✶

About this time the colonel's lady had received letters from her father in Scotland, who had expressed an anxiety to see them, as some events had occurred in the family which rendered a visit desirable. The following from the colonel, refers partly to that affair, and partly to the business of his commission.

Sabbath, June 24.

I received yours of yesterday, this forenoon. It is a satisfaction when letters come so soon to hand. I shall write to your father, God willing, when I can get leisure. You have done well in writing. I am hopeful he is not so anxious about seeing of you and me as you apprehend. I presume I know his temper as well as you do. He has affections that are strong enough, but they are masculine and reasonable, and that shew themselves more in doing good offices to his friends, than in fond desires of seeing them; and this is certainly the finest sort of love—most disinterested, for the other may rather be called self-love, the indulging of our own soft inclinations. But you must be a philosopher to enter into these sentiments and ways of reasoning.

I have been on command since I wrote last. I went out on Friday and came home yesternight. It was on a foraging party, an easy and short command; and the major was with me. I have spoken to my Lord Stair about my affair; he relishes it very well, and says he had employed Captain Kennedy to speak to Colonel Preston about it when the regiment went out of camp to Harlebeck.

We have not spoken about the terms, and there is no haste, for it cannot be finished until winter. I have not spoken of it to the colonel; only in general I have told him that he must allow me to make my retreat out of the army. So now that I have tabled the affair I commit it entirely to kind Providence. I desire not to be anxious about it; for why should we be eager about any earthly concern? It is not the change of place or employment that can make us easy.

When Captain M'Leod come here, I shall be very well satisfied, if I have time, to come and see you. For besides the attractive power that Courtray has by your being there, to bring me out of the army, it has also several other charms by the company I get there. But I should not tell this, for wives are jealous creatures. We are to be reviewed this week by my Lord Orkney, as

General of the Foot, and are busy about our recruits.
I am thine. J.B.
Madam Blackader, *chez* Mons. Col. Cunningham,
Commandant *à* Courtray.

******

July 5. Riding alone all day and coming to Lisle. I bless God who has defended and guarded me all this while in camp, where I was much exposed. This Lisle should be a continual remembrance to me, whenever I see it, for here I was compassed about with deliverance. (*September 12*, 1708.) I went in the afternoon and visited the post I had at the attack, and was thankful for my escape.

******

The passing of the French lines, which we have already mentioned as the first memorable exploit this campaign, took place on the 25th. It was effected by stratagem, and celebrated by the writers of the times, as a feat of the most consummate generalship. These lines ran along the Scheldt from Bouchain to Arras, and by getting possession of them, a way was opened for besieging the former place, and even penetrating into the interior of France. The design was executed with the greatest secrecy. The army had orders to march in the evening, so soon as it was dark enough to strike their tents without being perceived by the enemy. They advanced with incredible expedition, and had possessed themselves of the passes on the river, before Marshal Villars was apprised of their destination, or prepared to oppose them. By this bold *ruse de guerre* the Allies obtained a victory without striking a blow; and without losing one man, became masters of an important conquest which they would willingly have purchased at the expense of some thousand lives.

******

July 25. Last night we marched at nine o'clock, and continued it all night, and this day till three in the afternoon, and by the blessing of God have taken possession of the French lines without losing a man. This was performed by the excellent conduct, and to the great honour of our general, being one of the finest projects and best executed that has been during these wars. Not unto us, O Lord, but unto thee be the glory. It is thou who givest a spirit of judgement and conduct to those who have the direction and command, and a spirit of strength to those who are to execute these commands. Our enemies are taken in their own craftiness. We were long chained up, but when thy time comes, thou goest before us as the captain of our host, and then we do great things. This was a sore fatiguing march of ten or twelve leagues: most of the army fell ill by the way, so that in the afternoon, when the French made a mien to oppose us, we had but a handful of men to oppose them, no more than 60 or 80 in a regiment. But the enemy retired, and we lay at arms all night. I bless God I was very well; cheerful and thankful. The Lord makes good that promise to me. Isa. xl. 29-31.

July 26. This morning we marched forward, the enemy being also on their march to oppose us. Their army drew up on a plain before us. We hear that it was very nearly carried in a council of war, that we should attack them; but it was resolved otherwise to the regret of most part of the army. In such cases it may be said *vox exercitus vox Dei*. Our soldiers were much encouraged by their success in passing the lines, and the enemy much disheartened. I confess I was uneasy at it, for I look upon such fair opportunities of fighting as probably opportunities of defeating their army and ending the war. We are not to expect moral certainties; but when God delivers our enemies into our hand, and we let them escape, he often times lets them be more troublesome afterward. I pray God it may not be so with us.

On the other had, we are not to be suspicious of our general's conduct. We have more reason to admire it, and to believe he knows a thousand times better what is to be done than we do. Submissive obedience is our duty, and I give it heartily. If any man deserves implicit obedience I think he does, both in respect of his capacity and his integrity. The Lord be blessed for what he has done, and direct us by his counsel what is further to be done for the improving this success. May he send peace and truth upon the earth. We marched most part of this night also, and stormy weather it was. I slept a little in a soldier's tent till it was blown down about my ears, and the rain came in upon me. I bless God even for these little accommodations. We are more thankful in such circumstances for a small mercy, than for much greater ones when we are living at our ease and nothing to trouble us.

July 27. This morning we had a small march, and very bad weather. My mind was poring too much about public matters, and grudging lest the fruits of our good success be lost. This is not much my business; my duty is to be very thankful for the mercies we have met with. Providence will dispose of all for his own glory. Our design seems now to be the siege of Bouchain; and though this appears but a small thing, and no such enterprise as we might have hoped from our passing their lines, yet let us be thankful it is so well as it is, that we are gaining ground of the French in their own country, and baffling them. We are like to get a great deal of fatigue and trouble during this siege, the enemy's army being entire and strong.

July 30. Quiet these two days. We got a sudden alarm this day by the French passing the Scheldt and coming over to us. Our army drew out in great haste, and marched to the right to our line of battle, and there expected them. But it turned out only a feint to cover their design on the other side, and to amuse us till they should take post between us and Douay, which, it is said, they have done. I always thought they would make this siege troublesome to us, and that we should have fought them. The enemy soon retired over the river, and we returned to our camp. In the afternoon we marched again to the right to cover the general's quarters.

★★★★★★

In the following letter to his lady, of this date, he recapitulates very concisely the events of the preceding days.

Hordain, Tuesday, July 31.

I have received both your letters, and hope you have received mine giving account of our passing the lines. We have reason to be very thankful that God is pleased still to favour us with success, though we are so unworthy of it. But I observe also, that Providence does it in such a manner as seems to make the war spin out longer; for on whatever side France has the thickest and strongest nests of garrison. Providence turns our arms that way. He is dashing the potsherds of the earth together. Our march that time was very fatiguing; for we marched from nine at night till three in the afternoon next day; so that when we came to Arleux, where the French made some mien of opposing us, when the line drew up there was hardly above 70 or 80 of our regiment together that had not fallen by.

We had another night's march also on Wednesday's might crossing the Scheldt, and yesterday again the line was drawn out and formed the enemy having passed a considerable body of troops over the Scheldt towards us; so that everybody expected a battle: but the French drew off again. It was but a feint their coming over, to cover their design of taking post on the other side between us and Douay, where they well be troublesome and make the siege uneasy.

I bless God I am very well, and was never better than yesterday, when we expected to have come to an engagement. God forbid that I should boast of myself, for I find I have not that fund of natural gifts that some have, and may complain of much weakness. But in God will I boast. It is he that supplies me liberally with through-bearing grace. Of myself I can do nothing, but through him I can do all things. And, indeed, I am so weary of the war, that I am glad when I see it likely to come to a decisive action. Besides, the fatigues we have had, and are likely to have during this siege, make me believe that we should rather have brought it to a decision. But Providence does all for the best. It is our duty to obey and follow, and not to dictate or prescribe rules.

There are six British Regiments to be at this siege, and it comes just to us; so that we lie by for a warrant as we did at the siege of Douay. And in appearance it would be better to be at this, than the next which probably may be Valenciennes, both a stronger town, and a worse time of the year. But in this also, let us be very easy. The disposing of our lot, and every circumstance in it, is in the hand of a kind and gracious God. Let this make you easy and cheerful. It is better to have these experiences in our lot, than to be becalmed in the midst of our enjoyments, without these rousing providences. We are not lying in the line, but on the right of the army, covering the general's quarters. I would not for the price of my commission have been from the army upon this march. It was well ordered I came that day with General Murray. Give my humble service to Colonel Cunningham and his kind family. The Lord's presence be with you.

    Thine.   J.B.

Madam Blackader, *chez* Mons. Col. Cunningham,
 Commandant à Courtray.

★★★★★★

August 1. We are busy fortifying our camp, expecting alarms from the near neighbourhood of the enemy.

August 3. On command this day, overseeing the workmen at our trenches, which we have now put into so good posture of defence, that we do not fear the enemy's attack.

August 5. Sabbath. Much of my time spent in company and conversation, unsuitable to a Sabbath. Alas, how can it be otherwise, living in this army, where there is so much to check the growth of grace, and so little to strengthen it.—We were likely to have marched tonight upon some expedition about his siege, and it being referred to lot by throwing the dice. Providence ordered it so that we stay here.

August 10. Lying quietly these five days. I met with an occasion of being put out of humour, but I bless God, who, by his grace, subdues my corruption, and gives me any thing of a meek and quiet spirit. I find that heat and passion, and unreasonable humour, I am least able to bear of anything. I am fond, by all means, of living peaceably with all men, and would have them live so with me.

******

Of the proceedings and situation of both armies at this time, the letters contain more particulars than the diary. We shall therefore transcribe one or two of them.

Camp near Bouchain, August 5.

I received yours of Tuesday; but I cannot get writing so oft as I would incline, for it has been an unsettled sort of time since we passed the lines—much hurry and alertness, things being now to come to some better settlement, and the siege to have a much better aspect. The town is now fully invested, and it is not doubted but we shall be able to make the siege, and we even hope it will not prove so troublesome as we at first apprehended; and it is thought the French may march off when they find they cannot hinder it. We ought not to murmur that we do not immediately reap all the fruits that we proposed to ourselves; or that we find difficulties in prosecuting our good success. Providence could as easily have made us defeat their army, as surprise their lines; and as easily have opened a door to us into their country and their strongest towns, as into this fortress. But it is our concern to do our duty, and leave the disposal of events to him who orders all for his own glory.

I told you in my last what regiments are to be at the siege. Our regiment is upon command now too, lying out of the line on the right. We are very well entrenched over all, and lie very peaceably and quietly, though we are lying so near one another, that our soldiers and theirs sometimes speak together, the river only being between us. But both armies are well entrenched, so that here is no appearance of either of us making attempts upon each other. I have not got quarters here, the village being all occupied before we came. But I am very well in my tent. Keep your inclinations and humours, as to the possessing of our earthly comforts and satisfactions, for we should not consider what is pleasing, but what is best for us. The Lord's blessing and presence be ever with you.

Thine.　　　　　　　　　　　　　J. B.

Madame Blackader, *chez* Mons. Col. Cunningham,
Commandant à Courtray.

Camp, Friday, August 10.

Our post here is still very peaceable; for as near as we lie to one another, there is no disturbance. The siege is likely to go on very well. We have altogether cut off their communication with the town, so that this siege, we hope, will not be so tedious as we feared. (See note following letter). It is thought the enemy may make some movement, and march off from this post, when they cannot relieve the town. I can give no guess how long it may last, or what more will be done, or if any other siege will be taken in hand. No doubt, if time allow, they design to make as great progress as possible this campaign. But our great concern is to do our duty on every occasion where Providence posts us. Some of us are wishing to be on this siege, as being easier than it would be at the end of the campaign, at a stronger town and worse weather. For my part I have neither wishes nor fears upon the subject.

I think you have no reason to be uneasy about not hearing from Scotland. You know your father writes but seldom; if he were worse we would have heard. I have no letters or news from thence, but what the public gives us. You hear of that business of the Faculty of Advocates about that medal, and the Pretender. I do not well understand it; but there seems to be mad humours a-breeding and going through the island. I can scarce believe what they say, that the Lord Arniston has the chief hand in it. He was always looked upon as very well affected to the government. It is like enough to be his son indeed. There is good news that we hear yesterday of the Muscovites beating the Turks, and making a peace with them. This will be mortifying to the French king.

It is a great mercy, and we ought to be very thankful that Providence gives us such success. We are apt to be weary and discontented, because the steps are so slow, and that the war spins out so long that there is yet no prospect of ending it, by gaining those ends for which we entered into it. But God's ways and thoughts are as far above ours, as the heavens are above the earth; and there is a day coming wherein the infinite wisdom, and justice, and holiness of God shall be displayed before all the world, as to all that falls out hear.

We hear there are eleven regiments coming up, and Murray's is said to be one, and the fusiliers. Captain Dalrymple is gone down to Antwerp for money; let me hear if you want any, and I shall write him to leave you some as he comes through. We have no reason to want or to complain, we have enough, and I trust the blessing of God with it. My humble service to Colonel Cunningham; I shall give myself the honour to write him when I get more time.

    I am thine.   J.B.

Madam Blackader, *chez* Mons. Col. Cunningham,
Commandant à Courtray.

******

Note:—This communication between the enemy's camp and the town, was established through a morass where the water was pretty deep, though covered with willows and rushes. It was constructed on a narrow footway that ran through the middle of it, and a parapet carried on with fascines from tree to tree the whole way, defended by three redoubts. In order to get possession of these, the Duke of Marlborough ordered out 400 grenadiers who marched up to the middle, and some to the neck in water. They reached the parapet, and drove the enemy from their posts, though exposed to the cannon, both of the town and the entrenchments.

An ensign of Ingoldsby's regiment, who was at the head of fifteen grenadiers, being very short of stature, and seeing, when they had advanced into the water, that he must either drown, or give up his share of the enterprise and return, chose rather to get upon the shoulders of one of grenadiers and when they came to the parapet, he was one of the first to leap into the enemy's works.—*Lediard*, vol. ii.

******

Bouchain, August 13. Monday.

The trenches were opened on Saturday, on this side of the town. There is to be an attack also on this side; and we would have been upon it; but it is otherwise ordered. The whole army that lie on this side are to be concerned, and to carry it on, which will make it easy to us all. There are to be three regiments in the trenches every day, and there being sixty, it will not come above once to our turn. We broke ground last night on this side, with four battalions of Guards covering, with little or no loss. I was on command on Saturday, which was both short and easy, having gone out at nine in the morning and returned in the evening. We were perfecting the lines of our army in front. They are so strong, that we do not think the French will try them. Monsieur Villars is reckoned to have lost much reputation, since our passing the lines. They say most of his generals are much discontented.

Let us be living by faith, cheerfully committing future events to the direction of God, possessing our souls in patience. We are too hasty, and would have all great events crowded into our own times, that we might see God's enemies destroyed by battles and victories. But we should consider that providences run in a parallel to the time of the world's duration; some accomplished in one age, some in another, but all in their right and proper season, which will make a beautiful and comely prospect when all is perfected.

I am thine. J.B.

Madam Blackader, *chez* Mons. Col. Cunningham, *Commandant à* Courtray.

Colonel Preston, about this time, having obtained the appointment of brigadier, Colonel Blackader, had his ambition prompted him, might have risen to a higher command, but he had ceased to look upon these things with an eye of youthful vanity, or mercenary hope, considering them as encumbrances, to be shunned rather than coveted.

******

August 17. Abroad at court all the forenoon. He who is above me in the regiment, has now got a greater post which takes him, in a manner, out of the regiment, whereby my charge becomes greater. I do not now look upon it with the eyes of youthful vanity and ambition, as a step of rising and pushing forward. I view it as a heavier charge and burden upon my shoulders, which, the Lord knows, I am not able for. But this is all my hope and confidence, that he who sends none a warfare on their own charges, when he calls me to any duty, be it never so difficult, will give me grace to go through with it. I have greater inclination to leave this employment, than to rise in it. Our Brigadier's commission, we hear, is come over with Brigadier Panton.

August 21. Getting an alarm this morning between twelve and one; we marched to our alarm post, and remained till five. I was calm and composed. This post which the French have taken makes us uneasy.

August 22. This night we were again at arms all night, and marched to our alarm post, where we lay till sunrising. In the midst of all these confusions God is a refuge. This is all my comfort and peace, for from every other quarter, nothing but trouble. The humour of those we have to do with, and the society we live in, are among the greatest uneasinesses we meet with in the world. There is nothing I have a greater aversion and fear of than living in strife and contention. I would live with all the world peaceably, quietly, and innocently, and would have everybody about me calm and easy.

August 25. I visited the siege on all sides, seeing what was most observable and curious about all the works and trenches.

******

Of this alarm, and some other particulars, the colonel gives an account in a letter to his Lady, of this date.

Thursday, August 23. Since I last wrote to you we had an alarm which has given us both fatigue and trouble. On Monday night, about twelve, they gave the alarm at the village where we he, by firing upon a redoubt and battery we have. We hurried out immediately and marched down to our alarm post; but the French retired from this place, and in the meantime attacked Hordain, and took some of our generals there; but the regiments there repulsed them, and then they came up our side of the river and attacked a post we have at Etrum, and took it, and have fortified themselves there. But we, to prevent any trouble from them, have made a strong line between us and them, all the way from this to Hordain; so we reckon ourselves better and safer than we were before. It has given us fatigue; for Monday and Tuesday both nights we lay at our arms, upon our alarm posts; and our picquets are to lie at arms on the lines every night as long as the siege lasts.

This is one of the most troublesome sieges we have ever made, by the near neighbourhood of the French army; but yet we hope, by the blessing of God, to finish it with success and honour, which will indeed give a great reputation to our general. It is hoped we may have the town in eight days. Our regiment has not been in the trenches yet. We are to be in on Monday if the *Basse-Ville* be not over before that time. I bless God who strengthens me for fatigue, and carries me through the doing of my duty. I see his goodness in defending and taking care of every thing about us; for our regiment might have been at Hordain when it was attacked. We threw the dice for going there when we came to this village, and so we missed it. *The lot is cast into the lap, but the disposing of it is of the Lord.*

     I am thine.   J.B.

Madam Blackader, *chez* Mons. Col. Cunningham, *Commandant à* Courtray.

******

August 29. This day our regiment went into the trenches. I bless the Lord who made them safe and easy to us, and that we had no loss. I spent the day quietly though among the noise of cannon, bombs, &c., and no accident befell me.

             Thursday, August 30.

We are just come from the trenches, where we have had a quiet night; and none wounded save a sergeant of Captain Ferguson's. We still expect to be masters of the town in four or five days. Time runs away, this is the day the Battle of Tanniers was fought. The remembrance of the many experiences of God's goodness to us, should encourage us to trust in him cheerfully in time coming. I have got a house hard by the regiment, by Colonel Kerr's regiment marching out of this camp. I have got Mr. Harris' commission to give him; and I have thanked the brigadier for the regard he has paid to our recommendation. It is one of the greatest comforts I have if I were to leave the regiment, that I have got that charitable good office carried through.

You win excuse me not enlarging in this letter, being fatigued all yesterday, having no sleep last night, nor this day, nor will not till night. The Lord's peace and blessing rest with you.

J.B.

Madam Blackader, *chez* Mons. Col. Cunningham,
Commandant à Courtray.

September 1. I was on command yesterday, and came off this morning. Everything went on smoothly. The Lord makes all I do to prosper well. The town is capitulating this night. Blessed be God who countenances and gives success to all our undertakings.

September 4. I went in to see the town which we have just taken. It is nothing but a heap of rubbish; so ruined. Mankind are made the scourges of the earth to punish each other for their sins.

******

While the army was lying at Bouchain, Colonel Blackader was negotiating with the General respecting the disposal of his commission. As nothing remarkable occurs during this period of inactivity, we shall transcribe two or three of his letters for this month, which contain more particulars than the diary.

Bouchain, September 2.

You will probably have heard before this reaches you, that this town has at last fallen into our hands. They began to capitulate yesterday about two o'clock. They are to be prisoners of war; which still seems to throw the greater discredit upon Marshal Villars, to see a garrison taken prisoners in his sight, and that he could not relieve them. We have reason to bless God it is so well over, for our army has been in very critical circumstances, has had many posts to defend, and many accidents to fear. But the goodness of God has brought us well and honourably through, and to him be the praise, where it is originally due. It is thought we may lie here eight or ten days till we repair the works, and put the town in some posture of defence. What we shall do after that, time only can discover.

September 3. The garrison marched out this forenoon. The soldiers go to the French army, for we were in debt to them about 1500 men; but the officers are prisoners till they be relieved.—I am sorry that you are complaining. Take care of yourself. Be not anxious or melancholy, for you have no reason. God deals bountifully and kindly with us, and grants us the same blessings that he did to Jabez: He keeps us from all evil that it may not grieve us, and what would we have more? Should we complain that our enjoyments are out of our sight, and lying at the mercy of Providence? No; we should rather rejoice that there is an occasion of exercising faith and dependence, and a larger field of experiences of God's faithfulness in fulfilling his promises to us. We have need of all these things. If we look into our own hearts we shall find it so. We hear that Lord Albemarle is gone down to the Hague to advise about the further operations of the campaign.

The Lord's presence and blessing rest with you.

I am thine. J.B.

Madam Blackader, *chez* Mons. Col. Cunningham,
Commandant à Courtray.

Bouchain, September 8.

There is no news since my last. We are busy about this town; and would as gladly have it up now, as before to throw it down. I believe we shall yet lie here ten days. We are at an utter uncertainty still about our future operations Some are wagering we shall make another siege, others that we shall not; and every body wishes the last may gain. I see none so public-spirited in the army as to wish for another siege.

I am very well pleased with your scheme sent in your latest letter, for the rest of the campaign, to go and lie where the most and best forage is. It is really very naturally expressed, and one can see, from your style, that you profit by the conversation of men of business and commandants of frontier places. But if we should take your advice, to go and lie where there is best forage, what if that should prove to be about Ypres, and the neighbourhood of the poor Castellany of Courtray; then, I am afraid, some of your family would wish us back again at Cambray or Valenciennes. But without jesting, there is much a talk that our army, if we do no more, may come to lie thereabout to consume the forage about Ypres: so you had best advertise the boors to bring their corn to that town; it will be an act of charity done to the poor boors, and the governor will be no loser.

I shall also consider of your other scheme, which seems to be pretty well laid, except that of running over in a dogger, which I do not like. I know you mean only of taking that occasion of going to Ghent. I can give no resolution on that head till we see farther about us. I am ready to determine whatever way duty calls, which I think is a better temper than to be bent upon any thing. In such a case I generally find there is a snare. I desire to be seriously concerned to know what is duty, and beg grace to follow it when discovered; and I hope the Lord will direct by his spirit, and cause us to walk in a right way wherein we shall not stumble, Jerem. xxxi. 9, and be as a voice behind us, saying. *This is the way, walk ye in it.* Tomorrow is ordered to be kept a day of thanksgiving for the taking of Bouchain. It is to be wished that repentance and reformation were joined with it more than we see.

   I am thine.   J. B.
Madam Blackader, *chez* Mons. Col. Cunningham, *Commandant à* Courtray.

                September 23.
I am very glad to find your thoughts so just and moderate on the subject of my last. It is what I expected from one who is so reasonable, and so resigned to the will of God. It is a mercy that both of us are so easy upon that head, for this is a frame of mind I greatly desire, and for which I have often prayed.—I can say nothing yet about my obtaining leave to go to Scotland, the brigadier himself being yet undetermined about his own going. Meantime, let us put all our concerns into His hands, who taketh care of us, and knows best what is good for us.

I have just received yours, and your father's letters. I won I have not foresight enough to foresee or answer all the difficulties that can be proposed in the affair; and I believe it would be easy to find flaws and failures in all human securities and determinations; because such is the nature of human affairs, that they are not capable of an infallible security. All we can do is, to act according to the best of our judgement. When things come to an anxious perplexity, that they must be managed by a cunning dexterity, they are then above my reach and calibre. Everyone has their proper talents; artifice is not mine. I see no better foundation to put it on than this:

At such a day as I give, you are to pay me such a sum of money, and then you are to be lieutenant colonel; if you fail in payment, then I have my post, and you have your money. But I will not break my heart about these things. The Lord direct and

guide by this Spirit.
                    I am thine.   J.B.
Madam Blackader, *chez* Mons. Col. Cunningham,
Commandant à Courtray.

The person with whom the colonel was on terms regarding the disposal of his commission, was Lord Forrester. But the brigadier having signified that a fellow-officer would be more acceptable to him than a stranger, the major of his own regiment was advised to become the purchaser. The sum, however, which he was able to advance, £2000 sterling, not being thought adequate to the value of the commission, this project was laid aside, and the former negotiation continued.

                                        Saturday, September 29.
This proposal of the major's that I told you of is now over; for upon second thoughts he does not find it convenient for him. It was also the brigadier's advice to him not to lay out the small stock he had that way, for he thought it too great a risk for a man that has a family. So the affair is gone into its former train again, and my lord and I have very nearly agreed. I put it upon this foot.

I am to have £2600 sterling, for it, with a drawback of a shilling per pound; if free of this, then £2500. I give him till the 20th of March to pay the money; failing which, or if proper security is not given, the bargain is dissolved. I make £1600 to be paid in London, and the rest in Edinburgh. So let it take what course Providence pleases to give it.

My lord has a mind to go away, if he get leave, in three or four days; and I intend also to ask leave; but I know Lord Orkney is very nice in granting it. If I come, I think of bringing the chaise.

Tournay is now the ordinary road. The brigadier told me yesterday that both General Murray and Colonel Cunningham had intelligence from Ypres, that the French may probably have some design on the Lys, so it is expected some troops may march that way. I know not what to do with Andrew, (his servant,) I would gladly do something for him, now he is growing old. I propose getting him into Chelsea, as a sergeant. He inclines to stay in my service, and to dispose of the other which, he says, win give £30 or £40. I am just going on command, which, I hope, will be short, as it is but the piquet I came off in the morning.

I am thine.

J.B.

Madam Blackader, *chez* Mons. Col. Cunningham,
Commandant à Courtray.

The colonel readily obtained leave of absence, and took his departure; uncertain whether his arrangement with Lord Forrester might not miscarry, and call him back to the regiment next campaign. His apprehensions, however, were never destined to be realised, for the commission was disposed of, and the stipulations punctually fulfilled at the appointed time. Before quitting Bouchain, he addressed a petition to the commander-in-chief, soliciting permission to retire from the service, which was granted. The following is a copy of the petition:—

To His Grace the Duke of Marlborough,
The Petition of Lieutenant—Colonel Blackader, &c.
Humbly Sheweth,

That I have served in this regiment since the late happy Revolution, and have been several times wounded in the service, particularly at the battle of Blenheim, and at the siege of Lisle.

My Lord, If my natural strength and vigour were any way equal to the zeal with which I have served these twenty-two years, the hopes of seeing an end put to this long and troublesome war, by your Grace's wise and happy conduct, would still support me under all its growing fatigues: But, my Lord, my grey hairs increasing fast upon me, do give me notice that it is time I should think of a retreat. Also, the circumstances of my private affairs in North Britain, do require my attendance there.

May it therefore please your Grace to allow me (by disposing of my commission to a gentleman much better qualified for the service) to retire out of the army, and turn my sword into a ploughshare.

✶✶✶✶✶✶

October 1. Yesterday having taken my resolution to depart, I went in the afternoon to ask leave, and found all the generals so easy and accessible, that I met not with the smallest difficulty. This morning I left the army at Bouchain. The Lord only knows whether ever I shall return to it again. I refer my life to his will and disposal. If his presence go with me, I am glad to go; if it be his pleasure I should return, I am also satisfied. I was melancholy in the morning at parting with some of my kind friends, and the corps I have lived in these twenty-two years. But through the day I had a serene, thankful mind, while riding alone in my chaise. I applied that saying of Jacob's, Gen. xxxii. 10. So may I say, *I am less than the least of all his mercies,* for with my lieutenant's partisan, I passed over to this country about twenty-one years ago, and now the Lord sends me out of the army with abundance of reputation, and the conveniences of life; for I was ashamed to hear of the kind and obliging things which my Lord Duke spoke about me to the generals with him, after I was gone out.

I say not this to flatter myself, or to be fuel to vanity; but to sir up thankfulness. Oh the goodness and mercy with which God has followed me these twenty-two years since I came to this employment: how wonderfully preserved, protected, and honoured! in so much that there has scarce been an action in which I have been, but Providence did kindly make some accidents fall out, which procured me greater reputation in the army. Not unto me, but unto thee be the praise; for hadst thou withheld thy grace I should have misbehaved on every occasion; and had contempt and shame instead of honour.

I have seen officers more deserving in themselves, who have been toiling through fatigues and dangers for twenty or thirty years, and who had gathered a good stock of reputation,—I have seen them lose it all in one day, or in an hour. And it would have been so with me, if the Lord had left me; but he has always furnished me very liberally. I praise him who enabled me to live in such an army, suitable to the profession of religion, though, I confess, with much weakness, and many failings on my part. This is a great and wonderful mercy, and it is also remembered in the army, I hope, to the honour of God and the credit of religion.

I came safe to Tournay at night. I have not had more serenity of mind and thankfulness than I had all this day. I take this for a good omen that the presence of the Lord shall go with me. I spent the next day there quietly, meditating on the goodness of God to me. Thou hast been my hiding-place, my shield, my glory, the uplifter of my head.

October 3. Travelling to Courtray, where I arrived safe. I bless God for giving us a happy meeting and bringing the campaign to a comfortable issue.

October 9. We left Courtray and travelled all day to Ghent.

October 16. Left Ghent and came with an escort to Sas, where we intend taking ship for Rotterdam. We were to have sailed early next morning; but by an accident of a rope breaking, and the water failing, we were stopped all day. This at first made us uneasy; but it turned out very fortunate; for there came a very great storm, which might have put us in danger if we had gone. It frequently happens so with us, that things which we are vexed at and reckon to be crosses, are by the wise providence of God made to be our choicest mercies.

October 18. Sailed this morning, and with a good wind came to Rotterdam at twelve o'clock next day.

******

While at Rotterdam Mrs. Blackader was seized with a violent fever, in which she was dangerously ill, and confined for nearly a month. In December she recovered so far as to enable them to prosecute their journey.

******

December 25. This day we left Rotterdam. Thy goodness and mercy, Oh Lord, has followed us here; may thy presence be with us during this voyage.

December 28. This forenoon we embarked in the yachts that carry over Prince Eugene and the Prussian Ambassador to London. We essayed to get over the shallows and out of the Maese, but could not, and cast anchor and lay there all night. Next day we got over, and in the evening stood out to sea; but not finding the man of war that was to convoy us, we were obliged to come back and anchor before Helvoet, where we lay tossing all night

December 30. In the afternoon our convoy came out: we weighed anchor and prosecuted our voyage till midnight with a good wind. But the wind then turning contrary, we were obliged to change our course more northerly towards Yarmouth.

December 31. In the afternoon we came to anchor between Yarmouth and Harwich. There we were tossed for another night, and next morning we wrought up to Harwich and landed.

January 2. We had a pleasant voyage up the river to Ipswich, and in two days arrived safe in London. Now that thou has brought us to Britain again, Oh Lord, let us have thy presence and blessing here as we have had abroad.

******

The colonel continued in London until the 23rd of March, to await the final conclusion of his transaction with Lord Forrester. This matter was conducted amicably, and without further interruption, and terminated to the entire satisfaction of both parties.

> We have now finished our bargain about my post, according to our previous appointment, and having made my demission, I now look upon myself as out of the army. I remark the kind dealing of Providence with me; for the 25th, two days hence, is the day on which, by Act of Parliament, I would have lost my post if I had gone to a Presbyterian meeting.[1] Now by the goodness of God I am delivered out of this snare, for his law does not touch me, having no post. I knew not this, nor did I suspect it last summer when I entered into the agreement. But God who leads the blind by the way they know not, was leading me by the hand and taking me out of the army in the best and fittest time. I desire to adore and admire the mercy and goodness of God, to me in his providence, and to trust in him cheerfully in the time to come. Make thy way plain to me, that I who am a wayfaring man, and a fool may not err therein.

The remainder of the continental war presented nothing memorable. Marlborough being disposted, the command was bestowed on the Duke of Ormond; but as negotiations for peace had been set on foot, he had secret orders to refrain from offensive hostilities. This prevented him from co-operating with Prince Eugene, who was resolved to press the war with vigour; and in consequence, the French gained some advantages and recovered several of the towns they had lost. The whole campaign was, on the part of England, a studied artifice to deceive the Allies. But it was destined to be the last, for the conference which had been opened at Utrecht, in the beginning of the year, terminated in a treaty of peace, which was concluded and signed April 11, 1713.

---

1. This was a bill to prevent *Occasional Conformity*, by which all persons having places of profit or trust under government, should forfeit these if they were convicted of being present at any meeting for religious worship, consisting of more than ten persons besides the family, and where the book of Common Prayer was not used. This bill, which had formerly been much contested, now passed without opposition; and was to take effect on the 25th of March, as above,—*Burnet*, vol. ii.

CHAPTER 18

Domestic Sketches, 1712–1714

Having disposed of his commission, and obtained his final liberation from the army, Colonel Blackader left London. His stay there was not signalised by any thing particularly worthy of notice. He says:—

No place I ever was in gives me a greater idea of the vanity of the world, than this city. Most people walk in a vain show.

He several times visited the Duke of Marlborough then in London, but under disgrace, and shorn of his military honours, "a sad emblem," he remarks, "of the capricious inconstancy of all human things."

Now that the means of grace and of hearing the gospel were more within his reach, he gladly availed himself of these opportunities. Scarcely a day passed in which he did not attend public worship, either at the morning lectures, or some of the religious Institutions in the city. This he never considered as any hindrance or interruption to his secular concerns.

★★★★★★

April 5. I see that the service of God does not hinder business, but promotes it; for yesterday being employed in his service, and having several affairs yet to be despatched, I was afraid I should have too little time. But Providence brought my business to my hand, and also made it smooth and easy; so that it was well done, and soon over, and cost me neither trouble nor care. I see this in all the steps of my life, that though there is much weakness in my own management, he makes all I do to prosper, better than those who have much more wisdom and prudence. On Sabbath I heard the Bishop of Salisbury (Burnet) preach a very good sermon. I was edified by it; but I complain that impressions speedily wear out, and my affections soon grow cold.

******

It was on the 7th of April that he and his lady left London, but from the slow mode of travelling then in practice, it was more than two weeks before they reached Edinburgh. On the evening of the 21st, they came to Dunbar. While here, his thoughts immediately turned to an interesting object, fitted to call up, in his mind, images at once pleasing and melancholy. The solitary rock where his venerable father had languished in captivity, and which, it appears, he had then visited occasionally on the mournful errands of filial duty and affection, stands within a few miles of that shore. This naturally attracted his attention, and seems to have been the subject of his pensive meditations, leading him to contrast his former humble and desolate prospects in life, with his present honourable and comparative affluence. He says:—

> In the evening I stepped out, and walked towards the seaside, in sight of the Bass Island, which occasioned serious thoughts, and a thankful frame of mind, to think of the long train of mercy and goodness that has followed me these many years since I was there; when there was far from any appearance or expectation of such things as Providence has now done for me.

Next day they arrived in Edinburgh; and on the 24th, came to Craigforth, the seat of his wife's father, near Stirling. There he continued until the middle of August, when he fixed his residence for some time in Edinburgh. The rural quiet and retirement which he enjoyed at Craigforth, were much more congenial to his temper and habits, than the tumult and distraction of the army. His leisure hours were spent occasionally in the recreation of angling or field-sports, which he considered a more rational and harmless pastime, than the frivolous amusements, or the fashionable dissipations of cities. He says:—

> I pass my time quietly after the country manner. I find more peace and serenity of mind here, than in towns. There is something more sweet and innocent in rural life.

His company and conversation, as was to be expected, furnished many attractions for visitors, both friends and strangers; but he always grudged being compelled to sacrifice to the curiosity of his guests, more time than could be either instructive or edifying. Conversation, when it ceased to accomplish this object, he regarded as degenerating into idle entertainment, which ought to be checked, rather than encouraged.

> There is much of my time wasted in making formal visits of ceremony. A country life, I see, is subject to this inconvenience. I was in company all day, (*June 4.*) by strangers coming to the house. This is a kind of life I do not like to have all my time stolen from me, and trifled away. I could not well live without some intervals of retirement. To be continually in bustle, and in public, is contrary to a Christian life. It keeps me from private duty, from thinking and meditation.

Notwithstanding his assiduous attendance on the public ordinances of religion, and his peculiar warmth of devotion, he expresses himself no friend to that Pharisaic ostentation, which leads men to attach an undue value to external forms, while they are negligent to cultivate the no less essential duties of personal or domestic piety. The protracted services of the church, which it was then customary with some to extend to three or four hours without intermission, he objected to, as tending to fatigue the attention, and exhaust the mind, rather than to edify or improve it.[1] Among other remarks on this subject, he observes, while attending the preparation sermons before the sacrament at Stirling.

> I complain that I was preached more dead and flat, by being too much in public. I am sorry I cannot hold out better, but I am not capable of such intenseness of attention. My spirits become fatigued by long sermons. I think this is the fault of the custom here. There is too much time employed in public, and too little left for private devotions. And also, upon such occasions, there is too much pains taken to work up the affections and frame to a height, without taking equal care of a suitable growth and improvement in the judgement and conversation.

---

1. The Communion Service especially was then protracted to a very tedious and unnecessary extent. On the Preparation Sabbath they had in towns three long sermons, besides, in some places, two exhortations or addresses to intending communicants. On the Fast-day, Thursday, there were three services by two or three several ministers; on Friday evening a sermon; on Saturday two, or perhaps three. On Sabbath, there was the action sermon, as it is called; the table services which were seldom short, sermons in the tent, and an evening sermon in the church. The whole ceremony concluded on Monday, with two sermons, by two different ministers. These lengthened services which had there origin in times of persecution, when people could meet for worship only by stealth, and at the hazard of their lives, the church has now judiciously abridged; and it is a question with some, whether they might not be still farther reduced?

This makes fanciful, rather than solid Christians. We are generally more earnest to have the consolations and smiles of Christ, than careful to take on the whole yoke of Christ, or to walk in a course of obedience, mortifying and subduing our own wills and tempers.

It was a favourite text with him, that expression of the psalmist in his dedicatory prayer. *For we are strangers before thee, and sojourners as were all our fathers; our days on the earth are as a shadow, and there is nothing abiding.*

I heard a good sermon on a subject that I love well to hear preached upon. Oh learn me to live as I have heard, a stranger and pilgrim in the world. I thought my affections more warmed and raised by this sermon, than they were at the Lord's table. The spirit is free, and bloweth where it listeth. I desire not, as many do, to measure my Christian growth by the workings of my affections, but by solid resolutions of the will, guided by a sound judgment and understanding, and that guided by the word of God.

******

June 29. I went early to Airth on Sabbath, but did not communicate; and in the evening the ministers served a conviction upon me that I ought to have done it. I hope, however, I did it in effect, that is, I took hold of Christ in my heart, and fed upon him by faith. I desire to employ him for mortifying sin, and for sanctifying my soul.

August 6. I was abroad all day, attending a burial in the country. Most of the conversation and company there, was not desirable. It is wonderful to see what a perverse, malignant spirit is gone out among the gentry, especially against all that is good. Oh the madness of the people, that would sacrifice religion and liberty, and all that is valuable, to satisfy their humour; but *Quos Deus vult perdere prius dementat.*

******

Parties at this time in Scotland, both political and religious ran extremely high. This was a subject of Frequent regret and animadversion with Colonel Blackader. Although a man of no faction, and expecting neither post nor pension from government, yet he could not but lament the violence of party, and feel interested in the welfare of his country. The divisive interested spirit which rent both the church and the state, was his greatest uneasiness, and he will be found perpetually alluding to it in course of the diary.

On the 14th of August he left Craigforth, and came to Edinburgh. His first reflections, on this occasion, were those of gratitude and thankfulness.

> I bless God for his goodness, (which has been very great,) in bringing us back here to a quiet, peaceable habitation among our friends, after so many year's wanderings through dangers and difficulties. Now that we are to live here, let thy presence be with us, that our house may be a Bethel, and our hearts a temple where thou mayest delight to dwell.

Here, though he regularly attended the Established Church, not only on Sabbath, but at the weekly sermons, he united himself to a private society or association for prayer and religious fellowship. At the same time he extended the greatest liberality of sentiment towards others. To those who differed from him in opinion, he never shewed that asperity or intolerance of spirit, which unfortunately too much distinguishes the boasted liberality of more enlightened times. On the contrary, he reprobates these animosities as the hateful offspring of bigotry and virulence.

★★★★★★

September 10. I was most of this day in company, where too much heat was shewn in debate. Heat always produces heat, and passion draws out passion. Indeed, I suspect, that much of what some people call zeal, proceeds from heat and violence of temper which, I think, is natural to the Scots people above others; and I am afraid we are often led by our own humours, instead of the Spirit of God. It is the meek thou guidest in judgement. The meek thou clearly teachest thy way. Lord, make me so. Keep me from extremes, both on the right hand, and on the left. Let me not act or suffer for any thing but what is clear duty, wherein I may have thy approbation, and the peace and testimony of a good conscience. I dare not give myself up to be directed by any man, or set of men. Be thou thyself my guide.

(1713,) *February 3.* Hearing the morning sermon; and was afterwards surprised to hear of the sudden illness of a friend who seems to be dying. Lord, fit and prepare her for the change. Let her soul be bound up in the bundle of life. I find that the sight of dying person makes a deeper impression upon me now in cold blood, than ten thousand did in Flanders at battles. At night my niece died. Lord, sanctify the providence to those most concerned, and to us all. I perceive, that in a dying hour, an interest in Christ, and the sense of it, is worth ten thousand worlds; for all earthly comforts are then tasteless and useless.

******

In the end of March the colonel and his lady left Edinburgh, and spent the summer in visiting their friends in Stirlingshire. While at Doun, he observes:—

Here I was stirred up to a thankful frame of mind at the remembrance of all the mercies and deliverances that has attended me since I was last in this place, about twenty-three years ago.

The company of his friends and the relaxation of country diversions made his time pass very agreeably, and he sometimes exclaims with the ancient poet, but in a nobler sense, *Deus nobis haec otia fecit.* They left Craigforth in August and returned to Edinburgh.

******

September 10. I hear that our regiment is gone for Ireland. They cannot serve there unless they take the sacramental test.[2] (*Vide* chapter 4). I admire and adore the goodness of God to me, who brought me out of the army, just at the proper time; who allowed me to stay in it while service was to be done against his enemies, and honour to be got; and gave me a bountiful share of it, and of profit also. And I could never have managed my demission right, nor got the difficulties removed that are frequently in the way of such bargains, had not Providence made me almost passive in it, and sent a man who was fond of my post, and acceptable to those concerned, which made it easy, and let me off with honour and profit in abundance. May God give me grace to devote the lest of my life to him and his service.

November 5. This day heard sermon, and was made a member of the Society for Propagating Christian Knowledge.

******

---

2. The Test Act was passed in 1672, by all persons holding public offices, besides taking the oaths of supremacy and allegiance, were required to receive the sacrament, according to the rites of the Church of England. The act did not extend to Ireland till 1706, and is now repealed there. Dissenters from the English Church still regard it as a grievance; and it is now almost the only limitation of religious liberty in England; the Toleration Act of 1690, with its enlargement in 1779, having deprived all other laws against Protestant Non-conformists of force and effect.

In January 1714 the colonel was made an elder of the College Church, Edinburgh.[3]

> Lord, give me grace to do the duties of this post aright, so as I may have divine approbation, and the peace and testimony of a good conscience.

In his official visitations of the parish he was very assiduous; and the duties of this avocation, together with those of the fellowship meeting for prayer, and the Society for Propagating Christianity, kept him tolerably well employed. He was on the committee of this society, which consisted of fifteen members, chosen annually. Their office required both labour and attention. They transacted the whole business of the society, superintended their accounts, executed their orders, and managed their correspondence. Their meetings were held weekly, sometimes twice a-day, and never less than once a month. To these various duties he applied himself with diligence and cheerfulness, for he grudged neither time nor pains when they could be beneficial to the interests of religion or morality.

As a member of the Kirk-Session, he was sometimes brought into contact with the Presbytery. The ordinary discussions of that court, he thought, were conducted in general with too much acrimony and ill nature.

> Attending the Presbytery, and seeing there what is not very pleasant. Churchmen have their pride, their passions, and stiffness, like others. I believe there is much humour and wildfire mixed up with the zeal of many good people, which they themselves mistake for true zeal. There is much of that in Scotland. Our national temper, the *proefervidum ingenium* imposes upon us for zeal. But it is not all gold that glitters. The tongue is an unruly evil. Lord, rebuke and heal our divisions. Give us the ornament of a meek and quiet spirit—the wisdom that comes from above, which is first pure, then peaceable, gentle, &c. I do not like pride and ill humour in those who should have least of it.

His conduct upon another occasion, shews his conscientious independence in deciding according to the dictates of his own judgement, unbiased by the influence of any particular party.

---

3. It was then called the "North-East Kirk;" his only surviving brother was then an elder in the "New Kirk," which is now, I believe, the High Church. Both their signatures are subscribed to the Formulary in the Session-Clerk's Office, Edinburgh.

******

February 10. Waiting upon the Presbytery all day. I gave my opinion and vote not with the side that I gave it upon the other two days. It was according to my conscience, and I think it is a weakness to have the conscience tied to any party, but free and disengaged to receive the truth. I hope I was well directed; at least I was disinterested, and without bias in the matter; and I am sorry to see so much of it in those who should be the most free. I am always uneasy with brisk, forward, hot tempers. I like calmness, sobriety, and solidity, in debate; but mettle, resolution, and fire, when it comes to action.

February 22. Hearing our quarterly sermon against immorality. In the forenoon dining with a large company. I like not the brisk sparkling conversation of the wits so well as the wise and prudent, whereby we are edified and made better. At night had a meeting with our correspondents. Lord, direct and bless, else all our endeavours are vain and fruitless. This town is full of stories and rumours; there is a busy lying people spreading scandal on all sides, to rankle and irritate men's spirits. I know, I among others am the butt of this malice and rage,—but who shall harm us if we be followers of that which is good? Lord, counsel and guide us to just and proper measures for the security of our holy religion, our liberties, and properties, all of which seem to be in great danger.

March 17. At the Presbytery, and giving my opinion according to my judgment. I am chosen member for the General Assembly. Lord, give me grace to discharge my duty faithfully. I either mistake religion myself, or I think many in this country do. I think the best evidence of our sincerity, and of our being partakers of grace, lies in subduing our tempers, and those sins which most easily beset us. But I see many place their religion in strict opinions, in a fiery hot temper, and a forward practice conform thereto. This really scandalise me to see so much profession of strict religion, and other things not conformable.

April 27. Attending my duty in the *Synod*. I sought counsel and direction of God how to carry, that I may have no wrong bias upon my mind, no prejudices, but to have the glory of God and the good of his church always before me. I wish to have a just mixture of zeal and prudence, that I may be kept from extremes on the right or left hand.

May 6. Heard an excellent sermon at the opening of the Assembly.

Lord, direct and guide this Assembly by thy Spirit. Give them a spirit of unity and love, a spirit of zeal and wisdom to manage all we do for thy glory and the advancement of Christ's kingdom. Direct me in my affair. Put words into my mouth; for I may say, I am but of slow speech and a stammering tongue. I have not the gift of delivering my mind with eloquence.[4]

May 7. Walked with the commissioner, (the Duke of Athol.) Upon the Committee of the Assembly. Obliged to go out and sup, where we were kept intolerably late. Vexed at it, and out of order.

May 10. Still on committees: in the afternoon dined with the commissioner.

May 12. This day the affair I was concerned in came before the Assembly. I was sensible how weakly it was managed on my part. I was unwilling to take the commission, but I could not get by it.

May 17. This forenoon the Assembly rose, and a pleasant sight it was. such unity and harmony! I was much affected while singing the 133rd Psalm.

May 19. Waiting upon the Assembly's Commission, and representing the case of our old regiment as to conformity to the English Service.[5] I am apt to get too hot in debate: and I am sorry that too many in Scotland are so. I think religion runs greatly in the wrong channel, and may be called Presbyterianism rather than Christianity,—strict opinions in the head about public things, and oftentimes about doubtful points, where good men are on both sides; while the influences of it do not go through the conduct of their lives, in universal obedience and charity.

★★★★★★

---

4. His "affair" was the presenting of a call from the Scots congregation at Rotterdam, to Mr. Robert Baillie, minister at Inverness, to be their pastor: the case was considered, but Mr. Baillie was continued in his ministry at Inverness. A letter was written to the magistrates of Rotterdam, and another to the Scots congregation, containing reasons why the Assembly could not comply; and they empowered their commission to cognise upon any other process that might be brought before them for planting that congregation. *Vid. Acts of General Assembly,* 1714.

5 This was in reference to the grievance imposed upon them by the Test and Act already alluded to: it certainly was an obvious inequality of toleration, that those of the Scots communion employed in her Majesty's service in England or Ireland, should be obliged to conform to the English Church, while the same conformity was not required of Episcopalians in Scotland.

On the 2nd of June he quitted Edinburgh and fixed his residence in Stirling. At this time the country was in considerable fermentation, from the intrigues of the Pretender's friends and some unpopular acts of the administration. The death of the queen seemed also to throw an additional gloom over these apprehensions.

★★★★★★

August 3. This day we got the surprising news of the queen's being extremely ill, which put a damp upon my spirits and stunned me at first. Then being alone, and committing all to God by prayer, my heart was somewhat quieted and established. Lord, disappoint the designs of malignant restless enemies, and get glory by all events. Met in the afternoon with the magistrates and friends here, to concert measures for our security. Let our eyes be towards thee, and give us help from trouble, for vain is the help of man. We heard next day that the queen is better. I rejoice in it, and wish her recovery if it be God's will. We have had peace and truth in her time, and also liberty under the wings of her government, to lead quiet and peaceable lives in all godliness and honesty. If we have had hardships put upon us of late years, they must be attributed to the violence and rage of parties, and not to her temper. She has been virtuous, sober, clement, and devout in her own way. All this we ought to acknowledge with thankfulness to God, and also to her as the means.

August 5. We do not hear yet of the queen's death, although her life be despaired of. Lord, prepare her for, and receive her to, an immortal crown of glory. I am glad that all is going on quietly and peaceably, all seeming to go in heartily with the Protestant succession.

August 6. This day I came up in haste from Craigforth to Stirling, hearing the queen is dead. She died the first of this month. I assisted with the magistrates in proclaiming the new King George. Lord, send him over to us filled with the graces and gifts that may make him a great and lasting blessing to these nations. We hear comfortable accounts from all places of peace and quietness; and that there appears not a dog to move his tongue against the Protestant succession. This is the Lord's doings, and wonderful in our eyes, as what we did not expect. May the goodness of God lead us to repentance, else he can soon turn our hopeful beginnings into a sad end. He has many arrows in his quiver.

★★★★★★

The intestine jealousies and divisions to which the writer of the diary slightly alludes, had risen at this time to an almost unprecedented height. A very general discontent had been engendered in Scotland, by some late unpopular acts of the legislature; and as both parties were equally ready to put the worst construction on the sentiments and actions of each other, every measure was interpreted and regarded as bearing directly upon the grand subject of alarm, the Presbyterian religion, and the succession of the House of Hanover. The minds of the people were exasperated at the toleration granted to Episcopacy, and the permission to use the English Liturgy. This, with the restoration of patronage, against which the country had always entertained an inveterate prejudice, were looked upon as a pre-concerted scheme to overturn the whole establishment. Patrons, many of whom were disaffected, were invested with their ancient rights, on purpose, as was supposed, to fill up vacancies in the church with such presentees as were favourable to the interests of the Pretender.

Another, and a more solid ground of discontent was, the act obliging the Established Clergy to take the oath of Abjuration, which, in some parts of it, breathed a spirit directly at variance with Presbyterian principles. The church was thus divided into two factions. Jurors and Non-jurors, and the nation kept in a state of tumult and fluctuation. Attempts certainly were made to alter the succession into its hereditary channel, and promotion ran strongly in the interest of the exiled family. There were publications in which the rights of the Pretender were asserted, and openly defended: but the danger was magnified, and the alarm was industriously propagated to serve political purposes.[6] These projects were happily disconcerted by the wranglings of party in the cabinet, and the unexpected death of the queen; and the accession of the House of Brunswick met with no formal opposition.

******

August 12. Went to Edinburgh on business, and sat in the commission. When wise and good men have the management, things go well. Little else was done than drawing up an address to the king. This is a hot place on one side and other. I was in a company where there were some of contrary principles, high-fliers on both sides, and like to fire the house. I like not this high-flying on any side; and I dare say we mistake our temper often for zeal. I thought myself obliged to vindicate truth and matter of fact, and to own my own principles. It was

---

6. *Vid. Somerville's Hist*, and dissertation on the danger of the Protestant succession.

ill taken; and the gentleman in whose house we were, turned peevish with what I and a minister said, and ran away from his own table. I took no notice of this. However, he came to himself, and sent for me, and we parted good friends.

Where people differ from me, I would gladly carry towards them with that good nature, courtesy, and civility, as to engage them. I would comply in things indifferent; for I do not think religion obliges to a morose, captious behaviour, an opposing and contradicting every thing that those of a contrary persuasion say or do. There is great prudence to know the proper time when a testimony ought to be given. I desire at all times boldly to avow my own principles, and never to be ashamed of them; but I do not think this obliges me to be always attacking and disputing with others. It does much hurt, for it irritates instead of edifying.

August 18. I heard a sermon at Logie, being the preparation before the sacrament. I find on these occasions, too many follow divisive courses; and I do not like such separative ways, as makes this holy ordinance a communion of parties, which should be a communion of saints. My affections were not highly raised, yet I hope faith was in lively exercise. Lord, I desire, on this occasion particularly, to be thankful for the great things thou hast done for us, in disappointing the big hopes of enemies, and the fears of thy people; surprising us with mercy, breaking the snares that were laid to bring us into slavery and ruin, and bringing a Protestant Prince to the peaceable possession of our throne. Lord, make us a holy, humble, thankful people, and this will complete our deliverance.

September 23. This afternoon we got the good news of the king's safe arrival. Oh Lord make us thankful; thou dealest mercifully with us. Lord, make him a lasting and great blessing to these nations, and to thy church, to break the balance of Antichristian power in Europe. Assisting at night at the solemnity with the magistrates and officers of the regiment here. We were very cheerful, and good reason have we. We may see the moderation and lenity of a just and good government. Those who have been the greatest enemies to it are protected, and may appear in as great security as its best friends. But if a Pretender had come in, I doubt not but the country had become a field of blood; persecutors again triumphing, and glutting themselves with the blood of their countrymen; malice and vice again high in place, and good men hiding themselves. But the Lord be praised the snare is broken, and our soul has escaped as a bird out of the snare.

September 27. The gentlemen here met to address the king; disputes among them. Lord, direct me and my friends here, to carry and countenance the right side, who stand for liberty and religion against those who value neither.

October 20. Hearing a good sermon on this occasion (the coronation.) Thankful frame for the great things God has done for us: That he has broken the yoke of tyranny, popery, and slavery that was preparing for us by wretched men that have no regard to the security of our religion or liberty. Blessed be God who has turned their counsels into foolishness, and made their designs of no effect. Going in the afternoon to assist at the solemnity. This is a day of much joy and mirth through Britain, and it is to be feared of much sin also. Drunkenness is an ordinary sin on such occasions. I bless God who keeps me free from these temptations.

December 24. Christmas-day. I see much of a party spirit here in Scotland; a great heat in the head about strictness of principles, wherein the practice of true godliness is not much concerned. I do not see that strictness in the practice of those who are hottest in their heads about circumstantials. I would desire to be strict to myself in my own walk, but easy and charitable to others that differ in opinions from me. All the Protestant churches preach on Christmas-day, on the birth of Christ. We differ from them, but we should be moderate, and not run them down, as it were a sinful wicked custom. I wish professors in Scotland were warmer hearted and cooler headed in religion; but this is another instances of the *proefervidum Scotorum ingenium*. We often take that for zeal, which is nothing but natural temper.

December 31. I bless the Lord who adds to my days and years, and that I enjoy them in peace, contrary to my expectations. Lord, give me grace, so to number my days, as to apply my heart to heavenly wisdom.

Chapter 19

Rebellion in Scotland, 1715-1716

This year has been rendered memorable in British history, by the unsuccessful attempt of the Jacobites to replace the young Pretender on the throne of his father. Negotiations for his restoration had been secretly carried on between the Courts of England and St. Germains, for some time prior to the Rebellion. During the Tory administration, in the last years of Queen Anne, his interest was warmly espoused by the ruling faction and even the queen herself privately declared her inclination to take measures in his favour, on condition of his abjuring the Catholic religion, which was now become an insuperable barrier to the British throne. Could he have been induced to make this sacrifice, which every maxim of policy and prudence urged him to make, his friends professed their readiness to attempt the repeal of the Act of Settlement, and to recover by law, those rights which they subsequently attempted in vain by arms. But such was his infatuated bigotry, or weakness, that he was willing to renounce the hopes of an empire for a speculative point of faith.

Notwithstanding these, and other discouragements, his adherents prosecuted their schemes and intrigues with ardour; entertaining the most sanguine expectations of seeing the Hanoverian succession subverted, and the crown transferred to the hereditary line. The sudden death of the queen, as was noticed, rather disconcerted their plans which were then not ripe for execution; and the peaceable accession of the new king, tended for a while to increase their confusion and dismay. Their enmity against the existing government was doubly exasperated, when they saw themselves immediately cast out of favour and trust, and their political adversaries again become the ascendant faction.

This exaltation of their opponents to power and place, contributed to swell the number of the disaffected. The usual artifices of disappointed ambition were resorted to, for exciting clamour and discontent in the country. They seized every incident that could inflame the populace, or flatter their prejudices. To the malcontents in Scotland they held out the hope of procuring a dissolution of the Union, which had been always regarded as a national grievance. In England, disaffection was fomented by various machinations. Riot and tumult, always favourable to revolutions, were encouraged with the design of making these unhappy divisions subservient to their main purpose.

But all these arts and intrigues were baffled by the vigilance and activity of the government. Measures were adopted for the public safety, and the nation put in a posture of defence. New regiments were levied, and several disaffected officers were dismissed from the army. The Dukes of Marlborough and Argyle, the Earl of Stair, and others who had been disbanded under the late administration, were restored. Of the chief abettors of those intrigues, some were committed to custody, and others retired into banishment to escape the penalties of the law.

The death of Louis, the great supporter of the Stuart dynasty, was a final blow to the interests of the Pretender in France, and should have taught his friends to moderate that enthusiasm which was ultimately to bring ruin on their cause. But they had gone too far to recede; and with a fatal temerity, they resolved to erect the standard of rebellion, and try the fortune of war. The unsuccessful result of this experiment is well known, and cannot here be enlarged upon; we shall, however, advert again to the subject, when we have brought up our extracts from the diary, to the date when the Highlanders took arms under their commander-in-chief at the Castleton of Braemar.

In quelling this rebellion. Colonel Blackader, though not called to action, rendered his country some service; and his exertions were not overlooked by the government. He was still residing as a private gentleman in Stirling, but ready to obey the call of honour, when the religion and liberties of the kingdom were threatened with extinction. He volunteered to take the command, and submitted to the drudgery of training a regiment that was raised in the west, and posted at Stirling to guard the bridge of that town, one of the most important passes of the Forth. Of this, however, more hereafter.

******

March 9. Came to Edinburgh. Sat with the Assembly's Commission. Lord direct and guide men of all spirits. Warm the cold, and make men of hot and zealous tempers as much concerned and zealous for the peace of the church, for unity and charity, as they are for redressing grievances and reforming abuses.

March 14. In the morning I was with our society, and afterwards about business, recommending a young friend to one of the boards. When I see people hanging on and depending, I cannot be thankful enough, and admire the goodness of God who has provided for me without a life of dependence upon any but himself. I see plainly that bread is not to the wise, nor favour to men of skill. Others may fawn upon the great; I have nothing to ask of them but civility.

March 26. Returned home to Stirling; all going well.

April 7. Dined at home with much young company, and very merry. In the evening went to a concert, and was innocently diverted for two or three hours; but when they were going to turn it into a frolic by dancing, I shewed my dislike, and stopped it. I think music, right timed, an innocent amusement. It lays our humours and turbulent passions; makes the mind serene, and the temper sweet; at least I find these effects. But I prescribe not to others.

May 3. Went to Edinburgh, the Assembly being to sit this day. Was pleased, and I hope edified by the moderator's (Mr. Carstairs) speech to the commissioner, Earl of Rothes.

May 6. The Assembly taken up in answering the king's letter. I see two parties, the hot and the moderate, and these side themselves according to their light and temper. Lord, guide both to the same end, thy glory and the church's good. I hope it is the end of both, though they take different means. Let there be a right temperament made out of both; the zeal and heat of the one, to spur and stir up the cold and backward; and the prudence and moderation of the other, to check the rash and forward.

May 9. The Assembly deposed two ministers for not praying for the king. They gave great reason to suspect their disaffection to the government.[1] Dined with the commissioner.

May 11. This day they transported a minister, Mr. Black from Les-

---

1. These were Mr. James and John Maitlands from Aberdeenshire. They refused also to observe the thanksgiving appointed for the King's accession. *Vid. Acts of Gen Assembly.*

mahego, to go for Rotterdam. There was much heat and debate, and the evil of division and unwarrantable separation much exposed. I did all I was able in this affair.

May 12. An act was voted recommending unity, love, and charity, and against separation. I was sorry, and told publicly that I thought it a shame that in this venerable house there should be so much spoken against an act for unity, &c. I see too much of party-spirit and humour on all sides. There are some hot people that, in my opinion, would put us all in confusion. I bless God there are also wise and sober men who, I hope, have the wisdom that cometh from above.

May 20. This day I came home to Stirling, and dined with the Lords of the Circuit.

July 24. Alarmed with accounts of an intended invasion. Surprised and damped with it at first. But the name of the Lord is a strong tower. I desire to flee to it in an evil day. *What time I am afraid I'll trust in thee.* Oh that my heart were fixed, and then I shall not be afraid of evil tidings. Lord, turn the counsels of our enemies to foolishness. Give a spirit of judgement to them that sit in judgment, and strength to those who turn the battle from our gates. Our sins indeed make us obnoxious to thy wrath, but, Lord, pardon, and pour out a spirit of repentance and humiliation upon all ranks. I went out to see a rendezvous of some honest countymen who are hearty for the cause; but our help must come from thee, for vain is the help of man. Some trust in horses, and some in chariots, but our surety and sufficiency is in Jehovah. In him will we boast all the day.

August 3. Fast-day before the sacrament, and hearing very suitable sermons to the occasion. We get fair warning of our danger. O that we might take it. I desire, for my part, to take it, to flee from the wrath to come, to flee to the covert of blood, into the chambers of his attributes provided for his own to hide them in till these calamities pass over. This is a time I should be searching and trying my ways; and I find many things wrong. A falling from my first love, and first works: a decay of grace; indolence, and security; unprofitable mispending of time; vain lightness of heart, &c. I desire to have a humble frame, confessing my sins, and resolving better, to have more zeal for the glory of God and the interest of his gospel. Lord, give me strength to perform, else my resolutions signify nothing.

August 7. Sabbath. A sweet communion. Earnest in prayer in behalf of myself and the public. I wish a company of the righteous were raised up to wrestle against the designs of an Antichristian party, to stand in the gap and turn away thy wrath, which is the thing we have most to fear. They are busy raising troops for our defence; but a troop of wrestlers with God would do us more service than ten thousand armed men. And I trust, on this occasion there have been strong batteries of prayer raised against the Pretender and his Antichristian host, by which heaven may be prevailed with to defeat their projects. I bless God that we can still go about this work in peace. We were kept very late, till my spirits were fatigued. I cannot approve of this way of managing the affair, and lengthening out the public exercises, till we are made unfit for private duty. It is too like the *opus operatum*. But custom bears down all.

August 24. The alarms are renewed again of the invasion. I cannot say but it casts a damp upon my spirits always when I hear of it; though it need be no surprise, considering the mad schemes of confusion, blood, and all the calamities of a barbarous intestine war. God can in mercy disappoint our fears, as he has many times done; but we are a sinful people, and have reason to think God is angry with us. The staff in their hand is the rod of God's indignation; but do thou say to us, *Yet a very little while and mine indignation shall cease.* We have got account of the death of the King of France. We have been long looking for it, but God's time is the best time; and it has happened favourable at this crisis, when he had been laying designs, and was upon the point of sending a Pretender to invade us. Perhaps this intervention of Providence may defeat their designs; it certainly casts a great damp upon the spirits of the Jacobites, whose plight-anchor he was. And we bless God for it, follow what will; he was the main pillar and support of Antichrist's kingdom.

We hope it is a good omen. Antichrist will get a blow, and is near his end. But this should learn us to be humble and modest in judging. We make too homely in applying God's providences and judgments according to our own humours and passions. People thought, and I thought myself, that he would not go off the world without some remarkable judgment; and yet he died in peace, and without any horror, as we hear, but with composure and great presence of mind. God's ways are not as ours. We measure infinite wisdom by our own foolish and limited understanding.

September 3. Hearing good news from France. We hope the Pretender's measures will be broken, and that he will not get assistance there, now that the old oppressor hath ceased to deal treacherously. *He is now no more a terror to the land of the living, but gone down to the sides of the pit; lying among the uncircumcised, his sword under his head. Where is now the fury of the oppressor, and who art thou that shouldest be afraid of man that shall die, and the son of man that shall be made as grass?* I bless God that I have lived to see this great event which I wished so much, and was afraid never to see. There is also some glimpse of a reformation in France by the encouragement of Jansenism. Thou canst carry on these weak beginnings to a perfect reformation, and make a conquest of Antichrist within his own kingdoms.

September 17. There is now a great deal of company and military in this town, which obliges me to live more publicly than I incline. I visit the camp in the park here almost every day, and dine with the general (Wightman.) In the afternoon went out to meet the Duke of Argyle. I was with him next day at the review, and dined with him. Sensible of the too great freedom I took in conformity to the world, but I bless God I am now more seldom exposed to these temptations. When I see the army again, I am thankful that he has brought me out of that way of living, and given me a quiet habitation.

September 20. This day spent with the great folk; in the evening went out to see some honest people come from the west.

******

These "honest people" were a body of the citizens of Glasgow which was zealously attached to the Hanoverian succession. This city, as we noticed above, made an early stand for the preservation of their rights both sacred and civil: and on the present occasion they were equally ready to manifest a similar attachment to their king and country. They had watched narrowly the progress of the insurrection,—provided the town with guards and ammunition,—trained themselves regularly to the use of arms, and established a correspondence with various parts of the kingdom, by means of which they had timely advice of the Pretender's motions and designed invasion.

Upon the first news of the rising in the North on the 7th of September, they offered to raise a body of 600 men, and to maintain them for sixty days at their own expense; and on the 17th, when the Duke of Argyle arrived in Edinburgh to take the command of his Majesty's forces, which he found much inferior in number to the Rebels, he wrote instantly to the city of Glasgow to assemble and march the above corps of volunteers towards Stirling, for the defence of that place, as the Highlanders were on their way thither, having already seized and fortified the town of Perth. In compliance with this request, the Lord Provost put himself at the head of three battalions of well-armed citizens, making in all ten companies. It is mentioned in their address that they prevailed with Mr. Bruce, younger of Kennet, to be their major, and the Honourable Colonel Blackader to accept of the office of Colonel, for the better ordering their discipline; a task which, as we shall find, he cheerfully performed.[2]

******

September 21. Providence has brought a business to my hand that I was not expecting. I was desired to take charge of these honest men come from the West. I did it cheerfully. Lord, I devote both myself and them to thy care; let thy presence be with us. Next day I had another proposal of the same kind, but was already engaged.

September 23. Exercising my new battalions, and very well pleased with them. I hope God will bless and reward their zeal and forwardness, who have so willingly offered themselves. Let it not be the worse for them that I am put at their head. Let God be our captain, and through him we shall do valiantly. Without his commission, the best and strongest troops are but broken reeds. He can save by many or by few, and often works his purposes by feckless and unlikely instruments.

October 11. Exercising every day. The evening spent with my Glasgow friends; it was out of kindness to me. I bless God who gives me gifts and talents to make me any way useful and acceptable.

October 14. Rode out with the duke the length of Doun; all things going well. I was afterwards with the Duke of Roxburgh. Many of them are now leaving this town. I have been much delighted with the fine qualities and charming sweet disposition of my guest the duke, and the other gentlemen I have had the honour to have with me this month. It made me sad at parting with them; but this is a time to possess and enjoy as if we possessed not.

******

The occasion of the duke's departure was an express from Provost Campbell of Edinburgh, requesting his immediate assistance with a detachment of the regular troops; as a party of the Highlanders had

---

2. Rae's *History of the Rebellion.*

made a descent on the coast of Lothian, and were marching towards Edinburgh, hoping to make themselves masters of the metropolis before the army at Stirling could prevent or be apprised of their design. This was a body of above 1600 men, under Brigadier Macintosh, detached by the Earl of Mar to join the Rebels in Northumberland who were in danger of being attacked by General Carpenter. They coasted along the south shore of Fife, and crossing the Frith under cover of night about Crail and Ely, they landed before daybreak at North Berwick, Gulan, and Aberlady.

Having stayed at Haddington next night, (14th) instead of directing their course to the Borders, they marched suddenly towards Edinburgh, and were advanced to Piershill, within a mile of the town, when the approach of the duke compelled them to alter their rout. They turned to Leith, and seized the citadel, an old dismantled fort without gates; but the ramparts were entire. In this post they fortified themselves with beams of wood, carts, and other materials; having plundered the ships in the harbour of their provisions, ammunition, and cannon. They kept possession of the fortress for one day; and while the duke was in Edinburgh making the necessary preparations to dislodge them, they took the opportunity to decamp at night.

Favoured by the ebb of the tide, they marched off in silence round the Pier-head, along the sands, and established their next quarters at Seaton Castle, belonging to the Earl of Wintoun. Thence they took their rout toward the Borders, by Dunse and Coldstream, and joined he English Rebels at Kelso. Meantime the duke got notice, that the Earl of Mar, then at Perth, had given out that he intended to pass the Frith with his whole army, either at the bridge of Stirling or Doun, and that the vanguard was already advanced to Dunblane. This intelligence occasioned his immediate return, and he found the report confirmed by several countrymen whom the approach of the enemy had frightened from their homes. The arrival of the duke stopped the career of the rebels, and obliged them to retreat back to Perth.

October 18. Got accounts that the rebels have quitted Leith. Hearing also that the enemy are now coming nearer us: but the duke is returned. I keep exercising my battalions. Help us, Oh Lord, to look to thee in troublous times, for vain is the help of man. We are using the means, but safety and victory are from the Lord.

November 11. This day we got account that the enemy are advancing. I went out in the afternoon with the battalions, and was making ready for the battle; for I am willing to venture my life with them. But at night I was told we were to stay, and defend the town and the bridge. I was composed and submissive, though I would rather have gone; but I do not wish to be positive against Providence, for he knows infinitely better what is good for me than I do myself.

November 12. This morning our army marched out. I got my orders from the duke, and was much complimented; but if I know myself right I have no reason to be vain. I went out with the army a short way, and sent my best wishes and prayers along with them. Oh thou. Lord of hosts, go forth with our armies; and thou great Judge of right, judge between them and us. Plead the cause that is thine own. I have more fatigue with business than if I had been out with the army; but the post that Providence allots me is always the best. Alarmed at night by the enemy, and putting all the town in arms. I went down to the bridge with the Glasgow battalion, and continued there all night. It was a peaceable night, and I bless God for it.[3]

★★★★★★

This was the day before the Battle of Dunblane or Sheriff-muir took place, which, although a victory, did not prove decisive, part of the King's troops being put to flight. Matters had been for some time ripening for action. The Earl of Mar being joined by most of the chiefs of the Northern Clans, had seen his army augmented to above 10,000 effective men. Leaving a garrison in Perth, he set out on the 10th, in order to give battle. The two armies drew out upon an irregular piece of ground near Dunblane, and had scarcely time to form, when the action commenced. On the right wing, where the duke was in person, the king's troops completely defeated the rebels. But the left, commanded by General Whetham, was thrown into confusion; many of them were cut to pieces, and the rest with their general, ignorant of their success on the right, and apprehensive of being surrounded, fled towards Stirling, where they arrived about three in the afternoon, to the great dismay of the inhabitants.

The duke and General Wightman having put the left wing of the enemy to flight, and pursued them to the river Allan, more than two miles distant, returned to the field, and learning the fate of Whetham's division, prepared to attack the other wing which had formed on the top of a hill, to the number of 4000 men. But on his approach, the

---

3. "The bridge at Stirling was closed up with stake and faill, and the bridge at Doun cut down."—*Coll. of authentic Papers relating to the Rebellion.*

rebels began to disperse; upon which the duke retired to Dunblane, where the soldiers lay on their arms all night, expecting next day to renew the battle. The enemy, however, having preferred retreating to fighting, he marched for Stirling, carrying with him the standards, colours, and prisoners he had taken. The killed and wounded were nearly equal on both sides, being reckoned between six and seven hundred each. We now return to notice how the Glasgow battalion acquitted themselves at their post.

******

November 13. Sabbath. Being under arms all night, I slept two hours this morning, and then went to church. At the dismission we were alarmed; and, upon going out, I saw one of the most melancholy sights ever I beheld in my life—our army flying before their enemies! O Lord, what shall we say when Israel turn their backs and fly before the enemy? But we have sinned. I went down to the bridge with a heavy heart, the runners away coming fast in, and every one giving a worse account than another, that all was lost and gone. Indeed seeing is believing; all the fields were covered with our flying troops, horse and foot, all had the appearance of a routed army. Oh what dismal views we had, expecting to see the rebel Highland army at their heels. These and such thoughts filled my mind. Lord, thou hast turned our swords' edge, and hast not made us to stand in battle; thou hast poured shame and contempt upon us; thou goest not forth with our armies. Give us help from trouble, for vain is the help of man.

I took down all the Glasgow battalion to the bridge, and posted them in some entrenchments there; but indeed I had no great hopes of keeping the rebels out; for thinking our army was routed, I expected they would pass the Forth at some ford, and soon become masters of Stirling. Thus we spent all the afternoon very melancholy, till the evening when a better scene began to open. We got intelligence that the duke was still on the field of battle, after having been victorious, where he first was. Oh what a surprising turn! We could not believe it; we were as men that dreamed; but it was soon confirmed to us by eyewitnesses. Oh how hast thou turned our fears and griefs into joy and songs of praise! Providence has managed it so, that no flesh shall boast.

Our right wing did beat their left; but our left was attacked before the line of battle was formed; and so every regiment upon the long march, broke and drove back one upon another. We were too vain and conceited, and despised the enemy too much, and rested too much upon the arm of flesh. God humbles us, and lets us see all flesh is grass; yet he takes care of his own cause, and lets not our enemies triumph; at the same time he humbles our pride, and mortifies our vanity. I now see also the Providence was kind to me, and those who remained here. We would have been posted on the left or centre, and so have been surprised and broken as the rest were, and perhaps lost both life and honour. My prayer was. *If thy presence go not with me, carry me not up hence.* Thou hast heard me. Success was not to attend the left wing. I was not to be there. All is well ordered; thou takest care both of my life and reputation.

November 14. This day it is expected there will be another engagement; that the duke will attack them if they remain where they are.

November 15. We hear the rebels are retired. Lord be blest, who puts a bridle in their nose, and a hook in their jaws, and turns them back by the way they came. Oh what a merciful surprising turn of Providence; yesterday we were expecting a barbarous and cruel enemy at our gates by this time, and to be flying before them. God is our defence, our shield and buckler. The army came back in the afternoon, in much better condition than we expected. Lord be blest for this respite, and sanctify this providence,—this check to make us humble,—to repent and turn to thee. The regiments are cantoned round about us, and consequently the company here is very bad. No wonder though our carcases be made to dung the face of the earth. God can be glorified upon us, and work his own work without such vile instruments.

November 17. Yesternight we escaped a great danger from fire, by those sad neighbours of ours. Lord, thou keepest us from terrors by night, as well as dangers by day; thou puttest a hedge about us, and allowest no evil to befall us.

November 18. We got the news of the entire defeat of the rebels at Preston in England. Lord, thou rebukest them everywhere,—breakest their power, and crushest their designs.

November 19. In the morning I saw the duke review the regiments of foot. Some of them are sore shattered. They who stood and did their duty best, have suffered least. It generally happens so. But it was less the fault than the misfortune of the regiments on the left; they were attacked by surprise before they had formed.

November 22. The Glasgow regiment marched home. I convoyed them part of the way, and we parted with much affection on both sides. I bless the Lord who has sent them home safe, and that they were not exposed, nor suffered as others. They were committed to my charge, I committed them to thine, and thou hast been their defence. Thou also takest care of all that concerns me; even my name and reputation has been increased by their coming here. Lord, to thee be the praise; I lay all down at thy feet.

******

This body of volunteers, on their leaving Stirling, were handsomely complimented by the Duke of Argyle, as well as in the following letter which Colonel Blackader addressed to the Provost and Magistrates of Glasgow.

Stirling, November 29, 1715.

My Lord, and Gentlemen

I am honoured with yours by Captain Rodgers. I assure you it is a very sensible pleasure to me that I have had the opportunity put in mine hand I have long wished for, of doing any service to the good town of Glasgow. They have shewn so much zeal and forwardness for these valuable interests that ought to be dearest to us, that honest men should be ambitious to serve them: But, my Lord, with submission, you put the debt upon the wrong side: It is I that am laid under great obligations; it is I that owe my hearty thanks, which I do hereby with gratitude return to you. Gentlemen, to Provost Aird, and the other honest gentlemen with him, who were pleased to choose me to be their colonel.

And indeed, if my capacity for that post had been equal to the pleasure and zeal I had to serve them, and the interest they appeared here for, their choice had not been bad. I took the charge of them the more cheerfully, that I knew they were men that came out in the integrity of their hearts to offer themselves willingly in this good cause; and being resolved to venture my own life, I thought I could not do it in better company, than with those I was assured would fight from principle, in the defence of our sacred and civil concerns. And I am very well satisfied I had made a good choice; and that, if they had been called out to action, which they seemed much to desire, I doubt not but they would have fully answered the expectation his

Grace the Duke of Argyle, and everybody else, had conceived of them.

Providence, that manages all well, did order it otherwise; and, I doubt not, for the best. They did good service while here, both by their own good behaviour, and the good example they gave to others, of zeal for the service. For the pains I was at with them, it was so far from being a fatigue, that the tractable disposition, alacrity, and keenness they shewed to learn everything of our military art, made it a very great pleasure and diversion to me: and what I taught them to do in jest, I doubt not but they would, if tried, have practised to good purpose, in earnest. The officers that came here were generally such as might, with reputation, have carried the king's commission: and indeed, I do but justice to your whole body of volunteers to say. That, if I have any credit by taking the charge of them, it is owing to their good behaviour.

I hope there shall be no further occasion for you to put yourselves to such expense and trouble, as you have been at, in shewing your great concern for the government; though I doubt not but that, in case of necessity, the same zeal that put you on to make this handsome and seasonable appearance, would make you to do it again; which, if it should happen, I offer you, my Lord and Gentlemen, my hearty service and assistance in whatever I am capable of. I shall add no more, but to wish all happiness and prosperity to you and your good town; and that, as I have the favour of your goodwill and affection, I may have yet a further occasion to shew how much I desire to deserve it. I am, my Lord and Gentlemen,

    Your much obliged.

        Most obedient, and humble servant,

                              Jo. Blackader.

              ******

November 24. Hearing that the old regiment I was in has suffered much, and that the officer who succeeded me is wounded.

              ******

This was at the Battle of Preston in Lancashire, where the Cameronian Regiment, which had been recalled from Ireland, behaved with great gallantry. More than half of the killed and wounded was sustained by this regiment alone. Their lieutenant-colonel, Lord Forrester, Major Lawson, and several others were wounded.

******

November 28. Rode out this morning convoying the Duke of Roxburgh on his way. I was very sorry to part. I have hardly known any man with finer qualities, more sweetness of temper, meekness, probity, and integrity, which I most admire and am most charmed with. I am glad of this opportunity I have had of knowing him, and enjoying his friendship, which I do very much value. At night with honourable company, and very diverting, perhaps too much mirth. There should always be a check, for the mind grows vain and light by too much jollity, and loses its sober, spiritual sett.

November 30. This day riding out and convoying away the Earl of Haddington. The guests I have had here have much enlarged my heart, there has been so much good humour, easiness, and I hope innocence.

December 13. Went out in the morning with the duke and the generals to view the field of battle. It is folly to lay the blame upon each other, right wing or left wing. Time and chance happen to all. They who fled would likely on another occasion have behaved well and done their duty; and those who stood might, in the same circumstances, have fled as well as they did. The glory and praise of all belongs to God; and no cause of boasting to man. The general and great company were at our house in the evening.

******

The Battle of Preston may be said to have quelled the rebellion in England and the south of Scotland; most of the disaffected noblemen and gentlemen there being either killed or taken prisoners: the Highlands only remained to be reduced, and this was accomplished early in the next year by General Cadogan, the British Plenipotentiary in the Netherlands, who arrived in the end of November with 6000 Dutch troops. Meantime the Pretender himself, upon the repeated solicitations of his friends, embarked for Scotland, and on the 22nd of December landed at Peterhead. Soon after, he made his public entry into Perth, and solemnly took upon himself the functions of Majesty, by conferring titles and ecclesiastical dignities, appointing prayers and thanksgiving throughout the churches for his safe arrival, and issuing proclamations for all fencible men to repair forthwith to his royal standard.

The deep snows and inclemency of the season prevented the king's troops for a time from giving him any interruption in the exercise of these assumed prerogatives. But the scene speedily changed; for the Duke of Argyle, being joined by the Dutch troops, and a considerable train of artillery, set out (*January 29*) for Perth to dislodge the rebels. The intelligence of his approach was very unwelcome and very unseasonable, as it prevented the ceremony of the Pretender's coronation, and the meeting of his Parliament. Their greatest concern being now to secure a retreat, they deserted the place and retreated to Dundee, and thence to Montrose. The royal army went in pursuit; and on their rout to Perth, seized the garrisons of Braco, Tullibardine, and Auchterarder, which had been deserted. Perth, the metropolis of the rebels, was taken possession of, as was Dundee also.

But on reaching Montrose, they found the Pretender had made his escape, having slipped out privately on foot, accompanied only by one of his domestics; and finding a fishing boat, which carried him and the Earl of Mar on board a French ship, they put to sea, and in a few days landed near Dunkirk. (See note following). His deluded followers were obliged to disperse and fly to their hills. Some of them escaped to France, and others were taken in their wild concealments among the mountains. General Cadogan soon after reduced Inverness and the rest of the Highlands, and thus extinguished the last sparks of the rebellion.

★★★★★★

Note:—The Pretender was not popular with his party; he seemed from the first to consider his cause hopeless, and this discouraged his men. One of them gives the following description of his person and habits: "His person is tall and thin, seeming to incline to be lean rather than to fill as he grows in years. His countenance is pale, and perhaps he looked more pale by reason of an ague that seized him two days after he came on shore. He has something of a vivacity in his eye, that perhaps would have been more visible had he not been under dejecting circumstances and surrounded with discouragement. His speech was grave, not very clearly expressing his thoughts, nor over much to the purpose: but his words were few, and his behaviour and temper seemed always composed. What he was in his diversions we know not, for it was no time for mirth; neither can I say that I ever saw him smile. Our men began to despise him; some asked if he could come abroad among the soldiers, to see us handle our arms or do our exercise. I must say, that when we saw the person whom they called our King, we found ourselves not at all animated by his presence; and if he was disappointed in us, we were tenfold more so in him; we saw nothing in him that looked like spirit." *Proceedings of the Rebels at Perth.*

✶✶✶✶✶✶

When the Glasgow regiment were dismissed. Colonel Blackader joined the royal army under the duke, and marched to Perth, which the rebels had fortified, and were expected to offer battle in defence of their king and capital. He was very willing to have drawn his sword once more in the service of his country; but on this occasion he was disappointed by the sudden flight of the Pretender and his followers.

✶✶✶✶✶✶

(1716.) *January 3.* Visiting a person dying of his wounds. I had a conviction, that I should have taken more pains with him. I spoke seriously to him; Lord, bless it, and give me such a sight of Christ myself, such desires after him, such delight in him, that I may with warm and fervent affections hold out his usefulness and liveliness to others, to make them fall in love with him. Lord, pluck him as a brand from the burning; let free grace triumph and be magnified in redeeming and saving him.

January 6. Went to Glasgow with the duke, and was very kindly treated there, all the people in the town shewing a great affection for me. In the evening I was with my friends at a ceremonial entertainment.[4] It is thou, Oh Lord, who givest me honour and riches in abundance. Providence brought the occasion of my obliging this good town, just to my door without my asking for it. I am desired to come and live here among them; their kindness invites me, but I do not yet determine.

January 9. Came back to Stirling. We got there the certain account of the Pretender's being come over. This determined me to go with the duke to Perth. Lord, let thy presence go with us. I put my trust in thee, hide not thy face from me.

January 29. In hurry and confusion by the army's marching away.

---

4. For an account of this "ceremonial entertainment," see the Scots Courant for January 1716.

We got an alarm at Ardoch, and heard some firing. I recommended myself to God, and was easy, being on my duty. When we came to Tullibardine the business was over, and the house had surrendered. I supped with the general, and lay all night at a country house.

January 31. Marching onward, we got the agreeable news that the rebels had quitted Perth. About six in the evening we marched again, and came to Perth at three next morning. It was a cold, but pleasant moonshine night.

February 3. Finding the rebels flying before us, I took leave of the army and returned home. Getting great promises of friendship both from the duke and the general.

CHAPTER 20

Miscellaneous Extracts, 1716-1721

The time from the suppression of the Rebellion, until his appointment as Deputy Governor of Stirling Castle, the colonel spent in his usual retired manner, enjoying the recreations of the country, and the society of his friends. Many of his leisure hours he devoted to benevolent purposes, in doing offices of kindness and charity to the poor in his neighbourhood, or to the cultivation of his own mind in reading and study, for which he had always a predilection. In the Greek and Roman classics he took great delight, and had made considerable attainments in several of the branches of Natural Philosophy. The General Assembly of this year, to which he was returned a member, furnished him with some occasions of trying his talents as a public speaker; and if we may judge from the imperfect specimens he has recorded, his exhibitions in that venerable court do no discredit to his rhetorical powers. His oratory seems to have been entirely extempore—the unpremeditated expression of those feelings which rose in course of the debate. The subjects of discussion have now lost their interest; and the short abstracts of his speeches can serve no other purpose than to develop some characteristic features of his mind, when called into a new sphere of action.

******

April 25. This day kept for thanksgiving by appointment of the *synod*. God has done great things for us, an evil and ill-deserving generation; he has disappointed our fears, and broken the power of our enemies. It was not our sword nor our bow, but thy right hand that wrought our deliverance; for we saw enough to humble the pride of man.

May 3. The assembly sat down: Went to church with the commissioner, and heard a good sermon from Acts ix. 30. The king's letter was very kind, and the commissioner made a handsome speech.

May 5. Sitting on a committee all the afternoon, seeking council and direction to guide me right among the rocks and shelves of debate. Alas! I think there is not the spirit of love among us that should be, but a rankling party-spirit, churchmen siding themselves too much with state-parties. Lord, subdue passions, envy, pride, self-seeking, wrangling; restore peace, love, and unity.

May 8. This day in the committee of Instructions. There were many proposals about redress and representation of grievances. Some were for addressing the king alone; others, for addressing the king and Parliament; and a third party for endeavouring merely to get their grievances redressed. I said I was willing to go in with the second and last of these proposals, if we could fall upon a proper way to do it, but I disagreed with the first; for these grievances were now, many of them, enacted into laws, and so it is the legislative power alone that must help us; and for us to address the executive, when it is the legislative only that can help us, were the seeking a remedy where it is not to be found, and putting a thorn in the king's foot, and he gets too many of these.

Speaking of the Toleration, (which was one of the grievances,) I said it was my opinion, that it was not so much the legal toleration that was a grievance, as a connivance at practices beyond the law; and that if magistrates in towns, and justices in the country would execute the laws as they were empowered to do, and which the Toleration Act did not hinder them from doing, then there would be no such abuse or grievance in the toleration itself. For instance, I said, in this our capital, where the Assembly sits, there are twelve or fifteen Meeting-houses where either the Pretender is prayed for, or King George is not prayed for, and where the principles of rebellion are taught. Now the act does not allow this; and if these houses were shut up, as I suppose by law they may and ought to be under such circumstances, then the toleration could be no grievance; for I would have liberty, to all scrupulous consciences, to worship God in their own way.

Upon this, some went out and told the Provost of Edinburgh what we were about, as if we were reflecting upon him; and he came in immediately and justified himself, which, I told him, I was glad of, and that I had given him an opportunity to do it; for I was indeed informed by the best authority, that there was an order, directed to the

Provost of Edinburgh, come down a month ago, for shutting up the meeting-houses, if they did not pray for the king.

May 11. In committees, and in the Assembly all this day. In the address to the king, congratulating him on the happy ending of the rebellion, and conveying the thanks of the Assembly to the officers who had been, under God, instrumental to it, it was proposed by some that the Duke of Argyle only should be named. I rose and gave my opinion to this purpose.

Moderator.—It may be thought reasonable, that, after having mentioned his Grace the Duke of Argyle, with all the honour due to his great merit and eminent services, we should, in the next place, do justice to a gentleman and a brave officer, who had also deserved well of this country. Moderator, there is not a man within these walls has a greater honour and esteem for the Duke of Argyle than I have.

I have seen too many of his great actions, not to have a just esteem of them. But, Moderator, his Grace has such a fund of merit—such a stock of renown, that I am sure neither he nor his fiends (as I hope all of us are) will grudge us the doing justice, in the second place, to General Cadogan. Moderator, this gentleman is a stranger, and for that reason some would perhaps grudge him his share in our favour; but for my part, I think he ought, for that very reason, to have a stronger claim on our gratitude—to have his merits fully and duly considered. Moderator, General Cadogan neither affects it, nor does he want to have his services recommended to his royal master, or his merit proclaimed to the world by the mouth of a General Assembly. Moderator, Fame has taken care of that. But he is an officer who has, of a long time, deserved well of the Protestant interest and alliance abroad; and now Providence has put an opportunity in his hand of deserving well of us; and in ours, of being generous and thankful.

Finding several members proposing others to be named also in our address, I said. Moderator, there is, I think, a handsomer way of setting up great merit and great actions to light, than by mentioning names or pointing out the man, and that is, by touching the bright character of the person, and the circumstances of his exploits, for example, in the queen's time, when we spoke of a victorious general who had reflected lustre on her reign, and made her arms triumphant, who had curbed the insolence, and reduced the exorbitant power of France, nobody needed to name that personage, every man know it was the Duke of Marlborough. So in our case, when we speak of the great deliverance God has wrought of for us, by defeating the rebels, and frustrating their designs, then we all know it was the Duke of Argyle that led on the army to victory; and when we speak of reducing the highlands, and restoring peace and tranquillity to the country, we know it was General Cadogan had the management of it.

And I think this is the best expedient to make us unanimous, to name both, if we do name any; for by that it will appear, that the General Assembly is not actuated by any party spirit, but acting fairly and impartially. Whereas, if the duke alone be named, it may be thought to be done by a faction; but if we name General Cadogan also, it will be seen to the world, that whoever serves the king with fidelity, or deserves well of our country and our church, will have a good title to the favour and thanks of the General Assembly.

It was carried to name the duke alone, and I went cheerfully along with it. I know by this I lose the favour of both sides, but I hate to be a tool or a party man. I would join with both when they are right, and with none of them when they are wrong.

May 12. This day came on the affair of Mr. Webster and Mr. Simpson.[1] There seems to be much heat and party spirit about it. After some members had delivered their opinion, I spoke to this purpose.

Moderator, We have spent much time upon this business both in the last Assembly and in this. We have heard much reasoning about it, or to speak more properly, much speaking, and some reasoning; for where reason ends, there passion begins; and of that there is no end while there is so much fuel in our breasts to feed it. Moderator, if this business be ripe for the Assembly if Mr. Webster's first libel and answers to it be prepared by the committee, and if the last libel and answers to it be ready for the Assembly, then let us go on to the judging of it, in the name of God, in the fear of god, and in the love of truth; for I hope all of us are come here with upright and sincere hearts, to defend and maintain truth, and suppress error, but if this affair be not yet ripe for the Assembly, why is it so much pressed to come on? It

1. This was the noted case of Mr. John Simpson, Professor of Divinity at Glasgow, who was accused of teaching and preaching heretical doctrines, for which, by appointment of the Synod of Lothian, he was libelled by Mr. James Webster. The Assembly of this year, not having leisure fully to consider the erroneous points charged against him, remitted the case for more thorough examination. This intricate process agitated the country, and the Supreme Court of the Church, for fourteen or fifteen years. In 1729, the professor was, by a sentence of the Assembly, suspended from preaching and teaching, and all exercises of ecclesiastical power or function. *Vid. Acts of Ass. Periodical Pamph.*

ought to be left with the committee it was referred to.

And I am persuaded. Moderator, it will come to this; and I am told by several judicious members, that it will certainly land there. But, say they, it is too soon yet, it is not time yet. Moderator, are we come here without an object, to spend our fire upon one another—are we come here to spend our ill humours upon one another—are we come here to list ourselves under the banners of Mr. Webster and Mr. Simpson, with a factious spirit to fight and contend, not for truth but for victory? Or are we come here to afford diversion to the town; for it has now become the common street talk, *Come let us go into the Assembly and see sport.*[2] Moderator, and are we come to this—to make ourselves buffoons and laughing stocks for the public? I am afraid, Sir, it may be like the sport that Samson made to the lords of the Philistines, pull down the house about our ears, rend and divide the church, so that neither we nor our posterity may ever see cured.

Moderator, we call ourselves a Venerable Assembly; it is in everybody's mouth. *The Venerable Assembly.* What is it that makes this or any Assembly Venerable? It is not a great company of gentlemen in black coats and bands, and some with grey hairs, (and, Moderator, would to God there were more grey hairs among us.) It is not party-spirit, passion, heat, or wrangling. Moderator, you know, and can tell better than I, what it is that makes an Assembly Venerable. I shall only name two characteristics which I find in one of Paul's Epistles—two lists, and set the one against the other, the one is called the works of the flesh, anger, wrath, malice, hatred, variance, strife, envying, emulation, sedition, heresies. To be purged of these, moderator, will make an Assembly Venerable. The other list is the fruit of the Spirit, love, peace, joy, long-suffering, meekness, gentleness, goodness, faith, temperance.

To be endowed with these will make an Assembly Venerable, and answer the end of our coming together *to consult for the glory of God and the good of the church*, as every member binds himself to do in the works of his commission. Moderator, Let not the reverend brethren consider the insignificant person it comes from; but let every one of us lay our hands on our hearts, and see if it be true; and if it be so, then—*Pudet hoec opprobria nois et did potuisse et non potuisse refelli.* If it not be true, I humbly beg the pardon of this Venerable Assembly.

This speech, I found, was ill taken by some hot, stiff men on both

---

2. This practice, it would appear, had become so common and annoying, that the Assembly the following year passed an act prohibiting the admission of idle disorderly people who were not concerned.

sides; but it was approved of, and thought necessary by the more peaceable and moderate.

May 14. The business of the former day still continuing; some wishing it to remain with the committee, others pushing to bring it to the open Assembly. I said. Moderator, by bringing it into court, we shall not only wrong the cause of Mr. W. and Mr. S., but what is of infinitely more importance, the cause of truth; for we take it out of that way, and out of these hands where it was and will be managed calmly and judiciously, and judged fairly and impartially; and we put it into a way where it will be judged hastily, and I fear precipitately. For, , if I should judge in it now, I am persuaded it would be rashly; for, I must confess, I have not yet received that evidence and conviction in the affair as to make me able to judge of it distinctly, or with accuracy. So I propose it be put again into the committee's hands. Next day when the business was to be brought to a conclusion, I made some reflections to this purpose:

Moderator, —Now that this affair is going from us, I would beg leave to speak a word to it in concluding. The reverend brethren of this Assembly have shewn a commendable zeal against error. Much has been spoken, and well spoken, against several errors, particularly against Jesuitism, Socinianism, and Arminianism. For Jesuitism, I hope there is no great danger of it, so long as we keep the Pretender from the throne of Britain. For Socinianism, I hope there is no great danger of it either, especially the grosser part of it. For Arminianism, it is a dangerous error indeed; for it saps the foundation of all our religion, by overthrowing the doctrine of free grace, and setting up that of free will. It is a dangerous error, because all men are by nature Arminians, and the corrupt heart of man naturally falls into Arminian principles; therefore, the ministers of the Church of Scotland cannot shew too much zeal against it.

But, moderator, I would humbly recommend to these reverend ministers, that they would shew the same zeal against divisions and all practices tending that way. Let us not be like a general or an army that sends out all its sentries one way, and while they are looking out sharply that way, the enemy comes and attacks them in a different quarter, where they were not expecting, and therefore unprepared.

Moderator, the ministers of our church are our watchmen; and it is their duty to stand upon their watch-tower, and give us warning of our danger, from what quarter soever, whether from errors and vice on the one hand, or divisions on the other. Moderator, God has of his great mercy preserved this church, since the blessed Reformation, from the contagion of error; and I hope, by the vigilance of its pastors, he shall still preserve it. But we know that this church shall has been miserably rent and distressed, and brought, by divisions, into the utmost confusion. And I think I may, without offence, warn the reverend ministers of our church, that the nearest prospect of our danger comes from that quarter; for if ministers shall suffer themselves to be divided into parties, we may easily foresee, it threatens our ruin.

All I shall say more, Moderator, is to express my humble hope, that the reverend ministers in this Assembly will return home, cheerful and thankful, blessing God for the great deliverances he has wrought for us, and not let their spirits be soured or rankled by poring too much upon any grievances yet to be redressed. There are, indeed, grievances still, but these, I hope, shall be redressed in the due and short time. But though we may have some cause to complain, yet, blessed be God, our church is not in danger, and, I trust, never shall be, under the happy government of our good king, and his Protestant successors.

This speech was not well taken by some, and I observed, by those especially who have most need to be warned and put upon their guard against divisions. It was the sore heel that cannot be touched. But I have exonered my conscience in giving my testimony against heats and discord.

May 16. The Assembly closed with singing the 122nd Psalm. I returned in safety home to Stirling.

******

The remainder of this year furnishes few or no incidents in his life worthy of particular notice. His time was divided chiefly between the cares of his own family, and the calls of friendships or charity which were occasionally made upon him.

******

June 16. I was sent for in the morning up to the castle, to do a good office to a gentleman, a prisoner there, who had been taken in the Rebellion. I did it heartily, for as to matters of civility, we should heap kindness like coals of fire upon their head. We may shew zeal against their cause, and at the same time tenderness and humanity to their persons.

******

Next year he was nominated Deputy-Governor of Stirling Castle, an appointment which he did not solicit, and which was procured, in consideration for his services in the late Rebellion, solely by the interest of those noble friends with whom he had lately lived on terms of familiar intimacy.

★★★★★★

(1717,) *March 2.* This day I got my commission sent me from Edinburgh. Lord, fit me for whatever I am called to; I cast all upon thee. Thou knowest I was more afraid of the snares and temptations of great posts, than lifted up with the splendour and pageantry of them. I went up and intimated my commission. Some were making their compliments and wishing me joy, who, I knew, wished me little joy on the occasion. I desire to have the Divine approbation and the testimony of a good conscience, and then I need not much value their applause. I feel grateful to those noble persons who have honoured me with their friendship. I pray God I may deserve their favours. The best way to do this is to discharge well my duty. This is the best court we can pay to all good patriots and honest men.

March 12. I brought up my wife and family to the castle. I am more concerned about the duties of my post, than taken up with the honours of it.

March 26. Getting the news of a threatened invasion from Sweden. I laid my heart open before the Lord, and pleaded my case with him. Here am I posted among heaps of rubbish, and bare rocks, and almost defenceless walls, with a weak invalid garrison that I am a stranger to. There may be treachery or open mutiny among them. I know I have some enemies, and few to ask counsel of. These things look dark to the eye of sense and reason. But where sense and reason end, there faith begins. The Lord of Hosts, I trust, is on my side. He can make an invalid garrison invincible,—a ruinous and dismantled fortress impregnable. Through him we can do valiantly. It is not the Swedes or any foreign enemy we need fear. It is our own sins and backslidings that lay us open to the judgements and wrath of heaven. Putting the garrison in order, and providing the means of defence.

May 22. I have now qualified myself by taking the oath of Abjuration, a subject which has occasioned much heat and mischief. I desire to take it in singleness of heart, believing that it is a cautionary oath, and that the government has no ensnaring design in giving it, and that it does not oblige to anything contrary to the word of God, or to our principles. Many do scruple to take it; well, I do not condemn them that have not light to take it, nor should they condemn those who have clearness. Only I must say this, that many in their way of managing, raise scruples and objections, both in their own and other's consciences, rather than find them there. I see much design and cunning, under a pretence of strictness. I do not blame all, for I am persuaded many are upright and single-hearted. But artful and designing men always lead astray the simple and honest.

May 28. This being the king's birthday, I was much taken up in the solemnities of the occasion. I invited the magistrates and officers to a glass of wine in the castle. We then went to the cross, and next to the townhouse. I drank a good deal, but was nothing the worse. I do not justify myself, for there is sin in these things; but it is one of the snares that public posts are exposed to. Next day too there was some solemnity, but on a less deserving occasion; the restoration of a prince, (Charles II.) one of the worst that ever sat on our throne. But is the restoration of true monarchy that we celebrate.

June 23. Sabbath. Heard a sermon against legality. It is all very well to warn people against legality; but I see there is a party goes too far into the other extreme towards Antinomianism. I see generally where there are errors in a church, the orthodox side, the warm zealous party among them think they can never go far enough from the error, and so run themselves over a precipice on the other side. I desire to be found in the way of truth, shunning extremes on either hand. I know a pious minister who said, that he believed that serious, solid piety and religion have been upon the decline, since there has been so great an outcry against legal doctrine. It is not all gold that glitters. I think religion is much mistaken by many persons in Scotland, *who tithe mint and anise, and neglect the weightier matters of the law*, righteousness, truth, and sincerity. Lord, remove prejudices, and every thing that hinders our spiritual edification.[3]

---

3. "Legal preaching" at that time was so unpopular, as to be almost accounted heresy. Ministers who courted the favour of the people, were sometimes weak enough to accommodate their discourses to these prejudices, in a ridiculous degree. The colonel mentions a young preacher, a candidate for one of the charges in Stirling, at that time vacant, who gave in so far with the popular strain, as to use this expression in his prayers. *Lord, save us from the crooked path of morality!* The colonel's remarks upon this are rational and judicious. "Had he said the crooked path of self-righteousness, it would have been right; but I never lie to hear ministers (continued next page),

July 21. Sabbath. Hearing a stranger, our minister being dead. Lord grant, that the mantles of our departed Elijah's may descend on their successors. The town was much taken up with his preaching, and would give him a call. But I think it is not a minister's preaching alone that makes him a blessing to any place. It is his walk and conversation, holy, humble, self-denied. For without these, if he should preach like an angel, he will not edify or do much good; especially if he be found to be of a worldly, factious, designing temper.

August 13. Going this day for Glasgow. Meeting in the evening with some of my good friends, old Stirling acquaintances, who kept me too late. Next day I waited on the Duke of Montrose. Dined with him; he was very kind and civil. Staid late and supped with him. At my coming away next morning, my kind friends intended to give me a public convoy, but I slipped off very early, and shunned it, for I do not like parade and show.

August 28. Hearing the agreeable news of the great victory Prince Eugene has got over the Turks. Lord, turn it to they glory. Thou art dashing the potsherds of the earth together—the Turk against Antichrist. May it prepare a way for spreading the truth—for the kingdoms of the earth to become the kingdoms of our Lord Jesus Christ. Dry up Euphrates, and make a path for the Kings of the East. Make an inroad by the glorious light of the gospel into Satan's kingdom—into Mahomet's and Antichrist's kingdoms. Let the Captain of our Salvation ride prosperously, his sword girt upon his thigh, going forth conquering and to conquer. May all the kings of the earth pay him homage, till the uttermost ends of the earth be given him for a possession, and the islands receive his law. Amen.

September 12. This is the day I ought no to forget; one of the great Ebenezer's of my life—the siege of Lisle. God delivered and honoured me; he wounded and healed me. He gave his angels charge over me in that night—a night much to be remembered by me, when heaven and earth seemed to mix,—thunder and lightning from above,—cannons, bombs, and firearms round about. Bit my mind was staid on this promise, Isaiah xliii. 2. *When thou walkest through the fire thou shall not be burnt, &c.*

---

especially young men, speak slightingly of morality! But I observe, when a young man sets up for a high-flier, or to gain applause, and a name for strictness among country people, the best way to attain his end is, to run down morality and legality."

December 19. I was called to a meeting of the Session, Council, Deacons, &c. about calling a minister. As I had reason to think there had been some underhand work, I thought it my duty to discharge my conscience, and spoke to this effect:—

My Lord, (the provost being preses,) while we have this matter entire before us, and before we be much dipped into it, I would beg, as a well-wisher to the town of Stirling, to give my humble opinion and advice in a general way. All of us that are concerned in it, ought to lay by all prejudice, all wrong bias and ill humour, and cordially join together in calling a faithful gospel minister, who may feed us in the integrity of his heart, a man of a peaceable temper, free of all party-spirit,—a man who has no other design upon us, but to lead us to Christ. And it is much the interest of this town, at this time when people are so ready to be led into parties, to have a man of a healing quiet temper, in a word, a man that can say. *This is our rejoicing, even the testimony of our conscience, that in simplicity and godly sincerity, not with fleshly wisdom, but by the grace of God, we have had our conversation among you.*

I shall venture to say that the gospel never did thrive, and never will, in the hands of a party minister. As to the gift of preaching, I look upon that to be but a part of his qualifications. We ought to consider his conduct and conversation also, for a minister may preach like Paul himself, and by his conduct destroy more than he builds up. It was asked, that I should explain myself, if I had any insinuations; that the minister they were seeking was not such a man. I said I had no insinuations, only I thought we should be very cautious and wary to choose such a man as I had described.

(1718,) *January 14.* Hearing sermon on the occasion of moderating a call for our minister. I came to church with a peaceable, calm temper, to go along with the call, though I have been passive all the while. I complained, however, that I had but little opportunity of being acquainted with Mr. M. I had heard him preach, but knew little either as to his ministerial or prudential qualifications, to say whether he be fit for this place or not; and the town of Stirling know as little. In a matter of this sort, every man should be fully persuaded in his own mind, to give his vote with knowledge, understanding, and judgment. However he got a very harmonious and unanimous call. I thought it better to shew the meekness of a Christian temper, and signed the call with the Session. I hope it is a good choice, though rashly gone into by many; and I heartily pray God, he may prove a blessing to this place, and to myself in particular. Being appointed by the Session, I waited on the Presbytery to desire their concurrence. I said nothing to them about my own opinion. I did not think it proper, being there as the mouth of the Session.

January 23. This day visited by some young people from Edinburgh. We had coarse, rambling conversation, very unsuitable and unprofitable. I like mirth and diversion, but I hate gross, unpolished talk. One foolish or vicious person in a company, win put the conversation more out of order, than a dozen of polite people will put it right. The way of sin is easy and natural to the corrupt heart; the way of virtue and piety is harsh and severe to it. Lord pardon, and cleanse from the filth contracted in such society. It could not be helped, but it is a mercy I am not tied to them.

January 25. Yesterday we had a marriage. There was much mirth and gay conversation. We had music, and the young people dancing. I think these amusements very allowable on such occasions, while they are kept within the bounds of decency. My own temper is cheerful, but not frolicsome. The diversion, as usual, continued till late; and this day was also spent in mirth and jovial conversation. I stole from the company in the intervals to recollect myself, for I cannot long bear too light conversation, or too great jollity. Being Saturday, we dismissed the music early, and had family exercise.

February 1. The day spent quietly; but we supped abroad at night, which is the first time we have done so, I think these four years, since we came to Stirling. I do not like the practice; for it puts my family out of order, and unfits us for private duty.

★★★★★★

These extracts make it appear with what regularity and habitual reverence he was accustomed to maintain his intercourse with the Father of Spirits. Amidst the ceremonious cares of hospitality, or the levities of public company, he could steal a moment to offer up a pious thought, and rally his scattered mediations. Family devotion was a part of religion which he cultivated at all times, and under all circumstances in his own house. He acted at once as the priest and the father of his family. Whether alone or in company, (and he was seldom without visitors,) this duty was never neglected. When he officiated himself, he usually read a sermon; if a clergyman happened to be present, he was requested to offer prayers, which were sometimes preceded by an extempore lecture on some passage of Scripture.

******

February 18. This day I was betrayed into a fit of passion, for which I do not justify myself, though I had the right on my side. It was at my servants, who were colluding together with lies to deceive me, which I discovered, and could not bear, but gave them a sharp rebuke as they deserved. O Lord, pardon wherein I exceeded, for the wrath of man worketh not the righteousness of God. There is too much self even in our anger, and our zeal against sin. We know not what spirit we are of; there is much fuel within, which would soon break out if left to ourselves. Every one of us carries about with him, as it were, a barrel of gunpowder, and a lighted match to kindle it.

March 15. Busy all the forenoon, and troubled about rectifying disorders and abuses in the garrison, whereby it is likely I will get the character of being severe. But I see men will not do their duty without discipline and authority. Lord, do thou direct me to do my duty, and carry aright, avoiding all extremes.

April 1. Being appointed a member to the Synod of Glasgow and Ayr, I took journey yesterday and came to the *Synod* at Ayr. I observed a stiff and fiery spirit got in among them. Lord, rebuke their spirit; heal cur distempers and plagues; restore the spirit of love, charity, and meekness.

April 2. There was sad work this day in the *Synod.* Mr. Anderson gave in a violent libel against the ministers of Glasgow. [4] There was much wrangling and contention on both sides. A healing overture was proposed, but t displeased both parties, and both protested.. Next day we could not come to an agreement, and nothing but voting could bring the matter to a decision, when my opinion was asked, I said,

Moderator,—I have not inclined to speak upon this subject all this

---

4. Mr. Anderson was minister at Dumbarton, and figured much in the controversies of his time. He wrote with great virulence against Prelacy and the Liturgy; and was answered with equal scurrility by Mr. Calder, an Episcopal minister in Edinburgh. His call to Glasgow was favoured by many of the citizens and burgesses, but opposed by the clergy and University; and it was in answer to their complaints against him that he appeared at the Synod of Ayr. One of his opponents observed, "Why should the peace of the church be broken by one man? Let *Jonah* be thrown into the deep, and the storm shall be calm" "No," replied another, "let him rather be sent to the city to preach repentance." *Vid. Pamphlets on the Subject.*

while; now I shall give my mind freely upon the whole. This debate is between two parties, which I am sorry should be contending parties, and which should never be at variance, *viz.* the ministers and the people of a city. I see the business has been managed on both sides with much cross, ill humour. Both have committed faults; a great ferment has been raised, and a great fire kindled. It is not now so much our business to ask how it has been raised and fanned, as to lend a charitable hand to allay aid extinguish it. So the question comes, in short, to this.

Whether it will be more for the glory of God, the peace, unity, and comfort of the town of Glasgow, to translate Mr. Anderson there? I humbly think it will not; for. Moderator, how fit soever Mr. Anderson may have been before, and at the call, to be a minister there, and I shall not question his fitness then; yet now as the case stands, I think there is not a man in Scotland more unfit to be a minister in Glasgow than he. He is disqualified by his peculiar circumstances; for, being the occasion of so much division, and the bone of contention there, is there any chance, and likelihood, that he win ever be the cement of union? It must be a strong faith that can believe it.

And, Moderator, his conduct in all this affair gives us no reason to think that he win ever become a bond of unity. For at the beginning of the affair when he got his call, and saw a division arising about him, he had acted with a Christian spirit if he had come or written to the magistrates, *gentlemen,*—I thank you for the honour you have done me, in calling me to be one of your ministers, but I will not sow dissensions among you, I desire you to drop it. But instead of this, he sits within ten miles of Glasgow, and fans, and throws fuel into the flame; I mean his letter to the parish. Moderator, wherein, if I have any knowledge of religion, there is nothing written of a Christian temper, or a Gospel spirit, I see little else but banter, satyr, and burlesque. Moderator, my humble opinion is this: This Reverend Synod is the common father both of the ministers and the people of Glasgow. I think you should give them your charitable advice, and tell them freely.—Gentlemen, your minds are heated; in your present ferment you are not fit to choose a minister.

A man in a fever is not fit to choose what is good for him. Tell them to lay down these irascible passions of anger, malice, envy, back-biting, &c., and let their spirits cool, and then let them join heart and hand together, and choose a faithful, pious, peaceable, gospel minister; a man far from party-spirit, for I will venture to say, the gospel never did, and never will thrive in the hands of a party-man. Advise them to choose a man who has no other end in view, but to lead them to Christ; in a word, a man that can say on his admission, *I determine to know nothing among you save Jesus Christ and him crucified*; and the close of his ministry can say with the Apostle, *This is our rejoicing, even the testimony of our conscience, that in simplicity and godly sincerity, not with fleshly wisdom, but by the grace of God we have had our conversation among you*. And, Moderator, if they will choose such a man, assure them in your Master's name, that they shall have the blessing of God with him, they shall have peace, unity, and happiness with him; and if they do not choose such, they can expect nothing but strife and contention; and I cannot but say, as the case now stands, and from the debates I have heard, that the translating of Mr. Anderson to Glasgow must be productive of the worst consequences. For these reasons I am against his translation.

It was carried in the affirmative by a great majority, though it is not likely that he who so virulently libelled the ministers of Glasgow, will be fit to be a colleague with them. I left Ayr, and returned home to Stirling.

April 28. This has been a remarkable day to me; a merciful deliverance. Returning with some friends from a marriage-visit in the country, my horse threw me at a place where there was an ill step. All my face was sadly bruised and cut, but no bones broken. I was taken up senseless and carried into a house. There was much mercy in all this, for when my horse threw me, my foot stuck in the stirrup; and though my horse be very hot and fiery, yet he stood still til a servant came up and helped me. But they tell me that the horse was vicious, and offered to strike at me when I was lying on the ground. There is a great cut just beneath my eye, but the sight is mercifully preserved. I got a surgeon immediately, who took care of me; and next day got home in a chaise to Stirling. It was the beginning of June before I got completely recovered.

June 15. Sabbath. Serious in hearing. We have four exercises here on the Sabbath, and we had four different ministers; some expressing things one way, some another, yea, in seeming opposition to each other. These views, I confess, stumble me. Some that are called legal preachers, are blamed for leaning too much to the Arminian side; while others that call themselves evangelical, perhaps go too far to the Antinomian side. Lord, teach me thyself, for I dare not trust implicitly to any man. Lead me in the way I should go. The righteousness of Christ is the only foundation; it is through his strength alone that we can do any thing; but yet I would have the necessity of these duties pressed, *Crucify the flesh, Mortify your members, Pluck out the right eye,* &c. These are all spoken imperatively, and not in a passive style. *Let your lusts be mortified,* &c.

In short, I would have us as active and diligent in mortifying our lusts as if we could do it ourselves, and as if heaven were to be gained by it; and yet at the same time to believe that it is Christ must work in us both to will aid to do; and that we cannot mortify one vain thought of ourselves; it is the spirit of God and the power of his grace must do it; and to confess when we have done all we are but unprofitable servants. It is hard, I know, to do duties and not to rest some little upon them; but I desire to throw all away as to justification and acceptance, which must come through the righteousness of Christ alone. In the evening the whole congregation were disobliged by setting up a young preacher. Help us all to take the beam out of our own eye, and to look more into our own breasts, and we will be the more gentle to the faults and failings of others.

July 15. Busy all day preparing for a visit from the Lord Rothes, governor of the castle, and other great company. I rode out in the afternoon and met him near Alloa, but came home before him that I might receive him at the castle with all the honours. We had much company supping, and sat pretty late, but I hope without offence, though I will not justify myself. Next day we reviewed the garrison, and after dinner rode to Sheriff-muir. I had a distinct view and idea of the battle from my Lord, who was present and behaved very gallantly. Not unto us, but unto Thee be the glory of the day. The pride of man was stained on both sides.

July 23. This day our friends left us.

September 30. This day travelling to Leslie to visit Lord Rothes. Serene temper; for I am never in a better frame than when riding. We came there to dinner; cheerful company, and in the evening went out to diversion. I was invited at night to play, but shunned it. Next day we spent the forenoon in the bowling-green. In the evening when the company went to play, I got a book and read beside them.

October 2. This was a very bad day, which kept us within doors. We were sufficiently diverted by music. In the evening when the company went to play, I was more tempted than before, but got it shifted, and took a book and read till supper. We sat late as usual, but little drinking. This is rather an irregular way of living, and no friend to religion. I met with great kindness and civility. It is thou, Oh Lord, who givest me favour in the sight of any man.

October 13. At home writing letters; but perhaps shewing too much teeth in them. I should not be severe to others faults, as knowing I have many of my own. But I desire to have no resentment in my heart, though I do express myself sharply to correct their faults. Lord, give a meek and quiet spirit.

November 30. Sabbath. Serious in hearing, and desiring to be purged of all prejudices. Yet, alas! pestered with impertinent thoughts, though serious between hands. Ministers have learned me now to hear with a critical ear, sifting and examining everything I hear, perhaps too nicely; for now there are new plans and new schemes; but I am for the good old way. Many study vanity and applause, with a Pharisaical *Stand by, I am holier than thou.* Lord, teach me what is right.

December 13. Rode out upon an express from my Lord Rothes, to dine with him and others at a gentleman's house. There was cheerful company and diversion in the evening. I was only a spectator; but though I appear grave and sober on these occasions, my heart tells me I am in as great danger of temptation as any of them. We sat late, but innocent diverting conversation, and no insobriety. My advice was asked about certain affairs, which I gave. Lord, thou orderest all well that concerns me.

April 22. Visiting and using freedom in telling my mind freely to a minister in some points of doctrine and practice. I desire to be always under deep impressions, that it is only by grace I stand; and that without it I can do nothing; and that it is in Christ alone, and by his righteousness that I can be accepted. None in the world have more reason to exalt free grace than I have, or to be more humble.

(1719,) *January 1.* Lord, give me grace to spend my time better now that I am descending into the vale of years. Teach me to number my days that I may apply my heart to wisdom. I have not been faithful as I should have been, in witnessing against sin. Lord, pardon and give me more zeal for thy service. On this occasion I desire to take shame, and be humbled before thee, and flee to the covert of blood. Help me to employ Christ freely, and to rejoice in pardoning mercy.

January 16. Agreeably diverted all day, getting home a parcel of fine books, maps, globes, &c. We are apt to exceed in every thing; I was new-fangled about them, and spent two or three days among them. I reckon it one of the most innocent amusements.

April 18. Getting another alarm about the invasion, and that it is likely to fall upon us. If thou, Lord, plead not a controversy with us, we need not fear enemies. It is our sins and provocations that should make us tremble. Busily employed in the castle ordering things for our defence. But, alas! what signifies all this if the Lord watch not the garrison. If he appoint salvation for walls and bulwarks to us, we need not fear the whole Spanish Army.

※※※※※※

This projected invasion was another continental scheme in favour of the Pretender. It was headed by the Duke of Ormond, who set sail from Cadiz with an armament of ten ships of war, having on board 6000 regular troops, and arms for 12,0000 more. The king was apprised of these preparations against his crown and government, by the Duke of Orleans, Regent of France, who offered him at the same time twenty battalions for his service. Additional forces were raised at home, and foreign auxiliaries called in from abroad; 2000 men were brought from Holland, and six battalions from the Austrian Netherlands. Ormond's expedition suffered the fate of the Invincible Armada. The fleet was entirely dispersed by a violent storm off Cape Finisterre, except three frigates which landed in Scotland with about 300 Spaniards, under the Earls Marshal, Seaforth, and other Jacobite chiefs. They were joined by a small body of disaffected Highlanders, and took possession of some fortresses. But they were soon routed by General Wightman at the Pass of Glenshiel; the Highlanders dispersing to their hills, and the Spaniards surrendering themselves prisoners of war.

※※※※※※

April 24. Getting the good news this day of our enemies being scattered. Providence has long appeared in a signal manner for us, disappointing the plots of designing me; and does more for us than we can do for ourselves. Oh that his goodness might lead us to repentance. Help us to look to thee, to take refuge under the shadow of thy wings.

April 29. This day set apart for fasting and humiliation. We go about the outward duty, but, alas! there is little of the spirit of repentance in us. It is not the bowing down our heads as a bulrush for a day, but a confessing and forsaking of sin, everyone smiting upon his breast, and saying, What have I done? It is only a day of thy power that can do this. Lord, melt down our hard hearts, and fill them with evangelical sorrow, that we may look upon him whom we have pierced, and mourn. Pour out the spirit of grace and supplication upon all people. This would be stronger defence against our enemies than weapons of war or the strength of rocks. We have got a further confirmation of the dispersion of the Spanish fleet. *Thou breakest the ships of Tarshish with thy east wind; thou puttest a hook in their nostrils and turnest them by the way they came;* and we have no more to do but to be still, and know that thou art God. Be thou exalted among the heathen; be thou exalted in all the earth.

June 4. We have got a detachment of foreigners in the castle. I paid a visit to the Swiss colonel in the morning. They are a very civil people.

June 17. We have got the new of a victory in the North (at Glenshiel.) Oh, we admire the goodness of God who deals so mercifully with a wicked unthankful generation—who compasses us about with deliverance when we might expect wrath aid judgement.

June 26. Sabbath. At night the minister and good company supping with us. Alas! the best are but men. There was cross humour and resentment breaking out in one, who, I dare say, has much grace, yet he was not sensible of it. Corruption shewing itself strong; even these very failings he was ridiculing and running down in another, were just his own, which everybody but himself saw plainly to be his own predominants; and yet he is a clear-sighted man in everything else. Oh, what is man! no wonder we weak confused Christians know not ourselves, nor see our own failings, when wise men are so ignorant of theirs. All flesh is grass.

October 8. Rode out in the morning to pay a visit in the country. The gentleman not being at home, I went two miles farther, and there met with a providence that affected me very much; and acquaintance of mine seemingly dying, both to her own and others apprehension. Yet she was in the greatest serenity and composure, yea, spiritual rapture, rejoicing to die, and sorry to live. I staid some hours with her, and joined in conversation, confirming her in that frame of joy, believing it to be well-founded, and prayed with her. I came away both melancholy and joyful upon different accounts. There was company with us at night, and perhaps I went too far in holding out the things I had seen through the day, to some that may be were strangers to religion. I am weak. Lord pardon.

November 3. This is a new charge laid on me, a Justice of the Peace. Lord, give grace to discharge the duties of it, singly with an eye to thy glory, the suppression of vice, and encouragement of virtue, &c. Every post has its duties and burdens. Lord, keep me from the snares there may be in it. Thou knowest I had rather want the honour than be exposed to the snares of any post. Give grace to act so as I may have the Divine approbation and the testimony of a good conscience. I have again qualified by taking the oaths of abjuration and of allegiance, &c. I desire to swear in the integrity of my heart, being satisfied of the lawfulness of them. Lord, give grace to perform.

December 31. I bless thee, Oh Lord, for another year. The mercies of this year, as of all I have gone through, are great, yea, innumerable. A peaceable and quiet habitation, goodness and mercy following me all my days. O that thou wouldest quicken and revive me, and give supplies of grace as thou doest of all outward comforts. Well may I at the end of this year as of the rest say, *Hitherto the Lord has helped.*

(1720,) *January 8.* There is an order come down to put the laws in execution against ministers that do not qualify by taking the Abjuration oath. Lord, turn all to thy honour and glory; give light and counsel. If they be upright and single in the matter, aid have nothing but the glory of God before their eyes, the better for them; if otherwise, so much the worse, both for us and them. For my part I see nothing in the oath now, but what every Presbyterian ought to take cheerfully—every Protestant, and every Revolution man; for it is now a plain oath, swearing allegiance to the best of kings, and abjuring the restless Pretender. Finding some of the ministers refuse, I thought it my duty to go down and speak my mind freely to them about the matter.

I first offered my services as a Justice of the Peace to our minister, to qualify him in case he would yet come in; then I spoke to him as an elder, to put his ministry the charge of so many thousand souls—and the flock over which the Holy ghost had made him overseer, in one balance; and to put his metaphysical objections in the other, and see which has most weight; and if he could appeal to his master that this is a righteous cause—that he dare not, in conscience, swear allegiance to a Protestant prince—and dare not abjure a Popish Pretender, and if he could lay the stress of his suffering and his ministry on that point. Lord, send forth thy truth to lead and guide us, and in that purest light of thine, let us clearly see light.

January 20. This day our minister and another spoke to me from the brethren who scrupled to swear, desiring that I would write in their favour to the Duke of Roxburgh, &c. which I readily consented to do. Then we fell into debate about the oath; I was perhaps too harsh, yet I thought myself obliged in duty to speak freely, and to tell them that they were strengthening the hands of the Jacobites, and weakening the hands of the well-affected.

April 4. Busied all day about money concerns. Getting more of the world into my hands. Oh Lord, guide and direct. I believe it is thy blessing alone that makes rich; give me a token for good, that thou wilt add no sorrow with it. Take my heart off the world, and keep the world out of my heart. It was Providence brought this occasion in my way; I desire not to be rich. Lord dispose of me, and what thou givest me, for thy glory, and my own good. I am but a chamberlain, a trustee; pass it though my hands, to whom thou pleasest to give it. Enlarge my heart, as thou enlargest my estate; fill it with love to thee, and charity to thine,—the poor—the widow, and the fatherless. I would follow Jacob's example and vow. Gen. xxviii. 20-22. I have good reason; for the Lord has been with me, and kept me in all the way I have gone—through battles, sieges, and dangers these thirty years bygone. He has given me not only bread and raiment, but riches and honours in abundance. He has brought me again to my father's land in peace. He has enlarged my steps, and set my feet upon a rock. I desire then to say with the patriarch Jacob, *The Lord has been my God; and of all thou hast given me, I will surely give the tenth unto thee.*

July 3. Sabbath; heard a young man preach. I do not like this new fashion of preaching. I like a good style of language; but I would have a sermon take me by the heart, and not by the ears.

July 26. Went to Edinburgh to wait on the Duke of Roxburgh. Came in safe in the evening. There is something in a great town that destroys that serenity of mind that one has in the country. Here all are humming like bees; sharping upon one another; no idea of innocence. Living in a town is a perfect hurry and confusion. Waited upon the duke. It is the goodness of God that gives me favour in the sight of great men, and not skill or dexterity of my own. The more he raises me, may I be the more humble.

July 31. Went with his Grace to church, and heard a good sermon. Dined with him; and took the opportunity to recommend to him some persons, the widow and oppressed. It is the greatest privilege of the favour of great men to use it in doing good. Afternoon with him at church again.

August 1. Taking leave of the duke this morning. Busy using my interest, with people in power, for those that need protection and favour. There is a pleasure in doing good, and being serviceable to mankind, especially good people.

August 4. Returning home. Serene thankful temper; sitting alone in the chariot. Mercy and goodness follows me all the days of my life. I thought with myself, I am now the last of my father's family, born after my father was thrust out of his church, in destitute circumstances.. Now God has heaped riches and honours upon me. I see the children of Providence are better carried through and seen to, than the children of inheritance. Thou art the portion of my inheritance, and of my cup. *Truly the lines have fallen to me in pleasant places.*

August 11. This morning we were visited by the Duke of Argyle. I waited upon his Grace; he was very civil aid courteous. In the afternoon the duchess came up to the castle. I shewed her all the civility that lay in my power, and she was sensible of it. What am I, Oh Lord, and what is my father's house, that thou givest me such honour. Thou raisest up the poor from the dunghill, to set him with princes. At night I waited again on the duke; I pressed him to give the parole and orders, but he refused. He went away early next morning. I gave him eleven guns; so I hope I have not omitted any part of my duty.

September 1. Went on a visit to Leslie-House. Diverted with innocent country recreations.

September 10. The Duke of Roxburgh joined us today. We had cheerful conversation, but sat late. There are many temptations in greatness, and great men's company; though I must say I saw nothing but sobriety and modesty. Indeed I find the greatest quality always the politest.

September 12. Went out in the morning with the duke and other gentlemen a fowling, and got good sport; then went up to the top of the Lomond hills, and had a fine view of the country. Came home, where a splendid entertainment was prepared; at night there was music and dancing, and the young people very merry. I laid a restraint upon myself for fear of going too far, and joined but little, only so as not to shew moroseness or ill-breeding. We sat late, but the conversation was innocent, and no drinking but as we pleased. However, much time is spent; which I dare not justify. In all things we offend.

September 20. We came home to Stirling.

October 2. In the house of mourning; and at a funeral. The righteous man perisheth, and none layeth it to heart. I was concerned for the person—he was an honest man. Obliged to comply with that foolish custom of dirgee after the burial; and much idle, vain conversation, unsuitable to the day, and to the occasion; and though there was four ministers there, yet there was no help for it, where there is a promiscuous omni-gathering of idle graceless people.

★★★★★★

The death of another friend in Edinburgh, Mr. Balderstone, affected him also very much. The following is consolatory letter he addressed to Mrs. Balderstone on the mournful occasion.

Stirling Castle, Dec. 5. 1720.

The account of your dear husband's death was a surprise to us, having never heard of his illness. Probably it might have been so to yourself, and thus the stroke the heavier; but even in that case you must with Aaron hold your peace. His God hath done it; and whatever nearness to himself he pleases to admit any of his own to, yet he always reserves a liberty to himself, in the midst of the greatest familiarity, to shew some strokes of sovereignty, and he is not bound to reveal to us either what he is about to do with us, or the reasons of it, at the time. Elisha was a man who lived near God, and in much favour with him, yet he says. *Let her alone, for her soul is vexed within her, and the Lord hath hid it from me,* and hath not told me. God hath not given us absolute promises about temporal things, so neither should our faith go out peremptorily about them: but you have an absolute promise, that all things shall work together for good to them that love him.

You may take that, and I hope you find already in your sweet experience, that this *bitter* cup has that *blessed* effect.

But what I write of your surprise is mere guessing, for perhaps, as by his indisposition before, you got outward warning, so it may be you got some notice and intimations of it also upon your own spirit; but whether the one way or the other, be persuaded the way God has taken is the best for you. You need not doubt of mine and my wife's tender sympathy with you; but indeed, I almost thought it needless for me to trouble you on this sad occasion, or to offer any thing for your comfort: for you must go to the fountain of all comfort for that, and you live nearer the fountain-head than I do. You have also many dear and worthy friends about you, through whose hands the divine consolations are more likely to be communicated than by mine; but the long and intimate friendship between us, prevails with me to throw in my mite among others.

Your own melancholy will make you ready to pore too much on the dark side of the providence, but allow me to turn up another side of it, which is brighter; you have reason to be very thankful, and even to think with pleasure, that you have long enjoyed one of the best of husbands, with whom you have lived easy and comfortably as true yokefellows, and helps meet for one another, as heirs of the grace of life, strengthening one another's hands in the way of God; and in that good way you have led one another by the hand, even to the verge of life, to a good old age; and if he has got the start of you, and stepped in before you, why should you grudge at that? you are fast following, and will not be very long behind him; and this sharp providence will, through grace, wean you more from the world, make you sojourn in it as a stranger, and finding nothing in it to set your heart much upon, your affections will be more set upon the things that are above, where Jesus Christ is; and so by this sharp trial, you will be made more meet to be a partaker of that inheritance of the saints in light; and being made meet, you will desire to be dissolved and to be with Christ, where your heart and treasure is, and will, as a shock of corn fully ripe, fall into the grave.

The time is but short in this valley of tears; joy will come in the morning, and faith, at one view, can soon look over the few days or years of sorrow that are before you in time, into that fullness of joy that is in his presence, and those rivers of pleasure that are at his right hand for evermore; but as I said before, you are more capable of practising than I am to shew it you, and when, I hope, you have such access to the fountain of comfort yourself, you need it not from my hands.

    Yours, &c.   J.B.
To Mrs. Balderston, Edinburgh.

******

(1721,) *January* 6. Writing most part of the day about business, and in recommendations of one who, I believe, is wronged. There is a great pleasure in doing good offices to them that stand in need of us. Lord, give me more of this humour, kind, tender, and compassionate disposition to all fellow-creatures; especially to the members of Christ, to shew I am a member of the same body. Company in the evening, and a temptation laid in my way, but I escaped it. I bless the Lord who gives me so much of a meek and quiet spirit, as to slight little injuries, and stifle resentment. This is grace, for I have strong irascible appetites.

January 16. Getting an account of a disagreeable affair in the town; sin and villainy, which I think myself concerned to pursue, and get punished. I desire. Lord, to let thy glory be my chief aim in everything. Give us zeal and boldness for thee, that iniquity may be ashamed, and stop its mouth. I went next day to the Justice-of-Peace court, and told my mind very freely against Jacobitism, and stood up for the ministers. I spoke to the magistrates to this effect: *Gentlemen,* I believe you are satisfied that the libel is proven, and more than what was libelled. I believe you are fully convinced of the wicked designs of this man; designs of mischief, yea, I may say of murder, as appears by the probation, where he says he would venture to lose his life for it; that is, to be hanged for killing her.

You see also his implacable hatred and malice against one of the ministers of this place, by his cursing and waylaying him—a pious godly man who never gave him any provocation—who never offended him, except he took it for an offence, when the minister, from the pulpit, reproves fornication and drunkenness. The same spirit that carried him out to an unnatural rebellion, led him to curse and revile the minister; and the same spirit that made him curse his minister, would also lead him, if he had opportunity, to imbrue his hands in his blood. It is the same spirit that runs through all.

Now Gentlemen, I, as having the honour to command, at present, His Majesty's castle here, require satisfaction for the injury done to a family belonging to one of the king's soldiers. Next, as Justice of the Peace, I demand security and protection for the ministers of the place; and that wicked men, if the fear of God will not restrain them, the fear of punishment may. Gentlemen, I am very thankful, and I may say in the name of the town of Stirling, *we* are very thankful, that we have magistrates who will make it a conscience to do their duty—magistrates, who answer the end of their institution, to be a terror to evil doers, and a praise to them that do well. Now this is just what we demand of you, that you will tie up this wicked man's hands, and oblige him to give security for his good behaviour, under such a penalty, that he may be afraid of ever committing the like crimes.

The magistrates gave sentence accordingly to this effect, and he was committed to prison. I bless the Lord that vice is checked, and gets not leave to triumph, (though it prevails too much,) and that iniquity is put to shame, and hides its face before authority.

February 1. Hearing sermon, and the ministers dining with us. Went out with them afterward to meet with a man who pretends to the spirit of prophecy; but he would not speak to them. I took upon me to examine his pretensions a little. I believe he may be a good man, but weak, and perhaps not solid. The ministers have gone too far in it, and made too much noise; I wish religion do not suffer.

March 9. Going to the country to see an acquaintance who is ill; and Oh, we got a preaching there, humbling and edifying; seeing a poor man in miserable circumstances, dying in appearance, yet no sense of his condition, his mind filled with vanity and the world. Lord, pluck him as a brand from the burning, out of the jaws of hell and Satan; make him a monument of rich, free, efficacious grace. Let thy glory be exalted in redeeming and conquering such a soul from the power of sin and Satan. I was going to speak with him, and speak freely, and I had a great check afterwards that I did not. If the Lord give me another opportunity, I beg grace to be faithful to his poor soul.

June 18. Sabbath. Having sermon from a weak man; better have pity than prejudice on such occasions. Lord, quicken and revive, for without the influences of thy Spirit, neither law nor gospel will do the business. It must be a day of thy power. The minister supped with us. I had a check for being too rash in an expression concerning a person. Perhaps it was true, but it was uncharitable, and rash in me to say it.

June 28. The fast before the sacrament. Watching over my own heart, and against self-righteousness or self-working. I desire to come straight to Christ; I must have all from him of his free grace in the way of believing. Hearing two sermons in the forenoon; the last rather dead, and looking like legal work. I find I have much corruption, strong lusts and passions that war against the soul. I desire to come immediately to Christ, to get my heart filled with love to him, mixed with sorrow for sin to come to him as a Prince and Saviour exalted to give repentance and remission of sin. This is the frame I would be at. I have many things upon my heart, many complaints, many plagues, much wrong. I would come to Christ to plead that promise, *I, even I, am he that pardoneth your iniquities.* But, alas! I find not only a weakness and want of preparation, but a backwardness and unwillingness.

July 1. The Preparation. Hearing much of the love of God in Christ to sinners. He *that spared not his own Son, &c.* Oh this hard heart of mine that is not melted down and warmed with such love! Oh blessed Jesus, commend thyself to my soul; make thyself precious. I desire to embrace him in his full and free offer; and to go to the well-ordered covenant. I have many complaints of myself, deadness, formality, backsliding, falling from my first love, earthly mind, corruption strong, grace weak. What should I do with all these? Fruitless complaints will not help me. Oh then let me go straight to Christ; he is the life; he gives repentance and remission of sin; he washes us in his blood; he heals our backslidings, and loves us freely; he subdues our lusts; he is our righteousness and sanctification; he is all, and must do all for us and in us.

July 2. Sabbath. I cannot say my frame is lively, but I desire to act faith on Christ, to lay myself down at his door as a needy beggar. Oh to hunger and thirst after him! I would think that a good frame. May a sense of my need, sin, and guilt, chase me to Christ. The things I named before, still heavy on my heart; Oh to get them removed! not in a legal, but in a gospel way; by Christ, and not by working; yet I must not be idle. Serious in communicating, ejaculations, breathings of faith and love, God in my thoughts, my heart in heaven. Oh that such a holy frame were the native element of my soul! Let thy Spirit dwell in me for this is all I desire.

July 3. Thanksgiving. Serious in hearing. I have taken the cup of salvation in my hand. I hope I have also taken Christ and all his salvation. May my soul feed and rest upon him as my portion for ever.

July 9. Another death in the garrison; three within these few months. I was called up at three in the morning to see the dying person. I spoke to him, but, alas! I found not those impressions deep enough on my own spirit that I seemed to press home upon him; and I was grieved they made so little impression on him, through ignorance and stupidity. I ordered a military funeral for him. Lord, fit us all for our change. Thou art calling away the old men in this garrison pretty fast. Give us that inheritances which is incorruptible and passeth not away.

August 14. At home all day writing letters. My talent lies perhaps too much in writing facetious letters of wit, humour, and jest.. We should have a check upon ourselves in all things, even in those pleasures we think innocent; for though they may be innocent in their nature, they may become faulty by excess. Even our diversions should be seasoned with salt; the salt of grace rather than that of wit.

December 25. Christmas. I am not for observing of holidays; yet I think I was not ill employed this morning when I awakened, in thinking on these passage about our Saviour's birth. *Behold, I bring you good tidings of great joy, which shall be to all people. For unto you is born this day, in the city of David, a Saviour, Christ the Lord. And suddenly there was with the angel a multitude of the heavenly host, praising God, Glory to God in the highest, peace on earth, and good-will to men.* I thought it no superstition in meditating on these things. I see no command for the keeping of this day, yet I have no zeal against those who keep it religiously.

CHAPTER 21

Conclusion, 1722–1729

As the latter years of the colonel's life were not distinguished by any extraordinary events, it will be unnecessary to prolong the subject by multiplied extracts. Confined as he was within the narrow precincts of his office, and the limited circle of his friends, his character had less room to display itself in a manner sufficiently striking and diversified to command general interest. But though the concluding periods of his history be less chequered and eventful, still it was marked by the same tokens of divine care, and furnishes instructive incidents worthy of being recorded.

To him, the most retired situation—the most tranquil season, had its memorable occurrences. Every day afforded to his mind matter of useful observation; Every month had its calendar of mercies; every providence was noted in his journal, and thereby more deeply imprinted on the tablet of his memory. But the uniformity of his experiences had, in course of time, communicated a similar uniformity to his thoughts and expressions; and it is for this cause that his pious reflections have occasionally been omitted, as tending to fatigue the mind with needless repetitions. The same reason will apply to the remaining extracts, which are selected purposely of a desultory and miscellaneous kind, so as to exhibit his character under various shades of colouring. This explanation will obviate the supposition, which otherwise might have occurred, that the writer of the diary had become less devout, as if ease and prosperity, dangerous enemies to religion, had betrayed him into carelessness and security, or weaned his affections away from the things that belong to his everlasting peace, into a criminal conformity with the world.

As he advanced in years, he began to experience, in the loss of friends and relatives, some of those calamities and privations to which old age is necessarily exposed. He lived to witness the departure of many of his early acquaintances, and several of his distinguished patrons, among whom he records with much feeling, Marlborough, and the Earl of Rothes, his Fort-Governor. Of Lord Rothes' death, he has given a most tender and impressive description; a favour which, it is much to be regretted, none of his own friends did for himself.

******

January 21. Sabbath. Hearing a very good sermon in the main, yet some expressions in it, which I thought sounded otherwise than what I used to hear, and even otherwise than what I think the Scriptures and our divines express. My ill heart nibbled at these new ways of speaking, and hindered me from being edified by the very good things that were in it. Lord, help me *as a new born babe to desire the sincere milk of the word, that I may grow thereby.* A man that has a good appetite, and is hungry, will not quarrel with a meal, though it be not quite to his taste. It is a squeamish stomach that carps at a dish of meat, though there be a mote in it.

March 5. Alarmed in the morning by an express, that my brother is dying. I made ready, and immediately went for Edinburgh, but ere I got in, he was dead. I doubt not he has left this valley of tears—this weary wilderness, to enter into that fullness of joy,—those rivers of pleasure at God's right hand.

March 6. This morning, seeing another friend that was dying; and died two hours after. Lord sanctify these providences. Death is made familiar. I am handling it every day. O help me to be living as a stranger and pilgrim on the earth, sitting loose to all earthly enjoyments, that when death comes, I may look to it as a friend. *Oh death, where is thy sting?*

March 7. In the afternoon doing the last duty to my dear brother. Serious thoughts by the way. He is now happy; no more sin—no more sorrow—no more trouble. He is now singing that new song. *To him that loved us, and washed us in his blood, &c.* while we lay down the body to rest in the grave till the resurrection, in hope of a blessed immortality. It was his desire to be carried to the grave by ministers, and he got his wish; for all the Presbytery came in a body to the burial. At night I was again in the house of mourning with my other friend. It was a satisfaction that Providence brought me in to do these last duties, for I knew there was none in the world that they desired more to be near them at their death than myself. Oh, when I am laying my friends in the dust every day, make me remember I must lie down there shortly myself, but I know that my Redeemer liveth, and though after my skin worms destroy this body, yet I trust with these eyes, I shall see God.

March 8. Getting account that my Lord Rothes is very ill. I went over the water in the afternoon. This is a melancholy time; death striking on all hands. We were long upon the water, and had a troublesome landing. The night was dark, and the way bad. I got a guide, and got to Leslie, but found my Lord better than I expected.

March 10. I got opportunity this morning to speak alone to my Lord; I said but little. Lord speak thou; let him see his sin and danger, that he may cry out. *What shall I do to be saved!* Then let him see the remedy, Jesus Christ ready to receive him. *Come unto me all ye that labour, &c. Whosoever comes unto me, I will in no wise cast out.* I thought of returning home, but my Lord would not let me go, and kept me two days longer.

March 22. Giving a commission about buying a piece of land. I am easy about it, being more at friends' desire than my own. It is not time for an old man to be making projects for long life, and purchasing estates. Lord, be the portion of my inheritance, and of my cup. Make me meet to be a partaker of the inheritance of the saints in light. Let me think more of a removal, than of a purchase in this world. The most part of my time is over. I desire to live a stranger and pilgrim on earth, waiting till the day of my appointed time.

May 6. Took a sudden resolution again to go to Leslie, hearing my Lord is very ill. Riding alone all the day; serene, serious temper. Came to Leslie at night, and was much affected, and I hope edified, seeing my Lord's carriage. He called all his family together, and took leave of them solemnly; recommended them to the serious study of religion and holiness, as the one thing needful—as that alone which would make them happy in time and to eternity, and that when they came to be in the condition he was in, (death looking them in the face,) they would see it to be so. Then he prayed with them most fervently; this was very affecting to us all. He shewed the greatest submission and resignation; and though he was in much pain, yet the greatest patience, never uttering the least fretting expression; shewing a desire to be gone, yet submitting to the will of God, as to the time. About eleven at night, he caused his son, Lord Leslie, read the 36th Psalm to him and as he went along, he repeated the emphatical expressions of it, such as, *I sought the Lord, he heard me and delivered me, &c. This poor man cried, and the Lord heard him. Oh taste and see that God is good, &c.* I left him about twelve, being so much fatigued and affected, that I fainted away.

I waited on my Lord next day, and it was well spent time. He shewed a lively faith, trusting in God, relying upon his promises and his faithfulness, and gave solid reasons of his hope; declaring his full satisfaction with the Gospel method of salvation; and besought a minister that was present, and me, to deal plainly with him, and tell him if we thought he was wrong, or if we thought his faith was true and right founded; or if we thought it was presumption. For my part, I could not refuse to give testimony to the Spirit of God, and to the truth and reality of that gracious work of the Sprit, which, by all the skin and experience I had in religion, I thought I saw in him. So we encouraged him to go on believing, trusting, relying. He spoke to excellent purpose through the day; was very pertinent and ready in the Scriptures; prayed once I think publicly, and often privately, with his eyes so fixed and intent towards heaven, as if he were looking into it, and reminded me of Stephen, Acts vii. 55.

He desired the physician, and he himself frequently felt his pulse, not for the prolonging of life, but to observe how fast he spent and weakened; and was not pleased when they promised him long time to live; telling us he had no more to do here, and was well content to go out of a vain, sinful world, *and to be with Christ which was far better.* This humility and good nature he carried with him to the last; and even his brisk, cheerful temper, and pleasant way of speaking, when they told him that one of his physicians was gone, he said smiling, "The doctor thinks I will not die tonight, but perhaps I shall beguile him." I sat up with him till about one in the morning, and then I left him; for he pressed me to go, and said he would send for me when he grew weak.

May 9. Called in the morning, my Lord being weak. This day he prayed once in public with his family with great earnestness, recommending them to God; and prayed secretly, often with fixed fervent looks towards heaven. As he weakened, he began to be delirious; but whenever spiritual discourse was begun to him, he immediately came to himself again, and joined in it with the greatest seriousness; and he bade us that were about him, check him when we found him wavering, which we took the freedom to do, and which he took most kindly. About three hours before his death, his thoughts began much to waver, and the fever seized his head, and he became uneasy, but suddenly his spirit fled, and he went away calmly with little struggle. In a word, I never saw any man die more as a Christian hero, with so much natural fortitude, and such lively faith. He was pleasant in his life, and pleasant in his death. Oh keep the impression strong upon my heart forever, of what I have seen and heard here.

May 10. Came into Edinburgh this morning; waited on the commissioner to the Assembly, and went home.

June 22. Getting letters with the accounts of a new governor. Lord, let it be for thy glory and our good; thou doest all things for us well.

July 7. Going out early in the morning to Kilmadock, being the day before the sacrament. Heard two good and suitable sermons. Walking in the fields alone after sermon, meditating on the solemn ordinance. I complain of a hard, dead heart, carnal earthly affections, no relish for spiritual things. I desire to come straight to Christ by faith, to believe in him as a complete Saviour, able to heal all my plagues, to pardon all my sins, to stop all my complaints, to make up all my wants. Lord, give me such a sight of my self-pollution, and misery, and withal, such a view of the sufficiency and fullness of a Saviour, as may chase me unto Christ; give me such a sight of his love—of free sovereign pardoning grace, as may make sin terrible and odious to me.

July 8. Sabbath. Rose early in the morning, at four o'clock, and went out to the wood. There I endeavoured to pour out my soul, in confession and acknowledgement of sin, and bring my heart to mourn and be humbled for it. I sought more grace and more strength, for all I need. I will not speak of my resolutions and promises; it is not my promises to God I must trust to, to carry me through; it is God's promises to me, that he will perfect strength in my weakness. I was troubled all the day that I could not get love to keep pace with faith; now that I am old, the heart is not naturally so soft as in youth; the edge of the affections is blunted. I went down to the table, desiring that the plagues of my heart might be healed, that it might be more powerfully touched with grace; and it pleased the Lord to pour upon me a spirit of repentance and supplication.

The hard and stony heart was softened. I could not contain myself at the table, tears flowing out, which I strove much against; *first*, lest onlookers should think better of me than I knew I deserved, or think I had that which I had not; and again, I know the heart is deceitful and vain. However, I desired to have secret work between God and my soul, which none could be witness to. But Oh, let me not trust to my vows and resolutions as I have too much done: but to the well-ordered covenant and the promises of grace. I sat in the church all day serene and calm. At night, fatigued by long exercise.

August 2. The day of Blenheim, a day on which the Lord delivered and honoured me. This day also the great Duke of Marlborough is to be buried. This time eighteen years ago, was a glorious day for him; one of the greatest victories ever was obtained. I could not forbear to solemnize it by dropping guns with my tears, to the honour of my ever renowned, and ever to be remembered great general, under whose auspicious conduct, by the blessing of God, I have fought these thirty years bygone.

November 4. Hearing a stranger preach from a text that should be memorable to me from the time I was in the Bass, when Mr. Shields preached upon it.[1] Jer. ii. 2. *Thus saith the Lord, I remember thee, the kindness of thy youth, the love of thine espousals, when thou wentest after me in the wilderness, &c.* Oh for that first love, the love of espousals. Some are drawn in to Christ by the cords of love, others chased in by fear.

December 4. At night something came into my mind that passed in a public company the day before, wherein I thought I had justly given offence, especially to a minister, in speaking in too legal a strain, &c. I was uneasy at myself, and thought I was obliged to write a letter to him clearing myself, explaining my meaning, and declaring my principles and opinion on that head, which I think is sound, and I believe he thinks so too.

(1723,) *February 20.* Hearing a sermon; but not very well pleased with it. The distinction of legal and gospel preachers is too far pushed on both sides; and both go to extremes. Some err in pressing too much moral duties and holiness, without insisting enough from what principle they spring, *viz.* faith in Christ. Others again dwell too much on faith, without pressing holiness and moral duties. I do not like legal preaching; and indeed some sermons, such as Tillotson's, Barrow's, &c. are but like Seneca's discourses of moral virtue to me. I would have

---

1. Shields was confined for some time on the Bass. See a list of the covenanters imprisoned there. *Blackader's Memoirs, Appendix.*

ministers lead me to the spring—Jesus Christ, and faith in him, all to be done through his strength and by his grace; but I would have them often pressing—and warmly pressing obedience to his laws. There is certainly a middle way to be kept, and no doubt every minister thinks he is in the right way. Lord, lead me in the right way.

July 14. Not very well, and in the evening great and violent pain. But I bless God who mitigates and rebukes it, and makes it tolerable, and gives patience. Oh give the sanctified use of the rod. Let thy design be mercy to my soul. May affliction chase me unto Christ; and wean me from the world and its enjoyments. Sabbath, at home reading: serious and meditating. Lord, make up to me the want of ordinances.

August 21. In this Session, and after in the Presbytery. A foul scandal (adultery) of a great professor before us. O, we should not be high-minded, but fear. *Let him that thinketh he standeth take heed lest he fall.* Though some will not own it, I am afraid there are in Scotland both Antinomians and favourers of Antinomians; those who think themselves great proficients in grace, and that they stand high in favour with God above others, and treat them with a Pharisaical *Stand by, for I am holier than thou*; and that their sins, even gross sins, cannot cast them out of his favour, nor make them liable to his displeasure; that God sees not their sins as the sins of others, and is not angry with them as with others; and their views being only on free grace and pardoning grace, they do not entertain those frightful ideas of sin which they call a legal spirit: so that when they fall into even gross sins and scandals they are not uneasy. David's adultery and murder comes in to alleviate them; and they apply (or think so) the blood of Christ immediately, and take hold of the promise of pardoning grace.

There are others who do not fall into this way themselves, but from an excess of charity, and desiring to be much of a Gospel spirit, do favour these, and are easy to them, supposing them to be in a state of grace. Though they have made slips, they cannot find in their hearts to apply the threatenings of the law to them, but immediately apply the promises and consolations of the gospel. This is skimming over a wound before it be probed. I saw too much of this I thought this day in the Presbytery. I would magnify free grace; but I would also magnify the law. I would hold all by the tenure of free grace, but not so as to turn the grace of God into licentiousness, or take liberty to sin because grace abounds.

September 19. This is a remarkable day to me, the siege of Aeth. Particular providences happened to me that seemed awful and frowning at the first, but much mercy appeared after. I remember what a horror I was in alone for a little space in the trenches, from a providence that I brought upon myself and the regiment, which I did for the best, and to the best of my understanding, but which was like to turn ill out and endanger the lives of some soldiers, and indeed did cost some lives. This Satan drove home upon me as if I had been guilty of their blood, though it is as probable more might have been killed, if I had done the thing the other way. And at night, by another strange providence, I had almost been drowned after I had brought the regiment out of the trenches, coming home to the camp. All these had a terrible effect upon me. I thought upon that word our Lord said to Peter, *Satan has sought thee*, but I thought it was to destroy me. The damp of these providences continued upon me for several days: but I bless God who restored peace. The blood of Jesus Christ cleanseth from all sin.

October 1. Dining abroad; in company all the afternoon, and in the evening at a glass of wine. Cheerful conversation, perhaps too much upon the ramble. I comply too far with young rambling company; yet at the same time I was disputing against and keeping down wild mistaken notions, and debating on the side of truth. When I am grave at a bottle of wine, then I am reckoned morose, and a spy upon conversation; when I am cheerful, then it is a humour for drinking, and love of company. It is not easy keeping the middle way, therefore I go as seldom as I can into these occasions.

November 25. Burying a sergeant in the garrison. I was troubled I did not see him before he died; he was calling for me. I should embrace every opportunity of doing good to poor souls. Oh give more zeal for thy glory, more grace, to do my duty better.

December 30. Put out of humour by hearing, that he who is appointed to intimate the sentence of excommunication against that scandalous person, refuses to do it. It does indeed stumble me; for I have of a long time thought that Antinomianism is too softly and tenderly handled here; and this man seems to be a rank Antinomian. For, notwithstanding of these horrid scandals of adultery and perjury, he is enjoying a peace of conscience, that surpasses not only all natural, but all spiritual understanding. It does not shake his faith, no, nor yet his assurance. I am persuaded he breaks his neck upon such doctrines as these: *A believer has not to mourn or repent of his sins, &c. God does not see the sins of believers, &c., is not angry with them. And that God loves the be-*

liever as well when he is sinning as when he is holy. These are the doctrines they delude themselves with. Lord, send forth thy light and thy truth; let them be guides to me, and lead me in the way everlasting.

(1724,) *January 1.* Thou are still adding to my days and years. Oh Lord, give more grace to employ time better, and working out my salvation; that every year I may be made more meet for that inheritance of the saints in light. Then I might rejoice in old age, when every year, bringing me nearer the grave, might also bring me nearer heaven, by grace made ripe for glory.

January 13. Company coming up to the castle in the forenoon, great high-fliers. I wonder what heights and extravagances some men's violent humours will drive them to: and still the Church is the cry. By the *Church* they do not mean practical religion. It is not the Protestant succession. It is not King George. All these would be dropt; yea, a Pretender would be taken by the hand to get their grievances redressed. These lie at the bottom of their hearts; the breaking of the Union, &c. And there are too many that love to fish in troubled waters. A dice often thrown must cast up a lucky chance some time or other. Ambition, love of the world, &c. lie at bottom many times when we think we are acting from fair principles. I used freedom with them, and told them my mind. Lord, subdue those lusts that war against the soul, and blind the eyes of our understanding.

January 24. This day went to Dunblane to the burial of another old Bass friend. Pious company and suitable conversation.

February 13. Coming up from Craigforth in the evening, we met with a merciful preservation. The hill of Ballochgiech being slippery with ice, the horse fell, and the chariot ran back, and was nearly thrown over. I may still observe, that God gives his angels charge over us, to keep us in their hands, so that not a bone is broken. It might have been a melancholy night, and lives lost. We came out and got men who brought horses and chariot home safe.

March 25. Went to a Quarter-Sessions, where I thought it my duty to speak to the magistrates, to stir them up to do their duty in putting the laws in execution anent Popish Priests, and Jacobite Meeting-Houses. I told them I should feel myself obliged, by the post I was in, to represent it to government. Lord, bless and give success.

April 14. Sent for this day to hold a Justice court, a horrid murder committed this morning in the country; a woman and her daughter barbarously murdered and mangled. Several persons examined; and three others suspected and ordered to be seized. Lord, direct and guide us to discover the guilty. Strong presumptions of guilt upon two women; a long tract of malice, rage, revenge, and threatenings proven upon them, but they are most hardened obstinate wretches. Lord, make thou a full discovery. Let fall a spark of conviction on their consciences that they may confess and repent.

May 11. At home reading. Lord, make me more spiritually minded. We were alarmed with a great eclipse of the sun this evening; yet it did not appear remarkable, being very little darker than ordinary. The God of nature was pleased to spread a veil of clouds between the heavens and us; to stop the prying curiosity of vain man who would be wise to know every thing. It is our duty to be thankful for the daily kind returns of the sun to us; and that we are not scorched up as some climates are, or frozen with cold as others.

May 20-22. The judges coming in this morning; waited and went to church with them. Went to the court every day. They have been at all pains to find out the horrid murder of the woman and her daughter, and gave a fair hearing to the wretched culprits, appointing two advocates to plead for them, which they did as handsomely as the case would bear. The trial was long, and the judges had great patience. I ordered some refreshment for them. The jury gave in their verdict, finding the two women guilty. It was a melancholy sight. During the trial the panels had been quarrelling between themselves; and one of the women, upon receiving her sentence, fell into a violent rage at sight of the executioner who pronounced the doom, and tore and bit everybody near her. Oh may sinners be terrified by seeing thy righteous judgments against the wicked.

June 3. Hearing sermon in the forenoon. The three murderers who are under sentence of death were all brought into church. Yet I cannot say the discourse was suitable. He was too metaphysical about the law, when he should have held out the remedy of the Gospel.

June 9. I was desired by the minister to go along with him to visit the criminals. It was a melancholy sight; no contrition, nothing but curses, imprecations, and rage, against the judges and all who had any hand in their condemnation. I spoke to them honestly, telling them to confess and implore mercy and forgiveness of God. But I saw nothing but hardened obstinacy.

June 14. Sabbath. There was an affecting melancholy sight in church this afternoon, a child baptised of one of the criminals, a man that is to be executed here for killing his own mother. The man was present himself. The minister spoke well to the subject, and it drew tears from every eye.

June 27. Called down to Craigforth hastily in the morning, a child there dying. I was much affected and went out to the fields, offering up prayers to the throne of grace for the poor child. She, as well as the oldest of us, must be washed from original sin in the blood of Christ. She must have his righteousness imputed to her as well as we; she must have the corruption of nature taken away and cleansed, as well as we. I incline to have much charity for children. Our merciful Saviour said, *Suffer little children to come unto me, for of such is the kingdom of heaven.* I do not say all children will be saved, even of believing parents. But this is a point too deep for us; we must not meddle with the sovereignty of God.

July 27. Called down to hold a Justice Court, where I was sorry to hear some professors, and even good men, blamed for unfair practices. I thought myself obliged to give them a pretty severe reprimand in open court, to shew them that we do not approve of any such practices.

September 26. In the afternoon diverting with the officers that are come to this town; but put out of humour by their swearing, which I ought not to be witness to. I reproved them, but they cannot refrain. I resolve to withdraw from their company, one of them especially; for the rest are sober men.

October 21. Went this morning a mile to visit a curiosity; a man who is in good health, and yet has not been out of his house these twenty years. Was well diverted with him, he being a man of good sense, and great travel. Debating with him about his not coming to church to hear the Gospel; but I was too much on the banter; I should have been more serious and grave with him.

October 30. This being the prince's birthday, I was invited by the magistrates to drink the healths of the day. Very cheerful and merry. I went into the frolic of dancing, to avoid a greater frolic, drinking; for I thought it the more innocent of the two.

(1725,) *January 12.* At home writing letters to a friend. My vein is inclined to jest and humour. The letter was too comical and jocose; and after I had sent it away, I had a check that it was too light, and jesting foolishly. I sent and got it back, and destroyed it. My temper goes too far that way, and I ought to check it, and be more on my guard, and study edification in everything.

May 6. Went to Edinburgh, being chosen a member to the General Assembly.

May 11. An affair came on this day wherein I was solicited and inclined to favour a certain side; but upon hearing the cause, I was quite determined on the other side. I bless the Lord who keeps me from acting against light, or wronging my own conscience.

May 12. I was solicited by the town of Aberdeen to appear in a cause which comes on tomorrow. I do not like to be importuned, but to be keep free and unbiased. [2]

June 21. Went out to the country to see a dying Christian. I observe it is generally Christians of simplicity and godly sincerity, plain, simple hearted, that have most peace and serenity of mind at death, and most faith and joy; when the wise and prudent—the learned and subtle wits are often in the dark; and if they get their souls for a prey, yet they are not honoured to give such a testimony to the truth and reality of religion as the others. Worldly wisdom is good to defend us against the subtle serpents and ravening wolves of this world, but uprightness and sincerity give us peace at death.

August 2. This is one of my remarkable days. Hochstet. I resolved, as usual, to stay at home, and spend all the day at home. I went to my knees, and prayed over that Psalm which I had done the morning of the battle, in marching up to the enemy,—the 91st Psalm.

August 18. Reviewing old letters and papers; Oh what thankfulness and admiration should it raise; that I have been carried through so many snares of a cunning deceitful world, while others of more wisdom and prudence have misgiven. I see much truth in that, *The battle is not always to the strong, riches to men of understanding, nor favour to men of skill.* What dangers have I escaped, wherein I would have ruined and

---

[2]. This was an appeal from the Town Council against the synod, in reference to calling a minister. The magistrates had signed the call, and they synod disapproved. The Assembly appointed a new call to be moderated.

destroyed myself, hadst not thou held up my ways, and withheld me from leaping over precipices, into which my wicked heart and wild fancy would have precipitated me. How wonderfully preserved for twenty years wars, in battles and sieges! what great deliverances! Thou honoured me, and set me up as a monument of mercy in the army; took me out of it just at the right crisis, and brought me home to my native country among my friends, laden with riches and honours.

Again, Providence acted and provided for me. While others have been industriously toiling, running, projecting and plotting how to get posts and riches; yet crossed and thwarted in all their designs; Providence has laid them to my hand without anxiety, and often without the ordinary care and means. As an instance of this, how easily did I slip into this post. Many would have been glad of it, and courted it; I was not seeking it. I went from choice to Stirling to live; then came on the Rebellion which brought the great men and the army here, among these, the Glasgow regiment; then the different parties rising up, brought me into the castle.

Another instance, as to riches, was the South-Sea scheme, what labour and anxiety were some at! Riding, running night and day; hastening to be rich, their hearts and souls going after the world. Yet how was it converted into a trap to catch their worldly sins, and make them ruin themselves. Providence did all for me in that; I never stirred out of my chamber, but used the ordinary means, writing a few letters; and I came better off than they did with all their labour and pains. *Wait on the Lord, and keep his way, and he shall exalt thee.* As I desired to use the means with moderateness, so I desired to use the profit; and I might have had much more, for I gave nearly a third part of my profits to friends. God is the sovereign proprietor, he takes from one, and gives to another.

November 4. Bad weather, and extremely backward season. There is much corn upon the ground, and much not yet cut down. Lord pity, and deal not with us as our sins deserve, but according to the multitude of thy mercies.

November 8. Spent the day quietly about the garrison. I have now given over the diversion of chess-playing, as that which trifled away too much time, and made he spirit too keen about frivolities. Lord, give grace to spend my time better.

(1726,) *January 12.* Getting account of the king's landing. Lord be blessed for his preservation, for he was in great danger at sea, coming over in a great storm. Lord, preserve him long to be a lasting blessing to thy church, and these nations. Guide and direct him and his Parliament into right measures. Let them have thy glory more before their eyes, in all they do.

January 21. Writing and transcribing some memoirs that were lying by me, about the Earl of Rothes' death. They were demanded of me long ago by a minister who was employed in writing lives. I was in the wrong that did not send them sooner, for if I can do little good myself, I should do all I can to be helpful to others.

March 2. Good company visiting us. I should like to be so trysted in a place, to live where I might have a good man or minister, two or three say, to converse with freely, without reserve, to argue and debate with freedom, without jealousies or misunderstandings; a sympathy and good agreement between. Here I often dare not speak my mind out, for fear of giving offence.

April 5. Dull all day, and fit for nothing. I took up a play to read, a tragedy; but that did not answer. O give me grace to spend time better; to have more delight in religion, and then the day would not hang so heavy on my hands. I cannot now hold out reading or being long intent upon any thing, as I could have done before. The infirmities of age come on. If I had a spiritual mind, it would give a spiritual taste and relish; and I should not weary of spiritual duties.

May 3. Our friends going away; I felt melancholy at parting. No happiness in earthly enjoyments; all uncertain and unsatisfying. We are but strangers and sojourners here. All is vanity and vexation of spirit. Oh Lord, be thou my portion and my happiness, that when all other enjoyments vanish and perish, thou mayest be the eternal happiness of my soul. I went to the water, and diverted myself all the forenoon angling; but came up early to receive a visit from some persons of quality. Immediately when they were gone, another company came up that I was obliged also to drink a bottle of wine with. This made me uneasy; but I cannot help it. My post and station obliges me to entertain strangers.

May 21. Down at Craigforth all day. Going upstairs, I saw a melancholy employment, a painter drawing the portraits of two gentlemen, members of the family, both dead, and both my dear friends and relatives. I had serious thoughts; they were both cut off in the bloom of youth. *Tantum ostendunt terns nec ultra esse sinunt.* We cannot dive into the deep mysterious designs of Providence. The old gentleman had a great ambition and fondness to see himself and family represented, now that view is more distant.

June 16. At the water again all the forenoon angling. It is a delightful place, and a pleasant amusement. There is a calm and solitary serenity of mind about woods and water, which pleases me. Making some visits in my way home.

November 28. Busy through the day, and sitting close from two o'clock, till eight at night, writing letters, making up accounts, discharges, muster-rolls, &c. all coming at once; making up dispatches for Edinburgh, &c. All going on smoothly. Lord, thou makest all I do to prosper well. Oh give me grace to serve thee cheerfully, as I have good reason to do; and have my heart lifted up in thy ways. Fatigued at night. I did not think I would have been able to hold out so well and so long. Lord, thou art the strength of my heart, and my portion for ever.

(1728,) *January 5.* Paying a visit to the commandant. How pleasantly and cheerfully, (and as the world thinks) happily, do some men live; and all this, because they know nothing of their own hearts. But the Christian oftentimes, though outwardly in great prosperity, is seen hanging his head melancholy and cast down: *Wretched man, with this body of death.* And this is one reason why the carnal world reproaches religion and religions persons, as sour, gloomy, and splenetic. And alas! religious people are too seldom in that good, cheerful frame, so as to recommend their profession to a carnal world.

January 8. Writing letters this day (about purchasing more property.) Lord, keep my heart off the world, when my hands and thoughts are employed about it. I bless God my heart is not much set upon this affair. I should now, in old age, be thinking more upon dislodging, then settling in this world.

January 20. Applying to the magistrates for a supply to a person, or rather a community, which they granted. Some of them solicited again for a favour to a poor burgess, which I promised in my turn. *Rogatus rogo. Manus manum fricat.*

February 17. Serious in the forenoon reading. In the evening with our Society for prayer. O may every mean be blessed for strengthening grace, and making Christ more precious to my soul.

March 14. Sent for to see Craigforth, who is taken very ill. Found him very weak; he spoke little, and did not like to be spoken to. Our own ministers, and two others came and prayed with him. I desire to be much concerned about him. It is an awful, serious thing to see a friend dying. And I am sure I should hear this voice crying, to make ready for death, by fleeing to Christ; and this should be done when we are most lively and healthy. A deathbed is most unfit for this, when the body is oppressed with pain and sickness—the spirits languishing and weak. Oh give grace to be taken up this way, when I have such a call, such an impressive sermon on mortality, and the vanity of the world. In a short time he died; by which a business was thrown upon me I was not fit nor inclined for, as I could have wished to spend my old age in quietness, free from the cares of the world, that I might have time to mind better things. I was appointed tutor to the young heir, and to take the management of his affairs, which I would rather have shunned, not having skill in the law. *Cast thou thy burden on the Lord, he shall sustain thee; commit thy way to God; trust in him, and he shall bring it to pass.*

June 1. Sent for to a Justice-Court, upon a complaint against one of the Excise Officers. I took this occasion to give him a severe reprimand for his lewd, wicked way of living, scandalous and offensive to all sober people. My temper and spirit hot and keen in giving the rebuke; but it was all zeal, and I bless God who gives me opportunities of discouraging vice in this place. We petitioned the Board to get him removed elsewhere, which they granted.

June 22. Dining in company with officers here; cheerful conversation, but a great deal of loose language. I did not join them, but perhaps was too easy, and did not reprove. I think it would have done no good; yet sometimes I gave a check, as far as decency and good breeding would allow; and I do think that among polite gentlemen, this way is more likely to gain the end, than a solemn formal rebuke which would be but laughed at. I had but one diversion here, *viz.* the bowling-green, and I find I must give that over, though it be a very innocent recreation, upon prudential considerations; because I do not like the company of these officers. I am more the worse than the better of it.

July 18. Exercising the garrison, and reading over the Articles of war; giving orders against immorality, and putting them in execution immediately against a swearer.

August 24. Sabbath. I often wish much to hear oftener our friend at St. Ninians. I had a grudge that I could not get him heard this day, for fear of giving offence. And indeed it is a great grievance to me here, that I cannot get that edification I could get, and would fain have. I dare not go where I am most edified, for fear it be taken amiss. I think offence should not be taken at anybody for going occasionally where they get most instruction. It is the ill humours and narrowness of mind that makes ministers and others be offended. They should rather rejoice that any of their people get edification to their souls, by whatever instrument. It is a hard thing to be tied up from Christian liberty, by the prejudices and narrowness of people's humours. Lord, fill our hearts with mutual love and charity; there is not so much of that as should be among us.

October 10. Friends and acquaintances dropping off by degrees. Surprised with the sudden death of a young hopeful gentleman. Lord bless to me every providence. O give me grace to be living as a stranger and pilgrim, working out my salvation with fear and trembling; ready to go when called—ready in state—ready in frame.

★★★★★★

The routine of his military avocations, with the additional duties of the subordinate offices he had been called upon to fill in a civil capacity, afforded but little room for incident or variety in his life, and necessarily led his thoughts to run more in the beaten track of daily observation. This consideration, it would appear, weighed with him as an inducement to discontinue his diary, which breaks off at this time, when he was yet in tolerable health, and nearly a twelvemonth before his death. He closes his register at the end of the year, with an allusion to this uniformity in his manner of living, and making some cursory remarks on the review of his own history.

★★★★★★

It is needless for me to set down every particular day, when I have now so little to say that is worth saying—so little of variety, or remarkable as to my frame, or providence. Alas! my frame is too dead and formal, faith not lively, grace not vigorous. I am much taken up with business of one sort and another; yet still I do not want time for religion if I had but a spiritual mind and disposition. In the intervals of business I sometimes turn my thoughts upward, where there is prepared an eternal rest for the people of God.

I am reviewing my former diaries, beginning in 1701, when I was in London. I find great variety; many ups and downs; sad days of desertion, of melancholy, chagrin, and discontent with my own temper. But then, on the other hand, I had sweet ravishing communions and fellowship with God; noble actings of faith; delightful experiences; fervent prayer, and sensible returns of grace; faith vigorous; love ardent, and assurance strong. When I set up the one against the other, well may I say, that the light afflictions I met with, were not to be compared to these far more exceeding rich, and noble comforts and supplies. That which fretted and vexed me most was, that I was so little fitted for the business I was employed in; and met with so much ill company that I could not live with.

I had not suppleness to manage people's tempers and humours, wherein my antagonists had a great advantage over me, by conforming to the world, and putting themselves in every shape to gain their point; by cajoling, treating, bribing, they carried their cause, though it was, to every impartial spectator, palpably less fair and just. I had peace in the justice of our cause, and I took this, as an earnest of it, that I had so much of God's presence, though I was not supernaturally assisted above the sphere of human ability, nor contrary to the bias of my natural temper. I was always well helped to do my duty, and when any thing failed of success, it was not for want of assistance, but through the defect of my own management.

I find I complained also of a stiff reserved, unsociable temper; this was very uneasy and discouraging, but it had likewise its advantages; it kept me out of much sin and many temptations. My temper since has become more open, frank, and social; but then it often exposes me to too much conformity to the world, and to many snares. So we see every temper has its good and ill; but to follow and practise the good, and shun the evil. *Hoc opus, hic labor est.*

★★★★★★

Of the last year of his life, which we have now reached, and of the manner of his death, no memorials, so far as I know, have been preserved. It is, however, of less moment to know how a Christian dies, than how he lived; and there can be little doubt, that his closing scene would correspond with the general tenor of his walk and conversation; and that all his professions of religion would be amply substantiated and confirmed by his dying example. His health, as we observed, was yet comparatively fresh and vigorous, and though descending into the vale of years, his natural strength and spirits were not sensibly decayed. Though ripe as to age and honours, he may be said to have died prematurely as to constitution. The severe and repeated attacks of the malady with which he was seized, were beyond the power of frail nature long to resist or endure. For a considerable time before his death he suffered extremely from attacks of the stone, which, it appears, baffled all the efforts of medical skill to remove. This disease seems to have generated suddenly, as he never mentions, until a very late period, his being subject to calculus affections. These fits became more frequent and painful the nearer he approached his end; yet under the most excruciating anguish of bodily distress, his soul fled to that refuge, and his faith grasped with firm hold to those promises which had been the source of all his hopes and consolation. The following is a quotation from his diary for the 1st of May 1728; and among the earliest instances of his being seriously afflicted with his distemper.

★★★★★★

This last night I had one of the severest nights for pain I ever had in my life. I was seized about the middle of the night, and wrestled with my affliction for an hour or two, not wishing to awaken anybody, but found it would not do, the pains grew sorer and sorer; I arose and walked, and sat and tossed into twenty postures, seeking ease and using remedies which had little effect. I cried to God for pity and help, and prayed for patience, which was like to fail; but his everlasting arms were underneath, powerfully assisting me in the severity of my distress. Faith also was at work calling upon the Lord, and trusting in him as my God. But, alas! in the extremity of pain faith stands at a low ebb, and goes into little bulk. The thoughts become confused when the body is racked; I know not how it may be with others, but I find it so. At two in the morning I was directed to take some medicine, which, by the blessing of God, had so good an effect, that I got some rest and slept till nine, when I awaked much refreshed. O the kindness and compassion of God, who knows our frame, that we are but dust, and has no pleasure in afflicting his poor creatures. O may this be a rod to chase me to Christ;

and the fruit of all to purge away sin.

★★★★★★

The progress of this malady speedily undermined his constitution, and it was to its agonising pains that he ultimately fell a victim. When symptoms were discovered of its terminating fatally, physicians were sent for from Edinburgh, to give their advice and assistance; but their arts were of no avail, and the patient's only resource was to await the approach of that final deliverance, which was to exchange his momentary afflictions for an eternal weight of glory.

There is often something sublimely interesting in the death-scene of an expiring Christian, especially when earthly remedies can bring no relief, and human skill, foiled and exhausted, has pronounced recovery hopeless. The mind driven from all other resources, rises above its infirmities, and seems to rally its languid and scattered powers, as it were, to put forth one last collective effort of strength. Though the outward frame be racked with pains, or wasted to a shadow, the soul is often filled with secret raptures of heavenly joy.

It seems to acquire new vigour in proportion as the mansion of clay falls into ruins; and never longs more to be disencumbered of its chains than when about to quit its earthly prison. It is then that the spirit displays its superiority over the things of time, and makes its sublimest efforts of magnanimity. Then is the moment that faith completes her victory over the world,—that divine grace triumphs over all the doubts and the fears of nature. Even the timorous saint who has been all his life perplexed with discouraging apprehensions, viewing futurity through the dark and distempered region of his own thoughts, is often seen on the near approach of dissolution to exchange his disquieting fears for holy transports. The cloud that overcast his spirit is dispelled by the beams of the sun of Righteousness. That peace which passeth understanding shines in upon his soul with a setting splendour, and the lustre of his life never appears so bright as at the moment of its being extinguished.

Something of this kind seems to have been exhibited in the instance of Colonel Blackader. While he suffered the extremity of bodily pain, his soul appears to have burst from underneath the cloud of mental anxiety, and the pressure of severe distress. That temporary dejection of which he occasionally complained in earlier life, had entirely vanished. The gloom that sometimes intercepted the eye of faith in its contemplations of futurity, disappeared as the glories of the invisible world were more nearly revealed. A well grounded assurance of an interest in the Redeemer's merits had calmed all his solicitudes; and Hope, rising to full fruition, lighted up every dark spot in his anticipations. His mind retained to the last uncommon firmness, and his piety its usual fervour. When his physicians informed him that his distemper was beyond the reach of medicine,—that sympathy was now the only aid they could administer, he is said to have received the melancholy intelligence with the most resigned submission.

Raising himself on his bed, he surveyed his friends with a placid and dignified composure. He thanked all his attendants for their kind services, and having taken leave of his family, he breathed his last, expressing his firm hope and earnest desire of another and a better life beyond time and mortality. This took place on Sabbath morning the 31st of August 1729, when he was within a few days of completing his sixty-fifth year. His remains were interred in the West-Church of Stirling, within which, on the south wall, near the pulpit, is fixed a plain marble tablet, erected several years ago by one of his near relations, bearing the following inscription, which expresses briefly and modestly a general outline of his life and character:—

<blockquote>
Near this place are deposited the Remains of a
Brave Soldier and Devout Christian,
JOHN BLACKADER, ESQ,
Late Lieutenant-Colonel of the Cameronian Regiment.
He served under the Duke of Marlborough in
QUEEN ANNE'S WARS
and was present at most of the Engagements in that Reign.
He died Deputy Governor of Stirling Castle, in
August 1929. Aged 65 years.
August 1789, J. Y.[3]
</blockquote>

Having brought our extracts to a conclusion, it would now only

---

3. This marble was the tribute of his grand-nephew, Mr. John Young, Edinburgh, whose initials are inscribed upon it, with the date of its erection; grandson of his sister already mentioned. Of Mrs. Young's diary, and her husband's consolatory letter, entitled,: Faith promoted, and Fears prevented, from a proper view of affliction," we designed to give some further account, but the length to which our other extracts have extended, prevents us. She had two sons, John a merchant in Leith, father to the above, and grandfather to the present John Young, Esq. Edinburgh; William, who served as a surgeon in the Coldstream Guards during the Marlborough campaigns, and is often mentioned in the colonel's letters. He afterwards settled as medical practitioner, with his wife and family, in England, where his descendants still remain.

remain to lay before the reader some general sketch of the character of the individual whose papers have been submitted to his perusal. This, however, has been already anticipated, and in some measure superseded, by the criticisms which precede the diary, and the occasional remarks with which the whole is interspersed. Besides, the journal itself presents so true a mirror of his mind, and enters so fully into the minutiae of his life, as to furnish a more accurate and faithful portraiture than any laboured delineation from the hand of another. We shall, however, to aid the reader's conceptions, advert shortly to some of those circumstances with which he is already acquainted in the detail; and endeavour to place more immediately under his eye those characteristic features that lie scattered over so wide a surface.

In whatever light the particular shades of his life may be viewed, the general impression of the whole, by which alone the true estimate of any character must be fixed, will be such I am persuaded, as to bear out the monumental title which the affection of his relation conferred upon him, as a *brave soldier and a devout Christian*.

On his military qualifications it is not our purpose to enlarge; neither do we think these will be contemplated as the most illustrious or the most interesting parts of his character. The rank he acquired, and the esteem with which he quitted the army, bear honourable testimony to the high reputation with which he discharged the duties of his profession. There was scarcely an action in which he had been, (to use his own words,) "but Providence did kindly make some incidents to fall out," which raised him in the favour both of his general and fellow-officers; and when he left their society, he carried with him into his retirement the good opinion of one who was a competent judge of military character, and not given to flatter. He says:—

> I was ashamed to hear of the kind and obliging things which my Lord Duke spoke about me to the company with him, after I was gone out.

Bravery is reckoned the first and most shining quality in a soldier; and of this he never shewed any deficiency. On all occasions he seems to have behaved with abundant intrepidity, and in various instances acquitted himself with superior credit and distinction. Wherever his duty called him he was ready to go, without fear or hesitation; and in the hottest posts he never shrunk from danger, when example or encouragement made it necessary for him to expose himself. When he had opportunities of retirement and full leisure for his devotions, his courage, fortified by these internal resources, mounted to a pitch of boldness bordering on enthusiasm. Yet though daring, he does not appear rash or inconsiderate; we never find him courting unnecessary exposure, or rushing headlong into danger with a thoughtless and foolish temerity. His valour was of that cool and steady sort which is equally remote from callous insensibility and intemperate frenzy; it partook much of the general cast of his mind, solemn, grave, and deliberate.

There is another species of courage different from the former, but not less essential to the soldier, and that is a patient and passive endurance of the toils, fatigues, and privations which he must undergo in the vicissitudes of long and laborious campaigns. This necessary quality the colonel possessed in an eminent degree. Wearisome marches,—continuing under arms night and day,—the want of food and bodily repose,—the vexations of defeat and disappointments,—were endured with cheerfulness, and seem never to have extorted from him a single expression of discontent. He had the happy disposition of interpreting every occurrence in the most favourable light, and viewing every change in the fortunes of war, as working together, under Providence, for the general good. This "*kept his mind in perfect peace,*" easy as to the issue of doubts and difficulties. It inspired him with fortitude and encouragement under misfortune; it taught him confidence in the midst of perplexity, to turn even losses and disappointments into matter of gratitude. What, in some circumstances, might scarcely have been thought common mercies, in others, became luxuries. As he judged of all his comforts by comparison, this made him thankful for the smallest accommodation, were it but the shelter of a cottage, a soldier's tent, or a bed of straw.

Modesty, always the concomitant of true courage, was another conspicuous feature in his military character. His temper uniformly was to extenuate and never to exaggerate when speaking of his own achievements. His best actions, even such as were "distinguished by circumstances of reputation that gave them a peculiar lustre in the eyes of the world," he acknowledges to be but a compound of weakness and defects. In speaking of the regiment, he employs the same humbling and derogative language. When they had been "honoured in particular to do some very good service," he remarks, "It was the Lord's doing, and not by our sword or our bow; take thou the glory to thyself." That he considerably under-rated their services, "lest the arm of flesh should boast," appears from the historical fact, that during the preceding campaigns they received, for their gallant conduct, the thanks of the Duke of Marlborough, no less than seven different times.

In his backwardness to solicit preferment, his modesty was very remarkable, and in his shunning, rather than seeking those honours he had so meritoriously earned. He frequently mentions his incapacity to "fawn and cringe to the great," as he terms it; and he abhorred the smooth, but shallow artifices by which men of pliable and unprincipled ambition will insinuate themselves into favour. Many, by cunning and stratagem, by adopting base and contemptible expedients, from which an honest independent spirit recoils with disgust, will take precedence of real merit, and outstrip their more conscientious competitors in the race of preferment. To these arts he was an entire stranger. He had a dignity and elevation of mind that scorned ever to stoop or apply to them. It was his rule to pay no court to his superiors, except where merit and integrity paved the way to their favour. He says:—

> I never incline to go near the court, except when friends push and hector me to go; for I had always that bashfulness of nature, that I cannot endure to be where I think I am troublesome. Let others whose talent it is, get places by assurance and forwardness, I shall have mine by modesty, or want them. I cannot flatter and cringe; neither is it decent or becoming for a child of the house to be fawning upon the servants for a favour. A child of God should have a nobler spirit.

Those qualities of ambition, and bars to his advancement, were, in reality, the attributes that throw a peculiar lustre over his character; they are essential ingredients in the constitution of every noble and honourable mind. They formed no barrier in the way of his preferment, and they secured him ultimately, as they always will do, the esteem and confidence of his superiors.

The exemplary manner in which he discharged his regimental duties, has already been noticed, and will occur to the reader's recollection. He regarded the minutest parts of his office as a matter of conscience, and not merely of form. His attention to discipline was strict and assiduous, and his exertions were sometimes fortunate enough to attract the notice and the compliments of his commanding officer. Punishment was always a disagreeable part of his duty; and he shewed a tender reluctance to proceed to extremities, unless with incorrigible offenders, and where example could answer some salutary purpose. He took every opportunity of mitigating the rigour of the law, in favour of deserving objects, and mentions on one occasion his having saved "a poor creature's life, whom the whole court had sentenced to be executed, and would not recommend to mercy."

In cases where such interposition was unavailing, he made it his business to soften misfortune by acts of compassion, and temper even necessary severity with kindness. In the fate of a condemned criminal, he took an anxious and solemn concern. He would spend sleepless nights in prayer with God for the welfare of his soul, and attend him in his last moments, that he might teach him to flee to the blood of the atonement, for that pardon and reconciliation which he had forfeited at the hands of man. His sympathy for the "poor soldiers" under want and fatigue, and his charity to distresses of every kind, set the general benevolence of his character in a very amiable light.

He was not less attentive to morals, than to the military training of his regiment. These were to him a subject of great solicitude, and he was more apt to overlook or forgive disobedience to the rules of discipline, than a trespass against the laws of God. Here his zeal never shewed clemency, and would admit of no extenuation. Here he considered officers and men as alike amenable to the tribunal of his censure, and both frequently shared in his reprimands. Under all the obloquy, hatred, and reproach to which his strictness exposed him, he persisted in his efforts to correct and amend, in so far as compulsory power, and the influence of his own example could reclaim.

His ordinary mode for promoting their improvement, and enforcing obedience to his authority seems to have been very different from that in general practice. "Instead of cursing and swearing at my men," says he, "I ordinarily put them, by prayer, within the circle of God's protection." The immorality and profaneness of the army, which no coercive laws could restrain, form the prominent subject of complaint through the whole diary. This was his greatest uneasiness, and the most serious obstacle to his continuing in the profession. It made his soul "weary of the tents of sin."

The justice of the war in which he was engaged, was a subject to which he frequently adverts. His extreme tenderness of conscience in this respect, is visible from the whole tenor of his conduct. He was fully convinced, on his entering the army, that he was supporting the side of true religion, and vindicating the rights of his native land from the usurpation of a despot and a bigot. In consistency with these principles, he ever cherished an irreconcilable hatred to Popery and tyranny, and was always solicitous that they should never receive the aid of his personal services. He was satisfied "that the quarrel against France was a just one," but seemed less clear as to the lawfulness of carrying arms to assist the Austrians, seeing they had also been the oppressors and persecutors of the Protestant Church. He says:—

> This makes me afraid we shall not prosper. It is a sad thing to be in an army where I have not confidence to pray for success, and dare not seek it in a way of faith.

To ascertain at what point national wars cease to be just and necessary, by degenerating into ambitious conquests and wanton aggression; or how far an individual may make his own conceptions of their justice and necessity, a rule of conduct, are matters too intricate and casuistical to be here determined. We have said elsewhere, that the guilt of protracting the war from mercenary motives, attaches not to those who have unconsciously been made the dupes of designing policy, or the tools of selfish ambition. That Colonel Blackader acted with sincerity and singleness of aim to promote the glory of God, and the welfare of his country, nobody, we apprehend, will for a moment doubt.

The emancipation of Britain from the House of Stuart—from all the evils which that infatuated race had brought upon it by their bigoted zeal and inherent love of despotism—and from the attempts that were subsequently made to restore the exiled family, and bring all Europe under the yoke of a haughty tyrant,—was the grand attainment which he had always at heart. It afterwards attached him warmly to the Hanoverian Succession, and made him, in private life, the firm advocate and assertor of those liberties, civil and religious, which he has so honourably defended in the field.

In strictness and propriety of moral conduct, he certainly stands singularly prominent in the annals of military history. Seldom, we think, has there ever been exhibited in any situation of public life, especially in one exposed to so many and strong temptations, such universal circumspection in walk and conversation—such unceasing efforts to maintain a conscience void of offence—or such a successful struggle against the allurements of vice from without, and corruptions within. It was his constant and earnest endeavour to escape the pollution of sin—to keep himself pure and unspotted from the world. Exposed as he was perpetually to company, and that often of the worst description, it is astonishing, and seems impossible, except by the goodness of preventing grace, that he could have guarded with such vigilance against falling into some of the numerous snares which surrounded him, and into which he saw others falling every day. It was the terror and abhorrence of his soul, "to be chained on command with men whose tongues were set on fire of hell;" where nothing was to be heard but the confused ringing sound of oaths and blasphemies, which made his very flesh creep with horror.

He often shunned to mix in society, even when invited by the great, on no other account but that of unsuitable conversation, and an aversion to drinking, which was sometimes carried to excess. What others might think moderation, he reckoned intemperance;—

> I call that too much not when reason is disturbed, but when our heads are the least warmed, or that coolness of thinking marred which we should always be master of. And it is really astonishing to see men endowed with rational and immortal souls so degrade themselves, and led such poor, animal, sensual lives as they do. I know this would sound harsh with the genteel world, whose example has dignified these customs, and given them the reputation of virtues. But this does not change the nature of the thing.

Once, and only once, in the course of his life, was he himself overtaken with this vice, which he so justly reprobates in his associates. As truth requires us to be impartial, and not to throw a veil of concealment even over his failings, so we think this solitary instance of insobriety deserves to be recorded, not merely for the lesson which it teaches as to the imperfections of the best men, but for the example which it affords of a penitent humbled under guilt, shame, and remorse. No event seemed to have distressed his mind so much, and nothing could exceed the expressions of deep unfeigned sorrow with which he bewails his misconduct.

> This has been a remarkable day to me; one of the most humbling, melancholy days of my life, and also one of my greatest deliverances, having fallen from my horse, and narrowly escaped being killed. A mortifying, humbling day it has been to me, of sin, folly, and disgrace on my part; of tender mercy, pity, care, and compassion on God's part; love shining through anger; in the midst of wrath, mercy; a father chastening with one hand, and everlasting arms underneath preserving and protecting. I,

by sin and folly, plunging into trouble, and precipitating myself into danger: God in mercy giving his angels charge over me. O Lord, correct not in anger; let it be a fatherly chastisement to bring back a wandering son. Heal my backslidings; restore, quicken and revive. Oh sanctify the use of the rod, may it chase me to Christ; heal the plagues and distempers of my soul; repair what is wrong in my heart, and life, and practice.

The account of the matter he gives is this: He had gone from Stirling with a marriage-party; they had several visits to make in course of the forenoon, where etiquette required to drink the health of the young couple. They dined in the neighbourhood of Alloa, and spent the day with much hilarity.

Knowing the foolish fashion of treating young married men, I was resolved to be on my guard. I did not drink anything to do me hurt, but it was deceitful wine. We came away before five, afternoon; I thought I was well enough when we took horse, but the air and quick riding soon began to affect me, and coming to a bridge where there was a difficult step, my horse plunged and threw me: I was taken up insensible, and very much hurt.

This is the only instance recorded in which sociality threw him off his guard; and yet after all, it appears the intoxication was produced as much by external causes, as by the quantity or the quality of the wine. But such were his habitual impressions of that blamelessness of heart and life which become a true Christian, that his smallest faults were remarked and made the subject of reproof

Contemplating him as a pious and exemplary Christian, we are persuaded his character will appear to equal advantage. Rarely do we find an individual combining in his life, so much of the spirit and practice of true religion. It was the ruling principle of his conduct, and mingled with all he said and did, so that his ordinary actions were a continual proof and illustration of its power over his mind. We believe few instances will be found, all circumstance considered, of such habitual awe and reverence for religion—such lively and persevering faith—such ardent piety—such earnest aspirings after higher degrees of holiness—such constant spirituality of heart and mind—such separation from the vices and sinful customs of the world—such humility and submission to the will of Providence—such absolute dependence on the all-sufficiency of Divine grace,—and, finally, such grateful and unreserved ascription of all earthly enjoyments to the goodness of God, and of all hope of salvation to the merits of a Saviour.

Religion, with him, was a fixed and abiding principle. He endeavoured to keep the faith with undeviating and persevering constancy. That piety and devotion which were early implanted in his heart, were still cultivated in the midst of surrounding temptations, and grew, as he advanced in years, into a more perfect maturity of godliness. This, if not the only mark, affords at least the most unequivocal test of a Christian's sincerity. It is easy to assume a temporary profession, or submit to any rules and restraints for a time. The observance of outward and occasional forms, is common with many, who, as to the vital and essential attainments of a holy life, are remiss and deficient. But when a man obeys with the whole heart, when he applies the strict rule of the divine law to his whole deportment, and pursues a steady and uniform course of holiness, then he deserves the name of a sincere and consistent Christian.

His religion was of this sort. It was not put on to serve a turn, and laid aside when occasion permitted. It was his occupation and companion in retirement, as well as his delight in the sanctuary, and his profession before men. He did not conceal the absence of real godliness under the cloak of a sanctimonious phraseology, nor forget the author of his mercies in the day when he was crowned with riches and honour. In his private, and in his public life, he may be said to have exhibited a pattern of religion, singularly amiable and edifying.

In the superintending care and protection of divine Providence he reposed the most unlimited and unshaken confidence. Everything appeared to his eye under the inspection and control of a higher power. Armies and generals he regarded but as subordinate instruments in the hand of the Almighty. What others might call fate or destiny, with him were the fixed decrees of an overruling Providence; events which they traced to no higher source than he caprice of fortune or of chance, he uniformly ascribes to the unerring decision of infinite wisdom which could make victories or defeats alike to accomplish his purposes. To his firm belief and trust in the divine protection must we look for the true origin of his courage and resignation. This was his shield and buckler; the fortress and high tower, to which he fled for refuge. It was in the panoply of this spiritual and invisible armour that he wrapped himself up in the day of battle; and he esteemed its security a better defence than the strength of armies, or the weapons of war.

Going through the saps and trenches, where the bombs, cannon-balls, and grenades were flying pretty thick all the night. I believed I was even as safe there under the care of Omnipotence, as if I had been in garrison, or in my own chamber.

He reckoned himself, as well he might, the peculiar child of Providence; and his success and escapes might naturally suggest the reflection, when it is considered, that in battles, sieges, and skirmishes, he was personally engaged in nearly forty different actions.

Of these deliverances he ever entertained the most grateful recollection. It was to commemorate them that he every year set up his Ebenezers—not by erecting monumental pillars or material buildings, but by consecrating them in his memory, and engraving them on the living tablet of his heart. Every object that surrounded him he made the occasion of renewing these impressions, and stirring him up to fresh remembrances of his mercies. Fields, rivers, and ruined walls were in his eye, the hallowed monuments of his preservations. The anniversaries of his battles were observed with more solemnity than the day of his birth. Most of them, especially those in which he had experienced any signal deliverance, were religiously devoted, as long as he lived, to retirement, prayer and meditation. Such was his care to have these memorable events renewed and preserved in his mind, that he is said to have kept, as a memorial, a hat which had been *riddled* or perforated with bullets during the earlier period of his services.

That devout and spiritual frame which he seems on all occasions to have kept up, is also very observable. His mind seemed perpetually in a sanctuary; and he often enjoyed a heaven within, when all around him was noise, and oaths, and confusion. Piety and prayer formed, as it were, the nourishment and native habit of his soul in the midst of a barren wilderness. They were the sacred element which he found essential to his spiritual existence. He could not breath without intervals of devout abstraction and solemn communion with his God. When circumstances permitted him not to withdraw from company, he would often retire within the chambers of his own thoughts, and hold intercourse with society which the world knew not of.

It was often his custom while in the army to meditate alone in the fields, a practice which he afterwards continued when his comparative retirement gave him better opportunities of indulging it. Even his amusements were selected with this view, and made subservient to this favourite propensity. He preferred to the recreation of angling chiefly because it combined healthful exercise with solitude and meditation; and would spend many a summer day on the wooded and sequestered banks of some of the delightful streams in his immediate neighbourhood.

His love of retirement seemed to be a passion of his mind more than an acquired habit. It was no doubt strengthened by the wicked company he was obliged to associate with, and wished as much as possible to shun. But solitude with him, was not the effect of a morose unsocial temper, neither was it of a dark and gloomy piety. His mind was not in the least tainted with those ascetic principles that have peopled the desert with hermits, and driven the monk to the indolent superstitions of his cell. With him, solitude was the nursery of true devotion, the vehicle of spiritual improvement, the sacred armoury in which he fortified his soul with fresh supplies of divine grace against the assaults of temptation.

This, however, did not hinder him from paying respect to the institutions of religion.

His veneration for the Sabbath was supreme, and his attendance on public worship most regular and exemplary. One day spent in the courts of God's house he accounted better than a thousand. It was his greatest grief and regret, that in the army he could not get these sacred duties and that solemn day observed in proportion to the reverence and importance in which he held them. He was always sorry when compelled, by the duties of his profession, to engage in any business unsuitable or contrary to its solemnity. "*A Sabbath of rest in a camp*" was a mercy which he enjoyed with peculiar thankfulness and delight; and while others were amusing themselves with idle or criminal recreations, he either retired to the fields for meditation, or kept his tent reading his Bible. There was a solemnity in that holy day which he never forgot, which all the parade and profligacy of the army could not obliterate from his thoughts. He shunned, in devout remembrance of its appointment, the convivial board and the contagion of evil company; he shut himself up from viewing vanities, or mingling in the ordinary intercourse of society.

When opportunities of solitude were denied him, and all external respect seemed lost amidst the noise and confusion of military operations, he never suffered the hallowed distinction to be effaced from his mind, and would supply the want of outward observances by the homage and reverence of his heart. "In the morning," says he, after a long march, "I had almost forgot it was a Sabbath, but recollected myself and withdrew from company, (I mean in my thoughts,) and strove to keep up a spiritual habit of mind."

In proportion to his regard for this sacred day, and the pleasure he felt in seeing it observed, was his sorrow when its sanctity was violated and its ordinances despised. Almost every page in the diary is marked with expressions lamenting its sinful misemployment, or its open profanation.

He shewed by his own conduct, especially after his settlement in Scotland, that he accounted the holy of the Lord not merely honourable, but a delight. The earnest longings of his soul were towards the sanctuary. On sacramental occasions he was a regular attendant, and frequently joined as a communicant in many of the neighbouring parishes. His gratitude for the blessings of salvation, and the gifts of free grace, through Jesus Christ, was at all times in lively exercise; but more especially were his affections warmed and elevated on the days that were consecrated to the remembrance of his dying love. This unfeigned delight in the ordinances and solemnities of religion is one of the distinguishing marks of a true believer. It serves to discriminate between the real and the nominal professor. It is one of the surest tokens that grace prospers in the heart; and it throws an outward and visible lustre over the whole character.

To the established religion of his country he was sincerely attached; yet it appears he would not passively mould his opinions to any creed, nor implicitly follow any human system, without being satisfied of its conformity to the word of God. He had studied and investigated the scriptures for himself, and wished to make them the only rule of his faith—the only standard of his practice. He says:—

> I dare not give myself up to be directed by any man or set of men; Lord, be thou thyself my guide.

Wherever he discovered errors in doctrine or in practice, his zeal for truth and the salvation of souls made him strenuous in opposing and confuting them. All notions derogating from the divinity and atonement of Christ—salvation through free grace, and justification by faith alone, he reprobated as sapping the very foundations of Christianity, and extracting every thing from it of essential and vital importance. He disapproved highly of the extremes to which preaching was carried in his time by both parties, the one running too much upon a legal strain, the other misleading their hearers into absolute Antinominianism. Both of these he reprehended as equally unscriptural, and equally injurious in their effects. He never wished to hear the doctrines of the Bible separated from its duties, but to have religion treated in a rational as well as in a spiritual manner—to have the law preached as well as the Gospel, that the harmony and proportion of the whole system might be maintained.

To what he conscientiously believed to be the truth, and considered as sound and orthodox, his adherence was firm and inflexible. Whatever indifference of temper he manifested as to his secular concerns, he was most decisive in his religious persuasions. These he avowed honestly and fearlessly, and was prepared to defend whenever they were controverted. Yet with all this firmness, he cherished the greatest liberality of sentiment towards those who conscientiously differed from him. He had too sacred a regard for the rights of conscience, to exact from others a conformity to his own opinions.

"I would comply in things indifferent; for I do not think religion obliges to a morose captious behaviour, and opposing and contradicting every thing that those of contrary persuasion say or do. I desire at all times boldly to avow my own principles, and never to be ashamed of them: but I do not think this obliges me to be always attacking and disputing with others."

With the exemption of Roman Catholics, he was willing to tolerate dissenters of all kinds, provided they regulated their worship according to the prescriptions of law, and conformed in civil matters to the government of the country; and this, considering the state of party feeling then in Scotland, may be regarded as a stretch of charity by no means very general. He lived in habits of intimate friendship with many who differed from him on speculative points of theology. Several of the neighbouring clergymen were his constant guests, and his constant antagonists. Though separated in opinion on things of a doubtful or mysterious nature, he could associate with them as brethren united in more important matters than those which divided them. Honest and upright men he ever esteemed, and could expand his heart in charity to all of every denomination, who loved the Lord Jesus Christ in truth and sincerity.

His charity and affability in this respect were displayed in the several church courts of which he had the honour to be a member. There he was always the advocate of tolerant and conciliatory measures. When parties ran high, he shunned to appear in the front ranks of either, or to enlist as a partisan under the banners of any faction. He wished rather to steer between extremes, and to mitigate by gentleness the rancour of conflicting opinions. He was persuaded, that in matters of general debate there might be differences without animosity, and concessions without dereliction of principle; that it was possible to dislike the sentiments of an adversary, and yet to treat him with candour and respect; and that it was the duty of a Christian not to retaliate the harsh usage he might receive at the hand of an irritated brother.

The time alluded to above, was a stormy period in our spiritual courts. The Ark of the Church was in danger of being wrecked, more by the rashness of her pilots, than by the violence of political tempest. They were planting with their own hands the seeds of the Secession, which were nurtured in the hotbed of debate, until in a few years they sprung up with all the luxuriance of a rival growth. This was the effect of that "rankling party-sprit" which the writer of the diary so often laments, but of which he did not live to witness the consequences.

In his social and domestic character he appears equally amiable and exemplary. He never allowed his public engagements to supersede or interrupt his private duties; and mentions it as an unjustifiable neglect, that by staying too late abroad, he had been prevented from family worship, although it was a solitary instance, having occurred only once in the space of four years. In conversation he was always the strenuous supporter of truth and virtue, and the determined opponent of everything approaching to levity or immorality of speech. In companies where he could interfere, he was always ready to check improprieties of this kind; but where decency and good breeding did no allow him to reprove, he shewed his disapprobation by his silence:—

Which, among polite gentlemen, was more likely to gain the end, than a solemn formal rebuke which would be but laughed at.

There was, indeed, a gravity and composure in his manner which must have abashed the petulant, and extorted a reverence for his person from the most profligate.

His temper, however, was by no means severe or censorious. His disposition was cheerful, but not frolicsome; and he joined with the greatest hilarity in innocent diversions where mirth was restrained within the bounds of decorum. An austere and morose manner he considered as one of the reasons why the world reproached religion, and religious persons, as sour, gloomy, and splenetic; "and would have Christians, by a lively, cheerful frame, recommend their profession to a carnal world."

He had a vein of wit and humour, and was inclined at times to be facetious; but this was a talent he seldom indulged, as he wished his speech to be always seasoned with salt; "the salt of grace rather than of wit." Some of his letters which he thought too "comical and jocose," he recalled after he had sent them away, as bordering upon foolish jesting, and not tending to edification, which he desired to study in everything.

When arguing for truth, or "disputing against wild and mistaken notions," his zeal at times betrayed him into warmth of expression; yet such was his tenderness of giving offence, &en to an adversary, that if in the heat of debate he had dropped an injurious word, or used language which might be construed into intemperance or disrespect, he was willing to retract or make any proper apology; and mentions his having written a letter to a person with whom he had been disputing, upon recollection of something that passed in a public company the day before, wherein he thought he had given offence.

Of his great humanity and benevolence, abundant instances will occur. He was ever ready to assist the friendless—to visit the afflicted—and relieve the indigent. Providence had put the means in his hand, and he wished to be generous, to have his heart enlarged in proportion to his estate. Worldliness and love of money were not his faults. Earthly possessions he regarded with a jealous eye, and preferred to lay up treasures in heaven. He greatly enhanced his favours by his courteous and engaging manner of bestowing them. He was remarkably charitable, and at his death bequeathed £800 to the poor in his neighbourhood. He made various donations for religious uses, and conferred valuable legacies upon his friends and relations.

Upon the whole, we think his character altogether such as strongly to claim our reverence, and deserve our imitation. Few lives have been recorded more exemplary or more ornamental to religion. His piety, integrity, candour, humility, and benevolence, have seldom been exceeded. And we doubt not he will be ranked by posterity among the few of his profession, *who have fought the good fight*, who have been at once the defence and the glory of their country, and who have endeavoured *to live soberly, righteously, and godly in the present world.*

Brigadier Ferguson: A Soldier of 1688 and Blenheim

Contents

Prefatory Note	399
In the Scots Brigade	401
Colonel of the Cameronians	418
Brigadier at Blenheim	431
Appendix	452

Prefatory Note

The following sketch was originally written for the writer's personal pleasure, or the amusement of a limited circle. It has been suggested that it may have a wider interest, as illustrating distinct and well-defined type of Scottish character, and that, there may be a special interest in following the steps of a soldier of 1688, who afforded a characteristic specimen of the men who made the Revolution possible in Scotland. If the evils of a long protracted and embittered civil war, repeating the "Iliad of Woes" experienced by the previous generation, were avoided, this result was due, in the first place, to the statesmanship with which William of Orange used the power at which he had struck so boldly; and, in the second place, to the firmness and fidelity with which he was served by those who had become attached to his leadership abroad. There is much to be said for Burke's contention that the Revolution of 1688 was wrongly so called, and that it was "a revolution prevented rather than a revolution effected," but it is at least certain that the proceedings and the policy which the landing at Torbay inaugurated were dominated, not by the spirit of anarchy and disturbance, but by the spirit of order and discipline. It was to this that the British Constitution owed its solidity and stability, and the same qualities may be traced in the individual lives of many whose efforts contributed in lesser degrees to the history of the nation. The commander of the Cameronians was an adherent of the Prince of Orange, in a northern family mainly of Jacobite sympathies.

J.F.

Kinmundy
Old Deer, September, 1888

Major-General James Ferguson of Balmakelly

We have our good service to plead for us; and that we have been honest and loyal from the beginning, and will continue to the end.
    —letter of Brigadier Ferguson.

1.

In the Scots Brigade

Oh, Randal was a bonnie lad when he gaed awa—
A bonnie, bonnie lad was he, when he gaed awa!
It was in the Saxteen Hunner year o' grace and Thretty-twa,
That Randal, the laird's youngest son, gaed awa.
It was to seek his fortune in the Hie Germanie,
To fecht the foreign loons in their ain countrie,
That he left his father's ha' o' sweet Willanslee,
And mony sair hairts in the North Countrie.
  —Old Ballad.

"History," it has been said, "*is the essence of innumerable biographies,*" and the best way of judging a national movement often is to trace the career of a man. As there is always a deeper interest in politics, when to the stimulus of party and the inspiration of the great public cause is added the magic of the personality of a great leader, so in the narratives of the past we seem to see our way more clearly when subordinate events are allowed to group themselves around the achievements of some famous character who dominated the scene. It may be that in modern developments individuality is on the wane, yet the many works of fiction in which the author writes as an actor in the drama still pay a tribute to that human weakness which leads the student to place himself in the position of an eyewitness.

But apart altogether from personal narratives, or the principal actors who tread the stage, something of the same feeling ever lends interest to the lives of those who acted even small parts in great events, and contributed what in them lay to the determination of important issues. The composed fortitude of William of Orange and the "serene magnanimity" of Marlborough, never fail to impress; but there is also a charm in following the experience of an officer who served under them in a marching regiment or in subordinate command; for in so doing we seem to pursue a hitherto undiscovered by-way parallel to the great high road, which leads by nooks before unnoticed, and lends new interest to a familiar journey.

It would be difficult to overrate the advantage which the study of history has reaped in recent years from the opening up of immense stores of private correspondence and authentic documents long preserved in silence in the charter-chests and muniment rooms of old country houses. The materials have been in many cases afforded which enabled us to "contrast the hidden motive with the avowed pretext of public transactions," and if the revelation of the record, which was not written for history, sometimes "gilds refined gold," it sometimes explodes reputations. But there are scattered deposits as well as rich veins of such literary treasures, and there sometimes lurk in private repositories a few papers, which have a value of their own, either as contributing to the elucidation of obscure events, or as affording illustrations of types of individuals or classes who were important factors in national life.

Having occasion sometime ago to look through the contents of such a cabinet, we came upon a series of commissions and a few other documents, the dates of which corresponded in so interesting a manner with those of great public events, that the desire seized us, if possible, to reconstruct the career of the individual to whom they related. The period was an enticing one, for it was that of the generation who witnessed the final establishment of the Protestant character of this country, and the satisfactory settlement on a firm basis of the British Constitution.

The materials were somewhat scanty, for the home, to which the son of the soldier whose name heads these pages removed, was "harried" by Gordon of Glenbucket's Highlanders in the Forty-five, and such of his papers as had found a resting-place elsewhere did not escape perils of fire. He was the third son of William Ferguson of Badifurrow—a mansion situated on the braes that slope down to the Don, not very far from that prominent feature of Aberdeenshire landscape, Benachie,—who represented Inverurie in the first Scottish Parliament after the Restoration, which from the personal energy displayed by its members in celebrating the fact that "the king enjoyed his own again," obtained the designation of "the Drunken Parliament."

Tradition carried back the connection of his progenitors with the locality to the 14th century, and it has been said—with what truth is impossible now to ascertain—that one of the name "afforded ready and manly aid" to King Robert Bruce in the battle fought there, which initiated the chain of victories that culminated at Bannockburn. The Laird of Badifurrow left his property to his second son, for the eldest imbibed opinions unpalatable to his cavalier sentiments, and betaking himself to England, kept up little communication with his relatives in the North. History has assigned to him emphatically the title of "the Plotter." His varied experience embraced both parties and three competing ecclesiastical systems; he was for long the right hand man, and nominally the chaplain, of Lord Shaftesbury, who perhaps more than any other statesman is entitled to be called the founder of the Whig party.

When "the false Achitophel" fled into exile, the "Judas" of Dryden's satire was one of the two friends who alone remained with him to the last, and Shaftesbury "died in Ferguson's arms in Holland." He has been described as "the evil genius of the unfortunate Monmouth," and as he turned Jacobite and High Churchman after the Revolution, he secured the personal dislike of Burnet and the polemical denunciation of Macaulay. But the perusal of some of his own letters leads to a more charitable construction of his career than annalists have yet recorded; and a record he has left of the most involved passage in his life fits in remarkably with facts previously ascertained, and casts a fresh light on a fascinating and melancholy drama in English History. Though no careers could be more dissimilar, yet on one or two occasions the paths in life of "Ferguson the Plotter" and his soldier brother curiously crossed.[1]

The third son of a numerous family, the subject of our sketch, went like many other young Scotsmen of the time to find a career or a *quietus* in "the Lawlands o' Holland." For a small and impecunious country like Scotland, abounding with turbulent spirits, the old "Scots Brigade" was an admirable institution. It had for long been the fortune of the northern kingdom to provide other countries with their best soldiers; the fame of the Scots Guards in France was attested by many a stricken field, from the time when—

Swinton set the lance in rest
That tamed of yore the sparkling crest
Of Clarence's Plantagenet!

---

1. "*v. Robert Ferguson the Plotter.*" D. Douglas, Edinburgh, 1887.

—and Gustavus Adolphus, "the Lion of the North," owed many of his victories to the valour of his Scottish regiments. The Reformation in Scotland, and the revolt of the United Provinces opened a new field for the military spirit of the race, and so early as the year 1572, the famous brigade was formed, which won for itself the designation of "the Bulwark of the Republic." In 1578 the Scots regiments in the Dutch service bore the brunt of the action in the Battle of Reminaut against the Spaniards, "fighting without armour and in their shirts," and when more than 200 years later, owing to the spread of revolutionary principles in Holland, the traditions of "the old Brigade" were carried on in the 94th regiment of the British Army—it was among the oldest regular troops in Europe, and could boast of a long record of battles, storms, and triumphs won in "the classic land of fortified defence." [2]

At the time of which we write, these troops combined the service of the States with allegiance to their own sovereign, and as "the three Dutch regiments" formed a part of the fighting strength of Britain, while under the name of "the Scots Brigade," they constituted the most effective portion of the forces of Holland. Graham of Claverhouse was serving under their colours when he saved the life of William of Orange at Seneff, and it had been the failure to give him the promised command of one of the Scots regiments, which caused him to declare that "he would not serve a prince who had broken his word." He was destined to meet in the pass of Killiecrankie the very officer in whose favour he had been overlooked.

Young Ferguson, joining the Scots Brigade, entered the best school of discipline and practical warfare which the circumstances of the age afforded. The brigade, which had deteriorated owing to the admixture of foreign elements, had recently been reorganised by General Mackay, acting upon his spirited reply to the Prince of Orange, whom he assured that if it was recruited in Scotland, and commissions given to Scotsmen of good family, it would soon be as good as ever; and in 1685 it received a warm tribute of admiration from King James, who little realized for what that powerful weapon was next to be unsheathed. It is probable that, as was common at the time, his military service began as a gentleman-volunteer.

His first commission, dated 12th June, 1677, was as quartermaster in Colonel Macdonell's regiment. On 9th September of the following year, he received one as *"vendrigh"* in Captain van Zuylen's company,

---

2. Appendix, 1. "The position of the Scots Brigade," and commissions there printed.

and on 21st February, 1682, another as lieutenant in Captain Cuningham's company. On 10th June, 1685, a similar document describes him as Lieutenant of Captain Middleton's company," by exchange." That very day, in London, Luttrell made the note in his diary:—

> The three Scotch regiments that are in the service of the Dutch, are sent for over, in order to be sent into Scotland against the rebels.

But the insurrection, headed by the Earl of Argyle in the West of Scotland, was quelled before their services were required, and they were directed to London, threatened from another quarter. The unfortunate Monmouth, "so beautiful, so brave," had been received with enthusiasm by the peasantry of the West of England, and King James was mustering all his forces to crush him. On the third of July, "the three Scotch regiments which came from Holland, were drawn up in Blackheath before his Majestie, and the next day early they marched towards the west." They were, however, too late for the fight on Sedgemoor, in which Lieutenant Ferguson's more notorious brother, on the other side, had slightly forgotten his clerical character, and immediately returned to Holland.

Three years pass and another commission is followed by another voyage to England. But a great deal had happened in these three years, and the expedition of 1688 was under other banners and different auspices. Never perhaps had the tide of loyalty in England been in higher flood than when James succeeded to the throne, for the memory of the Ryehouse Plot was emphasized by the impending rebellion of Monmouth; and among the many loyal addresses which greeted the king's accession had been one from "the officers of the Scots and English regiments in Holland." It was the distinction of the policy he pursued to have changed all that; he had alienated the very classes who had most faithfully supported and suffered most for his father; and assailing the national church, he had converted the fidelity of a triumphant party into smouldering hostility, and prepared that coalition of parties, under the watchword of "Liberty, Property, and Religion," which made the Revolution of 1688 an enduring national act, and not the temporary *coup d'état* of a faction.

It was a significant fact that when, in 1687, he recalled the British troops in Holland, and the States, while forbidding the men to leave the colours, left the officers at liberty to follow their own inclinations, only 60 out of 240 obeyed the call. On the 22nd of March,

1688, Ferguson obtained his company, being appointed to Captain George Hamilton's, which had become vacant. But the importance of the rise in rank, and, it so happened, of the impending occasion, was typified by a larger document, dated 1st April, 1688. While his previous commissions, including that of 22nd March, are signed simply by "G. Prince d'Orange," this one is in duplicate, flowing both from the Prince of Orange and "*De Stated Generael der Vereeniehde Nederlanden*," and is engrossed on two pretentious pieces of parchment.

Captain Ferguson found himself on this occasion for a short time on the same side as his brother Robert, for both were on board the fleet which carried the Prince of Orange to the throne of Britain. When William disembarked in Torbay the first troops to land were Mackay's veterans of "the Old Brigade." They marched with him to London, but did not long remain there, for on 13th March, 1689, "the three Scotch regiments that came with the king from Holland went down the river in the companies' barges, to go on board some ships to carry them to Leith in Scotland, to secure the peace of that kingdom."

On the 25th of the same month, the Scottish Convention of Estates granted "warrant to the magistrates of Edinburgh to quarter two regiments under the command of Major-General Mackay, in Leith and the suburbs of Edinburgh." For by that time it was "up with the bonnets of bonny Dundee," and the authorities were not sorry to see the "wild westland Whigs" who thronged the Grassmarket, and the levies which Leven gathered off the streets of Edinburgh, supported by regular troops, and were eager to "acknowledge the great kindness and care of the King of England" in sending them. The next fact in Ferguson's career, as to which his own papers speak, presents him as having attained field-officer's rank, and entrusted with duty of difficulty and responsibility. But before that time arrived he had probably seen hard fighting. His regiment, which was that called, from its commander, Brigadier Balfour's, till Balfour fell before the Highland claymore at Killiecrankie, and afterwards Colonel Lauder's regiment, was one of those under Mackay's command during the campaign marked by that celebrated battle, in which "the vanquished triumphed and the victors mourned."

Lauder, then lieutenant-colonel of the regiment he was so soon to command, was in charge of the advanced guard—"picked men of the Dutch brigade"—which Mackay pushed forward to secure the Pass of Killiecrankie, when he set out from Perth for Blair; and when the

Lowland army debouched upon the open ground at the head of the gorge, it was Lauder's Fusiliers who first felt the enemy. According to Mackay's own account of his defeat:—"Lieutenant-Colonel Lauder was advantageously posted upon the left of all on a little hill wreathed with trees, with his party of two hundred of the choice of our army; but did as little as the rest of that hand, whether by his or his men's fault is not well known, for the General would never make search into the failings of that business, because they were a little too generally committed." In another account he says that Lauder was "abandoned by his party, and laboured without success to rally them"; and from the reflection of another contemporary, that "it is a pity to give green men to good men to command them," it would seem that the officers did their duty, but were not supported by the rank and file.

Luttrel mentions that letters from Scotland reported "that the fight was maintained very sharply for some time, but two of the Scots regiments that came from Holland would not fight, which occasioned a disorder among our men." Was it the recollection of old times, and a reminiscence of the Cavalier who "wore a white plumach" on the field of Seneff, which unnerved the picked men of the Dutch brigade? The Stuart papers mention a Captain Ferguson as having been taken prisoner at Killiecrankie; and Captain Crichton, the old dragoon and "persecutor" of the western Covenanters, whose recollections Dean Swift took down when living in the North of Ireland many years after, mentions that "next day, though victorious, the Highlanders suffered their prisoners to depart on parole that they would never take up arms against King James—Colonel Ferguson only excepted on account of his more than ordinary zeal for the new establishment."

The incident affords one of those curious coincidences and contrasts which give so much of the life and colour to the dry bones of history. For one of the first acts of the Royalists after the Restoration had been to collect the scattered remains of the Marquis of Montrose from every "port" and "airt" to which they had been dispersed, and to celebrate the "True Funerals" of the "Great Cavalier," and the companion of his campaigns who had suffered along with him, Sir William Hay of Delgaty, in the Church of St. Giles. Among those who took part in the ceremony was Captain Ferguson's father, the Laird of Badifurrow, who bore "the gumphion" before the bier of the Knight of Delgaty. It would be strange indeed if to the ears of the son, a prisoner of war, had floated the strains of "the Burial March of Dundee."

The character given him by Crichton quite accords with what

tradition has preserved as to his sentiments, and this little incident very well illustrates the contrast between "the Usurpation" and the Revolution of 1688, which indeed carried out the constitutional policy of wise reform originally advocated by Hyde and Falkland in England, and by Montrose in Scotland. An allusion in a letter of his own many years later indicates that Captain Ferguson saw no break of continuity between his father's loyalty to King Charles and his own fidelity to King William. If he was taken among the few who were left standing at their posts, when the mass of the Lowland army broke away before the sweeping onset of the clansmen, he must have been exchanged[3] or escaped,[4] for within a year he was conducting important enterprises as major without any reflection on his reputation, and much relied on by his commanding-officer.

It had for some time been a favourite project with Mackay to fix a thorn in the side of the Highlanders who adhered to King James, by constructing a fort and depot on the West Coast in an advantageous position, for controlling the mainland districts of Lochaber and Morven, bridling the island of Mull, where the Jacobites were very strong, and to which they sent their prisoners, and cutting communication between King James' supporters in Scotland, and the army of Irish and French auxiliaries he was himself at the head of in Ireland. Owing to the difficulties with which "poor, honest General-Major Mackay"—as Dalrymple calls him—had to deal, arising from the ambitions and intrigues which were rife in the Council at Edinburgh, and the lack of energy displayed in seconding his scheme on the part of the political authorities, a considerable time elapsed before he could get his project carried out. "At last," however, "he obtained his desire with regard to the fort at Inverlochy." The king ordered three 30 gun frigates with arms, ammunition, and implements to the West Coast of Scotland, and as the season was far advanced, Mackay proposed to the Council:—

That in the first place, in order the more to intimidate the

---

3. On 3rd September, 1689, the Privy Council wrote to General Mackay authorising an exchange of prisoners, "with such as you think meetest out of the enemies' hands." No Colonel Ferguson is recorded as present at Killiecrankie, and Crichton apparently gives the rank by which he was better known for many years, to the Captain of the Stuart papers.

4. The Clan Ferguson of Athole joined Dundee's army a day or two after Killiecrankie; it has been said that there was some old tradition of far-away kinship between them and their Aberdeenshire namesakes, and possibly in this may lie the secret of the captain's good fortune.

Highlanders, and force many of them to keep at home to guard their own property, a detachment of 600 chosen men should, in the meantime, be sent in the ships which were to sail with the materials and other necessaries.

But:—

Because of the emptiness of their coffers they were not able to despatch the detachment; and if the general had not got the provost and city of Glasgow to furnish the ships and materials, it had not been done for a month after, whereby the whole designed advantage of sending the detachment had been lost.

It was in the beginning of March, 1690, he writes, that he:—

. . . .engaged the city of Glasgow to hire ships, and make the necessary provisions for the speedy despatch of the 600 men, which he designed for the enemy's coast to make diversion under the command of Major Ferguson, a resolute well-affected officer to whose discretion and diligence he trusted much. He engaged the magistrates of the said city also to furnish and send away with the detachment 5000 palisades, with 500 spades, shovels, and pickaxes, to make up 2000 in all with the 1500 sent down from England, which he had ordered to Glasgow to be sent away with the party.

The historian of the House and Clan of Mackay, after quoting this passage, adds in a note a characteristic anecdote of the officer who had been thus selected as suited "to make diversion":—

When in Flanders he had on one occasion volunteered to go with a small party to guard a great number of prisoners to a considerable distance, after others had signified a wish to decline the service as being too hazardous. For the greater safety he cut the latchets of the prisoners' small clothes, which obliged them to march with one hand behind to hold them up. He had a brother of a very different cast known by the name of Robert the Plotter.

That worthy indeed had now become as hot a partisan of the exiled house as he had previously been of Monmouth and William of Orange, and was deeply engaged with Sir James Montgomery, the Earl of Annandale, Lord Ross, and others in a plot to combine the extreme Presbyterians and Jacobites in an effort for the restoration of James. An incident which General Mackay thus notices in his *Mem-*

oirs proves that he had hoped to persuade his brother to join in this intrigue, which, occurring at a very critical moment, and coinciding with renewed efforts in the Highlands, great exertions on the part of the French, and those endeavours in Ireland which were only defeated by the battle of the Boyne, caused much anxiety to Queen Mary and her advisers. Mackay says:—

> About the middle of April, though he (the general), to avoid all suspicion of himself, had delivered to the Commissary Melville's creature £4000 which the king had sent to the general towards the expedition: yet Major Ferguson was kept up about five weeks waiting for his provisions; and not only so, but the club who had joined in Parliament with the Jacobites, thinking to overrule that which was called the Court party, essayed to debauch Major Ferguson, after it had been publicly known that the general had appointed him to command the detachment of land forces along with the frigates: to whom the said major, who is a vigorous and well-affected man, discovered all their proposals not silencing a letter from a very near relation of his own to the same purpose; whereof the general gave present notice to the commissioner, and afterwards to the king.

In writing to King William,[5] Mackay described Major Ferguson as *"personne de probité et d'honneur comme aussi fidéle et affectionné au service de votre Majesté."*

In the beginning of May the preparations, thanks to the city of Glasgow, were complete, and from a burgess ticket of that town, dated 7th May, 1690, in favour of "James Ferguson, Major of the regiment of Colonel Lauder," it appears that the magistrates of the Metropolis of the West combined their services to the cause with a personal compliment to the commander. On the 15th of May he set sail from Greenock. The instructions:—

> For Major Ferguson, appointed to command in chief the detachment of 600 men, which are to be shipped at Greenock, and to go about to the isles and the coast of Lochaber, and for Captain Pottinger commanding their Majesties' ship the *Dartmouth*, with the rest of the squade under his command.[6]

—were of considerable length and couched in quaint phraseol-

---
5. *Lettre écrite au Roy le 16 Avril 1690 d'Edimbourg.*
6. Printed in the Appendix to *Mackay's Memoirs.*

ogy. The importance of harmony between the two services and commanders was insisted on. Nothing active was to be done but "upon visible and apparent advantages and humane assurance of success." A descent on Mull, with the assistance of the Campbells, was, however, suggested; and Ferguson was ordered to open communications and co-operate with the Laird of MacLeod. They were to "use with all the rigour of military executions such as shall continue obstinate in their rebellion with this proviso that women and children be not touched or wronged in their persons." And one touch shows distinctly the hand of the worthy old officer whom Burnet describes as the most pious of soldiers.

> The said major commanding in-chief shall have speciall care his men be keeped under exact discipline, both as soldiours and christians, to hinder cursing and swearing and all other unchristian and disorderly customs, and to chastise in their purs and persons such as persist in them after intimation.

The conduct of the expedition fully justified Mackay's choice of a commander, and expectations of the advantages to be gained.

> The gross of the rebels, particularly such as dwelt near the sea, with the inhabitants of the isles, staid at home to guard their country against the frigates with Ferguson's detachment, at the very noise whereof they were very much terrified.

It prevented the Western Clans "from coming in any considerable numbers to the assistance of Buchan and Cannon." Another writer observes that, as a consequence of its appearance:—

> The small islands between Kintire and Mull had put themselves under the protection of the Government, and the Earl of Seaforth with some others of the principal Highlanders were inclinable to do the same.

On the 30th May the Privy Council, being informed that:—

> Major Ferguson is arrived at the island of Mull, and is now lying at Dunstaffnage, and that several of the rebels have got together in a body within that isle in and about the castle of Dowart.

> —ordained the Earl of Argyle to order Colin Campbell of Ardkinglass to levy 600 men and march to reinforce him. The Council

allowed the Earl to nominate his own officers, and recommended the Lords Commissioners of the Treasury to order 400 bolls of meal to be sent to Inverary for the use of the 600 men. A letter of the time,[7] addressed "for Angus Campbell, of Kilberry," shows the steps taken to put this force in the field, the motives that were appealed to, and the blended influence of feudal power, and clan attachment wielded by the House of Argyle.

Edinburgh, 4th June, 1690.

Loveing Cousein,

Their Majesties' Privy Councill hes ordered us to raise six hundred men to goe to Dunstaffnage to meet Major Ferguson there. That this may be the better effectuate, wee ordered Sir Colin Campbell of Ardkinlass to go from this to meet you at Inverary, upon Thursday, the 12th day of this instant, for appointing these men to be raised, and for other things pertaining to the good of the country. Wee entreat you faill not to come there at that time and give your advyse, assistance, and concurrance in this matter. Wee expect that all of you will readily comply with the desyre of the Councill, both for the country's good and ours. And we hope, by your concurrance in this, (to have the) shyre exeemed from their resting public burdens. Those who will not concurr, they may expect little favour of this nature, and a dale of trouble for their disobedience, that at present they may avoid. There is four hundred bolls of victuall ordered to be sent ... for maintaining those six hundred men, and what else they will need, Major Ferguson will see them provided in. What farther we have to say in this matter, and what directions are necessary thereanent, shall be sent by Ardkinlass.

We are,

Your loveing Cousin,

Argyll.

I own I have ever found you most readie in what concerned me. I desyre you, upon this occasion, to be very active, and I have ordered you the command of the partie.'

An armistice, which had been the result of some make-believe negotiations, was soon recalled, and Mackay having sent an order to Ferguson to meet him at Inverlochy, set out from Perth on the 18th

---

7. Preserved among the Kilberry papers, and printed in the Appendix to the *Memoirs of Lochiel*.

of June with about 3000 horse and foot. On the 6th of July, Lord Melville wrote to the king:—

> I had not account from Major-General Mackay till just now, a post has come in from Inverlochy, showing that Major Ferguson, after he had burnt some of the islands, and taken assurance of some others not to join the rebels, not being strong enough to land in the Island of Mull, had come to Inverlochy, the place where Mackay designs to make the fort, and encamped at Lochyeall House this day sennight, and stayed till Mackay came to him, which he did Thursday or Frayday last.

For a government detachment to encamp at Lochiel House, was certainly establishing itself comfortably in the lion's den; and an account of the previous proceedings of the expedition is furnished in a despatch from Captain Pottinger to Lord Melville dated, "Aboard the *Dartmouth* in Duart Road, 19th July, 1690." Captain Pottinger excuses himself for not having written since leaving Greenock, on the ground of having been since then "scarce 48 hours in one place without motion," and of having:—

> Referred to Major Ferguson, who assured me of the tender of my most humble duty to your Grace upon several occasions, and that he would be more particular therein than I could or would have expected from the land part on't. But since Major Ferguson (who is a man of great diligence, zealously affected to the present government, and brave enough) is parted.

Captain Pottinger had to write his own despatches, and thus related what had been done.

> We divided our squades and boats they burning and destroying one way, our ships with the Major left nothing undone that was to be done the other way, in burning houses, breaking boats, and destroying the substance of such as was in actual rebellion; nor hath our appearance upon the coast had less effect in keeping these McClains of Mull, McDonalds, &c, all at whom if possible to preserve their interest; so that joining was prevented.

The *Dartmouth*, on board which this despatch was written, was one of the three ships that had relieved Derry not long before, having covered the advance of the *Mountjoy* when she broke the boom that stretched across the Foyle. (See note following). Mackay had arrived at Inverlochy on the 3rd July, and the construction of the fort, which Ferguson had commenced, was rapidly proceeded with. It was called Fort-William, after the King, and formed the first of the chain of fortresses, which raised at the centre and both ends of the great glen of Albyn, for years were so powerful a check on the unruly spirit of the Highlands.

******

Note:—Captain Pottinger, who wrote the despatch, was a gallant officer, but the *Dartmouth* was destined to be his last command. A record of his services is found in a resolution of the Scots Privy Council, dated 1st January, 1691, upon a petition presented by Thomas Pottinger, "the Sovereign of Belfast," on behalf of the widow and children of his deceased brother, Captain Edward Pottinger, commander of the frigate called the *Dartmouth*. The Privy Council recommended the widow and children to "the King's Sovereign Majesty his favour and bounty," on account of Captain Pottinger's "great zeal, and the signal services performed by him." The record bears that he had "evidenced great zeal and affection for the Protestant interest, as is not unknown to all that ever knew him." He had levied a company of men at his own expense, and defended Coleraine against the Irish army—the enemy being beat off "by his courage and skill in levelling and discharging the guns," all which was testified by a formal document, vouched by the Mayor and Aldermen of Coleraine.

As commander of a yacht, he had served with daring and credit at the siege of Carrickfergus, which was similarly testified by General Douglas. As captain of the *Dartmouth*, which "was ordered to cruise in the West Seas for their Majesties service in this kingdom, it is well known to the said Lords of Council with what faithfulness and diligence he behaved himself in the said service, and with what assiduity and carefulness he exonered himselfe of the trust and commission given unto him therein at all occasions, from the latter end of May that he came here till the month of October last, when by the violence of a great tempest and storme as happened not in many years at the dispensation and pleasure of God, he, with his men, ship, and furniture did all perish, (four or fyve excepted) to the exceeding grief and loss of his relict and fatherless children."

******

Mackay wrote to Lord Melville:—

> I recommend earnestly to your Grace the care of this post, which I look upon as the most important of the kingdom at present, and that which will at length make such as would sell their credit and service at such a deare rait to the King of no greater use nor no more necessary to him than a Lothian or Fyf Laird; therefore, by no means let it be neglected though other things should be postponed.

Before Mackay left Fort-William, on the 15th of July, he ordered a detachment to the Island of Mull. This detachment, though countermanded on the news of the naval reverse off Beachy Head, was subsequently despatched, and was commanded by Ferguson, for the Stuart papers record that the Highlanders who had received officers, ammunition, and provisions from James in Ireland, and had taken arms to second Sir James Montgomery's intrigues in Parliament, were "repulsed rather than defeated by Sir Thomas Livingston in the county of Moray, and by Major Ferguson in the Island of Mull." If his success was equal to that of Livingston on "the Haughs of Cromdale," thus similarly described, the repulse of the Jacobites must have been a total rout. Oldmixon says:—

> Major Ferguson was very successful against the rebels in the Island of Mull, while his brother, that vile apostate from all principles of morality, religion, and liberty, was in the depths of the Assassination and Invasion Plots in England.

> The progress of Major Ferguson in the Isle of Mull was so prosperous that it obliged Sir John MacLean, the proprietor, to submit to their Majesties' Government and deliver up his castles to their forces.

That his discharge of the duty entrusted to him received the approval of his commanding officer is proved by the general recommending him for promotion in a letter directly addressed to the king himself.[8]

Mackay wrote:—

> Et comme le bien du service, m' oblige de luy representer ceux qui en sont capables et si attachent avec zelle, le Lieutenant-Colonel Buchan merit que votre Majesté luy donne une meilleure poste, et Ferguson

---

8. *Lettre écrite au Roy peu de temps après le construction de Fort-William.*

seroit bien plus capable de commander le regiment de Lauder que Balfour,[9] s'il y avoit moyen d'accomoder celluy-ci autrement.

It affords an instructive illustration of the division of opinion which prevailed in Scotland at the time, to observe that of the two officers here recommended as zealous adherents of the Protestant succession, one was the brother of the commander-in-chief of the opposing army, while the brother of the other had been arrested a few months before by the order of King William, who was desirous that information should be forwarded on the strength of which he might be sent to Scotland, as otherwise it would be necessary by the law of England to release him, Ten years were to elapse before the measure that has been called the Scottish *Habeas Corpus* Act took its place in the statute book. Both soldiers, too, were Aberdeenshire men, for the Buchans were brothers of the Laird of Auchmacoy.

It would seem that after the reduction of the Western Islands, Ferguson's capacity and zeal were utilised on the Lowland side of the Highland line, for the records of the Scots Privy Council show that on 26th May, 1691, Sir Thomas Livingstone, Mackay's successor as commander-in-chief, laid before them a letter:—

> Directed to him by Major Ferguson in Perth, dated the 25th day of May instant, bearing that the prisoner which Major Munro was sending from Castle Blair made his escape about a mile from Perth, and that the ensign with the most of the party are gone after him, and that he has sent forward the money to Sir Thomas, and giving account that Sir Thomas's orders which the major caused publish at the church doors, had so good effect that Kindrogin, who commanded a party of the thieves was killed the last week with two or three of his followers in Glen Prossen, and since they have sent several more of that gang prisoners to Perth, and that the whole country do solicit they may be hanged, or an order got for their tryall or transportation.

The Council promptly ordained a Commission of Justiciary to be drawn, directed to the Magistrates of Perth, "for trying and judging such of the Highland thieves or robbers as are presently in the tolbooth of Perth."

The commencement of the Inverlochy Expedition had seen Ferguson admitted a Burgess of Glasgow, and its successful termination,

---

9. There had been two Balfours in the regiment at Killiecrankie. One was killed and one was taken prisoner.

and his subsequent services were recognised in a similar manner by a grant of the freedom of the City of Edinburgh on 30th October, 1691.

Within six months he was again in the Low countries, for his next commission as Lieutenant-Colonel in Monro's Regiment, which, unlike the others, is in the English form and superscribed by King William, is dated "at Our Camp at Lembeck the first day of August, 1692," just a few days after the bloody field of Steinkirk, where the British division, outnumbered and unsupported, had for long sustained unequal combat, and at last, exhausted and overwhelmed, only sullenly yielded to the impetuous charge of the famous Household Brigade,

The dread of Europe, and the pride of France.

"Let us see how these English bull-dogs will fight," had been the response of Count Solms to requests for reinforcement, and brave old Mackay, ordered to a post he knew to be untenable, after pointing out the fact in vain, had gone forward for the last time with the words "*The will of the Lord be done.*" His division left 3000 dead on the field, and, amongst others, Lauder's Regiment was severely handled, its colonel being taken prisoner.

2.

Colonel of the Cameronians

"Had Count Solmes, Trim, done the same at the Battle of Steinkirk, said Yorick, drolling a little upon the corporal, who had been run over by a dragoon in the retreat—he had saved thee—Saved! said Trim, interrupting Yorick, and finishing the sentence for him after his own fashion, he had saved five battalions, an', please your reverence, every soul of them. There was Cutt's,—continued the corporal, clapping the forefinger of his right hand upon the thumb of the left, and counting round his hand,—there was Cutt's—Mackay's—Angus's—Graham's—and Leven's, all cut to pieces: and so had the English Life-guards, too, had it not been for some regiments upon the right, who marched up boldly to their relief, and received the enemy's fire in the face before any one of their own platoons discharged a musket Had we drubbed them soundly at Steinkirk, they would not have fought us at Landen."—Tristram Shandy.

At Steinkirk, Ferguson had served for the last time in the old Scots Brigade, for the regiment to which he was now appointed was the famous one that had been raised three years before among the followers of Richard Cameron, the sternest of the Covenanters of the West. Its first colonel, the youthful Earl of Angus,[1] had fallen in the recent battle, and Lieutenant-Colonel Monro succeeding to the command, Ferguson was appointed in his place. Short as had hitherto been the career of the Cameronian Regiment, it had previously lost its Lieutenant-Colonel when Cleland was killed at Dunkeld, and a year after he entered it Ferguson obtained the colonelcy, when Monro died of

---

1. It was known first as Angus's, then as Munro's, then as Ferguson's, later as Stair's and Preston's, for long as the 26th (Cameronians), and now as the First Battalion of "The Cameronians Scottish Rifles."

sore sickness after the Battle of Landen (or Neerwinden).

Unique in its origin and organisation, it had, when embodied, 1200 strong on the holm of Douglas on 14th May, 1689, been formed on the model of a Presbytery, with a minister to the regiment and an elder to each company. Indeed, "their minister" exercised an influence not always conducive to good discipline and military subordination, and on one occasion his dislike to being quartered at Fort-William had been the source of some anxiety to the governor of that garrison. Mackay had at that time observed—"Angus's regiment ought to have a man of service put upon their head," and even in the Low Countries their chaplain continued to be a marked figure. In a diary of a tour in Holland in the year 1696, made by a west country Laird, William Mure of Glanderstone (afterwards of Caldwell), he records that at Gemblois, on 27th June—

> I went to Colonel Ferguson's regiment near to the rear of the lines, and heard worthy Mr. Shields preach.

And long after the Cameronians had little in common with the fierce zealots, who so gallantly defended Dunkeld against the Highlanders, it is said the tradition was maintained which placed a Bible in the knapsack of every soldier.

On 25th August 1693, shortly after the hard fought Battle of Landen, Colonel Ferguson succeeded to the command of the Cameronians.[2] He held it for twelve years, during most of which they served in the Low Countries in the campaigns of William, and subsequently under the brighter auspices of Marlborough. Indeed, when the British Army was reduced after the Peace of Ryswick in 1697, owing to a vote of the House of Commons that "all the forces raised since the year 1680 should be disbanded," they were for some time retained in Holland, in Dutch pay. A commission to Colonel Ferguson, as captain in his own regiment, dated 1st January, 1698, is in Dutch, and in the same form as those of the "Schotsche Brigade," except that it flows in the name of "*Sijne Majesteijt*" and is signed "William R."[3]

---

2. The Calendar of the Treasury papers contains this entry—"December 4 and 7, 1694, Paymaster Fox, his memorial for a warrant to pay £1800 to the Commissioners of Transports to be by them paid to Colonel Ferguson, for transport and provision of recruits shipped from Scotland to the Low Countries, dated 4th December, 1694. Letter signed, W. Lowndes, on the same subject, dated 7th December, 1694."
3. I am indebted to the courtesy of the officials of the "*Rijks Archief*" at the Hague, for the following extracts, which clearly authenticate, (continued next page),

On the 20th of the following February [4] leave was granted by:—

Walrad by der Gratien Godes, Furst van Nassau, Grave tot Sarbrucken, en Sarwerden, Heere tot Lahr Wiesbaden en Idsteyn, &c. Velt Maerschalck Generael van sijne Keyserlijcke Majesteyt, als mede van den Staet der Vereenighde Nederlanden, ende Gonverneur van's Hertogenbosch, &c.," to *"den Hre. Ferguson, Colonel oover een Regiment Schotten te voet in dienste van Lande . . sich van den dienst te mogen absenteren, en naer Schotlandt te gaen tot ver-sightinge van syne affaires.*

One of the affairs which required his personal attention, was probably of a matrimonial character, for he was married about this time to Helen, daughter of James Drummond of Cultmalindie.[5] The marriage was, unfortunately, of short duration, for Mrs. Ferguson soon died, leaving two little infants, a son and a daughter. The one trait of her character that has descended is recorded in the quaint words of an old memoir which describes her as "a seeker and server of God."

A few years before Colonel Ferguson had acquired the estates of Balmakellie and Kirktonhill[6] on the Kincardineshire bank of the North Esk, and it must have been a very welcome order which soon afterwards recalled the Cameronians to Scotland and stationed them

---

an interesting page in the history of the Cameronian regiment.—"*Resolutie Staten Generaal 29th October, 1697. Zijne Hoogheid de Prins van Oranjé geest kennis voornemens te zijn met het volgend jaar de Schotsche regimenten die sedert den jare 1689, in Zr Ms bezoldiging zijn geweest in dienst van den Staat terug te geven.* "*Resolutie Raad van State, 12th December, 1697. Teruggekeerd 6 Schotsche regimenten be-paling van de wijze waarop zij ter repartitie van de verschillende provincien zullen worden gebracht.* Gelderland, Lauder, Holland, Colyear, Ferguson, Schratnaver, Murray, Zeeland, Hamilton."

4. Printed form filled up in writing.

5. The Drummonds of Cultmalindie, an estate near the City of Perth, were descended through the houses of Invermay and Drummonderinoch, from Malcolm Drummond of Cargill, nth chief of the name, and progenitor of the Dukes of Perth. Their family history thus comprised the dark tragedy of Celtic savagery which furnished Sir Walter Scott with the character of Allan Macaulay in the *Legend of Montrose*. Who, that has read either the novel, or the *Tales of a Grandfather*, can forget the scene in the hall of Ardvoirlich when the lady of the house, offering her hospitality to the murderers of her brother, fled from the sight of his head upon the table, or the other in the old church of Balquhidder, recorded even more graphically in the quaint words of the Privy Council proclamation which ranged "the ire of the Drummonds" on the side of the Law when engaged in "taking sweet revenge for the death of their cousin, Drummond-Ernoch?" *v. App. iv.*

6. These Kincardineshire estates were sold by his son, who purchased, instead, the lands of Kinmundy and Coynach in Buchan.

at Perth. His leave (originally for three months) must have been extended, for, on 9th November, 1698, the freedom of Montrose was presented to "Collonell James Fergusone of Balmakellie." It is probable that the regiment came over in April, 1699, for in August of the previous year, he describes himself in granting a bond as "Commander of one of the Scots foot regiments in the service of the States Generall of the United Provinces," while a document attested as "compared with the books in the Exchequer," and headed "Abstract of the money due to Colonel Ferguson's regiment on the Establishment, from the 14th April, 1699, to the 1st December, 1700," may be taken as fixing the date of the transfer from Holland to Great Britain. (See note following).

★★★★★★

Note:—The document among the Kinmundy papers agrees exactly with the entries in the Dutch records.

Resolutie van de Staten Generaal, 6 September, 1698. Ontvangen eene missive van Zijne Majesteit waarbij wordt voorgesteld te licentieeren en naar Schotlandt terug te zenden het regimenten van den Kolonel Hamilton benevens de twee jongste compagnien van ieder de 5 overige regimenten, in het geheel 22 compagnien te voet, waartoe Zijne Majesteit wordt geauthoriseerd.

Resolutie van den Raad van State van 15 April, 1699. Is gelesen een request van James Ferguson en Johan Lord Strathnaver, Kolonels van twee Schotsche regimenten, te kennen gevende in substancie dat zij patent bekomen hebbende om te verlaten den dienst van den Lande en weder te keeren naar Schotland, te Rotterdam gekomen zijnde om de reis van daar voort te zetten, &c.

Verzoek om Restitutie van eenige gelden.

At the date of the Scotch document the arrears due to the officers of Colonel Ferguson's regiment were £2443 7s, with an additional sum of £1632 15s. 6d. for cloathing and reckonings. The colonel was £273 in arrear, the lieutenant-colonel £204 15s, the major £177 9s., each of the captains £109 4s., most of the lieutenants £54 12s., and most of the ensigns £40 19s. each. The whole amount payable to the regiment for the time mentioned was £10,593 16s. sterling. This was made up thus:—"For full pay for 8 companys for last 14 days in April, 1699, £221 4s. To *Do.* for 2 companys for the last week of April,

1699, £25 4s. To *Do*. for 10 companys conform to the Establishment, from 1st May, 1699, to 1st December, 1700, being 19 months at £544 12s. monthly; £10,347 8s.

Another paper, in less detail but in similar terms, is headed "The Lords Commissioners of the Treasury to Collonel James Ferguson's Regiment." It would seem, therefore, that if two companies were sent home in the previous year, they must have been disbanded, and the number was afterwards again raised to 12 or 13.

Before long there seems to have been another transference as far at least as pay was concerned. The Calendar of Treasury Papers contains the following entries:—

> Report of Mr. William Blaithwayt and Mr. W. Duncombe as to eight days' pay to Brigadier Ferguson and Col. Row for their regiments, due to them at the time they were sent from Scotland to Holland. Dated 23, March, 1703-4.

> Minuted 27 March 1704. D. Marlbro present. This canot be granted out of any of the English funds, these regiments being paid by English Mo. from ye very day of imbarcacon: but they are at libty. to apply to Scotl. where they should have been paid to their imbarcation.

★★★★★★

This paper gives a glimpse of the personnel of the officers, and shows both a touch of the clannish sentiment of the Scots nation, and how thoroughly the regiment was officered by Scotsmen. Commissions as captains were held cumulatively by the colonel, lieut.-colonel, and major, and the other captains were—Alex. Campbell, James Cranston, Henry Stewart, John Blackader (afterwards Governor of Stirling, and author of a diary, which has been published in his memoir by Dr. Crichton and makes up the first part of this Leonaur edition), George Murray, Andrew Monro, and James Aikman. Among the subalterns were several of the Colonel's own name. A Lieutenant John Ferguson was adjutant, while there were three ensigns, John, Robert, and James Ferguson. The last was possibly his son, who certainly a few years later formed an instance of the practice commemorated in the story of "the major crying for his parritch;" and two nephews, called respectively John and Robert, had entered the army. William Hamilton is designated as captain-lieutenant, and the names of the other Subalterns are the Scotch ones of Wilson (two), Lawson, Lindsay, Dickson, Gordon, Fairbairn, Boyd, Murray, Haddo, Maitland (two), Douglas, Bernard, Gray, Seton, Drummond, Glendinning.

It would seem that after their return to Scotland, the Cameronians were in great jeopardy of being disbanded. The correspondence addressed from Scotland to the politic Presbyterian ecclesiastic, who had the ear of King William, bears testimony to the anxiety felt by noblemen and others interested in the various regiments whose fate hung in the balance, when economy demanded a reduction of establishments. Among these letters to the future Principal Carstares, is one from Colonel Ferguson. It bears the stamp of the writer's individuality, and shews that he was a politician as well as a soldier, and sufficiently versed in the classics to be stung by lampoons in the dead languages levelled at the master whom he served.

The time was a critical one; the heats of the Darien controversy were skilfully fomented by the Jacobites, the popular mind was fiercely excited, and the national spirit of hostility to the "auld enemies of England" was fanned for ulterior ends by those who had other objects to promote. The ferment had taken a direction very dangerous to the Government; they knew that in the North-Eastern Shires they had not above four or five friends to the New Establishment in each County, and in a wild tumult the Edinburgh mob broke loose, threatened the lives of those who had roused their anger, and rioted to the tune of "Wilful Willie." So the situation gave force to their Colonel's appeal on behalf of the Cameronians, who were certainly the Proetorian Guard of Revolution principles north of the Tweed. On June 15th, 1700, he wrote thus to Mr. Carstares:—

> Dear Sir,—Since you went from this, things are grown rather worse than better: the ferment still continues, and new addresses are daily coming in from all parts of the country to be presented to the Parliament when they sit. God help us, we are ripening for destruction. It looks very like Forty-one. Yesterday, there came an address from the town of Glasgow to Powhill, their representative. Its much of the same nature with the rest; for redressing of grievances, a legal settlement of our company in Darien, and to be eased of all subsidies and taxes, There are likewise some officers who have been desiring the army to address for their arrears. You see, sir, what kind of people we are, and how the king, our master, is served by us.

But, God be thanked, there are more honest men amongst us than knaves. So I hope there will be no address from the army at this time. Monday last was a great day among the Jacobites here, being the birthday of the pretended Prince of Wales; and it was solemnised by a great many this year, who never did it before. I send a poem upon it, made by Dr. Pitcairn.

Its an allusion to that fable in Aesop of the frogs desiring a king from Jupiter, who gave them a stork. There are a great many satirical and obscene reflections upon the king in it.[7] You see, sir, that they are now above board with us; for treason is became so common that nobody takes any notice of it. They talk publicly that, unless the king will grant them the legal settlement of Caledonia, that they will address him again with forty thousand hands at it, and call a convention of States. We are all in flame; and I am sure the fuel comes both from France and England to keep it up. The Lord preserve our master and counsell from ought; and let all his enemies be confounded from Dan to Beersheba. I think, sir, you are very happy and safe where you are: but upon my word, I am not where I am, nor no honest man.

If our master be necessitate to break some regiments, I hope he will have a regard to his old servants; for there are four or five younger than that which I have the honour to command, *viz.*, Portmore's, Strathnaver's, Hamilton's, Maitland's, and Jedburgh's dragoons; for we were upon the Scots establishment before any of them. Besides, sir, we have our good service to plead for us; and that we have been honest and loyal from the beginning, and will continue so to the end. Pray give my most humble duty and service to our noble friend and patron. I have writ to him since you went from this. I hope he will continue his protection and favour to us; for we never will, nor ever did depend upon any but him, whom I pray God may long preserve.—*Adieu.*"

It is interesting to find a strong supporter of the government of William of Orange going back for a parallel to the existing excitement to the popular ferment that preceded the calamitous era of the Civil Wars. The observation, "it looks very like Forty-One," was probably accompanied by the recollection of how a year or two later that "Cavalier of stainless faith and purity," the Marquis of Huntly, had

---

7. Appendix.

stepped from the writer's father's door to raise the Royal Standard in the little market-place of Inverurie. "Our noble friend and patron "was probably the Marquis of Douglas, the father of the young colonel who had fallen at Steinkirk, or possibly the Duke of Queensberry, for the Cameronian Regiment was always associated with the Douglas name, and still bears on its appointments the mullet which was the badge of the most famous of Scottish Houses.

With the new century a new scene opened. In February, 1702, "Colonel Ferguson's regiment of foot was ordered immediately from Scotland to Holland." Next year we meet with him as brigadier-general, holding a command at Bois-le-Duc, an important fortress in Dutch Brabant. There occurred there a very curious incident which must be told in the words of the individual principally concerned. The notorious Simon Fraser, afterwards Lord Lovat, in the course of the mysterious intrigues he had been for some time carrying on, which perplexed the courts both of St. James and St. Germains, and procured him a lodging in the Bastile from the most Christian king, had made the acquaintance of Ferguson the Plotter in London.

They had, according to Lovat, whose word always requires to be taken with reservation, and is often absolutely unreliable—deep conferences on the prospects of King James. But "the old Plotter," who had, if not more natural talent for intrigue than Lovat, at least at that time more experience in the art, suspected his associate of being more intent on gratifying his private hatreds than advancing the Jacobite cause. He gradually unravelled the tortuous thread of a conspiracy to ruin the Duke of Athole, by the disclosure of which at the right time he managed both to spoil a very pretty piece of mischief and throw discredit on the existence of the alleged Jacobite design known as "the Scots Plot." Before, however, the unravelling process had been quite completed, the intriguers "parted with mutual protestations of friendship and esteem," and Ferguson gave Fraser:—

> A letter of recommendation to his brother, Major-General Ferguson, who had entered into the service of King William, and at that time commanded the Scottish regiments in garrison at Bois-le-Duc, entreating him to render the same services to Lord Lovat as he would to himself in his situation. This letter was the means of saving Lord Lovat's life about a fortnight after.

He was travelling through Holland, and being a suspected person, found himself in great danger among the Dutch. He says:

In this situation, he recollected the letter he had received from old Mr. Ferguson at London to Major General Ferguson, his brother, who commanded the troops at Bois-le-Duc. With this recommendation he determined to set out for that fortress; himself, his brother, and Major Fraser, having disguised themselves in the uniform of Dutch officers.

Having arrived there:—

In the evening he waited upon General Ferguson, who having read his brother's letter, entreating him to communicate to Lord Lovat everything he knew respecting the interests of the king, and to bestow upon him all the attentions in his power, desired that nobleman to sup with him alone, observing that he could inform him of several things of the last importance to the two courts. When Lord Lovat waited upon him in pursuance of his invitation the general assured him that, though he had been obliged for subsistence to enter into the service of King William and the Dutch Republic, he had always been in his heart faithfully attached to King James. He said that he should be charmed to meet with a favourable occasion of shedding his blood for the restoration of his prince.

The more unquestionably to prove his zeal for this interest, he gave Lord Lovat a copy of the secret intelligence that M. Ivoye, at that time governor of Bois-le-Duc and a general officer of the Dutch artillery, had received from the secretaries of M. Chamillard, the French Minister for the War Department. In these letters all the designs of France respecting Spain, Flanders, and the other countries that were the seat of war, were detailed: designs which the King of France conceived to be unknown to any person beside his minister and favourite, M. Chamillard.

This statesman, under the influence of a weakness fatal to his country, discovered them to his secretaries, who sold them again to the enemies of the king; and M. Ivoye had a round sum of money from the States of Holland for this business. It is indeed notorious, that this infamous traffic was carried on with more success under the administration of M. Chamillard than it had ever been before; it being extremely rare for Frenchmen to betray the interests of their monarch. Lord Lovat stayed with General Ferguson till after midnight: and the general told him that he would send his *valet-de-chambre* to introduce him again the next day by a private door.

In the morning, however, the commander found his garrison alarmed and mutinous. Some officers of the regiments of Orkney and Murray, relations and friends of Lord Athole, understood that Lord Lovat was in the town and had been addressed by several soldiers of the Fraser Clan, who were enlisted in their regiments. These gentlemen immediately spread a report, that he was come thither to debauch the Scottish garrison and induce them to desert. The officers in general had heard this report and represented it to their commander, desiring him to arrest Lord Lovat as an enemy to the State, and a partisan and emissary of France.

Upon this event General Ferguson despatched immediately a message to bring Lord Lovat incognito to his headquarters. He told him, with concern the great danger in which he was: that it was necessary he should disguise himself and set out upon the spot, since if the Dutch had the least rumour of the intelligence which had been spread by the Scottish officers it would be impossible for him to save his life, or hinder him from being cut into a thousand pieces. Lord Lovat thanked General Ferguson with great warmth, and told him that he was ready to set out instantly, provided he had the means of arriving in safety at Antwerp.

The affair was difficult, but Mr. Ferguson accomplished it by means of a sum of money, and by the assistance of a rich Dutch Roman Catholic merchant, whom he knew to be deeply attached to the French interest. This merchant brought to Mr. Ferguson and Lord Lovat a Catholic Postilion, whom he used when he went to Antwerp and Brussels in time of peace. The postilion had three saddle and one draught horse. He agreed to conduct Lord Lovat and his brother to Antwerp upon two of the saddle-horses, himself being mounted on the third; offering his little cart to convey Major Fraser and Lord Lovat's page. At the same time he demanded 100 *louis d'or* upon the spot in ready money, for the risk of his horses, and 50 for the risk of his life, both of them being forfeited in case of a discovery. Lord Lovat counted down the sum required, and, by the advice of Mr. Ferguson, disguised himself like a carter, in order to drive the cart out of the town. In this disguise he passed all the gates and redoubts of Bois-le-Duc.

Such is the story told by Lord Lovat in his *Memoirs*. It is a curious one, and scarcely consistent, in some of its details, with the career we have been tracing, or with the tradition of Brigadier Ferguson's family, which always represented him as a strong supporter of King William and the Protestant succession. When we are astonished by finding the commander of the Cameronians depicted as a Jacobite in disguise, we feel inclined to ask for more reliable testimony than the word of Lord Lovat, and remembering the confident opinions of General Mackay and Captain Pottinger, already quoted, as to his being "a man of probity and honour"—and old Mackay was well qualified to judge of probity—"faithful and enthusiastic in the service of King William," "vigorous and well affected," "of great diligence and zealously affected to the present government"—we seek for some other explanation of the hospitality afforded to the fugitive than is given in the confession, which he describes as made to him.

Nor is such difficult to discover. Apart from the natural feeling which would influence the general to protect "a kindly Scot" from the fury of the Dutch, there would be the desire to oblige his brother, and in the state of public affairs at the time, it was a much more grateful service to the Government to get a political busybody well away quietly, than to embarrass the Ministry with a State-trial. For during the reign of Anne, "a Stuart, yet Protestant, and prosperous," there was a tendency to treat the Jacobites leniently, and to regard their operations with half-closed eyes, until they became really serious, and it was the sudden resort to the opposite policy, with the triumph of the Whigs on her death, which precipitated the outbreak of 1715, and, in Bolingbroke's words, "dyed the royal ermines of a prince, no way sanguinary, in blood."

It is possible that Ferguson, like the great chief under whom he served, and many others, whose politics had been Tory though not Jacobite, having acted zealously in the Revolution, and .having, unlike Marlborough, served King William faithfully, had never wholly put out of sight the ultimate restoration of the old line under conditions securing the safety of the Protestant religion. We can well believe, that to him the words of the old covenanter at Dunse Law would have powerfully appealed—

> We desyred but to keep our own in the service of our prince, as our ancestors had done; we loved no new masters. Had our throne been voyd, and our voyces sought for the filling of Fer-

gus's chaire, we would have died ere any other had sitten down on that fatall marble but Charles alone.

There is an inherent improbability in one whose fidelity was not above suspicion being selected for such enterprises as he had been entrusted with in Scotland, or charged with the duties he is soon after found performing in the great campaign, which is strengthened by the conduct of his captors in 1689, and his own in 1690, while the articles under which the Cameronian regiment had been embodied stipulated "that all the officers of the regiment shall be such as in conscience and prudence, may with cordial confidence be submitted unto and followed"—"well affected, of approven fidelity, and of a sober conversation." Lovat, in describing his contemporaries, is always "over-violent or over-civil," and the strain of affectation which led him to pose as a classic patriot on the scaffold, inspires him to speak of transactions no better or worse than his own in language of elevated praise or equally eloquent abuse.

At this time a Jacobite plotter realised to his mind the ideal of heroic virtue, and to describe an acquaintance as such was probably intended as a high compliment. Certainly the sentences in which he speaks of Ferguson as "faithfully attached to King James," and "charmed to meet with a favourable occasion of shedding his blood for the restoration of his prince," have much more the ring of his peculiar personality, than of one who had been the trusted subordinate of Mackay, and friendly correspondent of Carstares, and was the superior of Elackader. They are far from harmonising with one or two references in a curious manuscript *Memoir*, written 40 years later by the daughter-in-law of Brigadier Ferguson, a lady whose sentiments may easily be gathered from a sentence in a letter written in 1746,[8] in which a clerical gentleman reminds his correspondent—

If you have any letters for Old Deer [9] remember that the Lady Kinmundy hath given it the name of Dear William.

It does not appear whether this remarkable, but fortunately evanescent designation was bestowed in honour of William of Orange or the Duke of Cumberland. The Lady Kinmundy refers with satisfaction to the fact that her husband's brother:—

Alone of all his father's family had been honoured to set up his

---

8. Printed in one of the Spalding Club Publications.
9. Old Deer was then included in the estate of Kinmundy.

standard about God's Tabernacle, I mean the Church of Scotland, and died a standard-bearer for the Protestant religion in the late French War, and was honoured to come over with our blessed deliverer, King William.

That the general talked politics in a guarded manner with an embarrassing guest, whose departure he was zealous in expediting is probable, and that Lovat misconceived or misrepresented the tenor of what passed is likely enough, but it does not appear that Fraser ever made any use in France of the information he says he received, and, even assuming the terms of the introduction to be correctly stated, it may be questioned whether they imported a very high degree of confidence. We may safely conclude that the effect of the General's wine had been to quicken Lord Lovat's always lively imagination, and that he romanced at length upon the foundation of a little Scottish hospitality in a foreign land. It is perhaps a coincidence worthy of notice that, when in 1746, Lovat was seized hiding in a hollow tree on an island in Loch Morar, by a party of sailors from the Furnace and Campbell Militia, the naval part of the force was commanded by a grand-nephew of the general who had entertained him at Bois-le-Duc. He met with less courtesy now, for as the sailors marched him off to the ship, the pipers of the Campbells played the Lovat March.

3

Brigadier at Bienheim

Malbrook s'en va t'en guerre.
—French air.

Lord Beaconsfield said:—

If there be any epoch of history more glorious, more satisfactory than another, it is the reign of Queen Anne. Then were our armies most brilliant with success, then were our victories most glorious; for even Waterloo, the most famed of battles, has not obliterated the memory of Blenheim.

And the high authority of Canning not only illustrates the reverence with which the men of a truly great time regard the past, but claims respect for the opinion that the reigns of William and Anne were "the best times of our history." Certainly the year 1704 was one of the most stirring in the annals of Great Britain, for there were all the elements which impress the mind in the contest she was carrying on. The scene of conflict was classic ground in military annals, and its fame "blazed broader yet in after years," yet the strife was to extend from the "Lowlands of Holland" to "Hie Germanie;" the forces were vast, and wielded by rare genius; and the adversary was that "old France," at once so chivalrous and mighty, then at the height of her power and prestige. The ostensible cause was the question "to which lion's paw," the Spanish Succession was to fall, but the real interests at stake in the earlier years of the war, were the Protestant Religion and the Balance of Power.

It was one of "those great conjunctures which call all the principal powers of the Continent into the field," and in Marlborough and Prince Eugene, its issue was to be determined by men equal to the occasion. Hitherto the war had dragged on without any decisive achievements, but now the crisis was at hand. The "*Grand Monarque*" had developed his great scheme for striking at the heart of the Empire, and Marlborough had resolved on a decisive effort to meet it, on which hung the fate of the civilised world. The English Cabinet had been re-organised by the admission of Harley and St. John; and in the spring Marlborough had set his troops in motion for that march to the Moselle, which was not to terminate till he had ascended the Rhine, and driven the veterans of France fugitives into the Danube.

Throughout this campaign the duke seems to have relied greatly on the experience and energy of Brigadier Ferguson, whenever there was special work to be done. He was to commit the care of his base and the defence of the line of the Meuse and the Low Countries to Dutch troops, and desired to review these forces in a body before finally embarking on his great enterprise. It was, therefore, necessary to temporarily supply their places in the garrisons, and especially at Maestricht, with British troops, and for this purpose, a body of four thousand men was ordered out of the several British garrisons in Holland in the beginning of March. A Journal of the campaign has preserved the exact route followed by this force, and the name of the officer to whom the command was entrusted. On the 9th of March all the detachments, from their several garrisons, joined at the Bosch, under the Honourable Brigadier Ferguson's command.

10th—The brigadier, with the said command, marched from the Bosch to, and cantoned in Osch, four leagues.

11th—Marched from Osch village to, and cantoned in the village of Wanray, five leagues.

12th—Marched from Wanray to, and cantoned in Grounock village, four leagues.

14th—Marched from Grounock to, and cantoned in Griffen-Swaert, on the west side of the Maes, near unto Venlo; and the next day crossed the Maes early in the morning, and marched thence through Roermonde to, and cantoned in and about the village of Harten (five leagues), a little southward from Roermonde; where the brigadier left Major Cornwallis with a reinforcement of nine hundred men, being the detachment of three battalions.

16th—The brigadier, with the rest, marched from Hart to, and cantoned in Spaubeck—six leagues.

17th—Marched from Spaubeck into, and reinforced Maestricht—three leagues. This journey contains about thirty-nine leagues.

21st—The Holland's garrison marched out of Maestricht, and left the keeping thereof to Brigadier Ferguson with the English detachment, and joined a great body of their own and auxiliary troops on Peter's Hill on the west side of the town."

For about five weeks, Ferguson seems to have commanded the garrison of Maestricht, and they must have been weeks full of occupation.

The Duke of Marlborough says his biographer Archdeacon Cox:—

> Reached Maestricht on the 10th of May. Here he continued till the 14th actively employed in assembling and organizing the army, superintending the formation of magazines, and pressing the march of the troops to the place of rendezvous.

On the 11th he reviewed the army, and the same day he wrote to the future Bolingbroke.

> On Wednesday next they pass the Meuse at Ruremond on their march towards the Moselle, and I may venture to tell you (though I would not have it public as yet) I design to march a great deal higher into Germany.

The quaint old town of Maestricht, with its spacious market places, and high sloping roofs, must then have been a busy place with troops marching, ammunition trains being despatched, and the conviction in the minds of all which the arrival of "the Great Captain" inspired, that a great enterprise was about to be entered on. Those who reflected on what lay before them, must have felt that if a splendid opportunity awaited them, they were also going to encounter great peril, and little as was known of the ultimate aim of the general, it was evident that the result of the campaign just opening must be either unequalled triumph or complete disaster. The military ascendancy of France in Europe had been for years unquestioned, and the prestige of the French soldiery was yet unbroken. The circumstances of 1704, were perhaps most nearly paralleled when the British infantry, under Sir John Stuart, gave the first check to the legions of Napoleonic France on the field of Maida, in 1806, but Blenheim was to be the Maida and Waterloo of that war in one.

The British had, it is true, fought with stubborn gallantry in the previous war amid the slaughter of Steinkirk and the carnage of Landen, and drawn from the reserved William the exclamation "See my brave English," but in both these battles the victory had been to the French, and they might have pointed to that practical demonstration which Marlborough was soon to cite to Tallard, which gives the pre-eminence over even "the best troops in Europe" to *ceux qui les ont battus*. And whatever reliance their own commanders might place on the mettle of the British troops, the bulk of the confederate army was composed of allies and auxiliaries. Had it been a question of reckoning probabilities, the odds would have been given largely in favour of France, and for those about to march under Marlborough's command, the occasion, if a very stirring, was also a solemn one. The bare dates even of musty documents become instinct with life, and even private papers of trivial importance have some public interest, when they speak of exciting surroundings and an important moment.

It is therefore not uninteresting to notice that Brigadier Ferguson, amid all the bustle of preparation for the march, found time to review and regulate his private affairs, and settle their disposal in the event of his falling in the battles about to be fought. "At Maestricht, the 12th day of May, 1704," is the place and date of a settlement of accounts between him and his nephew, Mr. James Ferguson of Pitfour, an advocate at the Scots bar, who managed his affairs in Scotland for him. It would seem as if the constant occupation involved in preparing his command efficiently for the campaign had rendered it necessary to delay finally setting in order his personal concerns, till the moment of leisure which often intervenes at the last between the completion of preparation and the commencement of action.

His will bears the same date, and purports to have been written by Mr. James Ferguson, advocate, but if the frame of the bequeathing clauses evidences the nephew's legal knowledge, the introductory sentences may perhaps be taken as preserving no mere words of style, but as showing the hand of the commander of the Cameronians himself. "Many a trait of character," the noble and cultured author of the *Lives of the Lindsays*, writes "may be read in the language and provisions of a will of the olden time," and "these intimations, so gratifying to posterity," are in this case at least characteristic of the time and the man:—

> Be it known to all men be thes present letters, me Brigadier James ffergusone of Bomakellie, forasmuch as noe thing is more

certain as death, nor more uncertaine as the time and manner thereof, And I being most earnest and desireous to leave my worldly affaires cleare where ever it pleases God to remove me from this transitory life, And being at present in perfect health of Body, and soundness in minde, Doe therefore make this my Latter Will and Testament as after follows to wit, I bequeath my Soul to God Allmighty to be saved by the allone merits of his only son, and my Lord and Redeemer, and I recommend my body to be decently and honourably Interred where it pleases God to call me. And for my worldly affaires and substance I dispose of them in manner following &c.

Two days later the bulletin, dated Maestricht, 14th May, 1704, contained the announcement:—

Our detachment under the command of Brigadier Ferguson will march from hence tomorrow, and my Lord Duke of Marlborough having concerted measures with the generals here will follow on Friday, and on Sunday we shall join all the English troops at Bedburg, near Cologne, and so pursue our march towards Coblenz.

On the Friday evening Marlborough caught up Ferguson's detachment, and marched with them from near Linnick to Bedburg where they joined the English forces and train of artillery under General Churchill.

Brigadier Ferguson's command was composed of a battalion of the First Guards (Grenadiers), a battalion of Orkney's Regiment (the 1st of the Line or Royal Scots), and Ingoldsby's (the 23rd or Welsh Fusiliers). It was a fine brigade, and bore the brunt of the fighting in the operations that followed, for it led and sustained the attack on the Schellenberg, and at Blenheim shared with Rowe's Brigade the protracted struggle round the strongest part of the French position. Without delay Marlborough pressed forward the execution of his grand design. From Bonn, marching early in the morning, and resting during the heat of the day, he proceeded up the left bank of the Rhine, "the stores and sick being sent up the river in boats, the men marching along joyously, quenching their thirst in Rhenish wines." At Coblentz he crossed the river, and advanced to Mayence, where the army was reviewed before the Elector, who was so much struck with the appearance of the troops that, alluding to an entertainment to be given in the evening to the officers, he remarked, "These gentlemen appear to be all dressed for the ball."

At last, at the end of June, the allied army found itself in front of the fortified height of Schellenberg, the key of Donauwerth, which they were anxious to secure as a *place d'armes* for the invasion of Bavaria. This position, strong by nature, and strengthened by art, was occupied by a Gallo-Bavarian force of 12000 men, whose right rested on the Danube and their left on the covered way of Donauwerth, while a line of entrenchments, uncompleted but formidable, ran along their front. Marlborough determined to lose no time in attacking, and, without waiting for the arrival of the main body of the Imperialists, selected a picked body of 6000 foot, to lead the assault. They were supported by 30 squadrons, and three battalions of Austrian Grenadiers on the right. A forlorn hope of 50 grenadiers of the English Guards, led by Lord Mordaunt, (of whom only ten, besides himself, came out of the action,) preceded them, and at six o'clock in the evening of the 2nd July, "they proceeded upon the attack, Brigadier Ferguson leading up the first line of foot, Count Horn and the other generals bringing up the rest: Lieutenant-General Goor commanding the whole."

They pressed forward exposed to a storm of grape from the entrenchments in front, and a flanking fire from the works of Donauwerth, and as they got nearer, the the enemy loaded with case which did "very great execution." The first discharge of musketry struck down General Goor, and many other officers, and an unfortunate error by which the men mistook a ravine they had to cross for the ditch of the entrenchment, and flung in their fascines, caused a momentary hesitation. The enemy then "came out of their trenches with bayonets in their pieces, but they were quickly obliged to return to them again," for the Guards stood their ground bravely, and the rest of Ferguson's Brigade "coming up at this critical moment rushed forward to their support."

But though the enemy were driven back into their lines, these were not yet won, and the defence was so vigorous that the assailants were twice repulsed, and the carnage was great. Then Lord John Hay dismounted his dragoons (the Scots Greys), and brought them up to the aid of the infantry, and the Imperialists forcing an entrance where the lines had been denuded of their defenders, called to meet the principal attack, the whole pressed forward, the entrenchment was carried, and the enemy fled in confusion.

The Duke of Marlborough coming in with the first of our

squadrons, found our foot pursuing the enemy, and, therefore, ordered Brigadier Ferguson to keep them to their colours and continue upon the field of battle, whilst he made a clear stage of the enemy with the horse only.

In this action, which Marlborough described as "the warmest that has been known for many years," and Blackader in his diary, as "one of the hottest I have seen," the regiments composing Ferguson's Brigade "suffered more than any others." Of his own regiment, the Cameronians, apparently not in his own brigade, only a detachment of 130 men were engaged; of its officers, Capt. Lawson and Lieut. Seaton were wounded, and it lost one sergeant and 18 privates killed, and three sergeants and fifty-seven privates wounded. The victory was complete, though its lustre soon paled before that of Blenheim; and the emperor, conscious that it had saved the House of Austria, might well write to Marlborough—

> This will be an eternal trophy to your most serene Queen in Upper Germany, whither the victorious arms of the English Nation have never penetrated since the memory of man.

A month passed in marches, negotiations, and laying waste the lands of the Elector of Bavaria; and again on the 12th of August, the combined troops of Marlborough and Eugene, confronted the united forces of Marshall Tallard and the Elector. The allied generals on that morning advanced, accompanied by the battalion of Guards from Ferguson's Brigade, of which Marlborough was himself colonel, and from the Tower of Dapfheim Church, observed the quartermasters of the Gallo-Bavarian army marking out their camp on the rising ground beyond the Nebel. They then returned to the camp of their own army behind the Kessel, and made preparations for attacking the enemy the next day. The French and Bavarian army, largely outnumbering the allies, stretched from the Danube, on which their right rested, to the high ground, bounding on the north the valley through which it flowed, and as the river was nowhere fordable, they could only be attacked in front.

The steep banks and marshy bottom through which the Nebel flowed down to the Danube presented an obstacle to the assailants, and several villages lent additional strength to the defence. Of these, the most important was Blenheim, on the right of the French position, and the advantages afforded by the houses and garden walls were increased by the construction of entrenchments, barricades, and palisades. It was occupied by a force of twenty-two battalions and six squadrons of the *élite* of the French Army, supported by artillery, which swept the approaches, and was regarded by Tallard as the most important part of his line. Indeed, his throwing so many men into Blenheim, by weakening his centre, largely contributed to lose him the battle, but it very much increased the difficulty and danger of the task allotted to the brigades directed against the village.

The British Army moved forward from their encampment early in the morning of the 13th, and picking up the force under Major-General Wilkes, which had been pushed forward the day before to secure the pass of Dapfheim, advanced in nine columns, and deployed into order of battle about seven o'clock. Lord Cutts had command of the ninth column, "upon the left of all by itself next the Danube," composed of Rowes' and Ferguson's British brigades, Hulsen's Hessian infantry, and the British cavalry under Wood and Ross. "Lord Cutts had orders with these troops to attack the village of Blenheim."

Marlborough's attack was delayed by the time required by Prince Eugene's forces to come into line of battle on the right. Divine service was performed by the chaplains at the head of each regiment, and Marlborough was "observed to join with peculiar fervour in this solemn appeal to the Giver of Victory." He then rode along the lines to find his troops impatient for the signal, narrowly escaping a French cannon ball which passed beneath his charger and covered him with earth. Under a heavy artillery fire, the British soldiers established six bridges over the Nebel.

At last, about mid-day, hearing that Prince Eugene was ready, Marlborough ordered Lord Cutts to begin the attack on Blenheim. His troops, descending to the Nebel, took possession of two water mills on its banks under a heavy fire of grape, and continued their advance up the slope, receiving the first small-arm discharge of the enemy at thirty paces. Rowe, whose brigade was leading, struck his sword into the palisades before he gave the order to fire, but in a few minutes he fell mortally wounded; his lieutenant-colonel and major were killed trying to carry him off; one-third of his men had dropped, and the brigade shattered and disordered, fell back on the Hessians. Cox says:—

> The enemy having placed four additional pieces of artillery upon the height near Blenheim, swept the fords of the Nebel with grapeshot. But, notwithstanding this destructive fire, the

brigades of Ferguson and Hulsen crossed near the lower watermill, and advanced in front of the village. The enemy therefore withdrew the guns within their defences and met the attack with such vigour that, after three successive repulses, the assailants halted under cover of the rising ground.

Lediard writes:—

> Whilst Row's brigade rallied themselves, that of Ferguson commanded by himself attacked the village of Blenheim on the left, but with no better success; and though both returned three or four times to the charge, with equal vigour, yet were they both still repulsed with like disadvantage, so that it was found impossible to force the enemy in that post without entirely sacrificing the infantry.

General Sir Frederick Hamilton thus describes the nature of the deadly combat in which those troops were engaged:—

> Upon Rowe's and Ferguson's Brigades crossing the Nebel, they halted under cover of the bank to reform. The First Guards, under Colonel Philip Dormer, were on the right of Ferguson's Brigade, and as they ascended the ridge which at first concealed them from the view of the troops in Blenheim, they found themselves opposite the centre of that village exposed to the direct musketry fire of its garrison. The soldiers, reserving their fire, steadily advanced in the most intrepid manner towards the palisades by which it was defended, but a deadly volley at thirty paces distant struck down many a gallant fellow, while the rest rushing forward attempted by sheer strength to drag away the palings; they fired through the intervals, or struck at the Frenchmen with their swords and clubbed muskets wherever an opportunity offered itself; but all efforts were unavailing. Dormer commanding the battalion was killed: Mordaunt lost an arm: and young Campion, one of the ensigns, was desperately wounded in the nearly successful attempt to pull away the wooden barrier.

> The French cavalry charged the right of Rowe's disordered troops, and were in turn charged by the British horse, who, coming under the fire of Blenheim, fell back behind the Hessians.

> In the meantime, Ferguson's Brigade with the First Guards, al-

ready much reduced by their gallant attack at Schellenberg, and by the stubborn resistance of the garrison of Blenheim, assisted now by the Hanoverians, renewed their attempt upon that village, but without cannon to breach the palisading, their efforts were again unavailing, and they stood exposed to the murderous fire of the garrison, until Marlborough, who had not been previously aware of the extraordinary strength of the post, desired Lord Cutts to withdraw for a time under the shelter of the rising ground.

Earned though they were in their endeavours to force an entrance, the troops of Lord Cutts held the ground they had won, and kept the twenty-two battalions occupying Blenheim employed until the battle was decided elsewhere, and it was from the tenacity with which he stood his ground in front of the village, in spite of the storm of bullets that came from it, that Lord Cutts received the designation of "the Salamander that lives in fire." After the French centre had been driven off the field in confusion, the veterans posted in Blenheim maintained their own, and as they were many in numbers, and in a very strong position, the task in which Lord Cutts had failed, seemed no easy one for the whole Allied Army. General Churchill took post in rear of the village, resting his right on the Danube, Lord Orkney approached from the north, while Lord Cutts, again advancing with Ferguson's and Rowe's Brigades, threatened it from the side of the Nebel. For some time there was sharp fighting, but it was the interest of both sides to put a stop to a struggle which might be bloody for the victors, and must be fruitless on the part of the vanquished. The French proposed to capitulate, but General Churchill insisted on unconditional surrender.

> No resource remained: to resist was hopeless, to escape impossible. With despair and indignation the troops submitted to their fate, and the regiment of Navarre in particular burnt their colours, and buried their arms, that such trophies might not remain to grace the triumph of an enemy. Twenty-four battalions and twelve squadrons, surrendered themselves prisoners of war; and thus closed the mighty struggle of this eventful day.

General Hamilton says:—

> The trophies of this victory, which saved the Austrian Empire, and for the time destroyed the power of France in central Eu-

rope, consisted of 100 guns, 24 mortars, 129 colours, 171 standards, 17 pair of kettledrums, 3600 tents &c. &c. The loss of the enemy in men was also very great, and the number of prisoners and deserters raised their total casualties to more than 40,000 men before the dispirited remains of the French army reached Strasbourg.

The victorious army bivouacked on the field of battle, and the weary troops, who had accomplished the march of the morning, and sustained the stress of the struggle round the village, forming a hollow square round the great crowd of prisoners "continued on their arms all night to secure them." Lediard, after mentioning the officers of higher rank who specially distinguished themselves, adds, "and Row, Ferguson, and Bernsdorff, Brigadiers of Foot, deserve particularly to be mentioned, for their great bravery and prudent conduct," and Oldmixon includes Ferguson in a similar list of those "whose names ought to live with honour as long as history can preserve them."

Though not forming part of the brigade he commanded, Ferguson's own regiment was hotly engaged, and interesting information as to its fortunes in the battle is afforded by a document headed "A State of the Respective Companys of the Regiment under the command of Brigadier James Ferguson after the battle of Blenheim, distinguishing the commission officers that were killed, wounded, or absent by sickness or order, and the non-commission that were killed, wounded, or absent by sickness or order, and the non-commission officers and soldiers that were disabled. As also an account of the widows and children of such officers as were killed." Among the officers the casualties were heavy.

Those present after the battle were, Colonel and Captain Brigadier Ferguson, Lieutenant-Colonel and Captain Livingston, Major and Captain Borthwick, Captain Cranston of the Grenadier Company, Captains Blackader, Munro, and Drummond, Lieutenants Dickson, Wilson, Douglas, Lindsay, John Ferguson, Bernard, Weems, and Ensigns Simpson, Dalrymple, Oliphant, Marshall, and Ogilvie, with the following staff-officers:—Adjutant Forge (?) Quarter-Master Stevenson, Surgeons Stewart and Man, and Chaplain Pitcairn. There were wounded Lieut.-Colonel Livingston, Captain Blackader, Captain Borthwick, Captain Lawson (hit at Schellenberg) and Captain Wilson, Lieutenants Robert Ferguson, Wilson, Leonard Ferguson, and Ensigns Dalrymple, Oliphant, Marshall, and Ogilvie, and Quartemaster Stevenson. Absent on order were Major Borthwick, Captain Aikman, Lieutenant Drummond and Ensign Morris, and through sickness Captain Hamilton and Ensign Gray.

Killed on the spot were Captains Campbell and Stewart, Lieutenants Seaton, Moncrief, and Douglas; Ensigns Hay, Bernard, Low, Maclain and Balfour. Seaton left a widow and three children, Moncrief a widow and one child, and Hay and Bernard each a widow. One sergeant and two corporals out of 34 sergeants and 33 corporals were disabled. There had been present before the battle 24 drummers, and 538 private soldiers, and the column which records the losses is unfortunately mutilated, so that it is only possible to read the first two figures which are 16. The paper which seems to have been an exact copy of the return actually sent in, is docquetted:—

> London,—of feby.,—1704/5, this is a true state of my regt. after the battle of Hoghstate.—Ja. Ferguson.

Another document entitled "The State of the Honorable Brigadier Ffergusone's Regt. after the two actions in Germanie, 1704," gives a complete roll of each company signed by "the commanding officer present with each company." [10] There were 13 companies, but one only mustered 20 rank and file, and the strongest 46. The state of the brigadier's own company is signed by his subaltern, "Ro^t. ffergusone"; and the whole was "justified and attested" as "just and conform to the state of the regiment," by himself, at the Bosch, in April, 1705.

The names of the officers speak for themselves, and from those of the rank and file, there can be no doubt as to the thoroughly Scottish character of the regiment. There had been taken prisoners no less than 11,000 men, and on the night of the battle, "our regiment," says Blackader, "was one of those that guarded them." 5,678 were assigned to Marlborough as his share, and their disposal raised a question of some difficulty, on account of their numbers, and the want of a place to secure them. Brigadier Ferguson was finally detached with five British battalions, to march them to Mayence, and take them down the Rhine. The bulletin, dated camp at Weissembourg, 12th September, 1704, states—

> Brig. Ferguson is marched this morning with five battalions of foot, *viz*., one of the royal regiment, (1st), General Churchill's, the Lord North and Grey's, Brig. Row's (21st Scots Fusiliers),

---

10. This is in duplicate, one copy having the actual signatures.

and Brig. Meredyth's regiments for Mayence, where they are to embark with the French prisoners, and conduct them to Holland.

And, on the 7th October, Marlborough wrote to the brigadier, (see letter following), ordering him to arrange for the disposal of the troops in the Dutch garrisons, with M. Slingelandt on behalf of the States. At Mayence, the Brigadier was joined by Captain Blackader, who had gone to the baths at Wiesbaden to recruit, and who now seems to have obtained from him the orders he had been hoping for, to go to Scotland in search of men to fill the vacancies caused by the campaign, as he accompanied him to Holland, and before long found he "was the first has yet reached Edinburgh, of any that were at the battles in Germany."

******

Note:—
    The Duke of Marlborough to Brigadier Ferguson.
            Au camp de Weissembourg le 7 Octobre, 1704.

Monsieur,
MM. Les Etats ayant souhaités que les cinq bataillons qui sont partis d'ici avec vous, et quatre autres des troupes Anglaises qui doivent s'embarquer en peu de jours puissent être disposés dans les garnisons sélon la Memoire ci-joint, je vous prie de regler le tout avec M. Slingelandt comme il se trouvera le plus commode pour les troupes eu égard aux quartiers où les cinq bataillons seront à présent, et de donner ses ordres aux quatre bataillons qui viennent á Nimègue á l'avenant; en cas que nous n'en envoyions pas deux droit á Ruremonde, dont on aura soin de vous avertir. Et comme leurs H. P. pouraient encore demander trois des regiments qui ont reste tout cet ete en garnison á Breda et Bois-le-Duc pour marcher á Maestricht, vous devez en ce cas donner les ordres á ceux qui sont dans le meilleur état de marcher deux de Breda, et un de Bois-le-Duc, selon les patentes quils recevront de M. M. les Etats.

       Je suis Monsieur, &c,   M.
           ******

At Nimeguen, the French prisoners were handed over to the Dutch authorities; three of the British regiments marched to Breda and two to Bois-le-Duc. The brigadier probably accompanied the latter, for about Christmas time he was married at Bois-le-Duc to Hester Elizabeth, daughter of Herr Abraham Hibelet "*predicant van der Waalse*

Gemeente"—i.e.. Pastor of the Walloon or Belgian Protestant church, there. Their marriage contract bears to have been signed *"binnen s' Hertogen-Bosch in huyse van de toekomende Bruyfs Vader op den ses en twintigste (26th) decetnber, seventien hondert vier"* and on the next day they were formally betrothed, (see note following), in the *"groote kerk"* or beautiful cathedral of Bois-le-Duc. They must soon have made a hurried visit to England, possibly in time to share in the last of the great rejoicings for the victories, for the brigadier signed papers in London in February, and his little children were sent up from Kirktonhill to meet him there.

******

Note:—I am indebted to the courtesy of M. Van der Does de Willebois, *burgomaster* of Bois-le-duc in 1887, for extracts from the registers of that town authenticating the betrothal, and the baptism of a daughter in the following year. The first is in these terms—*"Dat op den Zeven en twintigste der maand December Zeventein honderd vier alhier is onder trouwrd in de groote kerk de Herr Jacob Ferguson, weed? (weduwenaar), Brigadier van de troupen van haer Majesteyt van groot Brittagne met Jufforouwe Hester Elizabeth Gibelet j.d. (jonge-dochter) van den Bosch, wonende in de nieuwstraat.*
de tweede gebod opheden en het derde als toekomende Sondag te proclameren—den derden January, 1705."

The second is—

*"Dat op den elfden (11th) der maand Octobre Zeventein honderd vyf alhier is gedoopt in de Waalsche kerk; Anna Elizabeth nee le 8 Octobre fille de Monsieur Jacob Ferguson Brigadier des troupes Angloises de sa Majeste Britannique et de Madame Hester Elizabeth Hibelet, aiant pour parain et pour maraine Monsieur et Madame Hibelet grand-pere et grand-mere du susdit enfan*t."

******

In the campaign of 1705, in which the army acting on the Moselle experienced such hardships that "the Scots thought an army in their Highlands could shift better," and in which Marlborough performed the feat of forcing the French lines in Brabant, till then deemed impregnable, and nearly anticipated Wellington on the field of Waterloo, (see note following), Ferguson's brigade consisted of his own regiment, the Cameronians or 26th, the 16th, the 28th, and Stringer's, subsequently disbanded.

✶✶✶✶✶✶

Note:—On 2nd January, 1705, the Duke of Marlborough wrote to Major-General Wood from St. James's. "Application has been made here by the States Minister, that you might, upon any extraordinary occasion, be ordered to furnish proportionable detachments out of the Queen's forces as the service should require, which, being already in the instructions you have received, I shall add nothing on that subject more than to desire you will take care to communicate the same to Brigadier Ferguson and to the several garrisons, that they may comply therewith, so as, however, to have all due regard to the preservation of the troops, it being not intended by this that they should change their quarters, but only send out detachments on any emergency. I must likewise desire you will inform the brigadier, and the several regiments of foot at the same time, with Her Majesty's pleasure, that they provide as little wheel baggage for the campaign as possible, concerning which you may expect a regulation by the next post."

The diary previously quoted mentions that, on April 20th, 1705; Brigadier Ferguson, with the garrison of the Bosch, set out therefrom, all in great expedition, towards Maestricht, where our general rendezvous was intended," and tells how the brigadier, picking up the garrisons of Venlo and Ruremonde, "passed Maestricht and pitched at Buzee village, on the west bank of the river Maes, halfway between Maestricht and Liége, somewhat apart from Holland army, in Marshal Overquerque's command, who had then joined and lay encamped on Peter's hill, near the citadel of Maestricht."

Vide also Captain Blackader's diary and letters, for 1705, (April 12-August 20).

✶✶✶✶✶✶

He was not destined to share in the future triumphs of Ramilies and Oudenarde, for he died very suddenly at Bois-le-Duc on the 22nd October, 1705, a few days after the birth of his daughter. The tradition of his family attributes his death to poison. The old-fashioned words of an old MS. Are:—

He served in four reigns, still maintaining the character of a brave, valiant, and prudent officer, until his fame raising envy in the breast of the then commanding officer, he was cut off by very sinister means.

An entry in the diary which Colonel Blackader, to the mortification of the historical student, devoted rather to the record of his own personal religious experiences than the interesting events amid which he lived, illustrates how great a shock the news was to his friends:—

> I got the surprising account of our brigadier's death, with which I was greatly affected. *Man's breath goeth out, to earth he turns, that day his thoughts perish.* Oh the vanity of human grandeur! He was just come from court, where he was sent for that he might be raised a step higher for his services.

In accounts connected with the funeral, and letters written afterwards, he is described as major-general, and his name appears among the major-generals (1705) in the records of the British Army. But those who gave instructions for the inscription on his tombstone, designed him by the rank by which they were accustomed to know him; and the following letter from the Duke of Marlborough to M. Hibelez, reads somewhat strangely in the light of a promotion received for services in the field.

> *Au Camp de Calmpt-hout, le 24 Octobre, 1705.*
>
> Monsieur;
> *J'ai été bien affligé, je vous assure, de la triste nouvelle que vous venez me mander de la mort de M. Ferguson. C'était un officier de mérite pour lequel j'avais beaucoup d'estime, et que je ne puis assez regretter: le public y a une grande perte, aussi blen que sa famllle. Il est vrai que je faisais état d'abord que je serais arrivé en Angleterre, de prier la Reine de le faire général-major, et je ne doute point que S. M. y aurait consenti. Vous pouvez aussi faire fond que partout où il dependra de moi, je tâcherai de faire voir le cas que je fais de sa mémoire. Je vous prie d'en assurer Madame Ferguson et de me croire très-parfaitement.*
>
> Monsieur, votre, &c., M"

His name, however, occurs once again in the despatches, for replying on 28th January, 1706, to letters of the Earl of Galway who then commanded the British forces in the Peninsula, the duke wrote—

> By the former you desire Mr. Ferguson might be spared to supply the place of major-general in Portugal, but he had been dead near two months before the date of your letter.

"This day," says Blackader, writing in his diary two days after the former entry, "we were employed in the funeral of our brigadier;" and a few old accounts connected with the last scene have a certain melancholy interest, as showing how the obsequies of a general officer were conducted in those days in the Dutch garrisons. Eighty-four officers were provided with black scarves and gloves, twelve sergeants with crape, scarves, ribands, and gloves, and twenty-one ells of black cloth were obtained to cover twenty-one drums. There is an item for crape to cover Captain Ferguson's hat; so much for "24 ells of crape for ye four colours, six ells to each;" so much "for flambows and the men that bear them;" so much "more to the twelve sergeants that bore his corps to the grave;" so much "more for a sergeant and eighteen men who was the guard of his corps until his interment;" and a sum "payed to Bertram where the officers met with Captain Lawson."

The town of Bois-le-Duc rises out of a broad plain, which, in winter, becomes an extensive marsh, and with its imposing ramparts, bastions, and moat (as yet almost untouched), still recalls the days of the Grand Alliance, when it formed winter quarters and base of operations for the hosts of Marlborough. Above the ramparts cluster the red tiled roofs, and above them again is seen the pile of the beautiful cathedral of St. John, situated in the highest part of the town. The floor of the cathedral, perhaps the finest in the Dutch dominions, is covered with tombstones bearing the escutcheons of the *noblesse* of North Brabant, but in the choir is a simple slab showing these inscriptions. (See note following).

D. O. M. S.
d. Abr. Hibelet.
Ecclesle Gallo-Belg
Pastor.
obiit 2 mail
MDCCXX.
De H. Ed. Gestr. Heer Iames Ferguson.
A
Brigad.-General, &c.
obiit xxii oct.
MDCCV.

★★★★★★

Note:—M. Hezenmans "*l'archiviste de Bois-le-Duc*" has been good enough to furnish the following note on these abbreviations. "*Pierre tombale dans la cathedrale St. Jean à Bois-le-Duc (Hol-*

lande.) Coté sud-est du choeur. La seconde partie de 1'inscription se lit: De Hoog Edel Gestrenge Heer, &c." These words were the Dutch style of an officer of rank, and would be translated literally as "the high, noble, and powerful *seigneur*," or perhaps more accurately, as "the right honourable and gallant gentleman."

Curiously enough, in formal documents the date of General Ferguson's death has been variously given. That on the stone agrees with the Duke of Marlborough's letter, and perhaps, also, allowing for the difference of style with the date given in a paper headed "Brigr. ffergusone his abstract ending 11th October, 1705, he died," and also with Blackader's entry, which is dated the 13th. But, the Inventory prefixed to a formal copy of his will, bears to be of the goods belonging to "Umq^{ll} Brigadier ffergusone, of Bomekellie, the time of his deceise, who deceised at the Bosch, in Braband, the 14th day of October, 1705 years, faithfully made and given up be himselfe at Mastrich, the 12th day of May, 1704 years."

My first knowledge of the stone described above was obtained on a visit to Bois-le-Duc in 1887; and a more careful examination of old accounts on returning to Scotland, disclosed one in Dutch which contained entries of "*2 uuren luyden der klocken in de groote kerk*," and "*Het graft in 't choor.*"

One or two entries in the abstract corroborate Blackader's statement.

	Gilders,
16th October.—To ye Brigadier's Landslady and his fraught, from the Hague to Rotterdam, . . .	13 17
To Mr. Verdure at ye Hague, p. discharge given the Brigadier there,	173 0
17th.—for Lomond's at Rotterdam, Coach hier and passage money from Rotterdam to Gorkom, and for two botles of Bruntt Claret—in all,	10 0

******

The scene underneath the lofty arches of St. Jan's Kerk must have been an impressive one, on the October morning when the sergeant and 18 men moved up from the citadel beside the harbour with their charge, while the officers clustered round with their black scarves, and the colours and the drums were seen draped in black. Captain Lawson who took charge of the interment, and was a tutor under the will, would be busy and active; Lieut.-Colonel Borthwick wondering if the command was to come to him, which ultimately was given out of the regiment, and Captain Blackader musing on "the vanity of human grandeur." And when next the Scottish soldiers marched from Bois-le-Duc, one well-known figure was missing at their head; his charger was ridden by Major-General Murray; and the infant [11] baptized a few days before, and the elder children far away in Britain were never to meet in the home on the banks of the North Esk.

General Ferguson was succeeded in the command of the Cameronians by the Earl of Stair, who, on 13th January, 1706, granted a discharge to his children and executors, for "any sums laid out by me for arms and accoutrements for the use of the deceased Major-General Ferguson's Regiment, to whom I succeeded." Blackader's diary has told us the sensation of his comrades-in-arms on hearing of his death; Luttrell's preserves the ideas of the public.

Sat., Oct. 20, 1705. Yesterday we had three Dutch posts which advise ... that Major-General Ferguson is dead in Holland, and much lamented, being an officer of great experience.

Such is the story to which the old commissions led us, of the career of one who worked his way like a true Aberdeenshire Scot, and did his duty well in spheres continuously enlarging. As soldier of fortune, in civil strife, and in a more satisfactory position in the armies of his country abroad, he manifested the same qualities—if not so distinguished, at least happier in their final direction—which in his countrymen, Gordon of Auchleuchries and Keith of Inverugie, were so valuable to Peter the Great and Frederick of Prussia. He had been

---

11. The daughter, who so early lost her father, passed her life in Holland, marrying in 1730, M. Gerard Vink, Advocate, of Bois-le-Duc, grandson of M. Nieupoort, Ambassador to England, and brother of the Comptroller-General of the Dutch Fortifications. Madame Ferguson married again, her husband being Captain Hendrick Chombach. In the *"Naam Lijst en Wapen kaart der Leden van de Regering de Pensionarissen Griffiers en Secretarissen van 's Hertogen Bosch,"* a record of all those who have held honourable office in Bois le-Duc, since its conquest by the Dutch, occur the names and arms of M. Johan Hibelet, Madame Ferguson's brother, who married a grand-daughter of the famous Admiral Tromp, of M. Bastide, her brother-in-law, of M. Chombach, one of her sons by her second marriage, and of M. Vink, a relative of her son-in-law. Her other son (Chombach) entered the Dutch Army.

fortunate in his opportunities, for he seems to have been present at nearly every action of magnitude in which the British troops were engaged during his life-time, except the Battle of the Boyne.

The fell carnage of Killiecrankie had made him a major, the strewn fields of Steinkirk and Landen gave the remaining steps of regimental rank. The study of biography as subordinate and ancillary to history, affording sidelights and filling up the background, is calculated to correct an erroneous impression apt to be produced when we confine ourselves to accompanying the formal and dignified march of the national narrative. For there is a tendency to lose sight of the connection in the chain of events, and to consider different reigns and epochs, as if they were rather successive plays put upon the stage, than the development in various acts of one great drama. Nor is this tendency counteracted by the lives of those who performed the principal parts, and whose careers were crowded with events, for then we seem to be reading annals rather than memoirs, and time is forgotten in following action.

But, as in ordinary life some small circumstance sometimes calls up the past in its relation to the present, so for those who care to note it, and amuse themselves by reading between the lines of history, the reappearance of some personage unknown to fame, furnishes a standard with which to measure others, lets in a sudden light on a dry narrative, and points out better than the moralizing it suggests, how events grew out of each other which on the page of history seem very far apart. Killiecrankie and Blenheim are names which call up a totally different set of associations, yet the story we have been tracing shows that from one point of view they were only separated by the distance between major and general. Borthwick, the major of the Cameronians in the campaign of 1704, had been wounded in the fierce fight at Dunkeld; and a captain who was hit at Schellenberg, was again severely wounded in the action at Preston in Lancashire, which quelled the first Jacobite insurrection.

The father of Brigadier Ferguson had mustered under the banner of Lord Huntly in the Scottish "Troubles"; one grand-nephew was narrowly to miss capturing Prince Charles and Flora Macdonald after Culloden; while another received "a very high compliment" from Admiral Rodney for his conduct in the naval action off Guadaloupe in 1780, and the fall of a great-grand nephew at King's Mountain in the same year marked the turn of the tide in the contest for the Southern Colonies which governed the issue of the American Revolution.

Eighty-five years later the hoisting of the Federal flag on the Capitol of Richmond by a great-grand nephew of the American Loyalist officer, to whom fell the melancholy duty of surrendering on that occasion, signalized the preservation of a Union more fortunate in that respect, than the wider one of the preceding century.

The search for such coincidences perhaps deserves no better designation than mere historical gossip; and to pursue it further would be to transgress the limits prescribed when we resolved to trace this story of a soldier of the Protestant succession. His experience in its main features is probably an illustration of that of many others—comrades and contemporaries; but there is one peculiarity in it that arrests the attention, for who that knows the real Scotland of the 17th century would expect to find the Cameronians within four years of the day they were embodied receiving a colonel from Aberdeenshire?

The Duke of Wellington once observed that he could never make due allowance for, or understand the public men of William III. and Queen Anne's time till he had seen how the characters of the statesmen of France deteriorated during their Revolutionary period; and amid all the treachery, vacillation, and intrigue which marked even the Conservative Revolution, worked out under the motto, "*Je maintiendrai*" we turn with a sense of relief from the politicians, who betrayed the master whose bread they ate, to the straightforward soldiers who were true to their salt, and who, either as officers of King James bearing the pains and penury of exile without a murmur, or as steadfast supporters of William of Orange, in whose early battles they had won their spurs, maintained alike under the shadow of the Pyrenees, in the swift current of the Rhine, or on the banks of the Meuse and the Moselle, the truth of the old Continental proverb, *fier comme un Ecossais*.

Appendix

1

THE POSITION OF THE SCOTS BRIGADE IN HOLLAND.

Although the Scots Brigade were not in the pay of their own country until the year 1688, yet they had subsisted more than a century before by the authority of the Crown of Scotland, and were permanent on the Peace Establishment of that kingdom at the time they were sent last to the defence of the United Netherlands, since which time the order of the Sovereign by which they were employed abroad, remained in force until the year 1782.—*Preface to Historical Account of the Scots Brigade,* 1795.

The three English Dutch regiments that came over with King William, have ever since been on the establishment, and are now the 5th and 6th of the British line.

The three Scotch "came upon the establishment at the same time with the 5th and 6th."

The question of rank seems to have been decided betwixt the English and Scotch by the antiquity of the regiments; but as royal troops both always ranked before the troops of the United Provinces, or those belonging to German princes, which right never was contested with regard to the Scots Brigade, until the year 1783.—*Historical Account*

1678. Capitulation fixing footing of British Regiments in Holland.

Officers of the brigade serving in Holland took rank in Britain according to the date of their commissions, in whatever language they were written.

While the British regiments were in the pay of Holland the officers' commissions were in the name of the States, and it was not thought necessary they should have other commissions, even when they were upon the establishment of their own country, until vacancies happened, in which case the new commissions were in the king's name. Thus when Colonel H. Mackay came over to England on the recall of the Brigade in 1685, King James promoted him to the rank of Major-General, not considering him the less as a colonel in his army that his former commission was in the name of the States. And when the same General Mackay, who held his regiment by a Dutch commission, was killed, the regiment was given a few days after to Colonel Aeneas Mackay, whose commission is English and in the name of King William and Queen Mary.—*Historical Account.*

This is confirmed by General Ferguson's commissions. The earlier ones, prior to the Revolution, are all in Dutch and run in the name of the *Stadtholder* and the States. Unfortunately his commission as Major, the only one given when the Scots Brigade proper was serving on the British establishment, is not existent. It would have been interesting to have found it running in English. His Lieutenant-Colonel's commission is not so valuable as an illustration of the Scots Brigade, because of his transfer to a new regiment raised in Scotland. But, as it is, it agrees with Colonel Mackay's and runs in the usual British form. And when the Cameronians were actually on the Dutch establishment for a short period, his commission of 1698 (as captain) bears testimony to their anomalous position. It runs in Dutch, is granted by "His Majesty" at Kensington, but enregistered by the Dutch Council of State and the States of Zealand.

> At the Peace of Ryswick in 1697, the Scots Brigade, returning to Britain with the rest of the army, was mostly stationed in Scotland, being on the establishment of that kingdom; though we find that some Scotch regiments were then on the English establishment, such as the Earl of Orkney's regiment, known now by the name of the Royal, which consisted of twenty-six companies. The total of the troops on the English establishment in the year 1698, after the Dutch Guards and all the foreign troops had been dismissed, amounted only to seven thousand

men: that being the number to which the land forces were restricted by Parliament, besides those on the Irish establishment; so that the reduction must have been very great, for immediately after the Peace of Ryswick the number of the troops on the English establishment alone amounted to 20,943, besides the foreign troops then in English pay. If the troops of Scotland were reduced in the same proportion, the three regiments distinguished by the name of the Scots Brigade, must have made a very considerable part of the peace establishment of that kingdom. It appears that there was no intention of these regiments being again in the pay of the Dutch Republic, otherwise it is natural to suppose they would have been left in the Netherlands when the rest of the British troops came over at the Peace of Ryswick, or that they would have been sent to Holland in 1698, when the great reduction took place.

The extracts from the Dutch records quoted in the text and notes prove that this passage is erroneous. They show that Lauder's and Colyear's regiments, which appears to have been in Holland in 1690, and another, probably Murray's, being the three old Scots regiments, did remain in Holland in 1697; and the place of the three English Regiments that came over with the Prince had been temporarily supplied by three new Scottish regiments, including the Cameronians. In 1698 Hamilton's was recalled to Scotland, and in 1699 Ferguson's and Lord Strathnaver's. They probably were the regiments referred to as sent again to Holland in 1701, for the *Historical Account*, after mentioning the Dutch political co-operation with the king's policy at that time, continues—

> His Majesty in return did all that lay in his power to assist them; for which end he sent the three Scottish regiments retained in his own pay over into Holland. The States General in their instructions to their ambassador in England to thank the king, upon that occasion, make no mention of those regiments as having been formerly in their pay, but call them in general terms—three Scotch regiments, two of ten companies each, and one of eight; and instruct the ambassadors to request that the regiment of eight companies may be completed by drafts from the other Scotch regiments. . . . . During the war of the Succession three new raised Scotch regiments were added to the brigade, and the whole commanded by John, Duke of Argyll,

whose commission as Brigadier was from the States General.—*Historical Account.*

These new regiments were reduced in Holland in 1710, and in consequence of a financial dispute between Great Britain and Holland, £64,000 was granted by Parliament for payment of their arrears.

In the year 1782, it was resolved by the States General that an edict should be issued obliging the officers of the Scotch Brigade to declare that they acknowledged no Power but them as their lawful Sovereign; that his Majesty's Royal Colours, which had come off triumphant from so many battles and sieges, should be taken from them, and that the British uniform, sash and gorget, beat of drum, and word of command should be abolished, and the regiments totally changed into Dutch troops.—*Historical Account.*

The officers had hitherto (at least from 1757) taken the same oath of allegiance to the British Crown as those of other regiments. The Prince of Orange in his letter, of December, 1782, to the brigade, specially commanded that the uniforms should be made blue instead of red, and that orange sashes should be provided.

Some notes on the Scots Brigade were published in 1774, under the title of " Strictures of military discipline, in a series of letters, with a military discourse, in which is interspersed some account of the Scotch Brigade in the Dutch service, by an officer." Speaking of the position of the British, as compared with the Swiss in the Dutch service, the writer says,—

They enjoy no privilege as British troops, except the trifling distinction of being dressed in red, taking the right of the army when encamped or on a march, and having twopence a week more pay for the private men than the Dutch troops have.— See also Article on "The Scots Brigade" in the *Scottish Review* No. 6, April, 1884.

2

Commissions in the Scots Brigade.

1. Commisson as *Vendrig* or Ensign.

Alsoo de vendrigh's plaetse van de compagnie van den Capitain van Zuijlen Zijnde komen te vaceren noodigh is dat de selve met een ander bequaem person werde versien;

Soo ist dat Sijne Hoogheijt daer toe gestelt en gecommitteert heest, stelt en committeert mits desen James Ferguson

Lastende d'officieren en gemeene Soldaten van de selve compagnie den voornoemden james ferguson voor haeren vendrigh te houden en t'erkernen—gedaen in's Hage   den 9 September, 1678.
   (Signed)   G. Prince d'Orange.
                              Ter Orde. van S. Hoogh^t
                              J. C. Huijgens.

This commission is endorsed in name of the States of Zealand.

2. The first commission, of 22nd March, 1688, as Captain, contains the additional clause:—

Ende versoekende de Ed. Mo. Heeren, Raden van State hem met behoorlycke commissie te willen doen versien.

This commission is not endorsed, as most of the others are, on behalf of the States of Zealand, but the records in the *Rijks Archief* at the Hague contain this reference.

1. April, 1688. *Commissie als Capiteyn voor Jacob Ferguson in plaats van den Capiteyn George Hamilton op Holland.*

Which evidently relates to the following—

3. Commission as Captain, 1 April, 1688.

De Staten Generael der Vereeniehde Nederlanden. Allen den geenen die desen sullen sien Salugt. Alsoo de Compagnie van den Capitein George Hamilton sijnde comen te vaceren noodigh is, dat deselve wederom met een ander bequaem ende Crijgs erwaren persoen werde voorsien Doen te weeten dat wij ons betrouvende op de kloeikhejt ende erwarensheijt uit stuck van de Oorloge van den Lieutenant Jacob Ferguson hebbe denselven bij deliberatie van den Rade van State der voorse Vereenighde Landen gestelt ende gecommitteert, stellen ende committeren bij dese tot Capitein over de voorse comp^e tot alsuliken getalle als geordonneert is off noch geordonneert sal worden, gewapent ende getracteert volgens de Lijste ende ordonnantie van 'S Landswegen alreede gemaekt off noch te maecken. Gevende hem volcomen last, macht ende bevel over deselve Comp^e te gebreden. die te geleijden ende te gebrieijken tegens de Vijanden deser Vereenighde Nederlanden t' sij te velde ofte in guarinsoen tot bewaernisse van eenige steden ofte Sterikten, oock op den Schepen van oorloge des noot sijnde daer ende soot hem bij ons oft bij den geenen van ons last heb-

bende tot den voorse Landen dienst sal worden geordonneert ende bevoolen, houdende bij Capitein sijne soldatene in goede ordre, wacht, ende Criggs discipline, soo bij dage als bij nachte, souder te gedoogen dat sij de Bergere ende Ingesetene van de Steden ende platten Lande eenige Schade ofte overlast aen doen, ende voorts alles te doen dat een goet ende getrouw Capitein schuldigh is ende behoort te doen, achter volgende de Crijgs Ordonnantie ende artijikels Brieff, opt belegt vora der oorloge gemaeckt oft noch te maken, ende dit op de Gagie in de voorse Lyste gespecificeert, ter macnt tot twee en veertigh Dagen gerekent, daerop hij sijne Bevel hebberen ende soldaten Ons ende de voorse Landen getrouwelt sullen dienen souder eenigh weder seggen ende hun (?) oock seliken des vermaent sijnde on-weijgere laten monsteren des voort den voorm Ferguson gehouden van hem hierinne welende getrouwelt te quiten te doen den behoorte Eedt in hande van den geme Rade van State, ende dese sijne Commissie te doen registeren soo wel in de Secretarie van den selven Rade als bij de Heeren Staten van Holland ende Westvriesland op wiens Repartitie bij sal betaelt werden, daertoe hem oock behoor-lycke brieven van attache van den Heer Gouverneur ende Gecommitteerde Raden van denselven Lande sal werden verleem welck gedaen sijnde lasten ende ordonneren Wij den Lieutenant Bevelhebberen ende gemeene Soldates ende alien diene aengere mach den voorn Jacob Ferguson voor onsen bestelden Cap^n, te kennen hem te gehoorsaemen ende obedieren oock des noot en versocht sijnde alle be hulpende addres te doen ende dit alles tot Onse weder segge wenn wij sulx lot dienste van Lande bevoenden hebben te behooren. Gegeven ins Graven Hage den eersten April xvjc. acht en achtigh.

(Signed) P. R. Zoete de Laeke Van Villets.
Regter. Fol. 157

This is endorsed—

Ter Ordonnane van Ho. Mo. Heeren Staten Generael der Vereeniehde Nederlanden.
Ter Relatie van den Rade van State derselven Landen.
(Signed) G. Van Slingelandt."

On another fold it is also endorsed—

Jacob Ferguson heest op dese Commissie als Capitein gedaen den behoerlijcken Eede van getreuwigh in handen van de Ed. Mo. Heeren Raden van State der Vereenighde Nederlanden den eersten April 1688.

My present,
(Signed) G. Van Slingelandt.

A separate piece of parchment, attached by a seal and written in a different hand, is in these terms:—

Sijnne Hoogheijt Wilhem Henrik bij der Gratien Godes Prince van Orange ende van Nassau, Grave van Catzenellenbogen, Wianden, Diets (?), Buijren, Leerdam, en Marquis van den Meere ende van Vlissingen, Heere ende Baron van Breda der Stadt Grave, ende den Lande van Ouijck, Hiest (?) Grimbergen, Herstal, Oranendonck, Warneston, Arlaij, Roseroij, St. Wiit, Haelburgh (?), Polanen, Willemstadt, Rierwaert, ijsselsteijn, St. Maartensdijck, Steenbergen, Gertruijdenberg, en de hooge ende de lage Zwaluwe, Raaltwijck, en Duffburgh-grave van Antwerpen, ende Besancon, Duffmaarschalk van Hollandt, Duff-stadthouder ende Gouverneur van Hollandt Zeelandt ende Westvrieslandt. Capiteijn Generael ende Admirael der Vereeniehde Nederlanden, Mittgader de Gecommitteerde Raden van de Staten van Hollandt ende Westvrieslandt. Doen te weeten dat wij gesien ende gevisiteert hebben de geannixeerde Commissie de selve houden voorge-uitermeert, ende dat wij over sulx die in onse registre hebben doen registeren soo dat in conformite van dien aan Jacob Ferguson, eensamentlijck sijnde ouder hebbende Bevel hebberne ende soldaten de betalinge als in de selve Commissie bij ons versoreht worden naar behooren. Mits dat den voorn Capiteijn aan-nemen sal t' gemeene Landt te voldoen vant gene den afifgegaen Capiteijn aant Landt soude mogen schuldigh welen ende Zij van verschot van freminge bevoringe van wapenen vivres, ouder-hout van krane de soldaten off anders. Gelijck den selven Capiteijn mede aanden affgegaen Capiteijn sal moet en betalen alle t' gene den selven sal komen bewijlen aan de Compagnie ten achteren te welen, t' Zij van Leeimige kliedinge wapenen rant, Zoenement ofte anders tot ouder-hout van de selve verstreckt. Alles op freijne dat wij desen houden voor met geintermeert ofte geadmitteert nochte in de betalinge geconsenteert. Gedaen in den Hage ondert cleijne Segel van den Lande de ii. Aprill xvi. acht en achtigh.

Regt. die Sinantie van Hollant Fol. 158.
Ter Ordonnantie van Sijnne Hoogheijt ende de Gecommitteerde Raden.
    (Signed)   Simon van Beaumont.
Op-huij-den de ii. April, 1688, heest den Capitein.
Jacob Ferguson op dese Commissie gedaen die
behoorlijcke eede van suijveringe.
    Mij present,
        (Signed)   Simon van Beaumont.

4. Commission as Captain in the Cameronian Regiment.

Sijne Majesteijt, heest gestelt ende gecommitteert stelt ende committeert mits deesen tot Capiteyn over een Compagnie te voet den Collonel James Ferguson.

Lastende d'officieren ende geemene soldaten van de selve compagnie den voorn James Ferguson voor haeren Capiteyn te houden ende te erkennen. Ende versoekende de Ed. Mo. Heeren Raeden van Staeten hem met behoorlycke commissie te willen voorsien. Gedaen op kensington den ien January, 1698.

(Signed)   William R.
                                   Ter ordie. van Sijne Maj^t.
                                   by absentie van den Secretaris
(Signed)   S. van Huls.

This Commission is also endorsed on behalf of the States of Zealand. The seal on the face bears the British arms, with the lion of the House of Nassau in an inescutcheon of pretence. The stamp on the back shows the demi-lion rising from the waves of Zealand.

3

The following is the proclamation issued after Drummondernoch's murder:—

Edinburgh, 4th February, 1589. The same day, the Lords of Secret Council being crediblie informed of ye cruel and mischeivous proceeding of ye wicked Clangrigor, so lang continueing in blood, slaughters, herships, manifest reifts, and stouths committed upon his Hieness' peaceable and good subjects; inhabiting ye countries ewest ye brays of ye Highlands, thir money years bygone; but specially heir after ye cruel murder of umqll Jo. Drummond of Drummoneyryuch, his Majesties proper tennant, and ane of his fosters of Glenartney, committed upon ye ...... day of .... last bypast, be certain of ye said clan, be ye council and determination of ye haill, avow and to defend ye authors yrof quoever wald persew for revenge of ye same, qll ye said Jo. was occupied in seeking of venison to his Hieness, at command of Pat. Lord Drummond, Stewart of Stratharne, and principal forrester of Glenartney; the Queen, his Majesties dearest spouse, being yn shortlie looked for to arrive in this realm. Likeas, after ye murder committed, ye authors yrof cutted off ye said umqll Jo. Drummond's head, and carried the same to the Laird of M'Grigor, who, and the haill surname of M'Grigors, purposely conveined upon the Sunday yrafter, at the Kirk of Buchquhidder; qr they caused the said umqll John's head to be pnted to ym, and yr avowing ye sd murder to have been committed by yr communion, council, and determination, laid yr hands upon the pow, and in eithnik, and barbarous manner, swear to defend ye authors of ye sd murder, in maist proud contempt of our sovrn Lord and his authoritie, and in evil example to others wicked limmaris to do ye like, give ys sail be suffered to remain unpunished.

Then follows a commission to the Earls of Huntly, Argyle, Athole, Montrose, Pat. Lord Drummond, Ja. Commendator of Incheffray, And. Campbel of Lochinnel, Duncan Campbel of Ardkinglas, Lauchlane M'Intosh of Dunnauchtane, Sir Jo. Murray of Tullibarden, knt., Geo. Buchanan of that Ilk, and And. M'Farlane of Ariquocher, to search for and apprehend Alaster M'Grigor of Glenstre, (and a number of others nominatim), "and all others of the said Clangrigor, or ye assistars, culpable of the said odious murther, or of thift, reset of thift, herships, and sornings, qrever they may be apprehended. And if they refuse to be taken, or flees to strengths and houses, to pursue and assege them with fire and sword; and this commission to endure for the space of three years."

In his genealogy of the Drummonds (written in 1681), Lord Strathallan says that Thomas, the 4th son of Malcolm of Cargill, was the first Laird of Drummond-Irenoch.

> In his time that unlucky action of burning the kirk of Monyvaird fell out; after which, he being in the castle of Drummond in company with his nephew, David Drummond, second son to John Lord Drummond and brother to Malcolm, then master of Drummond, the hous was rendered to King James the Fourth; but this Thomas Drummond refusing to give himselfe up with the rest upon such insecure terms (fearing what happened soone after), leaped over the castle wall, and so escaped into the wood close beside the hous, and was, for that and some other bold pranks, called 'Tom unsained.' He fled first to Ireland, thereafter to London, where he procured favour from King Henrie the Seventh of England; by whose mediation and intercession he got a pardon from King James IV."

The lands he subsequently acquired bore testimony to his exile, the name being changed from Waigtoune to Drummond-Irenoch, "which signifies the Irish Drummonds' lands." His grandson was the father of John Drummond of Drummond-Irenoch, "killed by the clangreigors *anno* 1589," and also of David Drummond, "who, for his quantity, was called 'Mikel Davie'," the first Laird of Invermay. Lord

Strathallan says:—

Mr. James Drummond, second son to David Drummond, first Laird of Invermay, was the first of Cultmalindie. He married Elizabeth Stuart, daughter to Mr. Harie Stuart brother to Sir Thomas Stuart of Garntullie; she had to him two sons—David, who succeeded, and John Drummonds; and three daughters—Jean, Anna, and Helen Drummonds. 2. David Drummond, now of Cultmalindie, the son of Mr. James, yet a minor, but very hopeful.

The "unlucky action" of the Kirk of Monyvaird is the occasion on which the Murrays, finding the Drummonds too strong for them, shut themselves up in the church. Incensed by a shot fired from it, the Drummonds attacked and burnt the Church over their heads. It is said that "Tom unsained," whose mother was a Murray of Tullibardine, then saved the life of one of the Murrays, to whose good offices he afterwards owed his escape from Drummond Castle.

4

The following appeared in *Northern Notes and Queries* for December, 1886, in response to enquiries on the subject of old linen:—

40. *Old Linen* (No. 29).—I believe that linen of about the year 1700 is not at all uncommon in Scottish houses, and that some exists bearing witness to the Jacobite opinions of its early owners, There is at present in the Edinburgh Exhibition a little tablecloth, one of a set which has been in Scottish hands at least since 1705. This linen has always been called the "the Dutch linen," and vague tradition says that it was presented to one of Marlborough's generals by a foreign Court. It would seem to have been woven in commemoration of the victories of the Imperialists over the Turks in the campaigns on the Danube towards the close of the seventeenth century, in which Prince Eugene took part; and there was certainly a great interchange of courtesies between the Austrians under Eugene and the British under Marlborough, after Blenheim had saved the Empire.

The smaller pieces of the set have a border consisting of alternate trophies of crossed guns, crossed pikes, flags, drums, etc., and in the corners are shields with the two-headed eagle. The same arms occupy the centre of the cloth; above are representations of foot-soldiers, and below of horsemen, while lower still is depicted a town and a river running through it, and the word "Buda" woven into the cloth. "Pest,"

"Gran," "Nie" are also represented, and the rest of the cloth is filled with cannon, and on either side of the centre shield flying boys blowing trumpets, and carrying branches of laurel in the other hand. The larger pieces show the same pattern repeated, and the Danube flowing along the whole length of the cloth, with Buda and Pest alternately on the north and south of the river. This linen was brought home by Major-General Ferguson of Balmakelly, who "led up the first line of foot" at the Schellenberg, and commanded one of the brigades that assaulted the village of Blenheim. It now belongs, (1886), to his descendant, Mr. Ferguson of Kinmundy, Aberdeenshire.　　　　J. F.

October, 13th, 1886.

5

Losses of Ferguson's brigade at Schellenberg and Blenheim.

At Schellenberg the Guards had 4 officers, 7 sergeants, and 75 sentinels killed; 8 officers, 8 sergeants, and 127 rank and file wounded.

"Of the Earl of Orkney's first battalion of Scotch Royal" (probably the one in this brigade), there were 3 officers, 1 sergeant, and 38 rank and file killed; 10 officers, 3 sergeants, and 103 privates wounded.

(The second battalion had 2 officers, 1 sergeant, and 76 men killed: 15 officers, 12 sergeants, and 184 men wounded.)

Lieutenant-General Ingoldsby's Regiment (the Welsh Fusilier's) had 5 officers, 6 sergeants, and 60 men killed, 11 officers, 6 sergeants, and 156 men wounded.

At Blenheim, the guards lost the colonel commanding, killed, and had 5 officers wounded.

Lord Orkney's two battalions had 3 officers killed, and 8 wounded.

Ingoldsby's had 9 officers wounded.

Lediard, from whom these figures are taken, does not record the losses in rank and file at Blenheim.

A French general, writing to M. Chamillard, the Secretary of State, described the second attack on Blenheim, as delivered just after Marechal Tallard had made one of his visits to the village, "redoubling his care to secure that post." He wrote:

> They advanced to the very muzzles of our muskets, but were repulsed.

www.ingramcontent.com/pod-product-compliance
Lightning Source LLC
Chambersburg PA
CBHW031306150426
43191CB00005B/94